Appalachian Trail
Thru-Hikers' Companion
2015

The Appalachian Long Distance Hikers Association

Appalachian Trail
Thru-Hikers' Companion
2015

Robert Sylvester

Editor

APPALACHIAN TRAIL
CONSERVANCY®

Harpers Ferry

Cover art: On the front, McAfee Knob in June, © 2014 Douglas J. "Rylu" Labbe; on the back, © Brian "Evac" Wing.

Elevation profiles © 2013 Appalachian Trail Conservancy. **Derived from the 2012 Appalachian Trail Data Book *and other ATC sources.***

Maps developed or revised by Robert Sylvester in 2014.

Twenty-second edition

Published by the Appalachian Trail Conservancy
    799 Washington Street (P.O. Box 807)
    Harpers Ferry, West Virginia 25425-0807
    <www.appalachiantrail.org>

ISBN 978-1-889386-91-1

Contents

Foreword

Welcome to the twenty-second edition of the *Appalachian Trail Thru-Hikers'*
Companion. The 2015 *Companion* is a carefully conceived and diligently compiled and
designed book that belongs in the possession of every Appalachian Trail hiker. Our
hope is that the *Companion*, used in conjunction with Trail maps, will lead the reader
into making informed decisions about towns and services for resupply options.

This book is the culmination of the volunteer efforts of nearly forty ALDHA field
editors and ATC staff members who worked to make this edition as accurate and up-
to-date as possible. I'd especially like to thank Cynthia Taylor-Miller, aka "Mrs Gorp,"
who helped conceive the restyled tables and tirelessly updated them, and Brian King,
who, no doubt, worked long and hard putting all the pieces together. And, to everyone
else who contributed in some way to the publication of this book, many heartfelt
thanks!

A guidebook, like the Trail, is not static. Each hiker may discover something
previously unknown. Your contributions are vital to this process. Your comments are
most welcome—and requested! We rely on hikers' feedback to help us update future
editions. Please send your comments on this book to ALDHA at <companion@aldha.
org>, along with any corrections to Trail, shelter, or town descriptions.

Robert "Sly" Sylvester
Editor

The A.T. Hiker App

Guthook's Guides and ALDHA have teamed up to bring you a new way to plan and carry out your hike along the Appalachian Trail using an app for either the iPhone or Android platform. It taps into the latest info from ALDHA's *A.T. Thru-Hikers' Companion* and all the technical info you will need from actual GPS measurements of the trail by the app's creator, Ryan Linn, aka "Guthook."

Map | Guide | Profile

A portion of the proceeds supports ALDHA's trail programs.

For more information and to download the app, go to Google Play or the Apple App Store, or go to<www.sierraattitude.com/athikerapp.html>. You can also access the site with this QR code.

Additional Thru-Hikers' Companion content (and a PDF of the entire book) is on line at <www.aldha.org/companion/online>. Waypoints and maps to Trailhead parking; maps of post offices, hostels, and other lodging; The A.T. Mailing-Label maker; and much more, including periodic updates, can be found there.

About the *Companion*

The *Companion* is compiled, written, and edited by volunteers of the Appalachian Long Distance Hikers Association (ALDHA) and published by the Appalachian Trail Conservancy (ATC) as a service to those seeking to explore the Trail. It is intended for those making thru-hikes but is also valuable for those taking shorter section-hikes or overnight backpacking trips. The *Companion* provides you with details on shelters, water sources, post offices, hostels, campgrounds, lodging, groceries, restaurants, outfitters, and other related services along the Trail. In addition, the *Companion* offers information of historical significance about places you pass through while hiking the A.T. Unlike commercial guides, this book benefits from the latest information from volunteers who measure, maintain, and manage the Trail and those who hike it regularly.

Due to publication deadlines, we cannot guarantee that the information in this book will not change by the time you arrive in an area, despite the efforts of volunteers to acquire the most up-to-date information. Businesses close or change hours, hostels change rates and policies, and the Trail itself is subject to relocation. This edition was produced in the fall of 2014.

As you walk, talk to other hikers, and read shelter registers. The Conservancy's Web site periodically posts updates at <www.appalachiantrail.org/hiking/trail-updates/thru-hikers-companion>, which you can also reach by using a "smartphone" equipped with a QR reader and the code on the back cover of this book.

Inclusion in this book is not an endorsement by ALDHA or ATC, but rather a listing of services available and contacted by field editors. Likewise, the businesses listed do not pay for "advertisements" but are listed because of their proximity to the Trail.

ALDHA members do field research for each section of the Trail and are instrumental in gathering information. Without the hard work of the following ALDHA field editors, other volunteers, and ATC staff members, this book would not have been possible: **Georgia and North Carolina**—Scott Dowling (Pilgrim), Ann W. Thomas (Timberpixie); **North Carolina and Tennessee**—Lamar Powell (Hopeful), Sunny Riggs (Sunrise), Tom Bradford (10-K), Tim Steward (Mountain Squid); **Southwest Virginia**—Ken & Nora Bennett (Big Cranky & Dragonfly), Charles Davidson (Chase); **Central Virginia**—Laurie Foot (Happy Feet), Pat Ohleger, Leonard Adkins (Habitual Hiker); **Northern Virginia**—David and Sue Hennel (Gourmet Dave and The Real Gourmet), Alyson Browett; **West Virginia**—ATC Information Services Manager Laurie Potteiger (Mountain Laurel) and visitors-center assistant Reed Flinn; **Maryland and Southern Pennsylvania**—Mike Wingeart (Wingheart); **Central Pennsylvania**—ATC's Kelly McGinley and Bob Sickley in the Boiling Springs regional office; **Northern Pennsylvania**—Mary Ann Nissley (M.A. from Pa.); **New Jersey**—Debbie Melita (Baby Carrots); **New York**—Robert Cunningham (EZ), Mark Hudson (Skeeter); **Connecticut**—Tom Evans (Flatlander); **Massachusetts**—Kevin Reardon (Slider), Jim Niedbalski (High Octane); **Vermont**—Jeff Taussig, Cynthia Taylor-Miller (Mrs. Gorp); **New Hampshire**—Jeff Phillips and Jen O'Connor Phillips (Chaco Taco & Wakapak), Art Cloutman (Gabby); **Maine**—Sandie Sabaka (Bluebearee), Jennifer Friedrich (vonFrick), Rick Towle (AT Troll), Paul & Jaime Renaud (OleMan & NaviGator). Mileage figures are based on information from the 2015 edition of the *Appalachian Trail Data Book*.

TRAIL-MAINTAINING CLUBS AND REGISTERS

Trail-maintaining clubs are listed throughout the book. You may use the addresses provided to contact the clubs with any comments, suggestions, or feedback. Although often a thru-hiker will leave an additional one, the official shelter registers are the property of the maintaining club and should not be removed by hikers. The register is a useful tool for information on Trail conditions and other things that are happening in its section of the A.T. It may also help locate a hiker in case of an emergency. If you wish to donate a register (assuming that one doesn't already exist), you should include a note asking the maintaining club to forward it to you when it's filled.

GETTING TO THE TRAIL

Section-hikers looking for shuttle services should check the business and individual listings for the area in which they plan to hike. Also, check with ATC at (304) 535-6331, <info@appalachiantrail.org>, or check the ATC's A.T. shuttle and public-transportation list available at <www.appalachiantrail.org/hiking/find-a-hike/parking-shuttles-transportation>. (See page 1 for an important note on shuttles.) This same Web site will link to information on Trailhead parking.

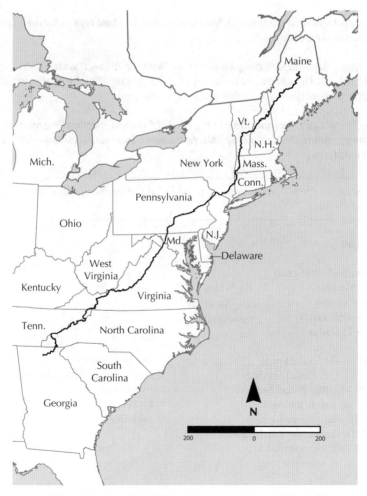

OVERVIEW OF THE APPALACHIAN TRAIL

Using the *Companion*

MAKING THE COMPANION YOUR OWN

Do not be afraid to abuse your paper *Companion*. While it has considerable information, it has been suggested that it could be made smaller. Unfortunately, no one agrees on what should be left out. So, here is an idea—do your own editing. Rip out what you don't want, use a hole-punch, a pair of scissors, or a highlighter. Send sections ahead to mail drops; mail completed sections home. Do some old-fashioned cut-and-paste. Make this book your own.

READING THE COMPANION

 Road-crossings and Trailheads with significant services nearby are indicated in south-to-north order.

Towns and post offices (including P.O. hours) are printed in **bold type**. A listing of post offices can also be found on page 253.

East and West—Regardless of compass direction, "**east**" or "E" and "**west**" or "W" are used as they are in the *A.T. Data Book* and the series of 11 A.T. guides: "East" is to the northbounder's right and the southbounder's left, when referring to the Trail.

Services—Major categories are indicated with ***bold italics***, specifically ***groceries, lodging, hostels, campgrounds, doctors or hospitals, restaurants, Internet access, laundries, veterinarians,*** and ***outfitters.***

Trail-Maintaining Clubs—Information is provided at the southern end of their sections and is offset by two rules.

Abbreviations—

In the body of the text:

M—Monday	F—Friday
Tu—Tuesday	Sa—Saturday
W—Wednesday	Su—Sunday
Th—Thursday	

FedEx—Federal Express	pp—per person
USPS—U.S. Postal Service	eap—each additional person
UPS—United Parcel Service	d—double
a/c—air conditioning	s—single
AYCE—all-you-can-eat	t—triple
B/L/D—breakfast/lunch/dinner	
CATV—cable television	

In the tables at beginning of each chapter:

B—bus	O—outfitter
C—campground, campsites	P—parking
cl—coin laundry	P.O.—post office
D—doctor, medical	R—road access
f—fuel	S—shelter
G—groceries, supplies	sh—shower
g—short-term resupply	T—train
H— hostels	nw—no potable water
L— lodging	V—veterinarian
m—miles	w—water
M—meals; restaurants	

Elevation—This column refers to the approximate elevation (in feet) of the landmark.

Comma—Services separated by commas are in the same location. For example, E–1.5m P.O., G means that the post office and grocery store are both located 1.5 miles east.

Parentheses—Services separated by parentheses are not all in the same location. For example, (E–0.2m C, S) (W–0.1m w) means that the campsite and shelter are east 0.2 mile, and the water source is west 0.1 mile from the Trailhead.

Shelters—May also be referred to as lean-tos. Shown in **bold print**, with distance and direction off Trail, water-source location, and distance to the next shelter (in italics, both north and south). **The distance to the next north and south shelter shown in the *Companion* includes the side-trail(s) distance from one to the other.**

 Indicates a designated Appalachian Trail Community™ mentioned in the text (several more communities participate but are outside the distance scope of the *Companion*). Towns and counties participating in this Appalachian Trail Conservancy program agree to help promote, preserve, and maintain the A.T. in various ways while ATC helps them with economic development.

Between Springer Mountain and the entrance to Shenandoah National Park above Waynesboro, Va., and again from the Massachusetts–Vermont line to the New Hampshire–Maine line, the A.T. runs mostly through national-forest lands. While ATC offers the official A.T. hiking maps (at <www.atctrailstore.org>), the U.S. Forest Service offers digital maps of the whole forests for iPhone and Android devices at iTunes and the Android Play Store. Prices range from 99¢ to $4.99.

Issues on the Trail

2,000-MILER CERTIFICATES

ATC recognizes anyone who reports completion of the entire Trail as a "2,000-Miler" with a certificate. The term "2,000-Miler" is a matter of tradition and convenience, based upon the original estimated length of the Trail. ATC operates on the honor system, assuming that those who apply for 2,000-Miler status have hiked all of the A.T. between Katahdin and Springer. In the event of an emergency, such as a flood, forest fire, or an impending storm on an exposed high-elevation stretch, blue-blazed trails or officially required roadwalks are considered viable substitutes for the white-blazed route. Issues of sequence, direction, speed, length of time, or whether one carries a pack or not are not considered. ATC assumes that those who apply have made an honest effort to *walk* the entire Trail. (P.S. The Shenandoah River is not the official Trail route.)

HUNTING SEASONS

Hunters are rarely an issue for northbound thru-hikers, but southbounders need to be aware of the hunting seasons, which may begin as early as mid-Oct, as you progress south toward Springer. Hunting is legal along many parts of the Trail, and ATC's Web site lists local hunting seasons. Wearing bright ("blaze") orange is a necessity in fall, winter, and spring.

SAFETY—OTHER HUMANS

If you tell friends you are planning a long-distance hike on the A.T., one of the first questions is likely to be, "Aren't you afraid? What will you do to protect yourself?" There are dangers in the backcountry, but, because of mass-media publicity and the popularity of backpacking, your friend was likely speaking of the dangers posed by other humans. Violent crimes have occurred on the Trail, with a frequency rate of less than two every *ten* years, on a footpath more than three million people use *each* year.

The difference on the A.T. and in any wilderness setting—other than people's expectations—is that you only have yourself and your instincts for protection. That means you must use common sense to avoid potential dangers. It is best not to hike alone. If you choose to, a few precautions can help keep you safe:

- Don't tell strangers where you are headed or plan to camp for the night; *don't post plans in real time on on-line journals or blogs.*
- If you run into a suspicious person, consider moving on to another location.
- Avoid camping or staying at shelters that are within a mile of a road crossing.
- Leave an itinerary of your trip with family or friends.
- If you use a Trail name, make sure the folks back home know what it is.
- Even with a partner, don't be lulled into a false sense of security. Two or more can also be vulnerable.
- Eliminate opportunities for theft. Don't bring jewelry. Keep wallets and money on your person rather than in your pack or tent. Leaving a pack unattended at trailheads or shelters is risky, even when it is hidden.
- Trust your gut. Always.

ATC and most long-distance hikers strongly discourage the carrying of a gun on the Trail. Guns are restricted (you can carry with all the proper permits but not legally discharge) on national park lands (40 percent of the route) and in many other jurisdictions through which the Trail passes. Report any crime or harassment immediately to the local police *and* ATC. Contact ATC at (304) 535-6331 or <incident@appalachiantrail.org>. Further advice can be found at <www.ap-palachiantrail.org/safetyawareness>.

SAFETY—MOTHER NATURE

While natural dangers are inherent to backpacking, many are misunderstood. For some, a hike in the woods conjures images of snakebites and bear attacks—both rare.

BEARS

Black bears live along many parts of the Trail and are particularly common in Georgia, the Shenandoah and Great Smoky Mountains national parks, and north of Shenandoah on into New York. While attacks on humans are rare, a startled bear or a female with cubs may react aggressively. The best way to avoid an encounter while you are hiking is to make noise by whistling, talking, *etc.*, to give the bear a chance to move away before you get close enough to make it feel threatened. If you encounter a bear and it does not move away, you should back off, and avoid making eye contact. Do not run or "play dead," even if a bear makes a "bluff charge."

The best preventive defense is preparing and storing food properly:

- Cook and eat meals away from your tent or shelter so food odors do not linger.
- Hang food, cookware, toothpaste, personal hygiene items, water bottles with drink mixes in a sturdy bag from a strong tree branch 10 feet off the ground, 6 feet from the tree, and away from your campsite.
- Use bear boxes, poles, or cable systems where provided.
- *Never* feed bears or leave food behind for them.
- A bear entering a campsite should be considered predatory. Yelling, making loud noises, and throwing rocks may frighten it away, but be prepared to fight back.
- If attacked, fight for all you are worth with anything at hand—rocks, sticks, fists.

Less dramatic threats to safety, such as contaminated water, dehydration, and hypothermia, afflict far more hikers—particularly those who are unprepared.

If you are unfamiliar with backcountry travel, ask questions, and read and learn about backpacking safely. Learn about dehydration, heat exhaustion, and hypothermia; learn safe ways of fording rivers and purifying water; learn how to avoid lightning, rabies, and Lyme disease—the most common threats to a hiker's well-being. A good resource for learning more about these topics is the ATC publication *Step by Step: An Introduction to Walking the A.T.* Before starting an end-to-end hike, take shorter backpacking trips until you feel confident in the backcountry. Finally, information and experience are useless if you forget one thing—common sense.

LYME DISEASE

In the Northeast, the heightened risk for Lyme disease (LD) is Apr to Jul and Oct to Nov, which coincide with the time frame thru-hikers pass through the states with the highest reported cases of the disease. Cases have been reported in all fourteen Trail states.

LD is a bacterial infection transmitted to humans by the bite of infected blacklegged ticks (formerly called "deer" ticks). Hikers should watch carefully for symptoms of LD, which may include "flu-like" reactions of fever, headache, chills, and fatigue and a characteristic "bulls-eye" skin rash, called *erythema migrans,* at the site of the tick attachment. Hikers should seek immediate medical attention for treatment.

Steps hikers can take to prevent LD include using insect repellent with Deet for exposed skin; spraying clothing items with the insecticide permethrin; removing ticks promptly; conducting a daily full-body tick check, including the head, underarms, and groin area; minimizing contact with high grass, brush, and woody shrubs; wearing long pants tucked into your socks; and wearing long sleeves, tucking your shirt into your pants to keep ticks off your torso.

LEAVE NO TRACE

With the millions who enjoy this place each year, the chances are great that any of us may inadvertently damage the natural environment along the Trail and mar the experience for others. Those negative effects can be minimized by adopting sound hiking and camping techniques which, while simple to learn, require some committed effort—think of LNT, wholly endorsed by ATC and ALDHA, as an educational and ethical program for responsible enjoyment of the outdoors, not a set of rules. If we are successful, the Trail will retain its essential natural qualities and continue to be a place where an extraordinary outdoor experience is available. Everyone's help is important. Please do your part by committing to these practices, and encourage others to learn about techniques that "Leave No Trace" on the Appalachian Trail. More information can be found at <www.LNT.org> and <www.appalachiantrail.org/lnt>.

PLAN AHEAD AND PREPARE

- Check Appalachian Trail guidebooks and maps for guidance and note that camping regulations vary considerably along the Trail. Travel in groups of 10 or fewer. If in a group of more than five, leave shelters for lone hikers and smaller groups.
- Bring a lightweight trowel or wide tent stake to dig a hole for burying human waste.
- Bring a piece of screening to filter food scraps from your dishwater and pack them out.
- Bring a waterproof bag and at least 50 feet of rope to hang food and scented articles.
- Repackage food in resealable bags to minimize waste.
- Prepare for extreme weather, hazards, and emergencies—especially the cold—to avoid impacts from searches, rescues, and campfires.
- Try to avoid areas when they are most crowded. If you are planning a northbound thru-hike, avoid starting on March 1, March 15, the first day of spring, or April 1.

TRAVEL AND CAMP ON DURABLE SURFACES

- Stay on the trail; never shortcut switchbacks. Take breaks off-trail on durable surfaces, such as rock or grass.
- Restrict activities to areas where vegetation is already absent.
- Avoid expanding existing trails and campsites by walking in the middle of the trail, and using the already-impacted core areas of campsites.
- If tree branches block the trail, move them off if possible, rather than going around and creating new trails.
- Wear gaiters and waterproof boots, so you may walk through puddles instead of walking around them and creating a wide spot in the trail.

DISPOSE OF WASTE PROPERLY

- "Pack it in, Pack it out." Don't burn, bury, or leave litter or extra food. That includes cigarette butts, fruit peels, and hygiene articles. Keep your trash bag handy, so you can pick up litter left by others.
- Use the privy for human waste only (feces). Do not add trash. If there is no privy, dispose of human waste by burying it in a "cathole," a hole 6-8 inches deep, 4-6 inches wide, at least 200 feet (80 steps) from campsites, water sources, and shelters, and well away from trails. Add dirt to the hole, and stir with a stick to promote decomposition. Push toilet paper to the bottom of the hole, and leave your stick in the hole. Don't hide your waste under a rock; this slows decomposition.
- Note that most "disposable wipes" are made from nonbiodegradable material that must be carried out rather than buried, burned, or left in privies. For those willing to go the extra mile, consider packing out your toilet paper, too. Animals' curiosity often brings toilet paper and other trash to the surface.

- Wash dishes, bodies, and clothing 200 feet away from water sources. Use biodegradable soap sparingly, or not at all. Avoid polluting the water by rinsing off at a distance to remove your excess sunscreen, bug repellent, *etc.*, before swimming in a lake or stream.
- Disperse dishwater and toothpaste, and urinate well away (at least 100 feet) from shelters and popular campsites. In that way, wildlife is not attracted close to camp. Animals sometimes defoliate plants to consume the salt in urine, so urinate on rocks or bare ground rather than on vegetation. Where water is plentiful, consider diluting the urine by adding water to the site.
- If you wish to donate items to other hikers (food, extra gear, clothing, books, *etc.*), don't leave them at shelters—use the hiker boxes at motels and hostels.

LEAVE WHAT YOU FIND

- Leave plants, artifacts and natural objects where you found them, for others to enjoy.
- Don't build structures or dig trenches around tents.
- Do not damage live trees or plants; green wood burns poorly. Collect only firewood that is dead, down, and no larger than your wrist. Leave dead standing trees and dead limbs on standing trees for the wildlife.
- Consider using rubber tips on the bottom of your trekking poles to avoid scratch marks on rocks, "clicking" sounds, and holes along the Trail.

MINIMIZE CAMPFIRE IMPACTS

- Use stoves for cooking—if you *need* a fire, build one only where it's legal and in an existing fire ring. Leave hatchets and saws at home. Burn all wood to ash.
- Do not try to burn trash, including foil, plastic, glass, cans, tea bags, food, or anything with food on it. These items do not burn thoroughly. They create noxious fumes, attract wildlife like skunks and bears, and make the area unsightly.
- Where campfires are permitted, leave the fire ring clean by removing others' trash and scattering unused wood, cold coals, and ashes 200 feet away from camp after the fire is cold and completely out.

RESPECT WILDLIFE

- Bears inhabit or travel through nearly every part of the A.T. Sightings have increased at shelters and campsites and even small food rewards teach bears to associate humans with food. When that happens, they often have to be killed to protect human safety. Dropped, spilled, or improperly stored food also attracts rodents. Even a few noodles are a large meal for mice. Clean up spills completely, and pack out all food scraps.
- Store your food according to local regulations. Store all food, trash, and scented articles (toothpaste, sunscreen, insect repellent, water-purification chemicals, balm, *etc.*) out of reach of bears and other animals. A safe distance is 12 feet from the ground and 6 feet from a limb or trunk.
- Keep a respectful distance. If hiking with a dog, keep it on a short leash. Do not follow or approach animals. Particularly avoid wildlife during sensitive times, *i.e.*, when they are mating, nesting, or raising young.

BE CONSIDERATE OF OTHER VISITORS

- Let nature's sounds prevail. Respect others by keeping loud voices and noise to a minimum. Do not use cell phones or audio equipment within sight or sound of other hikers, and turn ringers off.
- A.T. shelter space is available on a first-come, first-served basis in most (but not all) areas, regardless of the type of hiker or length of their hike.
- Limit-of-stay is generally two nights at any one shelter or campsite.
- If you are hiking with a dog, be aware of its potential impact on animals and other hikers. Keep your dog leashed and under control at all times, and learn where dogs are prohibited. Ask permission before bringing your dog into a shelter. If you find the shelter is crowded, be considerate and tent with your dog. Keep your dog away from springs and other water sources. Bury your dog's waste as you would your own.

TOWN CONDUCT

As a result of tension between hikers and some communities along the Trail, AL-DHA started an "Endangered Services Campaign" to educate hikers to be responsible for their actions. In town, consider yourself a walking, talking billboard for all backpackers and the Trail. Your actions have a direct impact on the businesses that provide services for the long-distance hiking community.

The success of a thru-hiker's journey depends on Trail towns and the services they provide. Remember that you are a guest of the community, no matter how large or small, even though you may be pumping money into the local

The Endangered Services Campaign

economy. Be courteous to those who earn their livelihood there, and remember that your conduct will have a bearing on how well—or badly—the next hiker is treated. As with so many other things in life, we are never truly alone. You are an ambassador for all those who follow you on the Trail. Nothing can turn a person or town against backpacking and the Trail quicker than an arrogant, smelly, and ill-behaved hiker.

Some business owners have reduced services or closed their doors to hikers simply because some hikers wouldn't respect their rules. Be a part of a movement that will reverse this practice and ensure that no one closes another door because of bad hiker behavior.

DONATIONS

Many hostels listed in this book suggest donations for the services provided. This means that the service should not be considered a gift or that it costs the provider nothing. The honor system of the Trail requires that you leave something.

GIVING BACK

If you would like to give back what was freely given to you by those who maintain the Trail or while you stayed in Trail towns, volunteer your time, effort, or money to the services and people who supported you. Consider contacting a Trail-maintaining club and working with them to organize or participate in a work trip, Trail-construction project, or regular maintenance. Every year, ALDHA sponsors work trips to Trail establishments. The Konnarock and other ATC crews seek volunteers during the summer, and you often will pass a Trail club working busily as you head along the path. Be sure to acknowledge their work with your thanks and respect. Giving back to the Trail and community helps keep the Trail safe and services available.

HITCHHIKING

Hitchhiking is illegal in certain states. It is your responsibility to know the motor-vehicle law as it applies to hitchhiking where you are hiking, to avoid being fined or hitching into worse trouble. Hitchhiking poses the risk of being picked up by an unsafe driver or someone who is personally dangerous. Hitchhiking is prohibited on interstate highways, the Blue Ridge Parkway, and Skyline Drive in Shenandoah National Park.

HIKING WITH DOGS

If you choose to hike with your canine companion, treat your dog as another backpacker. That means bury its waste as you would your own, and carry a water bowl so your dog won't drink directly from Trailside water sources. You are responsible for your dog, and you will be held accountable if it decides to steal another hiker's food or flop its wet body on another hiker's equipment. Keep your pet under control in camp, on the Trail, and in towns. Many hostels and other accommodations don't allow dogs, and, in those that do, a dog does not belong in the communal kitchen and sleeping areas. Closely monitor your pet's feet for torn flesh, bleeding, and other sores. After the weather warms up, check for ticks. It is best to keep your dog on a leash at all times; on national-park lands (40 percent of the Trail), regulations require it. Most post offices allow only guide dogs inside. Carry current rabies-vaccine certification papers in addition to a tag on the dog's collar. Dogs are prohibited in the Great Smoky Mountains National Park, the zoo area of Bear Mountain State Park in New York, and Maine's Baxter State Park. (For information on kennels near GSMNP and BSP, see entries for those sections.)

APPALACHIAN TRAIL MUSEUM SOCIETY

The Appalachian Trail Museum opened in June 2010 in Pine Grove Furnace State Park near the Trail's midpoint after years of work by the Appalachian Trail Museum Society (ATMS), formed in 2002. The group includes representatives of ATC and ALDHA and works with the National Park Service. The society is collecting items for eventual display in the museum and monetary donations. They are also in need of volunteers to help in many areas. Please contact ATMS, if you'd like to help, at <www.atmuseum.org>.

APPALACHIAN LONG DISTANCE HIKERS ASSOCIATION

The Appalachian Long Distance Hikers Association (ALDHA) is a nonprofit organization founded in 1983 to promote the welfare of the Appalachian Trail and the Trail community. ALDHA conducts work weekends on the Trail, speaks out on issues concerning the A.T. and its environs, and collects the information for this book. It has worked with various clubs and hostels to maintain areas widely used by hikers. ALDHA is open to anyone. A membership form is included at the back of this book. Annual dues are $10 per family (or individual). Benefits include the *Thru-Hikers' Companion* in pdf format, a membership directory, and a quarterly newsletter. For more information, visit our Web site, <www.aldha.org>.

THE GATHERING

Folks who want to learn what it takes to thru-hike the Appalachian Trail can find out everything they need to know at the fall Gathering. If you are already thru-hiking the Trail this year, the Gathering is also the place to receive an "ALDHA Way" certificate and patch for your accomplishment and find out what's next for your worn-in hiking boots. Slide shows and how-to workshops on the Pacific Crest Trail, Continental Divide, and other major foot trails help fill the weekend event. The 34th Gathering will be Oct. 9–11, 2015, at Shippensburg University, Shippensburg, Pa. For more information, visit <www.aldha.org/gathering>. **Special notice to 2015 thru-hikers and 2000-Milers: Bring your Trail-worn *A.T. Thru-Hikers' Companion* (or the Maine section in its entirety) and a completed-trail form to the registration desk, and your gathering fee is on ALDHA!**

AN INVITATION

This is the twenty-second edition of the *A.T. Thru-Hikers' Companion,* and ALDHA will again depend on comments, suggestions, and volunteers to update it in the fall of 2015. If you see information that needs correcting or come across information that should be included, or would like to be a volunteer field editor, please contact the editor at <companion@aldha.org>.

THE APPALACHIAN TRAIL CONSERVANCY

For additional information about the Appalachian Trail and a complete list of guidebooks, maps, and thru-hiking publications, contact the Appalachian Trail Conservancy at P.O. Box 807, Harpers Ferry, WV 25425-0807, or call (304) 535-6331, Monday through Friday except federal holidays, between 9 a.m. and 5 p.m. Eastern time. Its visitors center at Harpers Ferry is open year-round except Thanksgiving, Christmas, and New Year's Day. The e-mail address is <info@appalachiantrail.org>; the Web address is <www.appalachiantrail.org>. For direct access to the Ultimate A.T. Store, e-mail <sales@appalachiantrail.org>, call (888) 287-8673 weekdays between 9 a.m. and 4:30 p.m. Eastern time, or visit <www.atctrailstore.org>.

APPALACHIAN TRAIL PASSPORT

Appalachian Trail hikers can purchase a $7 "A.T. Passport" and use it to collect unique stamps at hostels, lodgings, and other landmarks. A list of participants appears near the end of this book in the "Hostels, Camping, and Showers" chapter. This document can become a keepsake for all hikers of the A.T. To learn more, and order your A.T. Passport, visit <www.atctrailstore.org> or <www.atpassport.com>.

Class of 2015: See the back of the book for a special invitation for you!

2015 Calendar and Key Dates to Remember

January

Su	Mo	Tu	We	Th	Fr	Sa
					1	2	3
④	5	6	7	8	9	10
11	12	13	14	15	16	17
18	19	**20**	21	22	23	24
25	26	27	28	29	30	31

February

Su	Mo	Tu	We	Th	Fr	Sa
1	2	③	4	5	6	7
8	9	10	11	12	13	14
15	16	17	**18**	19	20	21
22	23	24	25	26	27	28

March

Su	Mo	Tu	We	Th	Fr	Sa
1	2	3	4	⑤	6	7
8	9	10	11	12	13	14
15	16	17	18	19	**20**	21
22	23	24	25	26	27	28
29	30	31				

April

Su	Mo	Tu	We	Th	Fr	Sa
			1	2	3	④
5	6	7	8	9	10	11
12	13	14	15	16	17	**18**
19	20	21	22	23	24	25
26	27	28	29	30		

May

Su	Mo	Tu	We	Th	Fr	Sa
					1	2
③	4	5	6	7	8	9
10	11	12	13	14	15	16
17	18	19	20	21	22	23
24	25	26	27	28	29	30
31						

June

Su	Mo	Tu	We	Th	Fr	Sa
	1	②	3	4	5	6
7	8	9	10	11	12	13
14	15	**16**	17	18	19	20
21	22	23	24	25	26	27
28	29	30				

July

Su	Mo	Tu	We	Th	Fr	Sa
			①	2	3	4
5	6	7	8	9	10	11
12	13	14	**15**	16	17	18
19	20	21	22	23	24	25
26	27	28	29	30	㉛	

August

Su	Mo	Tu	We	Th	Fr	Sa
						1
2	3	4	5	6	7	8
9	10	11	12	13	**14**	15
16	17	18	19	20	21	22
23	24	25	26	27	28	㉙
30	31					

September

Su	Mo	Tu	We	Th	Fr	Sa
		1	2	3	4	5
6	7	8	9	10	11	12
13	14	15	16	17	18	19
20	21	22	23	24	25	26
㉗	28	29	30			

October

Su	Mo	Tu	We	Th	Fr	Sa
				1	2	3
4	5	6	7	8	9	10
11	12	13	14	15	16	17
18	19	20	21	22	23	24
25	26	㉗	28	29	30	31

November

Su	Mo	Tu	We	Th	Fr	Sa
1	2	3	4	5	6	7
8	9	10	11	12	13	14
15	16	17	18	19	20	21
22	23	24	㉕	26	27	28
29	30					

December

Su	Mo	Tu	We	Th	Fr	Sa
		1	2	3	4	5
6	7	8	9	10	**11**	12
13	14	15	16	17	18	19
20	21	22	23	24	㉕	26
27	28	29	30	31		

Circled dates denote full moons; new moons are bolded.

January 16–18	Southern Ruck, Nantahala Outdoor Center, Wesser, N.C.
January 23–25	Northern Ruck, Bears Den Trail Center, Bluemont, Va.
March 6–8	Appalachian Trail Kick-Off, Amicalola Falls State Park, Ga.
March 27–28	April Hiker Fool Bash, Sapphire Inn, Franklin, N.C.
April 3–5	A.T. Founders Bridge Festival, NOC, Wesser, N.C.
April 10–12	Trail Fest, Hot Springs, N.C.
April 11	ALDHA Steering Committee Meeting, Bears Den Trail Center
May 15–17	Trail Days, Damascus, Va.
June 5	Appalachian Trail Hall Of Fame Induction, Boiling Springs, Pa,.
June 6	National Trails Day; Hiker Festival at Appalachian Trail Museum
July 17–24	ATC Biennial Meeting, Shenandoah University, Winchester, Va.
September 25–28	21st ALDHA West Gathering <www.aldhawest.org>
October 9–11	34th ALDHA Gathering, Shippensburg University, Pa.

Getting to the Termini

An important note about shuttle services

Beginning in 1995, USDA Forest Service law-enforcement rangers in the South—who report to the regional office rather than the supervisor of an individual forest—began enforcing agency regulations on "special-use permits." The regulations say anyone taking money for a service involving Forest Service lands (including roads) must obtain a permit to do so; profit is not a factor. Permit-holders must pay a fee (up to $75) and, more prohibitively, carry high-premium insurance. Some A.T. shuttlers have been fined. Responding to questions from ATC and its Park Service partners, regional officials made it clear they will continue to enforce the policy and cited directives stating that it is to be enforced consistently and nationally. The A.T. crosses six national forests in the South and two in New England. ATC will continue to provide names of shuttle services, but keep that policy in mind—**call ahead to ensure the person is still performing this service.** You can check the ATC Web site, <www.appalachiantrail. org/hiking/find-a-hike/parking-shuttles-transportation>, for a downloadable copy of that list, or write ATC, Attn.: Shuttle List (address on page iv), for a copy by first-class mail.

Getting to Baxter State Park, Maine

No public transportation is available to or from Baxter State Park, but arrangements can be made to conclude or begin your journey with little difficulty. This usually means going through Boston, Portland, and/or Bangor, then to Medway, and then to Millinocket, still 20 miles southeast of the park. The nearest airport is in Bangor; the Portland airport is said to have more competitive rates, and Boston more so. Bus transportation is available from Portland to Medway and also from Boston to Portland.

LEAVING BANGOR

Cyr Bus Lines of Old Town, Maine, (207) 827-2335, (207) 827-2010, or (800) 244-2335, <www. cyrbustours.com>, serves northern Maine. A bus leaves Bangor/Hermon Greyhound bus station at 6:00 p.m. and Concord–Trailways bus station at 6:30 p.m. and arrives at Medway at 7:40 p.m. A bus leaves Medway at 9:30 a.m. and arrives at Concord-Trailways station at 10:50 a.m. and at Bangor/Hermon Greyhound station at 11:10 a.m. ($12 fare). The A.T. Lodge in Millinocket, (207) 723-4321, shuttles, as does Phil Pepin (A.T. thru-hiker, Trail maintainer, and registered Maine wilderness guide), (207) 991-7030, <www.100milewilderness. info>.

MEDWAY TO MILLINOCKET

From Medway, in the past, you would have to hitch on Maine 157 or call a taxi to go to either Millinocket, 10 miles to the west, or Baxter State Park, about 30 miles away. Today, however, transportation is available to and from BSP *via* shuttle from Maine Quest Adventures, (207) 746-9615, <www.mainequestadventures.com>, from Medway bus stop to BSP or Abol Bridge, $55 couple, $5EAP. Bull Moose Taxi, (207) 447-8070, charges $55 to Katahdin Stream Campground or to the A.T. Lodge in Millinocket. The A.T. Lodge also offers a SOBO special: pick-up in Medway, bed in the bunkroom, breakfast at the A.T. Café, and shuttle to Katahdin Stream Campground..

Baxter State Park—The park, (207) 723-5140, has 10 campgrounds available May 15–Oct 15 by reservation on a first-come, first-served basis—$30 per night per 4-person lean-to or 6-person-max-tentsite, except at the Birches long-distance hiker site, where the fee is $10PP/night. The Birches campsite, near Katahdin Stream Campground, is intended for northbound long-distance hikers who have hiked 100 miles or more contiguous with the park on their current trip. Hikers staying at the Birches must sign up at the information kiosk just north of Abol Bridge. Please see the entry for Baxter on page 246 for more information and details about camping and regulations near Katahdin. Southbound hikers should reserve a regular lean-to or tentsite at Katahdin Stream or Abol campgrounds. Reservations may be made four months in advance of the date you wish to stay in the park and can be made by mail or in person using a credit card. More information and a chart outlining real-time availability of sites is available at <www.baxterstate-parkauthority.com>. Inside the park, ranger stations do NOT accept credit cards. Every hiker must register *with a ranger* upon entering Baxter. Information kiosks are located at Abol Stream and Katahdin Stream campgrounds.

Pets—No dogs or other pets are allowed; see Medway and Millinocket entries for kennels.

Parking—No long-term parking is available, and parking at all trailheads and campgrounds is at a premium and is managed at the entrance gates. Check the park Web site, <www.baxter statepark authority.com>, for information on how to reserve a parking space. Advance reservations for day-use parking May 15–Oct 15 become available for Maine residents Apr 1; two weeks in advance of the day for nonresidents. When the spaces for a particular day have been reserved, that specific parking lot is closed. Plan ahead!

APPROACH TO KATAHDIN

A note for would-be southbounders—Katahdin is no stroll in the park. The profile and topo on the MATC's maps only give you a hint of what to expect—the single greatest sustained climb on the A.T. Get yourself physically prepared before you start at Baxter State Park (you will be on your own once you get past the ranger station). Northbounders routinely leave their full packs on the ranger's porch and hike up with daypacks provided there for that purpose. Every year, several stubborn southbounders, invariably much less-conditioned than seasoned northbounders, insist on carrying their fully loaded packs up the A.T. beyond Katahdin Stream Campground. This results in knee injuries and aborted climbs or even entire A.T. hiking plans. Take a hint from the northbound veterans: Hike Katahdin with a day pack, and pick up your full pack on your way back through the campground—you will still be a thru-hiker, and you will enjoy your day, rather than suffer the entire time and predispose yourself to any number of injuries or the need for a rescue on your first Trail day. The footpath below treeline is more rocks and roots than soil—no problem for the hikers who have been rock-hopping for 2,000 miles, but not a pleasant journey straight from the desk chair. Above treeline, you pull yourself over rocks in a few places and walk across slanted, roof-sized boulders in others. The climb is tough, even without a pack. The park re-commends you bring or borrow a day pack (plenty of water, lots of snacks, sunscreen, a first-aid kit, gloves, hat, and extra layers of clothing). If you don't want to retrace your steps, you might consider going up the Abol Trail (part of which is referred to as the "Abol Slide," because of the loose rocks and steepness formed by a nineteenth-century landslide) and down the Hunt Trail (A.T.). That requires a two-mile walk or ride from Katahdin Stream along the Perimeter Road to Abol Campground before starting your hike. The Abol Trail usually opens after the Hunt Trail; until the sandy, gravelly soils dry out, the trail is unstable, and boulders can become dislodged.

"Weather permitting," you can begin a southbound hike as early as May 31. Before then, trails are so wet, even without snow and ice, that foot traffic would irreparably harm the alpine and subalpine areas. However, even for the following few weeks, the tiny, biting blackflies can drive you out of the woods in agony and frustration, leaving behind a contribution of your blood to the North Woods ecosystem. Overnight camping season in Baxter is May 15–Oct 15.

Baxter Park will provide information on weather and conditions and recommendations regarding climbing but will remind hikers that your safety and good decision-making are your responsibility. The park is largely wilderness, and hikers should *not* expect timely rescue or assistance and *should* be prepared to self-rescue. Each morning, rangers at Chimney Pond (elev. 2,914 feet) make observations of conditions to determine both the safety of hiking conditions and the need to protect fragile alpine areas. At times, trails are closed for safety considerations and to protect the rare and endangered alpine plants, animals, and their habitat, as well as protecting unstable soils. Trail statuses and alerts then are posted at campgrounds throughout the park to provide hikers a guideline for planning their day's hike. Any park-wide alerts will be listed, including, for example, high heat index, blowdowns, thunderstorms, high water, snow, ice, *etc.* Be sure to check the posted weather report before embarking on your day's hike. Change plans if warranted.

Hikers who hike closed trails are subject to a court summons and fine and having park visitation privileges revoked. Those daily weather reports and trail alerts are posted at the trailheads at 7 a.m. during the hiking season.

Getting to Amicalola Falls State Park, Georgia

No public transportation is available to or from Amicalola Falls State Park, but hikers have several options from Atlanta, Gainesville (located 40 miles southeast of the park), and the mountain town of Dahlonega (located 16 miles east of Amicalola Falls).

LEAVING ATLANTA

If you fly into Atlanta, you can take Atlanta's rapid-transit trains (MARTA) from the airport to either the Greyhound bus station or the Amtrak station. To reach either station, take the MARTA train north from MARTA's airport station ($2.50 fare). To reach the Greyhound bus station, exit the train at Garnett Station. The bus station is located at 232 Forsyth Street, within sight of the entrance to the MARTA station. To get to the Amtrak station, continue north on the train to the Arts Center Station. From the Arts Center Station, bus No. 23 (departing the station every 10 minutes) will take you to the Amtrak station, located about 10 blocks north on Peachtree. If you wish to walk to the Amtrak station, follow Peachtree Street approximately one mile north; the station is on the left (west) at 1688 Peachtree NW. For more information, call MARTA, (404) 848-4711. Other options from the airport to the bus and train stations include taxis and the Atlanta Airport Shuttle, (404) 941-3440, a privately owned bus service. Atlanta Airport Shuttle vans leave the airport every 15 minutes, from south baggage claim, bound for the bus station and Amtrak station ($18.50 fare). Superior Transportation, (770) 457-4794, leaves Atlanta airport every two hours on the odd hour; $55 one way.

ATLANTA TO GAINESVILLE

Two buses and one Amtrak train leave daily from Atlanta for Gainesville. At publication time, Greyhound buses, (800) 229-9424, <www.greyhound.com>, departed the Atlanta station for Gainesville at 9:15 a.m. and 4 p.m. ($21.60) and arrived in Gainesville at 10:50 a.m. and 5:40 p.m. Buses departed Gainesville at 9 a.m. ($21.40) and arrived in Atlanta at 1:05 p.m. However, Greyhound routinely revises its schedule; call for current information. Amtrak's train was scheduled to depart from Atlanta daily at 8:04 p.m. and arrive in Gainesville at 8:59 p.m. ($16). A train was scheduled to depart Gainesville for Atlanta daily at 6:58 a.m. Reservations are required. Call (800) 872-7245, or visit <www.amtrak.com>.

Gainesville—*Lodging:* Motel 6, (770) 532-7531, $42.99 weekdays, $46.99 weekends, $3EAP, WiFi, pet-friendly; Lanier Center Holiday Inn, (770) 531-0907, $85–100D, no dogs, hot B, Internet; Country Hearth and Suites, (770) 287-3205, $55.99–$59.99D, B buffet, pets $15; Hampton Inn,

(770) 503-0300, $100–125, WiFi, no pets, hot B; Best Value Inn, (770) 534-0303, $50S–$55D, no pets. All are within four miles of the bus and train stations.

GAINESVILLE TO AMICALOLA FALLS STATE PARK

Tom Bazemore, (706) 265-9454 or (865) 209-1827, offers service to Amicalola Falls State Park; transports dogs and accepts cash (deposit may be required). Service to the Trailhead at USFS 42 available at an additional cost.

GAINESVILLE TO DAHLONEGA

Some hikers choose to stay in Dahlonega rather than Gainesville. The site of the country's first gold rush, in the 1830s, Dahlonega sits 16 miles east of Amicalola Falls and offers all major services. Tom Bazemore (see above) offers service to Dahlonega.

Dahlonega—■ *Hostel:* A.T. Hiker Hostel run by Josh and Leigh Saint, (770) 312-7342, <www.hikerhostel.com>, <hikerhostel@yahoo.com>, open year-round, by reservation; $80 thru-hiker's special (Feb 24–Apr 20) includes pick-up at North Springs MARTA station in Atlanta or bus/train station in Gainesville, bunk, fuel (8 oz. white gas or denatured, canisters extra), stop at outfitters if needed, B, and shuttle to Springer or Amicalola. Gear shipment to hostel available. Bunk & B $18, private room & B $42D, private cabin with B $55S–$65D. Fuel (white gas, canister & alcohol), free Internet/WiFi access. For guests only, shuttle service to all Georgia Trailheads (contact or see Web site for rates). Mail drops: P.O. Box 802 (USPS) or 7693 Hwy. 19N, Dahlonega, GA 30533 (FedEx/UPS). ■ *Lodging:* Hotel rates in Dahlonega vary with the season. After May 1 and on weekends, expect listed rates to increase. Holiday Inn Express, (706) 867-7777, $86–$169, $5EAP, includes hot B, no pets or smoking allowed; Super 8, (706) 864-4343, $50D, includes B, $8 for dogs, WiFi; Days Inn, (706) 864-2338, newly renovated, $49–$80, one room for pets $10, B, WiFi; Quality Inn, (706) 864-6191, $50–$80, includes B, pets <20 pounds $10 fee, Internet access and WiFi; Smith House, (800) 852-9577, <www.smithhouse.com>, $99–$229, no dogs, no smoking. The Smith House Restaurant, in operation since 1922, is famous for its family-style AYCE fare: L (beginning in April)

THE PROFILES THROUGHOUT THIS BOOK ARE BASED ON 2012 MILEAGES. WHERE THEY SIGNIFICANTLY DIFFER FROM THE CURRENT MILEAGES (USED IN THE TABLES), A NOTE TO CHECK THE TABLES HAS BEEN INSERTED.

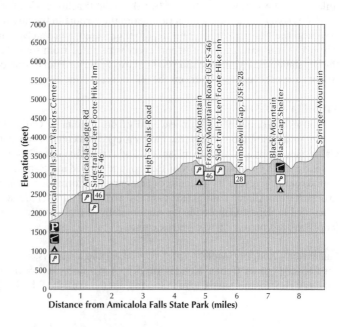

Distance from Amicalola Falls State Park (miles)

Tu–F 11–3, D Tu–F 4–8, Sa–Su 11–8. Hours are seasonal and may vary. Call ahead. *Outfitter:* Woodlands Edge, 36 N. Park St., (706) 864-5358, <woodlands.dahlonega@gmail.com>, M–F 10–5, Sa 10–5:30, Su 11–5, boots and apparel, limited gear.

ALTERNATIVES

Several Trail enthusiasts in the Atlanta area offer shuttles from Atlanta to the park and Springer Mountain. The ATC is continually updating its list. Many people who offer shuttles do so on their time off; arrangements are best made at least a week or two in advance. See page 1 for shuttle services.

AMICALOLA FALLS APPROACH TRAIL

Miles from Springer	Fr Last Point	Features	Services	Miles from AFSP	M A P
8.8	0.0	Amicalola Falls State Park; Visitors Center Archway (1,700') **AFSP "Max Epperson" Shelter**...*0.0mS; 7.3mN*	R, P, C, S, sh, cl, w (W–19m O)	0.0	
8.3	0.5	Base of Amicalola Falls (2,150')...*600+stairs*		0.5	
7.6	0.7	Amicalola Lodge Road (2,550')	R, P (E–0.1m L, M, w)	1.2	
7.4	0.2	+Len Foote Hike Inn Trail (2,600')	E–5m L, M, w	1.4	
7.2	0.2	USFS 46 (2,580')...*log steps on north side*	R	1.6	ATC N.C.–Ga. Map 4
5.6	1.6	High Shoals Road (2,800')	R	3.2	
4.0	1.6	Frosty Mountain (3,382')	C, w	4.8	
3.7	0.3	USFS 46, Frosty Mountain Road (3,192')	R	5.1	
3.4	0.3	+Len Foote Hike Inn (3,310')	E–1m L, M, w	5.4	
2.8	0.6	USFS 28, Nimblewill Gap (3,100')	R	6.0	
1.8	1.0	Black Mountain (3,600')		7.0	
1.5	0.3	**Black Gap Shelter** (3,300')...*7.3mS; 1.9mN*	S, C, w	7.3	
0.0	1.5	Springer Mountain (3,782')...*A.T. bronze plaque, register in rock*		8.8	

+ Fee charged

Amicalola Falls State Park—Its facilities nestled almost nine miles southwest of Springer Mountain, the park is the gateway to the southern terminus of the A.T. Scales to weigh packs and showers are located near the center entrance, as well as a rest room, snack machines, and water fountain. The visitors center sells guidebooks, maps, and gift items. The park holds UPS and USPS packages sent c/o Amicalola Falls State Park, 240 Amicalola Falls State Park Rd., Dawsonville, GA 30534. Indicate on the box to hold the package at either the visitors center or the lodge. The visitors center, (706) 265-4703, is open 8:30–5 daily. While at the park, sign the hiker register inside the visitors center. A $5/vehicle user fee is charged to all park visitors. Long-distance hikers may leave vehicles only in the parking area opposite the visitors center for up to 14 days before an annual pass is needed. Dogs must be on a leash within the park. ■ *Camping:* The park also offers campsites and cabins: campsites $25 with shower, coin laundry, 1- to 3-bedroom cabins (2-night minimum), call for pricing. ■ *Lodging:* The desk at Amicalola Lodge, (706) 265-8888, (800) 573-9656, <www.gastateparks.org>, is staffed around the clock; call for pricing on rooms, B included. Reservations suggested for cabins, campsites, and the lodge. ■ *Restaurant:* The lodge houses the Maple Restaurant, daily buffets, full-buffet B 7–10:30, L 11:30–3, D 5–8.

West 19 miles to *Outfitters:* North Georgia Mountain Outfitters, Travis/Shirley/ Whitney Crouch, (706) 698-4453, fax (706) 698-4454, <www.hikenorthgeorgia.com>, <info@hikenorthgeorgia.com>, 583 Highland Crossing, Suite 230, East Ellijay, GA 30540, Tu–Sa 10–6; full-service outfitter, Coleman and alcohol fuels by the ounce, canister fuels, short-term food resupply; will hold packages without fee; possible shuttles to Atlanta airport, Amicalola, Springer, and Neel Gap; call for possible delivery of packages and store items.

Amicalola Falls State Park Shelter (1993)—Located 50 yards behind the visitors center, sleeps 12, and available to thru-hikers at no charge. Built by a group of Trail backpacking enthusiasts from nearby Canton in memory of their friend, Max Epperson. The "A.T. Gang" spent 800 hours constructing the facility. Epperson hiked the Trail as far north as Connecticut before his health failed. Afterward, he continued to offer shuttles and support for his hiking friends. Water source and rest room 50 yards away at visitors center.

Approach Trail to Springer Mountain—From the park visitors center, it is an 8.8-mile trek to the first white blaze, most of it uphill. To cut off the steep, one-mile ascent of the falls, catch a ride to the top of the falls, and pick up the blue blazes there. The southern end was recently relocated just past its start at the visitors center.

Approach Trail *via* Nimblewill Gap—This alternative puts you 2.2 miles south of Springer Mountain on the Approach Trail but requires a bumpy, muddy drive up Forest Service roads. From the park entrance, go east 9.5 miles on Ga. 52 to abandoned Grizzles Store. Turn left on Nimblewill Road, and continue past Nimblewill Church at 6.6 miles. Just beyond the church, pass a road on the left where the pavement ends. Continue to the right on the unpaved road, and reach Nimblewill Gap at 14 miles. This is a very rough road and probably should not be attempted unless you have a vehicle with high ground clearance.

From Amicalola Falls to Springer Mountain *via* Forest Service roads—The easiest and quickest route takes you within one mile of the Springer summit; it is clearly outlined on ATC's new map for the area (item #135 at <www.atctrailstore.org>). From the park, go west on Ga. 52 for 13.6 miles to Roy Road, at Cartecay Church and Stanley's Store. Turn right, and proceed 9.5 miles to the second stop sign. At the stop sign, bear right, and go 2.3 miles to Mt. Pleasant Church on the left. Across from the church, turn right onto unpaved Forest Service Road 42. This well-graded gravel road, suitable for all vehicles, winds 6.6 miles to the A.T. crossing at Big Stamp on the north side of the road. To reach the summit of Springer Mountain, walk 0.9 mile south. If you don't want to retrace your steps on the A.T., an alternative is to continue 1.7 miles past the A.T. crossing to USFS 42's intersection with the Benton MacKaye Trail (BMT). The BMT leads 1.5 miles up Springer and joins the A.T. just north of the southern terminus.

Len Foote Hike Inn—(800) 581-8032, <www.hike-inn.com>. This $1-million lodge is similar to huts in New Hampshire's White Mountains. The 40-bed, 20-room inn is approximately 5.0 miles north of Amicalola Falls State Park facilities and 4.5 miles south of the Springer Mountain summit. The yellow-blazed Hike Inn Trail creates a loop with the blue-blazed Approach Trail that leads from the park to Springer. Overnight stays, which include family-style B/D, are $107S, $154D, rates subject to change; no dogs allowed. Amenities include linens, hot showers, composting toilets, and electricity (outlets in bath house only). Owned by the Georgia Department of Natural Resources, the inn is operated by the Appalachian Education and Recreation Services, Inc., a nonprofit corporation affiliated with the Georgia Appalachian Trail Club. Walk-ins are allowed, subject to availability. Registration is at the Amicalola Falls State Park visitors center, where you can check on room availability. Open year-round, guest rooms in the bunkhouse are heated. Sleeping bags recommended Nov–Mar.

Black Gap Shelter (1953/1995)—Sleeps 8. privy. Once the Springer Mountain Shelter, dismantled and moved to this location in 1995. This shelter is 1.5 miles south of the summit of Springer Mountain on the Approach Trail. Water is located 300 yards downhill to the right of the shelter.

Georgia

Miles from Springer	Fr Last Point	Features	Services	Miles from Katahdin	M A P
0.0	0.0	Springer Mountain (3,782')...A.T. bronze plaque, register in rock		2,189.2	
0.2	0.2	**Springer Mountain Shelter** (3,730')...1.9mS; 3mN Benton MacKaye Trail (southern terminus)	E–0.2m S, C, w	2,189.0	
1.0	0.8	USFS 42, Big Stamp Gap (3,350')	R, P	2,188.2	
1.9	0.9	Benton MacKaye Trail (3,430')		2,187.3	
2.8	0.9	**Stover Creek Shelter** (2,870') ...3mS; 5.7mN	E–0.2m S, C, w	2,186.4	
3.8	1.0	Stover Creek (2,660')	w	2,185.4	
4.2	0.4	Benton MacKaye Trail (2,580')		2,185.0	
4.3	0.1	USFS 58, Three Forks (2,530')	R, C, w	2,184.9	
6.0	1.7	Side trail to Long Creek Falls, junction with Benton MacKaye and Duncan Ridge trails (2,800')	w	2,183.2	
6.2	0.2	USFS 251, Hickory Flats (3,000')... shed, cemetery	R	2,183.0	
8.1	1.9	**Hawk Mountain Shelter** (3,200')...5.7mS; 8mN	W–0.2m S, C; 0.4m w	2,181.1	ATC N.C.–Ga. Map 4
8.6	0.5	USFS 42/69, Hightower Gap (2,854')	R, P	2,180.6	
10.5	1.9	Horse Gap (2,673')	R, P	2,178.7	
11.5	1.0	Sassafras Mountain (3,340')		2,177.7	
12.2	0.7	USFS 42/80, Cooper Gap (2,800')	R, P	2,177.0	
12.9	0.7	Justus Mountain (3,224')		2,176.3	
14.3	1.4	Justus Creek (2,550')	C, w	2,174.9	
15.8	1.5	**Gooch Mountain Shelter** (3,000')...8mS; 12.9mN	W–0.1m S, C, w	2,173.4	
17.3	1.5	USFS 42, Gooch Gap (2,821')	R, P (E–0.1m C, w)	2,171.9	
19.6	2.3	Ramrock Mountain (3,260')...rock outcropping		2,169.6	
21.1	1.5	Ga. 60, Woody Gap (3,173')...picnic area, spring **Suches, Ga. 30572**	R, P, C (E–7m H, f) (W–0.1m w; 2m PO, G, C, H, D, cl, sh, f)	2,168.1	
22.1	1.0	Big Cedar Mountain (3,737')...rock ledges		2,167.1	
23.4	1.3	Dan Gap (3,300')		2,165.8	
24.3	0.9	Lance Creek (3,050')...tent platforms	C, w	2,164.9	
26.2	1.9	Burnett Field Mountain (3,480')		2,163.0	
26.7	0.5	Jarrard Gap (3,250')...USFS Lake Winfield Scott Recreation Area	W–0.3m w; 1m C, sh	2,162.5	
28.1	1.4	Bird Gap, Freeman Trail (3,650') **Woods Hole Shelter**...12.9mS; 1.7mN	W–0.4m S, C, w	2,161.1	
28.4	0.3	Slaughter Creek Trail at Slaughter Creek Gap (3,790')...spring	w	2,160.8	

Miles from Springer	Fr Last Point	Features	Services	Miles from Katahdin	M A P
28.5	0.1	Slaughter Creek Campsite (3,800')... tent platforms	C	2,160.7	ATC N.C.–Ga. Map 4
29.3	0.8	Blood Mountain (4,461') **Blood Mountain Shelter** ...1.7mS; 10.3mN	S, nw	2,159.9	
30.7	1.4	Flatrock Gap(3,450') Trail to Byron Reece Memorial	W–0.2m w	2,158.5	
31.7	1.0	U.S. 19 & 129, Neel Gap (3,125')	R, P, H, O, cl, sh, f (E–0.3m L, g) (W–3m C, G, cl, sh)	2,157.5	
32.8	1.1	Bull Gap (3,690')	C, w	2,156.4	
33.2	0.4	Levelland Mountain (3,942')		2,156.0	
33.9	0.7	Swaim Gap (3,470')		2,155.3	
34.7	0.8	Rock Spring Top (3,520')	w	2,154.5	
35.4	0.7	Wolf Laurel Top (3,766')		2,153.8	
35.9	0.5	Baggs Creek Gap (3,800')	C, w	2,153.3	
36.7	0.8	Cowrock Mountain (3,842')		2,152.5	
37.7	1.0	Ga. 348, Tesnatee Gap (3,138')	R, P	2,151.5	
38.4	0.7	**Whitley Gap Shelter** (3,370')...10.3mS; 6mN	E–1.2m S; 1.5m w	2,150.8	
38.6	0.2	Ga. 348, Hogpen Gap (3,450')...A.T. plaque	R, P, w	2,150.6	
39.5	0.9	White Oak Stamp (3,470')		2,149.7	
40.6	1.1	Poor Mountain (3,620')		2,148.6	
42.4	1.8	Sheep Rock Top (3,600')		2,146.8	
43.2	0.8	**Low Gap Shelter** (3,050')...6mS; 7.3mN	S, C, w	2,146.0	ATC N.C.–Ga. Map 3
44.6	1.4	Poplar Stamp Gap (2,990')	C, w	2,144.6	
47.0	2.4	Cold Springs Gap (3,300')		2,142.2	
48.2	1.2	Chattahoochee Gap (3,500') Jack's Gap Trail to Ga. 180	E–0.5m w	2,141.0	
48.9	0.7	Red Clay Gap (3,485')		2,140.3	
49.6	0.7	Campsite (3,600')	C	2,139.6	
49.8	0.2	Spring (3,500')	w	2,139.4	
50.4	0.6	Spring (3,890')...water for Blue Mountain Shelter	w	2,138.8	
50.5	0.1	**Blue Mountain Shelter** (3,900')...7.3mS; 8.1mN	S, nw	2,138.7	
51.4	0.9	Blue Mountain (4,025')		2,137.8	
52.9	1.5	Ga. 75, Unicoi Gap (2,949')...A.T. plaque **Helen, Ga. 30545** Cleveland, Ga.	R, P (E–9m PO, G, L, M, cl; 17m O, D) (W–4.8m C, L, G, cl, f; 11m all)	2,136.3	
53.5	0.6	Stream (3,300')	w	2,135.7	
54.3	0.8	Rocky Mountain (4,017')	C	2,134.9	
55.6	1.3	USFS 283, Indian Grave Gap (3,113')	R, P	2,133.6	
56.3	0.7	USFS 79, Tray Mountain Road (3,580')	R	2,132.9	
56.6	0.3	Cheese Factory Site (3,590')	C, w	2,132.6	

Miles from Springer	Fr Last Point	Features	Services	Miles from Katahdin	MAP
57.3	0.7	USFS 79/698, Tray Mountain Road, Tray Gap (3,847')	R, P	2,131.9	
58.1	0.8	Tray Mountain (4,430')		2,131.1	
58.6	0.5	**Tray Mountain Shelter** (4,200')...8.1mS; 7.7mN	S, w	2,130.6	
59.6	1.0	Wolfpen Gap (3,600')		2,129.6	
60.2	0.6	Steeltrap Gap (3,490')		2,129.0	
60.8	0.6	Younglick Knob (3,800')		2,128.4	
62.2	1.4	Swag of the Blue Ridge (3,400')		2,127.0	
63.3	1.1	Sassafras Gap (3,500')	w	2,125.9	
64.2	0.9	Addis Gap to USFS 26 (3,304')	C (E–0.5m R, w)	2,125.0	
65.2	1.0	Kelly Knob (4,276')		2,124.0	
66.0	0.8	**Deep Gap Shelter** (3,550') ...7.7mS; 8.6mN	E–0.3m S, w	2,123.2	ATC N.C.–Ga. Map 3
67.2	1.2	McClure Gap (3,650')	C	2,122.0	
67.4	0.2	Powell Mountain (3,850')		2,121.8	
68.4	1.0	Moreland Gap (3,200')		2,120.8	
69.0	0.6	Streams (2,650')	w	2,120.2	
69.6	0.6	U.S. 76, Dicks Creek Gap (2,675') ...picnic area **Hiawassee, Ga. 30546**	R, P, w (W–0.5m H, f; 11m PO, all)	2,119.6	
70.7	1.1	Campsite (3,150')	C, w	2,118.5	
71.4	0.7	Cowart Gap (2,900')		2,117.8	
72.9	1.5	Bull Gap (3,550')		2,116.3	
74.1	1.2	**Plumorchard Gap Shelter** (3,050')...8.6mS; 7.5mN	E–0.2m S, w	2,115.1	
74.8	0.7	As Knob (3,460')		2,114.4	
75.4	0.6	Blue Ridge Gap (3,020')...dirt road		2,113.8	
76.4	1.0	Campsite (3,500')	C, w	2,112.8	
76.6	0.2	Rich Cove Gap (3,390')		2,112.6	
78.5	1.9	Georgia–North Carolina State Line (3,825')...tree register		2,110.7	

The Trail in Georgia begins at Springer Mountain and follows a rugged, often rocky terrain, reaching a height of more than 4,461 feet and never dipping below 2,500 feet. It passes through five major gaps and more than 25 smaller ones. Thru-hikers starting their journey in March or April will probably see snow, which can add to the difficulty. Spring melts give way to many of the wildflowers common throughout the mountains, including bloodroot, trillium, and azalea. Forests are mostly second-growth hardwoods of hickory, oak, and poplar. Half of the Trail lies within five designated wilderness areas in the forest.

Georgia Appalachian Trail Club—GATC maintains the 78.6 miles from Springer Mountain to Bly Gap, just over the North Carolina line. Correspondence should be sent to GATC, P.O. Box 654, Atlanta, GA 30301; (404) 494-0968; <www.georgia-atclub.org>; <gatc-trail_supv@ charter.net>.

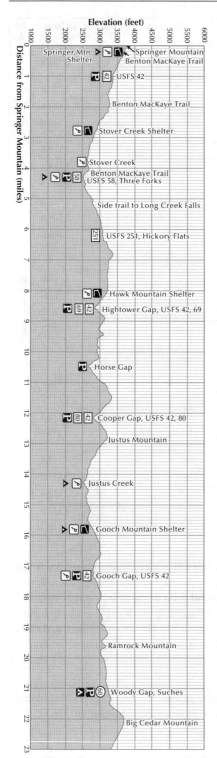

ALL PROFILES THROUGHOUT THIS BOOK ARE BASED ON 2012 MILEAGES. WHERE THEY SIGNIFICANTLY DIFFER FROM THE CURRENT MILEAGES (USED IN THE TABLES), A NOTE TO CHECK THE TABLES HAS BEEN INSERTED.

Chattahoochee National Forest—The Trail in Georgia winds through the Chattahoochee National Forest, created by Congress in 1936. By that time, much of the land had been laid bare from intensive timber harvesting. Today, little virgin timber remains, but the hardwoods have reestablished themselves with the help of 77 years of management and protection.

Bear problems—With the loss of habitat from development in the mountains, black bears are roaming farther in search of food. To combat this problem, the GATC and the USFS are placing bear cables for hanging food at the shelters most affected. If bear cables are not available, secure food using bear-proof techniques. *See page xiii.*

U.S. Forest Service rules (effective through June) require using a bear canister while camping overnight between Jarrard and Neel gaps, a five-mile stretch that includes Woods Hole and Blood Mountain shelters and Slaughter Gap Campsite. **Plan accordingly.**

Springer Mountain—Springer has served as the A.T.'s southern terminus since 1958. Before that, Mt. Oglethorpe, to the southwest, was the southern terminus. In 1993, GATC members and the Forest Service installed a new plaque marking the Trail's southernmost blaze. The hiker register is located within the boulder on which the plaque is mounted. The original bronze plaque marking the southern terminus, one of three intended for road crossings, was created in 1934 by GATC member and amateur sculptor George Noble at a cost of $20—a hefty amount in those days. Warner Hall, the club's second president, served as Noble's model and coined the phrase, "A footpath for those who seek fellowship with the wilderness." That plaque was moved to the mountain in May 1959; keep an eye out for the other two plaques at road crossings along the Trail in Georgia. The overlook at the 3,782-foot summit provides views to the west—a nice sunset spot.

Springer Mountain Shelter (1993)—Sleeps 12. Privy. Tentpads. Bear cables. Near the summit, 250 yards north of the bronze plaque, then east 200 yards on a blue-blazed side trail. Water source is a spring 80 yards on a blue-blazed trail in front of the shelter; spring may go dry in times of drought.

Stover Creek Shelter (2006)—Sleeps 16. Privy. Tentpads. Bear cables. Water source is the creek. No tenting near water.

Hawk Mountain Shelter (1993)—Sleeps 12. Privy. Bear cables. Army Rangers from nearby Camp Frank D. Merrill use the area for training exercises and have been spotted all times of the day and night. Water source is 300 yards on a blue-blazed trail behind the shelter.

Gooch Mountain Shelter (2001)—Sleeps 14. Privy. Bear cables. Additional tenting space 1.6 miles farther north at Gooch Gap, near the old shelter site. Excellent water source is 100 yards behind the shelter.

Ga. 60/Woody Gap/Suches—Parking area, picnic tables, and chemical toilets. A spring is on a poorly marked side trail 0.1 mile west of the A.T. on northern side of the gap.
  East 7 miles to *Hostel:* A.T. Hiker Hostel, 7693 Hwy. 19N, Dahlonega, GA 30533; (770) 312-7342, <www.hikerhostel.com>; owners Josh and Leigh Saint, open year-round. Bunk & B $18, private & B $42D, private cabin with B $55S–$65D; 5 p.m. pick-up at Woody Gap, Feb 24–Apr 27. Fuel, Internet/WiFi, coin laundry, shuttle service for guests to all Georgia Trailheads.
  West 2 miles to **Suches, Ga. [P.O. ZIP 30572: M–F 12:15–4:15; (706) 747-2611].**
■ *Hostel:* Wolfpen Gap Country Store (short-term resupply), 12905 Wolf Pen Gap Rd., Suches, GA 30572 ; (706) 747-2271; $15PP includes shower (towel, soap, shampoo); nonguest shower, $5; coin laundry with detergent (fee); fuel, hot L; WiFi; ATM; accepts UPS drops. Store open M–F 7:30–8, Sa 7:30–9, Su 9–7; also a designated Village Post Office (VPO). Free guest shuttles to Woody Gap; shuttles (fee) to all Georgia Trailheads. ■ *Other services:* Don L. Pruitt, M.D., (706) 747-1421, open M–Th 9–4, walk-ins 9–11. Jim and Ruth Ann Miner, (706) 747-5434, live in town and are available if you need help. ■ *Shuttles:* Wes Wisson, (706) 747-2671; <dwisson@windstream.net>.

Lance Creek—Campsite with 4 tent platforms, built by the ATC Konnarock crew. Good water.

Jarrard Gap—**West** 1 mile on blue-blazed trail to USFS Lake Winfield Scott Recreation Area; tentsites, showers, $15; dogs must be leashed.

Woods Hole Shelter (1998)—Sleeps 7. Privy. Bear cables. Located 0.4 mile west on a blue-blazed side trail, this "Nantahala design" shelter is named in honor of the late Tillie and Roy Wood, original owners of the Woodshole Hostel near Pearisburg, Virginia. Water source is an unreliable spring along the trail to the shelter.

Bird Gap—From here, the Freeman Trail leads 1.7 miles around the south slope of Blood Mountain and rejoins the A.T. 1.1 miles from Neel Gap. Those who choose this blue-blazed route miss the climb to the Trail's high point in Georgia; it serves as a foul-weather route around Blood Mountain.

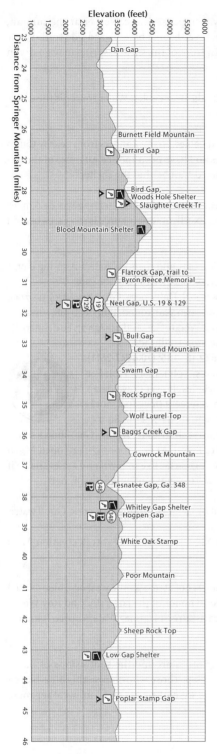

Elevation (feet)

Distance from Springer Mountain (miles)

Dan Gap

Burnett Field Mountain

Jarrard Gap

Bird Gap,
Woods Hole Shelter
Slaughter Creek Tr

Blood Mountain Shelter

Flatrock Gap, trail to
Byron Reece Memorial

Neel Gap, U.S. 19 & 129

Bull Gap

Levelland Mountain

Swaim Gap

Rock Spring Top

Wolf Laurel Top

Baggs Creek Gap

Cowrock Mountain

Tesnatee Gap, Ga. 348

Whitley Gap Shelter
Hogpen Gap

White Oak Stamp

Poor Mountain

Sheep Rock Top

Low Gap Shelter

Poplar Stamp Gap

Slaughter Gap—Slaughter Creek Trail leads to tentsites near Slaughter Creek that ease the load on Blood Mountain. *In an effort to counter visitor impact, fires have been banned along a 3.3-mile section between Slaughter Gap and Neel Gap.*

Blood Mountain—According to tales of the Creek and Cherokee, a battle here between the two nations left so many dead and wounded that the ground ran red with blood. Blood Mountain is the most-visited spot on the A.T. south of Clingmans Dome, and the impact of more than 40,000 visitors a year has taken its toll. Vandalism in and around the shelter is a chronic problem.

Blood Mountain Shelter (1934)—Sleeps 8. Privy. Located atop the highest peak on the A.T. in Georgia (4,461 feet), this historic two-room stone structure was last refurbished in 2012. No water or firewood available; no fires permitted. Northbounders can get water from a stream 0.3 mile north of Bird Gap or on a blue-blazed side trail at Slaughter Gap, 0.9 mile from the shelter. Southbounders can get water at Neel Gap or at a spring located on the blue-blazed trail to Byron Reece Memorial, 0.2 mile from where the trail joins the A.T., 2.4 miles south of Neel Gap.

U.S. 19 & 129/Neel Gap— Mountain Crossings at Walasi-Yi Center, 12471 Gainesville Hwy., Blairsville, GA 30512; (706) 745-6095, <www.mountaincrossings.com>. A full-service *Outfitter* with all stove fuels and gift shop (short-term resupply). Operated by new owners Georgeanna Morton & Logan Seamon. UPS and USPS packages held, $1 donation. ■ *Hostel:* Walasi-Yi, open year-round, $17PP, shower, coin laundry, nonguest shower $4, pets outside.

East 0.3 mile to *Lodging:* Blood Mountain Cabins, (800) 284-6866, <www.bloodmountain.com>, limited resupply. Cabins with showers, kitchens, and satellite TV sleep 4; thru-hiker rate $60, free coin laundry, Internet access, no pets. A trail leads from the Walasi-Yi Center to the resort office.

West 3 miles to *Camping:* Vogel State Park, (800) 864-7275, <www.gastateparks.org>. Tentsites with shower $20–$28, showers only $2.

Camp store (limited resupply) has snacks; coin laundry (detergent $1); and cabins, reservations suggested. Leash dogs inside the park.

Whitley Gap Shelter (1974)—Sleeps 6. Privy. Bear cables. This shelter is located 1.2 miles east of the A.T. down a steep side trail. Water source is a spring 0.3 mile beyond the shelter.

Low Gap Shelter (1953)—Sleeps 7. Privy. Bear cables. Water source is crossed at the shelter; a second source can be found 30 yards in front of the shelter.

Chattahoochee Gap—A blue-blazed side trail leads east to Chattahoochee Spring, source of the Chattahoochee River, which supplies drinking water to Atlanta and almost half of the state's population. Some 500 miles from this point, the river empties into the Gulf of Mexico.

Blue Mountain Shelter (1988)—Sleeps 7. Privy. Bear cables. Located on a short side trail. Water source is a spring on the A.T. 0.1 mile south of the shelter.

Ga. 75/Unicoi Gap—East 9 miles to **Helen, Ga. [P.O. ZIP 30545: M–F 9–12:30, 1:30–4, Sa 9–12; (706) 878-2422].** ■ *Lodging:* Helendorf River Inn, (800) 445-2271, $35–80 Su–Th, coin laundry, pets $20 in designated rooms only, B, WiFi, heated pool; Econolodge, (706) 878-8000, $45–$180, $10EAP, WiFi, B, $20/pets under 20 lbs. in selected rooms; Super 8 Motel, (800) 535-1251, next to coin laundry, hiker rates ($35S, $10EAP) exclude weekends, B, microwave, refrigerator, no pets, WiFi, Internet access, heated pool; Best Western, (706) 878-2111, $50–$65, WiFi, hot B, no pets, free possible shuttles to Trail M–F; America's Best Value Inn, (706) 878-8888, $40–$80, $6EAP, pets up to 30lbs. $15, WiFi, B; Jamison Inn, (706) 878-1451, $39D, B, no pets; Quality Inn, (706) 878-2268, $39–$99, $10EAP, B, $20/pet under 20 lbs., WiFi; Days Inn, (706) 878-4079, $39D, B, pets allowed $10; RiverBend, (706) 878-2155, hiker rate $39–$169, $10EAP, cabins up to 4 people $99–$250, pets $12.50 ea.; Alpine Valley Inn, (706) 878-2141, $40–$70 in off-season, $5EAP, pets less than 15 lbs. $10, heavier $15, B; Helen accommodations, <www.helenga.org>. ■ *Groceries:* Betty's Country Store and Deli (long-term resupply), ATC books, open daily 7–8, free shuttles 8 a.m.–6 p.m. ■ *Restaurants:* numerous. ■ *Internet access:* White County Library, Helen Branch. ■ *Other services:* bicycle rentals available at Woody's Mountain Bikes, (706) 878-3715; pharmacy. ■ *Shuttles:* Woody's.
    East 17 miles to **Cleveland, Ga.** ■ *Outfitter:* Smoky Mountain Trader, (706) 865-7296, <www.smokymountaintrader.com>. ■ *Medical:* Northeast Georgia Physicians Group, (706) 865-1234, M–F 7:30–4:30.

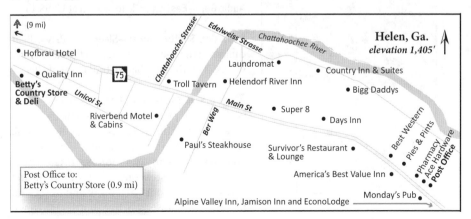

↑ (9 mi)

Helen, Ga.
elevation 1,405' ↑

- Hofbrau Hotel
- Quality Inn
- **Betty's Country Store & Deli**
- [75]
- Edelweiss Strasse
- Chattahoochee Strasse
- Chattahoochee River
- Laundromat •
- Troll Tavern •
- • Helendorf River Inn
- • Country Inn & Suites
- • Bigg Daddys
- Unicoi St
- Main St
- • Super 8
- Riverbend Motel • & Cabins
- Ber Weg
- • Days Inn
- • Paul's Steakhouse
- Survivor's Restaurant • & Lounge
- Best Western
- Pies & Prints
- Pharmacy
- Ace Hardware
- **Post Office**

Post Office to:
Betty's Country Store (0.9 mi)

- America's Best Value Inn •
- Monday's Pub •

Alpine Valley Inn, Jamison Inn and EconoLodge ⟶

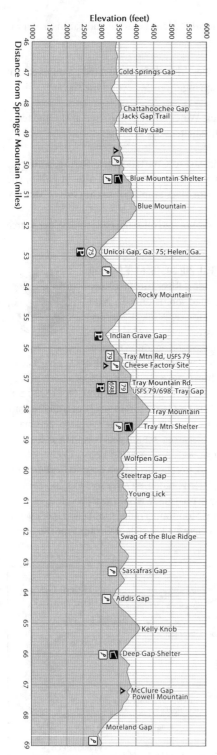

West 2.3 miles, then left 2.5 miles on Ga. 180 to *Lodging:* Enota Mountain Retreat, 1000 Hwy. 180, Hiawassee, GA 30546; (800) 990-8869, <www.enota.com>; waterfalls, organic gardens, and an animal sanctuary; $10 membership per visit and $5 campfire fee; tent-sites $25 with access to bathhouse, motel-type room $80D, cabins $110–$165, dogs $5. Free long-distance phone, coin laundry with soap, B Sa–Su, D F–Sa with advance notice, satellite TV, video library, Internet access, Jacuzzis in some cabins, massage 1½ hours $100, possible shuttle to Trail for fee. General store (short-term resupply) open 8:30–8, including Coleman, alcohol, and canister fuels. Holds packages for guests only.

West 11 miles to **Hiawassee, Ga**. (see below).

Tray Mountain—Spectacular views from the 4,430-foot summit and probably the southernmost breeding area in the United States for Canada warblers. These small, active songbirds may be spotted in the rhododendron thickets along the southern approach to the summit. Males are blue-gray above and yellow throughout the chest. Look for the distinctive "necklace" on both the males' and females' chests. The Canada warbler's song is an irregular burst of beautiful notes.

Tray Mountain Shelter (1971)—Sleeps 7. Privy. Bear cables. Excellent spot for taking in the sunset and sunrise from the summit or from viewpoints along the 0.2-mile trail to the shelter. Water source is a spring located 260 yards behind the shelter.

Addis Gap—**East** 0.5 mile to stream at USFS 26.

Deep Gap Shelter (1983)—Sleeps 12. Privy. Bear cables. On a 0.3-mile side trail to the east. Water source is on the blue-blazed trail to the shelter.

 U.S. 76/Dicks Creek Gap/Hiawassee—Parking lot, picnic tables, and small creek.

West 0.5 mile to *Hostel:* Top of Georgia Hostel and Hiking Center, 7675 U.S. 76 East, Hiawassee, GA 30545; (706) 982-3252, <www.topofgeorgiahostel.com>; full-service hostel and small-scale outfitter, bunk and towel $20, tenting with shower $10; free shuttles into town

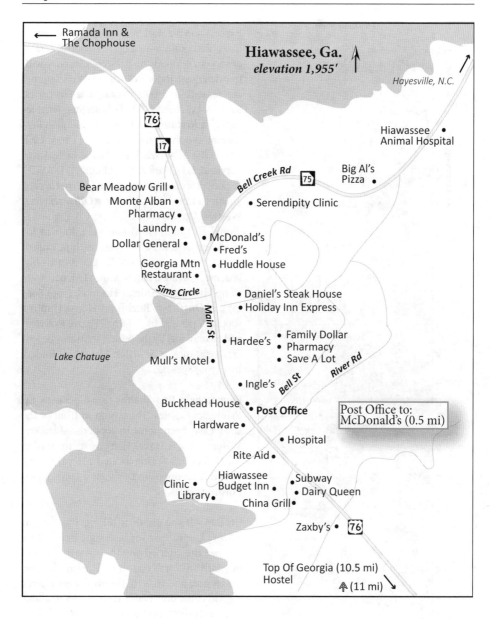

← Ramada Inn &
The Chophouse

Hiawassee, Ga.
elevation 1,955'

Hayesville, N.C.

76
17

Hiawassee •
Animal Hospital

Bell Creek Rd   75

Big Al's
Pizza •

Bear Meadow Grill •
Monte Alban •
Pharmacy •
Laundry •
Dollar General •

• Serendipity Clinic

Georgia Mtn
Restaurant •

• McDonald's
• Fred's

• Huddle House

Sims Circle

Main St

• Daniel's Steak House
• Holiday Inn Express

Lake Chatuge

Mull's Motel •

• Hardee's

• Family Dollar
• Pharmacy
• Save A Lot

River Rd

• Ingle's   Bell St

Buckhead House •
• **Post Office**

Post Office to:
McDonald's (0.5 mi)

Hardware •

• Hospital

Rite Aid •

Clinic •
Library •

Hiawassee
Budget Inn •

China Grill •

• Subway
• Dairy Queen

Zaxby's •   76

Top Of Georgia (10.5 mi)
Hostel   (11 mi) ↘

twice daily, other Trailheads for fee; hot food available; full-service laundry $5; Internet; free LD; holds/ships packages (see Web site for labeling).

West 11 miles to **Hiawassee, Ga. [P.O. ZIP 30546: M–F 8:30–5, Sa 8:30–12; (706) 896-3632]**. *See map.* ■ *Lodging:* Mull's Motel, 213 N. Main St., (706) 896-4196, $55 and up, pets allowed (fee), holds packages for guests only; Hiawassee Budget Inn, 193 S. Main St., (706) 896-4121, <www.hiawasseebudgetinn.com>, $39.95–$49.95s, $5EAP each, tent set-up with shower $10, one evening restaurant shuttle, coin laundry, Internet/WiFi access, short-term resupply, well-stocked in-house outfitter, free Mar–Apr shuttle for guests only from/to Trail at Dicks Creek or Unicoi gaps at 9 and 11 a.m. (fee for nonguests), $5 per person other months, holds UPS packages only for guests; Holiday Inn

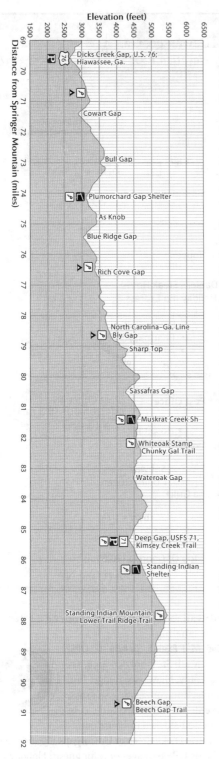

Express, 300 Big Sky Dr., (706) 896-8884, <www.
hiexpress.com/hiawasseega>, special hiker rates
of $69–$120, $6EAP, no pets, coin laundry with
free detergent, indoor whirlpool, WiFi/Internet
access, will hold UPS packages. ■ *Groceries:*
Saves-A-Lot, Ingles (ATM), both long-term resupply. ■ *Restaurants:* Georgia Mountain Restaurant, B only on weekends, L/D; China Grill
AYCE; Big Al's Pizza, L/D AYCE; Monte Alban
Mexican, L/D; Daniel's Steakhouse, L/D AYCE;
various other fast-food places. ■ *Internet access:*
Towns County Public Library. ■ *Other services:*
Western Union; coin laundry; Chatuge Regional Hospital, (706) 896-2222, known for
treatment of blisters; Serendipity Clinic (urgent
care), (706) 970-1154, M–W, F, Sa 12–8, cash only;
pharmacy; dentist; banks with ATM; hardware
store; Hiawassee Animal Hospital, (706) 896-
4173. ■ *Outfitter:* Buckhead House (limited
supply), operated by "Mama" Fagan; Coleman
and alcohol fuel by the ounce, shuttle info, general assistance. ■ *Shuttles:* Hiawassee Budget
Inn, (706) 896-4121.

Plumorchard Gap Shelter (1993)—Sleeps 14.
Privy. Bear cables. The stump in front of the
shelter has been home to copperhead snakes.
Water source is a creek that crosses the trail to
the shelter or a spring located 200 yards west
of the A.T., opposite the shelter trail. Food-
hoisting cables.

Bly Gap—If you are thru-hiking, it is time to
celebrate your first (or last) state line. When
you see the gnarled oak in a clearing, you're
officially in North Carolina. The gap, with its
grassy area and views to the northwest, makes
a good campsite. Water from a spring about
100 yards south on the A.T.

North Carolina

Miles from Springer	Fr Last Point	Features	Services	Miles from Katahdin	M A P
78.5	1.9	Georgia–North Carolina State Line (3,825')...tree register		2,110.7	
78.6	0.1	Bly Gap (3,840')...gnarly oak tree	C, w	2,110.6	
79.1	0.5	Sharp Top (4,300')...vista		2,110.1	
80.5	1.4	Sassafras Gap (4,300')		2,108.7	
81.4	0.9	**Muskrat Creek Shelter** (4,600') ...7.5mS; 4.9mN	S, C, w	2,107.8	
82.2	0.8	Whiteoak Stamp (4,620')	w	2,107.0	
82.4	0.2	Chunky Gal Trail (4,700')		2,106.8	
83.3	0.9	Wateroak Gap (4,490')		2,105.9	
85.4	2.1	USFS 71, Deep Gap, (4,341'), Kimsey Creek Trail to USFS Standing Indian Campground	R, P, w (W–3.7m C, G, sh)	2,103.8	
86.3	0.9	**Standing Indian Shelter** (4,760') ...4.9mS; 7.6mN	S, C, w	2,102.9	
87.8	1.5	Lower Trail, Ridge Trail (5,498') Standing Indian Mountain	(E–0.2m summit) (W–0.2m w)	2,101.4	
90.7	2.9	Beech Gap Trail, Beech Gap (4,460')	C, w	2,098.5	
92.4	1.7	Coleman Gap (4,200')		2,096.8	
93.5	1.1	Timber Ridge Trail (4,700')		2,095.7	
93.9	0.4	**Carter Gap Shelters** (4,540') ...7.6mS; 8.6mN	S, C, w	2,095.3	
94.9	1.0	Ridgepole Mountain (4,990')		2,094.3	
97.6	2.7	Betty Creek Gap (4,300')	C, w	2,091.6	
98.5	0.9	USFS 83, Mooney Gap (4,400')	R	2,090.7	
98.8	0.3	Spring (4,500')	w	2,090.4	
99.3	0.5	Bearpen Gap (4,700')		2,089.9	
99.8	0.5	USFS 67, Bearpen Trail (4,790')	R	2,089.4	
100.1	0.3	Albert Mountain (5,250')...firetower		2,089.1	
102.5	2.4	**Long Branch Shelter** (4,503') ...8.6mS; 3.5mN	S, C, w	2,086.7	
103.5	1.0	Glassmine Gap, Long Branch Trail (4,400')		2,085.7	
106.0	2.5	**Rock Gap Shelter** (3,760') ...3.5mS; 8.5mN	S, C, w	2,083.2	
106.1	0.1	USFS 67, Rock Gap (3,750') USFS Standing Indian Campground	R, P (W–1.5m C, G, sh)	2,083.1	
106.7	0.6	Old U.S. 64, Wallace Gap (3,738')	R	2,082.5	
109.8	3.1	U.S. 64, Winding Stair Gap (3,770') ...piped spring **Franklin, N.C. 28734**	R, P, w (E–10m PO, H, all)	2,079.4	
110.7	0.9	Campsite (3,970')	C, w	2,078.5	

ATC N.C.–Ga. Map 2

Miles from Springer	Fr Last Point	Features	Services	Miles from Katahdin	M A P
110.9	0.2	Swinging Lick Gap (4,100')		2,078.3	
111.8	0.9	Panther Gap (4,480')		2,077.4	
114.0	2.2	**Siler Bald Shelter** (4,600')...8.5mS; 7.3mN	E–0.5m S, C, w	2,075.2	
115.7	1.7	N.C. 1310, Wayah Gap (4,180')...picnic area	R, call H	2,073.5	
117.0	1.3	Wilson Lick Ranger Station (4,650')		2,072.2	
117.5	0.5	USFS 69 (4,900')...piped spring	R, w	2,071.7	
118.0	0.5	Wine Spring, Bartram Trail (5,290')	C, w	2,071.2	
119.9	1.9	Wayah Bald (5,342')...stone observation tower	R, P	2,069.3	
120.3	0.4	Campsite, Bartram Trail (5,200')	C, w	2,068.9	
120.8	0.5	**Wayah Shelter** (4,480')...7.3mS; 4.8mN	S, C, w	2,068.4	ATC N.C.–Ga. Map 2
122.1	1.3	Licklog Gap (4,440')	W–0.5m w	2,067.1	
124.4	2.3	N.C. 1397, Burningtown Gap (4,236')	R, P, call H	2,064.8	
125.6	1.2	**Cold Spring Shelter** (4,920')...4.8mS; 5.8mN	S, C, w	2,063.6	
126.3	0.7	Copper Ridge Bald Lookout (5,080')		2,062.9	
127.5	1.2	Trail to Rocky Bald Lookout (5,030')		2,061.7	
127.8	0.3	Spring (4,900')	w	2,061.4	
129.2	1.4	N.C. 1365, Tellico Gap (3,850')...powerline	R, P, call H	2,060.0	
130.6	1.4	Wesser Bald observation tower (4,627')	E–0.1m	2,058.6	
131.3	0.7	Spring (4,100')	w	2,057.9	
131.4	0.1	Wesser Creek Trail (4,115') **Wesser Bald Shelter**...5.8mS; 4.9mN	S, C, w	2,057.8	
133.0	1.6	Jump-up Lookout (4,000')		2,056.2	
136.3	3.3	**A. Rufus Morgan Shelter** (2,300')...4.9mS; 7.7mN	S, C, w	2,052.9	
137.1	0.8	U.S. 19, U.S. 74, Wesser, N.C. (1,723') Nantahala River, Nantahala Outdoor Center **Bryson City, N.C. 28713**	R, P, H, G, L, M, O, cl, sh, f (E–1m G; 13m PO, G, L, M, D, cl)	2,052.1	
138.7	1.6	Wright Gap (2,390')	R	2,050.5	
140.2	1.5	Grassy Gap (3,050')		2,049.0	
143.1	2.9	Swim Bald (4,710')		2,046.1	
144.0	0.9	**Sassafras Gap Shelter** (4,330')...7.7mS; 9.1mN	S, C, w	2,045.2	ATC N.C.–Ga. Map 1
145.2	1.2	Cheoah Bald (5,062')...sweeping vistas	C	2,044.0	
147.6	2.4	Locust Cove Gap (3,690')	C, w	2,041.6	
148.6	1.0	Simp Gap (3,700')		2,040.6	
150.7	2.1	N.C. 143, Sweetwater Road (3,165') Stecoah Gap...picnic table Robbinsville, N.C.	R, P, w (W–2m L; 10m G, L, M)	2,038.5	
151.7	1.0	Sweetwater Gap (3,270')		2,037.5	

Miles from Springer	Fr Last Point	Features	Services	Miles from Katahdin	M A P
153.1	1.4	**Brown Fork Gap Shelter** (3,800') ...9.1mS; 6.1mN	S, C, w	2,036.1	
153.3	0.2	Brown Fork Gap (3,600')	w	2,035.9	
155.1	1.8	Hogback Gap (3,540')		2,034.1	
155.9	0.8	Cody Gap (3,600')	C, w	2,033.3	
158.3	2.4	N.C. 1242, Yellow Creek Mountain Road (2,980') Yellow Creek Gap	R, P	2,030.9	
159.2	0.9	**Cable Gap Shelter** (2,880') ...6.1mS; 6.7mN	S, C, w	2,030.0	ATC N.C.–Ga. Map 1
160.6	1.4	Black Gum Gap (3,490')		2,028.6	
162.0	1.4	Yellow Creek Trail, Walker Gap (3,450')	W–2.5m Fontana Village	2,027.2	
162.4	0.4	Campsite (3,200')	C, w	2,026.8	
164.7	2.3	N.C. 28 (1,810') **Fontana Dam, N.C. 28733**	R (E–6m L, f) (W–2m PO, G, L, M, O, cl, f)	2,024.5	
165.9	1.2	**Fontana Dam Shelter** (1,775') ...6.7mS; 11.1mN	R, S, sh, w	2,023.3	
166.3	0.4	Fontana Dam Visitors Center (1,700')	R, sh, w	2,022.9	

At Bly Gap, northbounders enter the Nantahala National Forest with 4,000-foot gaps and 5,000-foot peaks. Nantahala is Cherokee for "land of the noonday sun." Long climbs between the Stecoah–Cheoah Mountain area and Cheoah Bald offer panoramic views of western North Carolina. Don't rush; enjoy the landscape from an observation tower or two.

Nantahala Hiking Club—NHC maintains the 58.5 miles between Bly Gap and the Nantahala River. Correspondence should be sent to NHC, 173 Carl Slagle Rd., Franklin, NC 28734; <www.nantahalahikingclub.org>.

No road access to the A.T. is available between Bly Gap and Rock Gap during Jan, Feb, and part of Mar. The Forest Service closes USFS 71 to all vehicular traffic until Mar 1 and USFS 67 until Mar 15. Frequently used Trailheads at Deep Gap, and others, are inaccessible.

Muskrat Creek Shelter (rebuilt 1995)—Sleeps 8. Moldering privy. This shelter uses the "Nantahala design." Water source is just south and visible from the shelter.

Deep Gap—From here, the Kimsey Creek Trail leads 3.7 miles west to the Forest Service's Standing Indian Campground (see next page).

Standing Indian Shelter (1996)—Sleeps 8. Privy. "Nantahala design" shelter. Water source is a stream opposite the side trail to the shelter. Recent bear sightings; *use bear-proofing techniques.*

Standing Indian Mountain—The 5,498-foot summit of the mountain 0.2 mile east is reached *via* a blue-blazed side trail. Cliff-top views to the south gave it the nickname, "Grandstand of the Southern Appalachians." At the top are flat areas for camping and views south toward Blood Mountain. A spring is located 0.2 mile downhill on an unmarked trail near the A.T. junction

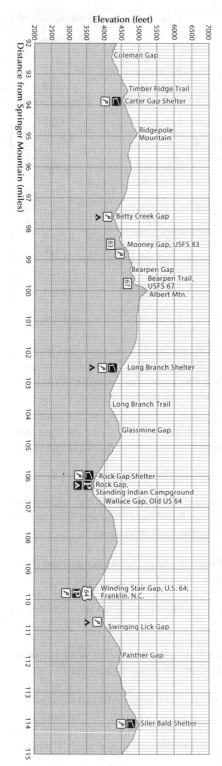

Elevation (feet)

Distance from Springer Mountain (miles)

Coleman Gap

Timber Ridge Trail
Carter Gap Shelter

Ridgepole
Mountain

Betty Creek Gap

Mooney Gap, USFS 83

Bearpen Gap
Bearpen Trail,
USFS 67
Albert Mtn.

Long Branch Shelter

Long Branch Trail

Glassmine Gap

Rock Gap Shelter
Rock Gap,
Standing Indian Campground
Wallace Gap, Old US 64

Winding Stair Gap, U.S. 64;
Franklin, N.C.

Swinging Lick Gap

Panther Gap

Siler Bald Shelter

with Lower Trail Ridge Trail. Please tread lightly if you choose to camp here; the area receives tremendous use.

Carter Gap Shelter (1959 old/1998 new)—Two shelters, the old and the new. Old shelter sleeps 6; new shelter sleeps 8. Privy. The new shelter uses the "Nantahala design." Water source is a spring located downhill behind the old shelter, on the west side of the Trail.

Mooney Gap—This gap has been identified as among the wettest places in the eastern U.S., with an estimated annual precipitation of 93.5 inches.

Long Branch Shelter (2013)—Timber frame, sleeps 8. Privy. Water is on right of side trail to shelter.

Rock Gap Shelter (1965)—Sleeps 8. Privy. Bear cables. Located only 0.5 mile from the road. Water source is a spring to the left and behind the shelter.

Rock Gap/Standing Indian Campground— West 1.5 miles on a paved road to the Forest Service campground with tentsites $16, restroom, warm showers ($2 shower only); small campstore with snacks open M–Sa 9–12, 2:30–5, Su 1–5 Apr–Nov; will hold packages shipped UPS to 2037 Standing Indian Campground Rd., Franklin, NC 28734.

U.S. 64/Winding Stair Gap— East 10 miles to **Franklin, N.C. [P.O. ZIP 28734: M–F 8:30–5, Sa 9–12; (828) 524-3219].** *See map.* The 11th Annual Hiker Bash, organized by Ronnie Haven, (828) 524-4403, <www.hikerfoolbash.com>, will be held Mar 27–28 and include food, music, and entertainment at 6 o'clock each evening at the Sapphire Inn Motel on East Main Street. This is a great venue for thru-hikers to share stories and meet former A.T. thru-hikers. Although a bit spread out, most major services are within walking distance along Business U.S. 441; <www.franklin-chamber.com>. ■ *Hostel:* The Hiker's Den Hostel, open Mar 1–May 31, $15; call Haven's Budget Inn for more information. ■ *Lodging:* Haven's Budget Inn, 433 E. Palmer St.,

(828) 524-4403, <www.ronhavenhikerservices.com>, $39.99S $5EAP, microwave, refrigerator, Internet, WiFi, daily shuttles in season to/from town and Trail for guests only, pets $10 with $50 refundable deposit, in-room phone, free local calls, coin laundry room with free detergent, will hold packages; The Sapphire Inn, 761 E. Main St., (828) 524-4406, <www.thesapphireinn.com>, $39.99S $5EAP, microwave, refrigerator, Internet, WiFi, free daily shuttles in season to/from Trail for guests only, pets $10 with $50 refundable deposit, in-room phone, free local calls, coin laundry room with

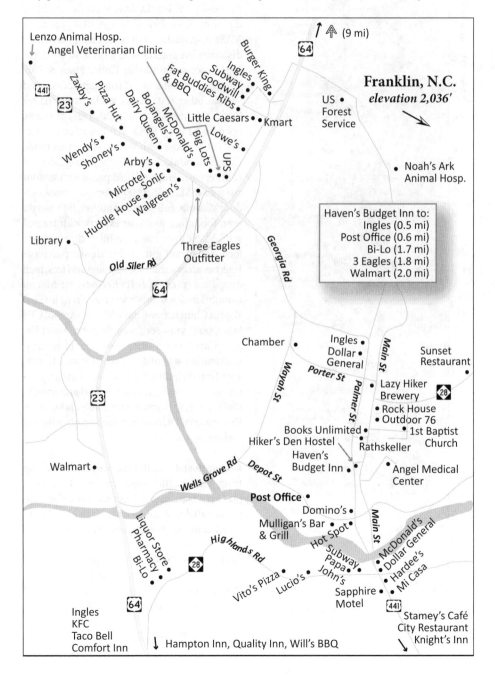

Lenzo Animal Hosp.
↓ Angel Veterinarian Clinic

Burger King
Ingles
Subway
Fat Buddies
Goodwill
& BBQ

64

Franklin, N.C.
elevation 2,036'

US •
Forest
Service

441
23
Zaxby's
Pizza Hut
Dairy Queen
Bojangles'
McDonald's
Little Caesars • • Kmart
Big Lots
Lowe's
UPS

• Noah's Ark
Animal Hosp.

Wendy's •
Shoney's •
Arby's •
Microtel •
Huddle House •
Sonic
Walgreen's •

Haven's Budget Inn to:
Ingles (0.5 mi)
Post Office (0.6 mi)
Bi-Lo (1.7 mi)
3 Eagles (1.8 mi)
Walmart (2.0 mi)

Library •

Old Siler Rd

Three Eagles
Outfitter

Georgia Rd

64

Chamber •

Ingles •
Dollar •
General

Main St

Sunset
Restaurant
•

Waynh St
Porter St
Palmer St

• Lazy Hiker
Brewery
• Rock House
• Outdoor 76

28

23

Books Unlimited •
Hiker's Den Hostel •
Haven's
Budget Inn •
Rathskeller
• 1st Baptist
Church

Walmart •

Wells Grove Rd
Depot St

• Angel Medical
Center

Post Office •

Domino's •
Mulligan's Bar •
& Grill
Hot Spot •

Main St

McDonald's
Dollar General
Hardee's
Mi Casa

Liquor Store
Pharmacy
Bi-Lo

28

Highlands Rd

Subway
Papa •
John's

Vito's Pizza •
Lucio's •

Sapphire
Motel •

441

Ingles
KFC
Taco Bell
Comfort Inn

64

↓ Hampton Inn, Quality Inn, Will's BBQ

Stamey's Café
City Restaurant
Knight's Inn

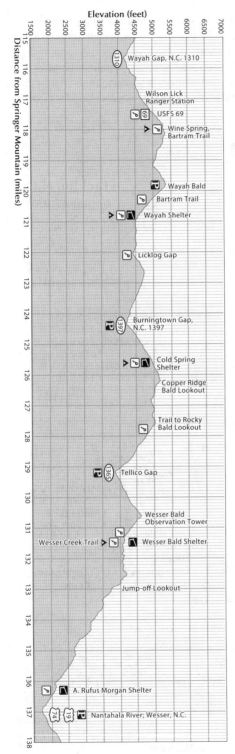

free detergent, will hold packages; Microtel Inn & Suites, (828) 349-9000, $62–$80, pets $20 up to 20 lbs., free long-distance phone (U.S.), B, WiFi. ■ *Groceries:* Ingles Supermarket, BiLow (long-term resupply). ■ *Restaurants:* Shoney's, AYCE; Sunset Restaurant, (828) 524-4842, M–Sa, 6 a.m.–8 p.m., B/L/D, daily specials, 10% hiker discount; Rock House Lodge, (828) 349-7676, M–Sa 10–7, quality craft beers on tap, 10% hiker discount, live entertainment on most F–Sa, Internet access; Rathskeller Coffee Haus & Pub, Tu–Th 11–7, F–Sa 11–11, Internet access; and various other restaurants. ■ *Outfitters:* Three Eagles Outfitters, , 78 Siler Rd., (828) 524-9061, open M–Sa 10–6, Su 12–4, full-service outfitter and coffee house with WiFi and Internet kiosk, Coleman and alcohol fuel by the ounce, Esbit and canisters, will ship and hold packages; Outdoor 76, 35 East Main St., (828) 349-7676, <www.out-door76.com>, full-service outfitter, lightweight gear, food, fuel, footwear experts with trained staff, M–Sa 10–7, 10% thru-hiker discount, $10 local-restaurant gift card with $50 purchase, Internet access, shuttles, shipping services, mail drops accepted. ■ *Internet access:* Macon County Library. ■ *Other services:* Franklin First Baptist Church, free B daily Mar 14–Apr 10; UPS Store, (828) 524-9800; coin laundry; Angel Urgent Care Center, (828) 369-4427; pharmacy; veterinarian. ■ *Shuttles:* Macon County Transit, $3PP from Winding Stair Gap to Franklin year-round, (828) 349-2222; Larry's Taxi and Shuttle, (828) 421-4987, <spunkman101@yahoo.com>; Roadrunner Driving Services, (706) 201-7719, <where2@mac.com>.

Aquone Hostel—Call Steve Bennett for pick-up from Wayah, Burningtown, or Tellico gaps, (828) 321-2340, $20PP. Hot food and hiker supplies available. Mail drops to 63 Britannia Dr., Aquone (or Topton), NC 28781.

Siler Bald Shelter (1959)—Sleeps 8. Privy. Bear cables. Located 0.5 mile on a blue-blazed loop. Water source is 80 yards down a blue-blazed trail from the shelter.

Wayah Bald—The stone observation tower at the summit of Wayah Bald (5,342 ft.) was built in 1937 by the CCC and renovated in 1983. Wayah is Cherokee for "wolf."

Wayah Shelter (2007)—Sleeps 8. Privy. Five tentsites. Nantahala-style. Water source is Little Laurel Creek, 600 feet west of A.T. on blue-blazed trail. This shelter was built by NHC in memory of Ann and Larry McDuff, thru-hikers and ALDHA members who were killed about a year apart in eerily similar accidents, hit by vehicles while riding bikes near home.

Cold Spring Shelter (1933)—Sleeps 6. Privy. Bear cables. Shelter built by the CCC. Tentsites on the east side of the Trail 200 yards north on A.T. Water source is 5 yards in front of the shelter.

Wesser Bald—Formerly a fire tower, the structure atop Wesser Bald is now an observation deck offering panoramic views. The Great Smoky Mountains and Fontana Lake dominate the view to the north.

Wesser Bald Shelter (1994)—Sleeps 8. No privy. Bear cables. This was the first of the "Nantahala design" shelters. Tentsites in clearing where the blue-blaze leads to the shelter. Water source is a spring 0.1 mile south on the A.T., then 75 yards on a blue-blazed trail.

Rufus Morgan Shelter (rebuilt 1989)—Sleeps 6. No privy. Located in a small cove, this shelter is named after the Nantahala club's founder. The water source is a stream across the A.T. from the shelter.

U.S. 19/Nantahala River/Nantahala Outdoor Center—At U.S. 19, the A.T. passes through the Nantahala Outdoor Center (NOC), (828) 488-2175 or (800) 232-7238, <www.noc. com>, an outdoor-adventure center with many services for backpackers; call ahead for shuttles. Between the outfitter and River's End Restaurant, the A.T. crosses a pedestrian bridge over the Nantahala River. ■ *Lodging:* NOC, office hours Nov–Feb 9–5, Mar–May 8–5, Jun–Aug 8–9, Sep–Oct 8–5; Internet access during office hours if available; after hours, go to Base Camp, a winterized hostel that may be full on weekends, $20 and up for bunk space; motel rooms winter rates $65–$79 ($80 Mar 1). NOC Nantahala Inn, winter rates $65–$90, satellite TV, pets in two rooms only, cabins $150 and up with cleaning fee. Reservations recommended, especially for after-hours arrival. ■ *Groceries:* Wesser General Store (snacks), open 7–9 Mar–Sep. ■ *Restaurants:* River's End Restaurant, open 11–6 Nov–Feb L/D, 8–7 Mar–Oct B/L/D, WiFi; Big Wesser BBQ and Brew, 10 a.m–11 p.m., snacks, light meals, drinks, open seasonally. ■ *Outfitter:* NOC Outfitters (short-term resupply), 10–5 (varies with season), offers backpacking gear, Coleman and alcohol fuel by the ounce, Esbit and canisters, ATM, stamps, coin laundry detergent, ATC publications, WiFi. Coin laundry with detergent by the scoop during office hours, restroom, and shower with towel $2 (except with bunkroom) are located on the southern side of U.S. 19. NOC accepts USPS, UPS, and FedEx packages sent to 13077 Hwy. 19W, Bryson City, NC 28713. Check with the front desk; packages must be marked "Hold for A.T. Hiker." NOC can ship packages *via* USPS up to 10 lbs. max (add $1 processing fee); extra charge on weekends.

    East 1 mile to ■ *Groceries:* Nantahala Food Mart (short-term resupply), daily 7 a.m.–8 p.m.

    East 13 miles on U.S. 19 to **Bryson City, N.C. [P.O. ZIP 28713: M–F 9–4:30, Sa 10–12; (828) 488-3481]**. Bryson City is a large town with many services, including Ingles Supermarket (long-term resupply), pharmacy, coin laundry, several restaurants, banks with ATM, Western Union, hospital, and several hotels.

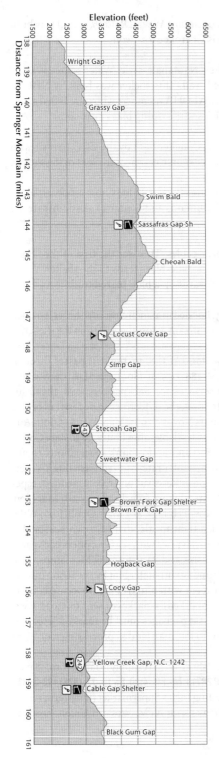

Elevation (feet)

Distance from Springer Mountain (miles)

Whitewater Rafting—The Nantahala marks the northbounder's first chance at Trail-side white-water rafting. The French Broad River in Hot Springs, N.C., and the Nolichucky River in Erwin, Tenn., are also whitewater hot-spots. Guided tours on the Nantahala are available through NOC for about $25 on nonpeak days, but you can rent a raft or "ducky" for less, with shuttles to the put-in point upstream included. Mountain biking, zipline, and horseback riding also available.

Smoky Mountains Hiking Club—SMHC maintains the 101.5 miles between the Nantahala River and Davenport Gap. Correspondence should be sent to the SMHC, P.O. Box 51592, Knoxville, TN 37950; <www.smhclub.org>.

Sassafras Gap Shelter (2002)—Sleeps 14. Privy. Located in a ravine 100 yards in on a blue-blazed side trail, this wood-framed shelter features a covered porch and benches. Water source is a reliable spring in front of the shelter.

N.C. 143/Stecoah Gap—West 10 miles to **Robbinsville**, N.C., with groceries, restau-rants, and motels. A good spring can be found by following the paved road west 200 feet to an overgrown logging road. Spring is located down the logging road on the left. *Lodging:* Cabin in the Woods, 301 Stecoah Heights Rd., Robbins-ville, NC 28771; (828) 735-1930, <www.thecabi-ninthewoods.com>, 2 miles from gap; 3 cabins $15–$70/night; B/D extra, WiFi, laundry, show-ers, pets allowed; shuttle and slackpacking/re-supply service; mail drops accepted. Buffalo Creek B&B, (828) 479-3892, <www.buffalo-creekbedandbreakfast.com>, rooms $70D, bunks $50; season is Apr–Oct, call for avail-ability Nov–Mar; will shuttle to and from Ste-coah Gap free and other locations for a fee; free laundry and B (D extra), Internet access; pet-friendly.

Brown Fork Gap Shelter (1996)—Sleeps 6. Privy. Constructed by the SMHC, Konnarock Crew, and the USFS. Water source is a reliable spring to the right of the shelter.

Cable Gap Shelter (1939/1988)—Sleeps 6. Privy. Shelter originally built by the CCC. The water source is a reliable spring in front of the shelter.

Walker Gap—The Yellow Creek Trail leads 2.5 miles west to Fontana Village. However, it is a poorly marked, difficult short-cut to the resort.

N.C. 28/Fontana Dam—**East** 6 miles to *Lodging:* The Hike Inn, (828) 479-3677, <www. thehikeinn.com>. A hikers-only service, owned and operated by Jeff and Nancy Hoch since 1993. Please call, e-mail, or visit Web site for more information, reservations (advance only), and directions.

West 2 miles to Fontana Village Resort. **Fontana Dam, N.C. [P.O. ZIP 28733; M–Th 11:45–3:45, closed F–Sa; (828) 498-2315],** is located 2 miles from Fontana Dam within the Fontana Village Resort. *Please note: Some services may close or be under reduced hours during off-season, and supplies are limited; most services available by late Mar.* ■ *Lodging:* Fontana Lodge, Fontana Village, 300 Woods Rd., Fontana Dam, NC 28733; (800) 849-2258, <www.fontanavillage.com>; $59–$69D weekdays, EAP up to 4 no charge; $69–$99 weekends; no pets in lodge (cabins only); reservations recommended; will hold packages at lodge. ■ *Groceries:* Fontana General Store (short-term resupply). ■ *Outfitter:* Hazel Creek Outfitter, limited hiker gear and all stove fuels, shuttles available. ■ *Other services:* minimart, restaurant, ATM, coin laundry, detergent at outfitters 50¢, ice cream/soda fountain (open in May) with Internet access, disc golf, mountain-bike rentals, and fitness center.

Fontana Dam Shelter (1982)—Sleeps 24. Restroom with showers and water located at shelter. Known as the "Fontana Hilton," this spacious shelter is located 0.3 mile south of the dam on TVA land. Shower facilities also are located at the dam; see below.

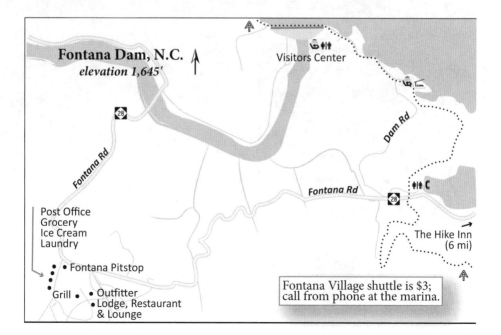

Fontana Dam, N.C.
elevation 1,645'

Visitors Center

Dam Rd

Fontana Rd

Fontana Rd

The Hike Inn (6 mi)

Post Office
Grocery
Ice Cream
Laundry

Fontana Pitstop

Grill • Outfitter
• Lodge, Restaurant
& Lounge

Fontana Village shuttle is $3; call from phone at the marina.

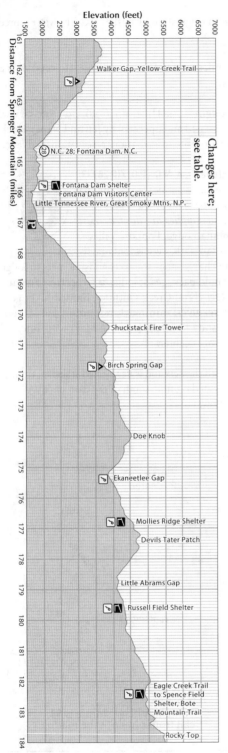

Fontana Dam—At 480 feet, Fontana Dam is the highest dam in the eastern United States. This facility offers a visitors center with restrooms and shower that is normally open May–Nov, 9–7.

TVA says that hikers should not be affected by work atop the dam in 20-15-2016.

Great Smoky Mountains National Park

Miles from Springer	Fr Last Point	Features	Services	Miles from Katahdin	M A P
166.3	0.3	Fontana Dam Visitor Center (1,700')	R, sh, w	2,022.9	
166.7	0.4	Fontana Dam, Little Tennessee River (1,740'); southern boundary, **Great Smoky Mountains National Park**	R	2,022.5	
167.3	0.6	Lakeview Drive West (1,800')	R, P	2,021.9	
170.7	3.4	Shuckstack Fire Tower (3,800')	E–0.1m	2,018.5	
171.9	1.2	Birch Spring Gap (3,680')...tentsites, spring	C, w	2,017.3	
174.2	2.3	Doe Knob (4,520')		2,015.0	
175.6	1.4	Ekaneetlee Gap (3,842')...spring west 300ft.	w	2,013.6	
177.0	1.4	**Mollies Ridge Shelter** (4,570') ...11.1mS; 2.8mN	S, w	2,012.2	
177.6	0.6	Devils Tater Patch (4,775')		2,011.6	
179.0	1.4	Little Abrams Gap (4,120')		2,010.2	
179.8	0.8	**Russell Field Shelter** (4,360') ...2.8mS; 3.1mN	S, w	2,009.4	
181.2	1.4	Little Bald (5,200')...vista		2,008.0	
182.7	1.5	Eagle Creek Trail to **Spence Field Shelter** (4,915')...3.1mS; 6.5mN Bote Mountain Trail	E–0.2m S, w	2,006.5	
183.9	1.2	Rocky Top (5,440')...vista		2,005.3	
184.5	0.6	Thunderhead (east peak) (5,527')...vista		2,004.7	
184.8	0.3	Beechnut Gap (4,920')...spring west 200ft.	w	2,004.4	
185.5	0.7	Mineral Gap (5,030')		2,003.7	
186.3	0.8	Brier Knob (5,210')...vista		2,002.9	
187.9	1.6	Sugar Tree Gap (4,435')		2,001.3	
188.7	0.8	Chestnut Bald (4,950')		2,000.5	
189.0	0.3	**Derrick Knob Shelter** (4,880') ...6.5mS; 5.8mN	S, w	2,000.2	
189.2	0.2	Sams Gap (4,995')...spring west 300 ft.	w	2,000.0	
191.8	2.6	Buckeye Gap (4,817')...spring east 600 ft.	w	1,997.4	
194.8	3.0	**Silers Bald Shelter** (5,460')...5.8mS; 1.7mN	S, w	1,994.4	
195.0	0.2	Silers Bald (5,607')...vistas		1,994.2	
196.5	1.5	**Double Spring Gap Shelter** (5,505') ...1.7mS; 6.8mN	S, w	1,992.7	
198.9	2.4	Mt. Buckley (6,582')...vista		1,990.3	
199.4	0.5	Clingmans Dome (6,643')...observation deck	E–0.5m R, P, w	1,989.8	
200.6	1.2	Mt. Love (6,446')		1,988.6	
202.8	2.2	Sugarland Mountain Trail **Mt. Collins Shelter** (5,900')...6.8mS; 8mN	W–0.5m S, w	1,986.4	

Miles from Springer	Fr Last Point	Features	Services	Miles from Katahdin	M A P
205.6	2.8	Indian Gap (5,286')	R, P	1,983.6	
207.3	1.7	U.S. 441, Newfound Gap (5,045') Rockefeller Memorial...restrooms **Cherokee, N.C. 28719** **Gatlinburg, Tenn. 37738**	R, P, w (E–20m PO, all) (W–15m PO, all)	1,981.9	
210.0	2.7	Boulevard Trail (5,695') to Mt. LeConte	W–5m L, M	1,979.2	
210.3	0.3	**Icewater Spring Shelter (5,920')** ...8mS; 7.8mN	S, w	1,978.9	
211.2	0.9	Charlies Bunion (5,500')...west 0.1m on loop trail		1,978.0	
213.1	1.9	Porters Gap, the Sawteeth (5,577')		1,976.1	
216.4	3.3	Bradley's View (5,200')...vistas		1,972.8	
217.7	1.3	Hughes Ridge Trail to **Peck's Corner Shelter (5,280')** ...7.8mS; 5.6mN	w (E–0.4m S, w)	1,971.5	
220.4	2.7	Mt. Sequoyah (6,069')		1,968.8	
221.9	1.5	Mt. Chapman (6,417')		1,967.3	
222.9	1.0	**Tri-Corner Knob Shelter (5,920')** ...5.6mS; 7.7mN	S, w	1,966.3	
224.1	1.2	Guyot Spur (6,360')		1,965.1	
224.7	0.6	Guyot Spring (6,150')...on A.T.	w	1,964.5	
224.8	0.1	Mt. Guyot Side Trail (6,395')		1,964.4	
226.7	1.9	Snake Den Ridge Trail (5,600')		1,962.5	
230.0	3.3	Cosby Knob (5,150')		1,959.2	
230.6	0.6	**Cosby Knob Shelter (4,700')**...7.7mS; 7.1mN	S, w	1,958.6	
231.3	0.7	Low Gap Trail (4,240')		1,957.9	
233.4	2.1	Mt. Cammerer side trail to fire tower (5,000')	W–0.6m	1,955.8	
233.9	0.5	Spring (4,300')...on A.T.	w	1,955.3	
235.5	1.6	Spring (3,700')...east 80ft.	w	1,953.7	
236.7	1.2	Chestnut Branch Trail (2,900')	E–2m Ranger Station	1,952.5	
237.7	1.0	**Davenport Gap Shelter (2,600')** ...7.1mS; 10.7mN	S, w	1,951.5	
238.6	0.9	Tenn. 32, N.C. 284, Davenport Gap (1,975'); eastern boundary, **Great Smoky Mountain National Park**	R (E–1.3m Ranger Station; 2.3m C)	1,950.6	

National Geographic Smokies Park Map

Established in 1934, the Smokies is the most visited of the traditional national parks; for that reason, it is especially important to practice Leave No Trace here. The highest elevation on the A.T. is here at Clingmans Dome at 6,643 feet. The Smokies also has the most rainfall and snowfall on the A.T. in the South, and many hikers are caught off-guard by the snow and cold temperatures that the high elevation means.

Great Smoky Mountains National Park—<www.nps.gov/grsm>. The Trail through the park officially begins for northbounders on the northern side of Fontana Dam; for southbounders, Davenport Gap is the beginning. In recent years, the park has hosted more than nine million visitors annually. Home to the most diverse forest in North America, the park includes more than 100 species of

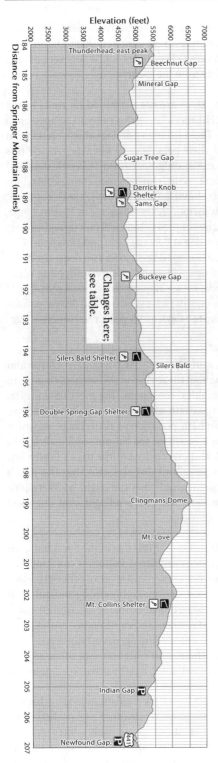

trees, 1,570 species of flowering plants, 60 species of mammals, more than 25 different salamanders, and 2,000 varieties of mushrooms.

Seasonal and temporary closures can be found at <www.nps.gov/grsm>.

*Backcountry Permits—***Backcountry permits** <u>**must be obtained**</u> **before entering the park—the thru-hiker fee is $20 for a seven-night permit. Purchase permits on-line** <u>**up to 38 days**</u> **before your planned entry of the park at <www.smokie-spermits.nps.gov> or by telephone at (865) 436-1297. You will need a paper copy; don't count on finding a computer and printer on the way.** Anyone caught without a permit may be issued a ticket! Additional rangers are being deployed in the backcountry to enforce this new-in-2013 fee.

*Human Waste and Privies—*In past years, the park's administration shunned privies at backcountry facilities. Instead, "toilet areas" were designated where backpackers are supposed to dig cat holes and bury their waste. A privy-building campaign, underwritten by ATC and SMHC, resulted in new facilities at the shelters by 2010. Although privies mainly provide an aesthetically acceptable way to deal with many hikers' refusal to use proper Leave No Trace methods, they are costly to maintain and a management last resort. The best decision is to do your business away from the shelter area before you get to camp or after you leave. Pick a spot far from any trails and 200 feet or more from any water, and practice Leave No Trace methods.

*Horses—*Within the park, half of the A.T. is open to horseback riding; horse users may also share A.T. shelters. SMHC and ATC have made a concerted effort to resolve issues with the horse users, who have helped with major rehabilitation and other projects along the Trail in that half.

*Bears—*Between 400 and 600 bears reside in the park. They become more active in the early spring and remain active through the fall. Following a few simple guidelines can help keep bears and other animals away from people and safe within the park. Be sure to hang food on the provided bear-

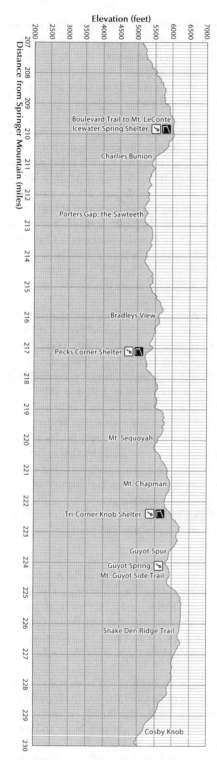

bag system, and do not feed or leave food for these wild creatures to eat. Shelters no longer have chain-link fences to keep bears out. Whenever possible, eat away from the shelters.

Dogs—Dogs are not permitted on trails in the park. Hikers violating this rule will be fined up to $500. Those hiking with dogs should arrange to board their pets. Several kennels provide this service: Standing Bear Farm Hiker Hostel, (423) 487-0014, <curtisvown@gmail.com>; contact for details. Loving Care Kennels, (865) 453-2028, <www.lovingcarekennels.net>, in Pigeon Forge, Tenn.; owner Lida O'Neill will pick up and/or drop off your dog at Fontana Dam and Davenport Gap for $300 for one dog, $450 for two dogs; also holds mail drops, will shop for delivery. Rippling Water Kennels, <www.ripplingwaterkennel.com>, (828) 488-2091, will pick up, board, and deliver pets for $250, up to 7 days; $50 deposit, reservations neces-sary.

Pests and Disease—At Clingmans Dome and throughout the park, you will witness changes in the Smokies' ecosystem. The most obvious has been the death of conifers at higher elevations. Atmospheric pollution weakens the trees, which makes it easier for the balsam woolly adelgid to attack and eventually kill the park's Fraser firs. Other pests and diseases affecting the park's ecosystem include chestnut blight, southern pine beetle, hemlock woolly adelgid, and dogwood anthracnose.

Air Pollution—This is one of the Smokies' most conspicuous problems. Pollution can drop vis-ibility from 93 to 22 miles on an otherwise clear day. Ozone can make breathing difficult and causes visible damage to black cherry, milkweed, and thirty other species of plants in the park. The park's ozone, nitrogen, and sulfur levels are among the nation's highest and often remain high longer than in nearby urban communities.

Shelter Policy—Park regulations require that you stay in a shelter. While other backpackers must make reservations to use backcountry shelters, thru-hikers are exempt from this shelter-specific regulation from Mar 15 to Jun 15. If the shelter is occupied by reservation, thru-hikers should tent close by and use the bear cables. Because only thru-hikers are permitted to tent-camp at shelters, the burden is on them to make room inside shelters for others who have reserved space; that is also the regulation.

Shelters South of Newfound Gap—Seven shelters and a campsite are located between the Little Tennessee River (Fontana Dam) and Newfound Gap.

Birch Spring Campsite—Spring water, bear cables, and tentpads.

Mollies Ridge Shelter (1961/2003)—Sleeps 12. No privy. Bear cables. Legend says the area was named for a Cherokee maiden who froze to death looking for a lost hunter and that her ghost still haunts the ridge. Water source is a somewhat reliable spring 200 yards to the right of the shelter.

Russell Field Shelter (1961)—Sleeps 14. No privy. Bear cables. This section of Trail is popular with riders. Water source is a spring 150 yards down the Russell Field Trail toward Cades Cove. A short walk beyond the spring is an open, grassy area with views into Cades Cove; the Russell Gregory family grazed stock here in the 1800s.

Spence Field Shelter (1963/2005)—Sleeps 12. Privy. Bear cables. Shelter is located 0.2 mile east on the Eagle Creek Trail. This section of Trail is popular with riders and bears. Spence Field, to the north of the shelter, offers azaleas, blueberries, and open views into North Carolina and Tennessee from the largest grassy bald in the Smokies. Water source is a reliable spring 150 yards down the Eagle Creek Trail.

Derrick Knob Shelter (1961)—Sleeps 12. No privy. Bear cables. Water source is a reliable spring near the shelter.

Silers Bald Shelter (1961/2001)—Sleeps 12. No privy. Bear cables. The increasingly overgrown bald 0.3 mile north of the shelter offers views of Clingmans Dome and sunsets over Cove Mountain. Water source is to the right; a trail leads 75 yards to a reliable spring.

Double Spring Gap Shelter (1963)—Sleeps 12. Privy. Bear cables. Gap was named to indicate the existence of two springs, one on each side of the state line and both now unreliable. The better water source is on the North Carolina side, 15 yards from the crest; second source is on the Tennessee side, 35 yards from the crest.

Clingmans Dome—At 6,643 feet, this is the highest point on the A.T. There are no feet-on-the-ground views from the tree-clad summit, but the observation tower provides 360-degree views. The summit is usually busy; a park road leads to within 0.5 mile of the tower. From here to the northern end of the park, Fraser firs and red spruce are now dying *en masse*—a dramatic change from the southernmost 30 miles of the park.

Mt. Collins Shelter (1960)—Sleeps 12. Privy. Bear cables. Nestled in spruce thicket. Water source is a small spring 200 yards beyond the shelter on the Sugarland Mountain Trail.

U.S. 441/Newfound Gap—The only road crossing along the Trail in the Smokies. Plenty of traffic goes through the gap with its large parking lot and scenic overlook; usually an easy hitch into Gatlinburg.

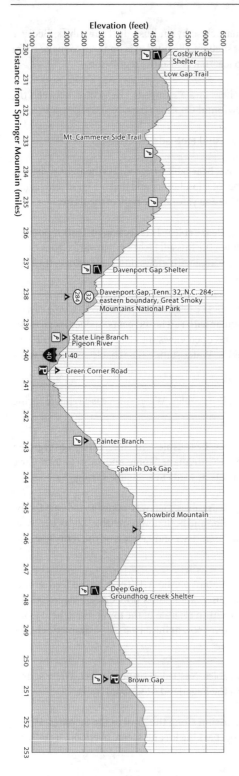

East 18 miles to **Cherokee, N.C., [P.O. ZIP 28719: M-F 9-4:30; (828) 497-3891]**, <www.cherokee-nc.com>, home of the Eastern Band of the Cherokee, with more than 40 motels and most major services. Attractions include the Museum of the Cherokee Indian, Unto These Hills Mountainside Theatre, Qualia Arts & Crafts center, and Harrah's Hotel & Casino. *Lodging:* Microtel Inn & Suites (828) 497-7800, <www.microtelchero-kee.com>, contact for rates; free phone, WiFi, B, pool; coin laundry.

West 15 miles to the resort town of **Gatlin-burg, Tenn. [P.O. ZIP 37738: M-F 9-5, Sa 9-11; (865) 436-5464].** ■ *Lodging:* Grand Prix Motel, 235 Ski Mountain Rd., (865) 436-4561, <www.grandprixmotel.com>, near edge of town closest to the park, hiker rate, B, Internet access, coin laundry, shuttles to Trail, accepts mail drops. Nearly 100 other hotels and motels. ■ *Restaurants:* More than 70, including Shoney's, with AYCE B and soup/salad bar. ■ *Groceries:* Food City *et alia* (see map). ■ *Outfitter:* NOC's Great Outpost, 1138 Parkway, (865) 277-8209; full-service outfitter, free showers for thru-hikers, Internet access, white gas and alcohol fuel by the ounce. Mail drops accepted; may ship as well. ■ *Other services:* Banks with ATM; doctor; A Walk in the Woods kennel, <www.awalkin-thewoods.com>, (865) 436-8283, hiker shuttles, dog-shuttling and boarding.

Boulevard Trail—This side trail, located 2.7 miles north of Newfound Gap, leads 5 miles to the summit of Mt. LeConte. A shelter and LeConte Lodge, (865) 429-5704, <www.lecontelodge.com>, are located at the top (reservations required; $132PP includes B/D). The round-trip to this spectacular peak is worth it, if you have the time.

Shelters North of Newfound Gap—GS-MNP has five shelters between Newfound Gap and Davenport Gap.

Icewater Spring Shelter (1963/1999)—Sleeps 12. Privy. Bear cables. Water source for this heavily used shelter is 50 yards north on the A.T.

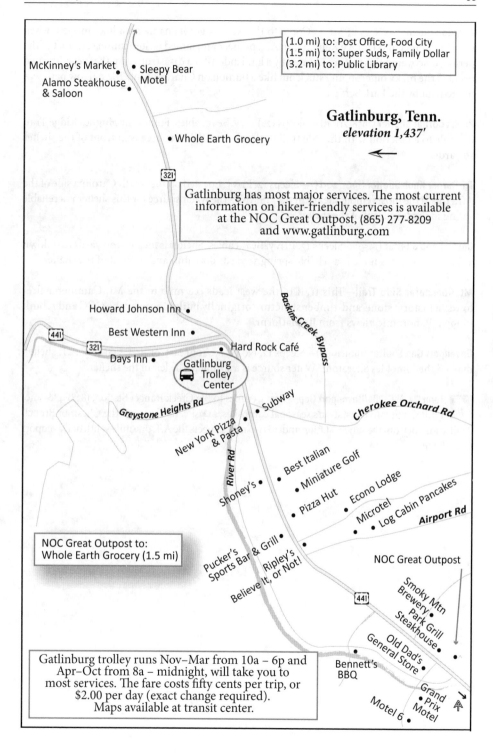

(1.0 mi) to: Post Office, Food City
(1.5 mi) to: Super Suds, Family Dollar
(3.2 mi) to: Public Library

McKinney's Market
Alamo Steakhouse & Saloon
Sleepy Bear Motel

Whole Earth Grocery

321

Gatlinburg, Tenn.
elevation 1,437'

Gatlinburg has most major services. The most current
information on hiker-friendly services is available
at the NOC Great Outpost, (865) 277-8209
and www.gatlinburg.com

Howard Johnson Inn
Best Western Inn
441
321
Days Inn
Hard Rock Café
Gatlinburg Trolley Center

Baskins Creek Bypass

Greystone Heights Rd
Subway
Cherokee Orchard Rd

New York Pizza & Pasta
River Rd
Best Italian
Miniature Golf
Shoney's
Pizza Hut
Econo Lodge
Microtel
Log Cabin Pancakes
Airport Rd

NOC Great Outpost to:
Whole Earth Grocery (1.5 mi)

Pucker's Sports Bar & Grill
Ripley's Believe It, or Not!

NOC Great Outpost

441

Smoky Mtn Brewery
Park Grill
Steakhouse

Old Dad's General Store

Bennett's BBQ

Gatlinburg trolley runs Nov–Mar from 10a – 6p and
Apr–Oct from 8a – midnight, will take you to
most services. The fare costs fifty cents per trip, or
$2.00 per day (exact change required).
Maps available at transit center.

Motel 6
Grand Prix Motel

Charlies Bunion—Views of Mt. LeConte to the west. It got its name on a hike in 1929, when Charlie Conner and Horace Kephart, an A.T. pioneer and famed writer/conservationist of the period, discovered this feature, created by a landslide after a disastrous rain that year. The two decided the rocky outcropping stuck out like a bunion on Charlie's foot. The narrow path was blasted out by the Park Service.

Pecks Corner Shelter (1958/2000)—Sleeps 12. Privy. Bear cables. Follow the Hughes Ridge Trail 0.4 mile to a junction with the side trail to the shelter. Water source is in front of the shelter 50 yards.

Tri-Corner Knob Shelter (1961/2004)—Sleeps 12. Privy. Located on the North Carolina side of the A.T., this is the most remote shelter in the GSMNP. The water source for this shelter is a reliable spring 10 yards in front of the shelter.

Cosby Knob Shelter (1959)—Sleeps 12. Privy. Bear cables. Shelter is located 100 yards east down a side trail. Water source is a reliable spring 35 yards downhill and in front of the shelter.

Mt. Cammerer Side Trail—This trail to the west leads 0.6 mile to the Mt. Cammerer fire-tower, a historic stone-and-timber structure originally built in 1939 by the CCC and rebuilt in 1994. Panoramic views from its platform.

Davenport Gap Shelter (1961/1998)—Sleeps 12. No privy. Your last, or first, GSMNP A.T. shelter, dubbed the "Smokies Sheraton." Water source is a spring to the left of the shelter.

Tenn. 32, N.C. 284/Davenport Gap—East 1.3 miles to Big Creek Ranger Station, (828) 486-5910; 1 mile farther to the station's seasonal campsites, $14/site, no showers. The Chestnut Branch Trail leads out from the ranger station and, in two miles, meets the A.T. one mile south of Davenport Gap Shelter.

North Carolina & Tennessee Border

Miles from Springer	Fr Last Point	Features	Services	Miles from Katahdin	MAP
238.6	0.9	Tenn. 32, N.C. 284, Davenport Gap (1,975'); eastern boundary, **Great Smoky Mountain National Park**	R (E–1.3m Ranger Station; 2.3m C)	1,950.6	
239.9	1.3	State Line Branch (1,600')	C, w	1,949.3	
240.1	0.2	Tobes Creek Road, Waterville Road (1,400'), Pigeon River	R	1,949.1	
240.5	0.4	I-40 (1,500')...underpass	R	1,948.7	
240.6	0.1	Green Corner Road (1,525')...steps	R	1,948.6	
241.0	0.4	Green Corner Road (1,800')	R, P (W–0.15m H, G, cl, sh, f)	1,948.2	
243.3	2.3	Painter Branch (3,100')	C, w	1,945.9	
244.2	0.9	Spanish Oak Gap (3,730')		1,945.0	
245.7	1.5	Snowbird Mountain (4,263')...FAA tower		1,943.5	
246.2	0.5	Campsite (4,100')	C, w	1,943.0	
248.2	2.0	Deep Gap (2,900') **Groundhog Creek Shelter**...10.7mS; 8.4mN	E–0.2m S, w	1,941.0	
251.1	2.9	USFS 148A, Brown Gap (3,500')	R, P, C, w	1,938.1	
253.8	2.7	N.C. 1182, Max Patch Road (4,380')	R, P	1,935.4	
254.6	0.8	Max Patch Summit (4,629')		1,934.6	
256.4	1.8	**Roaring Fork Shelter** (3,950') ...8.4mS; 4.9mN	S, w	1,932.8	
260.0	3.6	N.C. 1182, Tenn. 107, Lemon Gap (3,550')	R, P	1,929.2	
261.3	1.3	**Walnut Mountain Shelter** (4,260') ...4.9mS; 9.9mN	S, w	1,927.9	
263.7	2.4	Bluff Mountain (4,686')		1,925.5	
265.3	1.6	Big Rock Spring (3,730')	w	1,923.9	
267.8	2.5	Garenflo Gap Road, Garenflo Gap (2,500')	R, P	1,921.4	
271.2	3.4	**Deer Park Mountain Shelter** (2,330') ...9.9mS; 14.2mN	S, w	1,918.0	
274.4	3.2	U.S. 25 & 70, N.C. 209 (1,326') **Hot Springs, N.C. 28743**	R, P, PO, H, C, G, L, M, O, cl, sh, f	1,914.8	
275.8	1.4	Lovers Leap Rock (1,820')		1,913.4	
277.7	1.9	Pump Gap (2,130')		1,911.5	
279.3	1.6	Campsite (2,490')	C	1,909.9	
280.3	1.0	U.S. 25 & 70 overpass, Tanyard Gap (2,278')	R	1,908.9	
282.6	2.3	Rich Mountain Fire Tower Side Trail (3,600')	C, w (W–0.1m tower)	1,906.6	
283.7	1.1	USFS 467, Hurricane Gap (2,900')	R	1,905.5	
285.4	1.7	**Spring Mountain Shelter** (3,300') ...14.2mS; 8.6mN	S, w	1,903.8	
286.9	1.5	Spring (3,190")	w	1,902.3	

ATC Tenn.–N.C. Map 4

Miles from Springer	Fr Last Point	Features	Services	Miles from Katahdin	M A P
289.1	2.2	N.C. 208, Tenn. 70, Allen Gap, Paint Creek (2,234')	R, P, G (W–350yds w)	1,900.1	
290.7	1.6	Log Cabin Drive (2,560')	R (W–0.7m C, G, L, M, sh, f)	1,898.5	
294.0	3.3	**Little Laurel Shelter** (3,300') ...8.6mS; 6.8mN	S,w	1,895.2	
295.3	1.3	Bald Mountain Road, Camp Creek Bald (4,750')	R (W–0.2m to fire tower)	1,893.9	
297.0	1.7	Spring, creek (4,390')...blue–blazed trails both sides of A.T.	w	1,892.2	
297.1	0.1	White Rock Cliffs (4,450')	E–0.1m	1,892.1	
297.3	0.2	Blackstack Cliffs (4,420')	W–0.1m	1,891.9	
298.3	1.0	Big Firescald Knob (4,360')	w	1,890.9	
300.8	2.5	**Jerry Cabin Shelter** (4,150') ...6.8mS; 6.4mN	S, C, w	1,888.4	
302.7	1.9	Big Butt (4,750')	C	1,886.5	
304.0	1.3	Spring (4,480')	w	1,885.2	
304.3	0.3	Shelton Graves (4,490')		1,884.9	
307.2	2.9	**Flint Mountain Shelter** (3,570') ...6.4mS; 8.9mN	S, w	1,882.0	
308.1	0.9	Campsite (3,400')	C, w	1,881.1	ATC Tenn.–N.C. Map 3
309.9	1.8	N.C. 212, Devil Fork Gap (3,100')	R (E–2.5m C, g, cl, sh)	1,879.3	
310.4	0.5	Rector Laurel Road (2,960')...several stream crossings on A.T. north of road	R, w	1,878.8	
313.2	2.8	Frozen Knob (4,579')		1,876.0	
313.8	0.6	Big Flat (4,160')	C	1,875.4	
314.8	1.0	Rice Gap (3,800')		1,874.4	
316.0	1.2	**Hogback Ridge Shelter** (4,255')...8.9mS; 10.2mN	E–0.1m S; 0.3m w	1,873.2	
316.6	0.6	High Rock (4,460')		1,872.6	
318.4	1.8	Flag Pond Road, U.S. 23, I-26, Sams Gap (3,800')	R, P, H	1,870.8	
319.1	0.7	Springs (4,000')	w	1,870.1	
320.7	1.6	Street Gap Road, Street Gap (4,100')	R, P	1,868.5	
322.1	1.4	Low Gap (4,300')	C, w	1,867.1	
324.1	2.0	Spring (4,850')	w	1,865.1	
324.9	0.8	Big Bald (5,516')		1,864.3	
325.2	0.3	Big Stamp (5,300')	W–0.3m C, w	1,864.0	
326.1	0.9	**Bald Mountain Shelter** (5,100') ...10.2mS; 10.6mN	S, w	1,863.1	
326.5	0.4	Campsite (4,890')	C, w	1,862.7	
327.5	1.0	Little Bald (5,220')...wooded summit		1,861.7	
329.5	2.0	Whistling Gap (3,650')	C	1,859.7	
329.8	0.3	Trail to High Rocks (4,100')		1,859.4	
331.3	1.5	Campsite (3,490')	C, w	1,857.9	

Miles from Springer	Fr Last Point	Features	Services	Miles from Katahdin	M A P
331.8	0.5	U.S. 19W, Spivey Gap (3,200')	R, P, w	1,857.4	
332.4	0.6	Oglesby Branch (3,800')	w	1,856.8	
336.5	4.1	Spring (3,300')...water for No Business Knob Shelter	w	1,852.7	
336.7	0.2	**No Business Knob Shelter** (3,180') ...10.6mS; 10.5mN	S, C, nw	1,852.5	ATC Tenn.–N.C. Map 3
339.1	2.4	Temple Hill Gap (2,850')		1,850.1	
343.0	3.9	River Road (1,700') Chestoa Bridge, Nolichucky River **Erwin, Tenn. 37650**	R, H, C, sh, cl, f (W–1.3m L; 3.8m PO, G, L, M, D, V, cl, f)	1,846.2	
343.1	0.1	Chestoa Pike (1,700')	R (W–0.8m C, L)	1,846.1	
344.3	1.2	Jones Branch Road, Nolichucky River Valley (1,780')	R	1,844.9	
347.2	2.9	**Curley Maple Gap Shelter** (3,900') ...10.5mS; 12.8mN	S, w	1,842.0	
351.3	4.1	Tenn. 395, N.C. 197, Indian Grave Gap (3,350')	R, P, C (W–7m Erwin, Tenn.)	1,837.9	
352.4	1.1	USFS 230, Beauty Spot Gap Road (3,980')	R	1,836.8	
353.6	1.2	Beauty Spot (4,437')		1,835.6	
354.1	0.5	USFS 230, Beauty Spot Gap (4,120')... spring across road at gate	R, w	1,835.1	
355.1	1.0	Deep Gap (4,100') **Groundhog Creek Shelter**...10.7mS; 8.4mN	C, w	1,834.1	
355.7	0.6	USFS 230, Unaka Mountain Road (4,660')	R	1,833.5	
356.7	1.0	Unaka Mountain (5,180')		1,832.5	
358.9	2.2	Low Gap (3,900')	w	1,830.3	
360.0	1.1	**Cherry Gap Shelter** (3,900') ...12.8mS; 9.2mN	S, w	1,829.2	
363.1	3.1	Tenn. 107, N.C. 226, Iron Mountain Gap (3,723') **Unicoi, Tenn. 37692**	R (E–3m G, f) (W–10.3m PO, M, D, g)	1,826.1	ATC Tenn.–N.C. Map 2
364.4	1.3	Campsite (3,950')	C, w	1,824.8	
367.2	2.8	Greasy Creek Gap (4,034') ...old roadbed to Greasy Creek Road	C (E–0.6m R, H, C, M, g, sh, f) (W–0.2m w)	1,822.0	
368.0	0.8	Campsite (4,110')	C, w	1,821.2	
369.1	1.1	**Clyde Smith Shelter** (4,400') ...9.2mS; 8.5mN	W–0.1m S, w	1,820.1	
370.2	1.1	Little Rock Knob (4,918')		1,819.0	
372.4	2.2	Hughes Gap Road, Hughes Gap (4,040')	R	1,816.8	
375.4	3.0	Ash Gap (5,350')	C, w	1,813.8	
376.4	1.0	Trail to Roan High Bluff (6,200'), USFS Cloudland Rhododendron Garden Road Parking Area	R, P, w	1,812.8	
377.5	1.1	**Roan High Knob Shelter** (6,285') ...8.5mS; 5.2mN	S, w	1,811.7	
379.0	1.5	Tenn. 143, N.C. 261 (5,512') Carvers Gap...picnic area, spring	R, P, w	1,810.2	

Miles from Springer	Fr Last Point	Features	Services	Miles from Katahdin	M A P
380.9	1.9	Side trail to Grassy Ridge (5,770')		1,808.3	
382.7	1.8	**Stan Murray Shelter (5,050')** ...5.2mS; 2.1mN	S, w	1,806.5	
384.6	1.9	Yellow Mountain Gap (4,682') **Overmountain Shelter**...2.1mS; 18.2mN	(E–0.2m w; 0.3m S, C)	1,804.6	
386.2	1.6	Little Hump Mountain (5,459')	C	1,803.0	
387.5	1.3	Bradley Gap (4,950')	C, w	1,801.7	
388.4	0.9	Hump Mountain (5,587')...plaque		1,800.8	ATC Tenn.–N.C. Map 2
390.8	2.4	Doll Flats (4,600') North Carolina–Tennessee State Line	C, w	1,798.4	
393.2	2.4	Spring (3,060')	w	1,796.0	
393.8	0.6	U.S. 19E (2,895') **Elk Park, N.C. 28622** **Roan Mountain, Tenn. 37687**	R, P (E–2.5m PO, G, M) (W–0.3m H, C, L, sh, f; 2m M; 2.5m G; 3.4m PO, G, M, D, V; 7.5m C)	1,795.4	

This section has plentiful 360-degree views and ever-changing scenery flowing from rich mountain coves, boreal forests, and heath balds. Highlights are Max Patch, Big Bald, Beauty Spot, Unaka Mountain, Roan Mountain at 6,285 feet, and the open, grassy bald of Hump Mountain.

Carolina Mountain Club—CMC maintains the 93.2 miles between Davenport Gap and Spivey Gap. Send correspondence to CMC, P.O. Box 68, Asheville, NC 28802; <www.carolinamountainclub.com>.

Due to trailhead vandalism, the supervisor of trails for the CMC advises, "We do not recommend leaving cars at trailheads for anything more than a day trip."

Water sources—*Several water sources are located between Davenport Gap and Deep Gap. State Line Branch may be polluted.*

Green Corner Road—West 0.15 mile to *Hostel:* Standing Bear Farm Hiker Hostel, 4255 Green Corner Rd., Hartford, TN 37753; (423) 487-0014, <www.standingbearfarm.com>, <curtisvowen@gmail.com>; owners Maria Guzman and Curtis Owen; bunkhouse or tenting $20PP, cabin $25PP, tree house $25PP, studio $25PP, free WiFi (for guests), full kitchen, campstore with frozen food, dry and canned goods; fuels by the ounce; overnight parking $5; kennel services (call for details); credit cards accepted. Holds packages ($3 for nonguests). *Directions:* After walking under I-40, continue north on the A.T. 1.0 mile beyond the stone stairs to the first gravel road (Green Corner Rd.), turn left, walk 200 yards to hostel on right.

Groundhog Creek Shelter (1939)—Sleeps 6. Privy. Stone shelter located 0.2 mile on a blue-blazed side trail. Water source is a reliable spring to the left of the shelter.

Max Patch—The site of an old homestead and logging camp, Max Patch was originally forested, but early inhabitants cleared the mountaintop to graze sheep and cattle. The summit also has been used as a landing strip for small planes. In 1982, the USFS purchased the 392-acre grassy-top mountain for the A.T. and now uses mowing and controlled burns to maintain its bald appearance. The wide summit, at 4,629 feet, offers panoramic views of the Smokies to the south and a glimpse east to Mt. Mitchell (at 6,684 feet, the highest peak east of the Mississippi).

Roaring Fork Shelter (2005)— Sleeps 8. Privy. Two water sources, both located on the A.T., 800 ft. north and south of side trail to shelter.

Walnut Mountain Shelter (1938)— Sleeps 6. Privy. Bear cables. An old shelter, with a water source located down the blue-blazed trail to the left of Rattlesnake Trail; difficult to locate, may be seasonal. The neighborhood bears show no fear of hikers.

Deer Park Mountain Shelter (1938)—Sleeps 5. Privy. A former farmstead; the water source is located on the trail to the shelter.

 N.C. 209/ Hot Springs, N.C. [P.O. ZIP 28743: M–F 9–11:30 & 1–4, Sa 9–10:30; (828) 622-3242]. The A.T., now marked by special A.T. diamonds in the sidewalk, passes through the center of Hot Springs on Bridge Street, and most services are located on the Trail. ■ *Hostel:* The Hostel at Laughing Heart Lodge, 289 NW U.S. Hwy 25/70, (828) 206-8487, a stone's throw from the A.T. as you exit the woods. Bunks, $17, private rooms $28, pri-

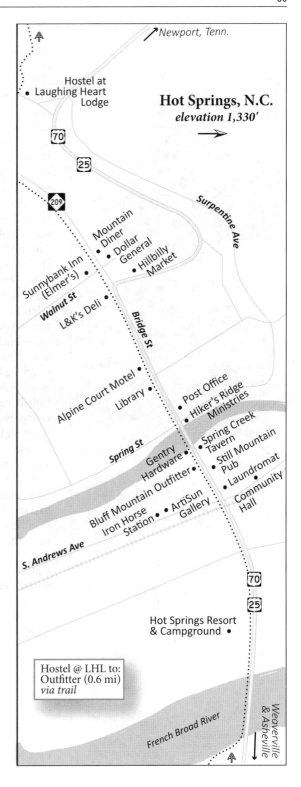

Newport, Tenn.

Hostel at Laughing Heart Lodge

Hot Springs, N.C.
elevation 1,330'
→

70

25

209

Mountain Diner
Dollar General
Hillbilly Market

Sunnybank Inn (Elmer's)
Walnut St
L&K's Deli

Surpentine Ave

Bridge St

Alpine Court Motel
Library

Post Office
Hiker's Ridge Ministries

Spring Creek Tavern
Still Mountain Pub
Laundromat

Spring St
Gentry Hardware
Bluff Mountain Outfitter
Iron Horse Station
ArtiSun Gallery
Community Hall

S. Andrews Ave

70

25

Hot Springs Resort & Campground •

Hostel @ LHL to:
Outfitter (0.6 mi)
via trail

French Broad River

Weaverville & Asheville

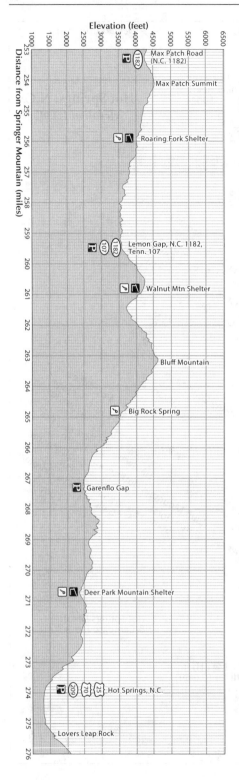

vate double $45 all with shared bath; hot showers (towel, soap, shampoo), pillows and linens, tenting $10, kitchen facilities; laundry $5, and shuttles; massage therapist by appointment; mail drops accepted. ■ *Lodging:* The Sunnybank Inn, 26 Walnut St. (P.O. Box 233), (828) 622-7206, owned by Elmer Hall, located at the white Victorian house across the street from the Dollar Store; thru-hiker rates $20PP, private rooms available, all with shared bath, pillows and linens; hot showers (towel, soap, shampoo); legendary AYCE organic vegetarian meals, $6 B, $10 D; work exchange is possible; no pets or tents allowed; holds packages for guests. Alpine Court Motel, (828) 206-3384, call for rates; credit cards not accepted; no dogs permitted in rooms. Hot Springs Resort and Spa, (828) 622-7676, <www.hotspringsnc.com>, thru-hiker cabin rate $50–$72, $6EAP up to 5; primitive tentsites $10PP up to 4; shower only, $5. Iron Horse Inn, (866) 402-9377, <www.theironhorse-station.com>, special hiker rate $55/night. Laughing Heart Lodge, (828) 622-0165, <www. laughingheartlodge.com>, $100 up, private bath, B included. ■ *Groceries:* Bluff Mountain Outfitters and Hillbilly Market (both long-term resupply); L&K's Deli (short-term resupply); Hot Springs Camp Store (short-term resupply). ■ *Restaurants:* Smoky Mountain Diner, B/L/D; ArtiSun Gallery, (828) 622-3573, expresso bar, home-baked goods, Ultimate ice cream, wine bar, free WiFi. ■ *Outfitter:* Bluff Mountain Outfitters, 152 Bridge St. (P.O. Box 114), (828) 622-7162, <www.bluffmountain.com>; owners, Dan Gallagher and Wayne Crosby; a full-service outfitter with fax service, ATM, Internet access, shuttle; mail drops accepted; ships UPS and FedEx packages. ■ *Internet access:* library, 88 Bridge St. (on A.T.), call (828) 622-3584 for hours. ■ *Other services:* coin laundry; bank; Dollar General; Gentry Hardware. ArtiSun Gallery and Marketplace (see above); sign up with Sunny for a new ALDHA membership and save 25%; will hold UPS and FedEx drop boxes (sorry, no USPS) sent to 16 S. Andrews Street, Hot Springs, NC 28743. Hiker's Ridge Ministry Center, next to PO, free WiFi, use of computers, open Mar 15–May 15 9 a.m.–3 p.m., closed Su.

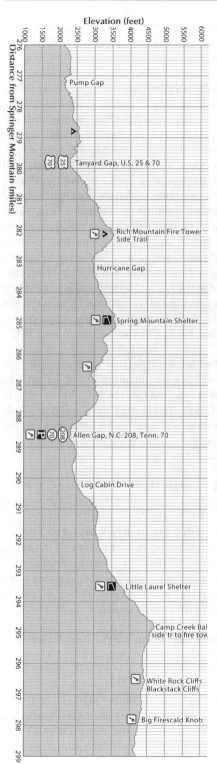

Elevation (feet)

Distance from Springer Mountain (miles)

Pump Gap

Tanyard Gap, U.S. 25 & 70

Rich Mountain Fire Tower
Side Trail

Hurricane Gap

Spring Mountain Shelter

Allen Gap, N.C. 208, Tenn. 70

Log Cabin Drive

Little Laurel Shelter

Camp Creek Bal
side tr to fire tow

White Rock Cliffs
Blackstack Cliffs

Big Firescald Knob

Southbound permits for Smokies—*Southbounders must have a backcountry permit before entering Great Smoky Mountains National Park (see page 29 for details). Permits can be obtained at Bluff Mountain Outfitters, (828) 622-7162, Sa–Su 9–5.*

Whitewater Rafting—Rafting companies offer guided trips on the French Broad River: Huck Finn River Adventures, (877) 520-4658; Nantahala Outdoor Center, (800) 232-7238; Hot Springs Rafting Co., (877) 530-7238; Blue Ridge Resort, (800) 303-7238.

Hot Springs Spa—(828) 622-7676. At the northern end of town, on the southern bank of the French Broad River, the spa offers baths and massages at the famous therapeutic mineral baths for which the town was named.

Spring Mountain Shelter (1938)—Sleeps 5. Privy. The shelter is on the west side of the Trail. Water source is 75 yards down a blue-blazed trail on the east side of the A.T.

Allen Gap—*Groceries:* Mom's Store, (828) 628-3224 (short-term resuply). Paint Creek is 350 yards west, but water quality is questionable.

Log Cabin Drive—**West** 0.7 mile to *Lodging:* Hemlock Hollow Farm Shoppe and Paint Creek Café, 645 Chandler Circle, Greeneville, TN 37743; (423) 787-0917, <www.hemlockhollowinn. com>; open all year. Go west for a few hundred yards on a dirt/rock road to Log Cabin Drive (gravel road). Turn left, and follow for 0.6 mile to paved Viking Mountain Rd. Shop is across the road on right. Heated cabins (seasonal) $25–$60 with linens; heated bunkhouse with kitchenette $20; linens $5; tentsite $12 per person; shower & towel and ride back to Trail included with all stays; shower & towel only, $4; hiker dogs $5/day; free WiFi for guests. Campstore; good variety of hiker foods, cold drinks, fruit; all types of fuel; first-aid and outfitter supplies. Accepts mail drops. Shuttles available. Paint Creek Café open, accepts most credit cards.

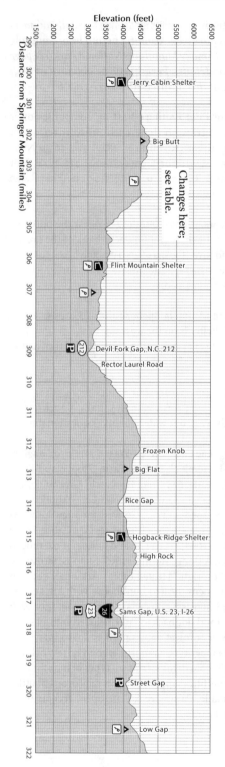

Little Laurel Shelter (1967)—Sleeps 5. Privy. Water source is 100 yards down a blue-blazed trail behind the shelter.

Jerry Cabin Shelter (1968)—Sleeps 6. Privy. Water source is on a small knoll, up a path found on the opposite side of the A.T. CMC member and honorary ALDHA life member Sam Waddle was the caretaker of this shelter and 2.9 miles of the Trail, from Round Knob to Big Butt, for 26 years until his death February 1, 2005. Sam had a good sense of humor and was responsible for a light bulb and telephone installed on the shelter wall. Sam's volunteer efforts transformed this shelter from "the dirtiest shelter on the entire Trail to one of the cleanest," according to Ed Garvey, by hauling out an estimated 20 bushels of litter. He was devoted to the A.T. and an inspiration to all volunteers who share the commitment it takes to make a difference. The electric outlet and telephone may be gone, but Sam's legacy will live forever.

Shelton Graves—North of Big Butt is the final resting place of William and David Shelton, who lived in Madison County, N.C., but enlisted in the Union army during the Civil War. While returning to a family gathering during the war, the uncle and nephew were ambushed near here and killed by Confederate troops.

Flint Mountain Shelter (1988)—Sleeps 8. Privy. Water source is on the A.T. north of the shelter.

Tenn 107/N.C. 212/Devil Fork Gap—East 2.5 miles to Laurel Trading Post, 11761 Hwy 212, Marshall, NC 28753; (828) 656-2492; snacks, drinks, sandwiches, light resupply, bathroom; camping $10PP, laundry $10 with detergent, shower $5, fuel by ounce; mail drops accepted.

Hogback Ridge Shelter (1986)—Sleeps 6. Privy. Water source is a spring 0.3 mile on a side trail near the shelter.

Sams Gap—*Hostel:* Mother Marian's, (828) 680-9944, free pick-up/return from Sams Gap or Big Bald, bunk $20PP, private room $50D, WiFi, TV with NetFlix, laundry $4, credit/debit cards accepted.

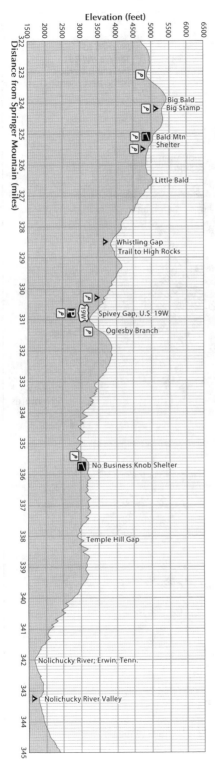

Elevation (feet)

Distance from Springer Mountain (miles)

Big Bald
Big Stamp

Bald Mtn
Shelter

Little Bald

Whistling Gap
Trail to High Rocks

Spivey Gap, U.S. 19W

Oglesby Branch

No Business Knob Shelter

Temple Hill Gap

Nolichucky River; Erwin, Tenn.

Nolichucky River Valley

Big Bald—True to its name, Big Bald offers 360-degree views at an elevation of 5,516 feet. From 1802 to 1834, the bald was inhabited by a cantankerous hermit named David Greer. Spurned by a woman, he retreated to the mountaintop where he lived in a small, cave-like structure (no longer visible). He declared himself sovereign of the mountain and eventually killed a man, only to be acquitted on grounds of insanity. The life of "Hog Greer," called so by the neighbors because he lived like one, ended when a local blacksmith shot him in the back (but was never charged). Greer Bald eventually became known as Big Bald. A golf and ski resort, Wolf Laurel, is clearly visible from the summit of Big Bald. A spring and campsite can be found by following the A.T. 0.2 mile north of the summit to a dirt road and then walking west 0.3 mile down the dirt road.

Bald Mountain Shelter (1988)—Sleeps 10. Privy. One of the highest on the A.T. (5,100 feet). The surrounding area is too fragile for tenting. Water source is a spring on the side trail to the shelter.

Tennessee Eastman Hiking & Canoeing Club—TEHC maintains the 133.6 miles between Spivey Gap and the Tennessee–Virginia line. Correspondence should be sent to TEHC, P.O. Box 511, Kingsport, TN 37662; <www.tehcc.org>.

No Business Knob Shelter (1963)—Sleeps 6. No privy. Surrounded by large Fraser magnolias and mammoth hemlocks, this concrete-block shelter was built by the Forest Service. Reliable water is found 0.2 mile south of the shelter on the A.T.

 Chestoa Bridge/Erwin, Tenn. [P.O. ZIP 37650: M–F 8:30–4:45; Sa 10–12; (423) 743-9422]. *See map on next page.* *Hostels:* Nolichucky Hostel and Outfitters; 151 River Rd.; (423) 735-0548, <www.unclejohnnys.net>; owners, John and Charlotte Shores. Hostel $20/night; private cabins $25–$45S, $45–$85D; camping $10PP; showers and towel free with stay, shower without stay $4; laundry $4 load; dog-friendly; free town shuttles for guests; section-hike and

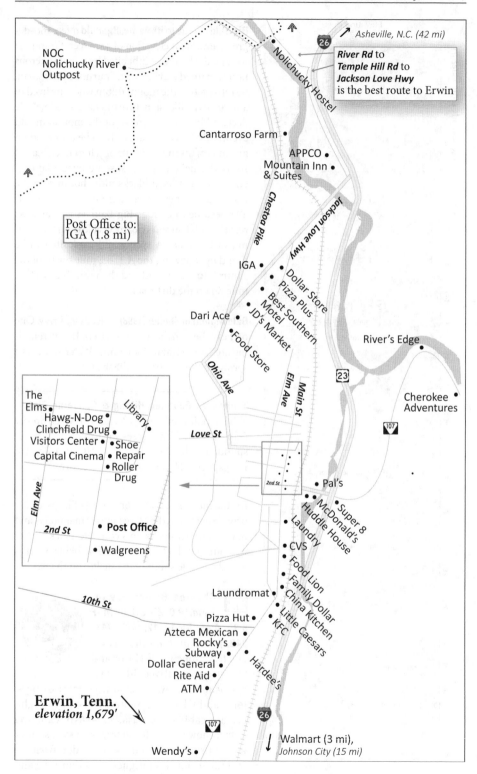

NOC
Nolichucky River
Outpost

Nolichucky Hostel

↗ Asheville, N.C. (42 mi)

River Rd to
Temple Hill Rd to
Jackson Love Hwy
is the best route to Erwin

Cantarroso Farm •

APPCO •
Mountain Inn •
& Suites

Chestoa Pike

Jackson Love Hwy

Post Office to:
IGA (1.8 mi)

IGA •
• Dollar Store
Pizza Plus
Best Southern
Motel
• JD's Market
Dari Ace •
• Food Store

River's Edge

Ohio Ave

Elm Ave

Main St

23

Cherokee
Adventures

The
Elms •
Hawg-N-Dog •
Clinchfield Drug •
Visitors Center • • Shoe
Capital Cinema • • Repair
• Roller
Drug

Library

Love St

107

Elm Ave

2nd St

2nd St

• Pal's

• **Post Office**

• Walgreens

McDonald's
• Super 8
Huddle House
• Laundry
• CVS
• Food Lion
• Family Dollar
• China Kitchen
• Little Caesars
KFC

Laundromat •
Pizza Hut •
Azteca Mexican •
Rocky's •
Subway •
Dollar General •
Rite Aid •
ATM •

10th St

Hardee's

Erwin, Tenn. ↘
elevation 1,679'

107

26

↓ Walmart (3 mi),
Johnson City (15 mi)

Wendy's •

slackpacking shuttles; free Internet, WiFi, and bicycles available. Outfitter store sells most normal fuel and gear. Shipments accepted addressed to ATTN: A.T. Hiker & Name. Cantarroso Farm, 777 Bailey Lane, (423) 833-7514, on Nolichucky River, private cabin with bath $25PP, private room with bath in home $45PP, tent and shower $15PP, laundry $5, town shuttle $3, mail drops for guests, WiFi/Internet.

West 1.3 miles to *Lodging:* 0.5 mile on River Road (best hitch), then 0.8 mile on Temple Hill Road to Mountain Inn & Suites, 2002 Temple Hill Rd.; (423) 743-4100; $79.95D per night (4 max), no pets, hot B buffet, Internet in lobby, guest coin laundry, hot tub and swimming pool (both seasonal), parking for section-hikers, mail drops accepted.

West 3.8 miles to ■ *Lodging:* Best Southern Motel, 1315 Jackson Love Hwy., (423) 743-6438, $39.95S, no pets, mail drops accepted; Super 8 Motel, 1101 N. Buffalo St., (423) 743-0200, $49.95S, $59.95D includes B, Internet, no pets, accepts mail drops. ■ *Restaurants:* many: *See map.* ■ *Groceries:* Food Lion, IGA (both long-term resupply); Dollar General (2 locations); and Family Dollar. ■ *Outfitter:* Mahoney's, (423) 282-8889, in Johnson City, 13 miles north. ■ *Internet access:* public library; Chamber of Commerce, (423) 743-3000, M–F 8–5, Sa 9–1, also has information on shuttles. ■ *Other services:* banks; ATM; barber; coin laundries; thrift stores; hardware; dentists; 24-hour emergency center; Walgreens; Walmart (4.5 mi. off I-26); shoe repair; movie theater; art gallery; veterinarian.

Whitewater Rafting—Rafting companies offer guided trips on the scenic, free-flowing Nolichucky River: NOC, (800) 232-7238; USA Raft, (800) USA-RAFT; High Mountain Expeditions, (800) 262-9036; Wahoo's Adventures, (800) 444-RAFT, which also provides rafting on Watauga River near Hampton–Elizabethton.

Curley Maple Gap Shelter (1961, renovated 2010)—Sleeps 12. No privy. Water source is a spring south on the A.T.

Unaka Mountain—With a large stand of red spruce atop its 5,180-foot summit, Unaka will remind southbounders of the Maine woods. Unaka is the Cherokee word for "white."

Cherry Gap Shelter (1962)—Sleeps 6. No privy. Water source is a spring found 80 yards on a blue-blazed trail from the shelter.

Tenn. 107, N.C. 226/Iron Mountain Gap—**East** 3 miles to *Groceries:* Buladean Shell Gas & Grocery (short-term resupply), (828) 628-4850, Su–Sa 7 a.m.–8 p.m., with made-to-order sandwiches, ice cream, and Coleman fuel.
    West 10.3 miles to **Unicoi, Tenn. [P.O. ZIP 37692: M–F 8:45–12 & 1–3:45 Sa 8:30–10:30; (423) 743-4945]**, with Clarence's Restaurant B/L/D, Maple Grove Restaurant, minmarts, and a doctor.

Greasy Creek Gap—**East** 0.6 mile to *Hostel:* Greasy Creek Friendly (short-term resupply), 1827 Greasy Creek Road, Bakerville, NC 28705; (828) 688-9948; bunkhouse $10PP, one room (twin beds) $15PP, camping $7.50PP, includes shower/towel/soap for guests; nonguest shower $3; restricted kitchen privileges; shuttle, coin laundry, prepared meals, ice cream, fuel, Internet; no dogs inside. Accepts mail drops. *Directions:* At gap, opposite blue-blaze, go through campsite "down" old dirt road past old barns through service gate to first house on right; do not use the "unfriendly" neighbor's drive.

Clyde Smith Shelter (1976)—Sleeps 10. No privy. Water source is a spring 100 yards behind the shelter on a blue-blazed trail. Renovations include new roof and porch.

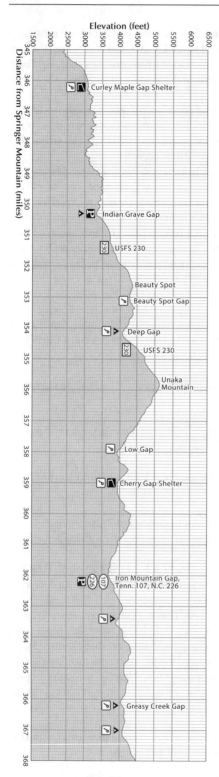

Roan Mountain—For northbounders, this will be the last time the A.T. climbs above 6,000 feet until Mt. Washington in New Hampshire. At the top is a parking area, with restroom and running water (May–Oct). Roan Mountain is arguably the coldest spot, year-round, on the southern A.T. Upon reaching the top of the main climb (for northbounders), enter a clearing, and pass the foundation of the former Cloudland Hotel. The Tennessee–North Carolina state line ran through the center of the hotel's ballroom when Cloudland was a thriving resort during the late 1800s and early 1900s. It was demolished in 1915, after loggers harvested the fir and spruce on the mountaintop. Much of the Catawba rhododendron was dug up and sold to ornamental nurseries. The remaining rhododendron flourished after the logging and covered the slopes of Roan, hence the famous rhododendron gardens. The peak blooming time is usually around Jun 20. The gardens can be reached by following the Forest Service road (visible from the hotel foundation) west, uphill, along the top of the mountain, where an information station is located.

Roan High Knob Shelter (1980)—Sleeps 15. No privy. The highest shelter on the A.T. (6,275 feet). Originally an old firewarden's cabin. The loft is known to leak. An unreliable water source can be found on a 100-yard, blue-blazed trail near the shelter. More reliable sources are south on the A.T. at the Roan Mountain restroom, when open, or a spring at Carvers Gap picnic area, 1.3 miles north.

Gray's lily—A protected, red, nodding lily can be seen blooming on the slopes of Round Bald, Grassy Ridge, and Hump Mountain in Jun–early Jul. The lily is named for botanist Asa Gray, who found it here during the 1840s. He called the Roan range, "without a doubt, the most beautiful mountain east of the Rockies."

Roan Mountain to Hump Mountain—Between Roan Mountain and Hump Mountain, the Trail crosses several balds. Round Bald (5,826 feet) is the site of a USFS experiment in which goats were used to keep briars and brambles from encroaching on the bald. Although the southern Appalachians do not rise above treeline, there are many

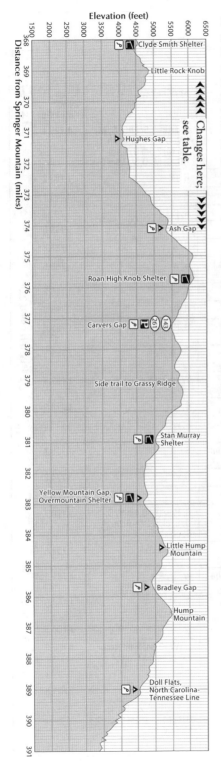

Elevation (feet)

Distance from Springer Mountain (miles)

Clyde Smith Shelter
Little Rock Knob
Changes here; see table.
Hughes Gap
Ash Gap
Roan High Knob Shelter
Carvers Gap
Side trail to Grassy Ridge
Stan Murray Shelter
Yellow Mountain Gap, Overmountain Shelter
Little Hump Mountain
Bradley Gap
Hump Mountain
Doll Flats, North Carolina-Tennessee Line

balds, the origins of which remains a mystery to scientists. Some point to the harsh conditions at high elevations, while others claim Indians cleared the mountains for religious ceremonies. Many believe extensive grazing and cropping led to treeless summits. The 6,189-foot summit of Grassy Ridge is reached by following a side trail to the east before the A.T. begins its descent off the ridge to Stan Murray Shelter. It is the only natural 360-degree viewpoint above 6,000 feet near the Trail. (Clingmans Dome has its observation tower, and Mt. Washington's summit in New Hampshire is covered with numerous buildings.) To avoid potential damage to endangered species, please do *not* camp between the summit and the southern peak. For northbounders, the A.T. veers west from the North Carolina/Tennessee line into Tennessee at Doll Flats, where it remains until crossing into Virginia 3.5 miles south of Damascus.

N.C. 261/Carvers Gap—Picnic area and parking area with restrooms; piped spring beyond restrooms. North out of Carvers Gap, the Trail has been relocated with switchbacks to control erosion and heal the vivid scar of the old treadway. Please stay on the new treadway to allow this area to recover.

Stan Murray Shelter (1977)—Sleeps 6. No privy. Formerly the Roan Highlands Shelter, this shelter was renamed for the former chairman of the ATC and originator of the Appalachian Greenway concept. Water source is a spring on a blue-blazed trail opposite the shelter.

Overmountain Shelter (1983)—Sleeps 20. Privy. A large, red, converted barn once used as a backdrop for the movie "Winter People." Fires and cooking are permitted on the ground floor only. Water source is a spring found to the left once you reach the old road before the shelter. There are two separate water sources here, depending on the dryness of the year.

Tennessee

Miles from Springer	Fr Last Point	Features	Services	Miles from Katahdin	M A P
393.8	0.6	U.S. 19E (2,895') **Elk Park, N.C. 28622** **Roan Mountain, Tenn. 37687**	R, P (E–2.5m PO, G, M) (W–0.3m H, C, L, sh, f; 2m M; 2.5m G; 3.4m PO, G, M, D, V; 7.5m C)	1,795.4	
394.0	0.2	Bear Branch Road (2,900')	R	1,795.2	
397.1	3.1	Buck Mountain Road (3,340')	R	1,792.1	
397.4	0.3	Campbell Hollow Road (3,330')	R, P	1,791.8	
400.2	2.8	Campsite (3,590')	C, w	1,789.0	
402.4	2.2	Campsite (3,130')	C, w	1,786.8	
402.6	0.2	**Mountaineer Falls Shelter** (3,470') ...18.2mS; 9.6mN	S, w	1,786.6	
403.4	0.8	Campsite (3,260')	C, w	1,785.8	ATC Tenn.–N.C. Map 2
404.2	0.8	Walnut Mountain Road (3,550')	R, P	1,785.0	
405.4	1.2	Stream, Howard Harrison Road (3,400')	R, P, w	1,783.8	
405.9	0.5	Viewpoint (3,350') ...memorial bench	W–0.2m H	1,783.3	
406.4	0.5	Upper Laurel Fork (3,290') ...footbridge	W–0.3m H	1,782.8	
410.3	3.9	Campsite (3,410')	C, w	1,778.9	
412.2	1.9	**Moreland Gap Shelter** (3,815') ...9.6mS; 8.2mN	S, w	1,777.0	
413.5	1.3	Tower Road, White Rocks Mountain (4,206')	R	1,775.7	
414.4	0.9	Campsite (3,700')	C, w	1,774.8	
416.8	2.4	Trail to Coon Den Falls (2,660')		1,772.4	
418.5	1.7	USFS 50, Dennis Cove (2,550')	R, P, w (E–0.4m H, C, G, L, cl, f) (W–0.2m H, C, cl, sh, f)	1,770.7	
419.6	1.1	High water bypass to Laurel Fork Shelter (2,200')	(E–0.5m S)	1,769.6	
419.7	0.1	Laurel Fork Falls, Laurel Fork Gorge (2,120')	w	1,769.5	
420.4	0.7	**Laurel Fork Shelter** (2,450') ...8.2mS; 8.6mN	S, w	1,768.8	ATC Tenn.–N.C. Map 1
420.7	0.3	Waycaster Spring (1,900')	w	1,768.5	
421.2	0.5	Side trail to U.S. 321 (1,900')	w (W–0.8m Hampton, Tenn. below)	1,768.0	
424.0	2.8	Pond Flats (3,780')	C, w	1,765.2	
426.6	2.6	Campsite (2,200')		1,762.6	
427.1	0.5	U.S. 321, Shook Branch Picnic Area (1,990') **Hampton, Tenn. 37658**	R, P, w (W–2m PO, H, G, L, M, D, f; 9m G, L, M, D, V, cl)	1,762.1	
428.6	1.5	Griffith Branch (2,100')	C, w	1,760.6	

Miles from Springer	Fr Last Point	Features	Services	Miles from Katahdin	M A P
429.0	0.4	Watauga Lake Shelter (2,130') ...8.6mS; 7.2mN **(closed due to bear activity)**	S, w	1,760.2	ATC Tenn.–N.C. Map 1
430.2	1.2	Lookout Road, Watauga Dam (north end) (1,915')		1,759.0	
431.5	1.3	Wilbur Dam Road (2,250')	R, P	1,757.7	
434.5	3.0	Spring (3,400')	w	1,754.7	
436.2	1.7	**Vandeventer Shelter** (3,620') ...7.2mS; 6.8mN	S (W–0.3m w)	1,753.0	
440.0	3.8	Spring (3,900')	w	1,749.2	
441.4	1.4	Turkeypen Gap (3,840')		1,747.8	
442.8	1.4	Spring (4,000')...water for Iron Mountain Shelter	w	1,746.4	
443.0	0.2	**Iron Mountain Shelter** (4,125') ...6.8mS; 7.6mN	S, C, nw	1,746.2	
444.3	1.3	Nick Grindstaff Mounument (4,090')		1,744.9	
444.4	0.1	Spring (4,090')	w	1,744.8	
446.8	2.4	Stream (3,500')	w	1,742.4	
447.6	0.8	Tenn. 91 (3,450')	R, P	1,741.6	
449.7	2.1	Campsite (3,990')	C, w	1,739.5	
450.6	0.9	**Double Springs Shelter** (4,060')...7.6mS; 8.3mN Holston Mountain Trail	S, C, w	1,738.6	
454.1	3.5	U.S. 421, Low Gap (3,384')...picnic table, spring **Shady Valley, Tenn. 37688**	R, P, w (E–2.7m PO, G, M)	1,735.1	
456.0	1.9	Double Spring Gap (3,650')	w	1,733.2	
457.4	1.4	McQueens Knob (3,900')		1,731.8	
457.8	0.4	USFS 69, McQueens Gap (3,680')	R	1,731.4	
458.9	1.1	**Abingdon Gap Shelter** (3,785') ...8.3mS; 19.9mN	S, C (E–0.2m w)	1,730.3	
465.4	6.5	Tennessee–Virginia State Line (3,302')...Mt. Rogers NRA sign		1,723.8	

Here, you will stroll along the Elk River, pass Jones and Mountaineer falls, see the impressive 50-foot Laurel Falls in the Pond Mountain Wilderness, look over the 16-mile-long Watauga Reservoir, and climb Iron Mountain. *Water sources between Wilbur Dam Road and Tenn. 91 often are unreliable in late summer.*

 U.S. 19E—Numerous incidents of vandalism have been reported at this parking area. Overnight parking not recommended.

East 2.5 miles to **Elk Park, N.C. [P.O. ZIP 28622: M–F 7:30–12 & 1:30–4:15, Sa 7:30–11; (828) 733-5711].**
■ *Restaurants:* Betty & Carol's Place, cash & take-out only, Tu Th–Sa 11–7:30, W 11–6; Sissy's Country House, M–Su (closes earl;y on Su). ■ *Other services:* J's Market (short-term resupply), hardware store with Coleman fuel and denatured by the ounce.

West 0.3 mile to *Lodging:* Mountain Harbour B&B and Hiker Hostel, 9151 Highway 19-E, Roan Mountain, TN 37687; (866) 772-9494; <www.mountainharbour.net>. Hostel open year-round; hiker cabin/hostel over barn $25PP, semiprivate king bed $55; includes linens, shower with towel, full kitchen, wood-burning stove, and long-term resupply. Tent sites $10 includes

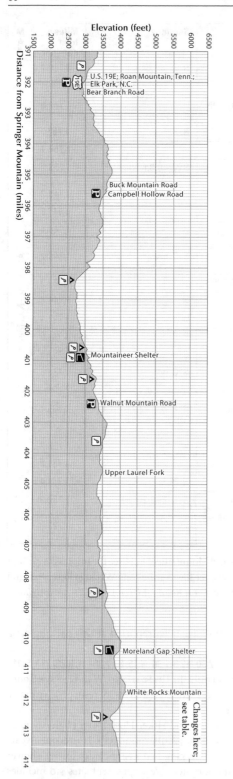

Elevation (feet)

Distance from Springer Mountain (miles)

U.S. 19E; Roan Mountain, Tenn.;
Elk Park, N.C.
Bear Branch Road

Buck Mountain Road
Campbell Hollow Road

Mountaineer Shelter

Walnut Mountain Road

Upper Laurel Fork

Moreland Gap Shelter

White Rocks Mountain

Changes here;
see table.

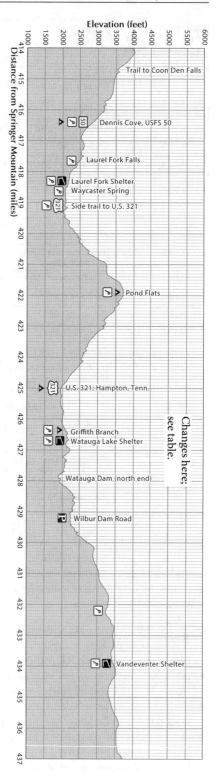

Elevation (feet)

Distance from Springer Mountain (miles)

Trail to Coon Den Falls

Dennis Cove, USFS 50

Laurel Fork Falls

Laurel Fork Shelter
Waycaster Spring

Side trail to U.S. 321

Pond Flats

U.S. 321; Hampton, Tenn.

Griffith Branch
Watauga Lake Shelter

Watauga Dam (north end)

Wilbur Dam Road

Vandeventer Shelter

Changes here;
see table.

shower, B&B rooms $125–$165. Shower without stay $4 with towel. Laundry available. Complimentary white gas and denatured alcohol; canisters available. Will hold mail drops (free for guests, $5 for nonguests). B available for $12 during peak hiker season. Shuttles priced by trailhead with reservation (shuttle parking $2/day). Secure overnight parking $5/day.

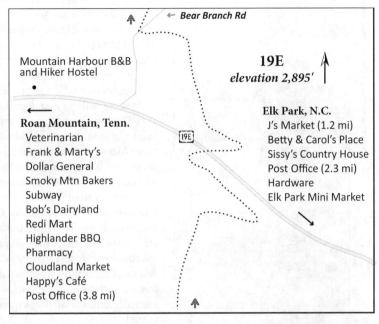

Mountain Harbour B&B and Hiker Hostel

19E
elevation 2,895'

Roan Mountain, Tenn.
Veterinarian
Frank & Marty's
Dollar General
Smoky Mtn Bakers
Subway
Bob's Dairyland
Redi Mart
Highlander BBQ
Pharmacy
Cloudland Market
Happy's Café
Post Office (3.8 mi)

Bear Branch Rd

19E

Elk Park, N.C.
J's Market (1.2 mi)
Betty & Carol's Place
Sissy's Country House
Post Office (2.3 mi)
Hardware
Elk Park Mini Market

West to ■ *Restaurant:* 2.0 miles to Frank & Marty's, pizza/subs T–W Sa 4–9, Th–F 11–9, closed Su–M. ■ *Other services:* 2.5 miles, Dollar General.

West 3.4 miles to **Roan Mountain, Tenn. [P.O. ZIP 37687: M–F 8:00–12 & 1–4, Sa 7:30–9:30; (423) 772-3014].** ■ *Restaurants:* Smoky Mountain Bakers Pizza; Bob's Dairyland, M–Sa 6–9; Happy's Café, 7–3; Highland BBQ, W–Sa 11–8; Subway. ■ *Other services:* several small grocery stores (long-term resupply); bank with ATM; pharmacy; medical center, open M–F; veterinarian.

West 7.5 miles to *Camping:* Roan Mountain State Park on Tenn. 143, (423) 772-0190; <tn-stateparks.itinio.com/roanmountain>, campground with showers, primitive campsite, campsites with water and electricity, cabins; visitors center, and swimming pool. Reservations suggested.

Mountaineer Falls Shelter (2005)—Sleeps 14. No privy. Water source 200 feet on blue-blaze. Tent camping 0.2 mile south of the shelter.

Trail to Vango Memorial Hostel—(423) 772-3450, <vangoabby@gmail.com>; run by "Scotty," 14,000-miler and Trail-maintainer. Bunkrooms $5 or $10/night, shower $2. Private room with deck, queen bed, linens, a/c, TV/VCR, computer, $20S–30D. Free WiFi, tenting, resupply available 4–8 p.m.; basics, ice cream, pizza, beverages, stove fuels. Holds mail drops if mailed 10+ days in advance to P.O. Box 185, Roan Mountain, TN 37687. No parking, access *via* A.T. side trails only. *Access:* (1) From A.T. vista with memorial bench (2 miles north of Walnut Mountain Rd. crossing), take side trail at height of land (SW) under powerline, 0.2 mile to hostel; (2) from hand-railed Upper Laurel Fork Creek A.T. footbridge, take blue-blaze along creek 0.3 mile to hostel. Pets OK; no druggies, alcoholics, or yellow-blazers. Cash only. Porch piano for musically inclined.

Moreland Gap Shelter (1960)—Sleeps 6. No privy. Water source is 0.2 mile down the hollow across from the shelter. Northwest exposure; wet during storms.

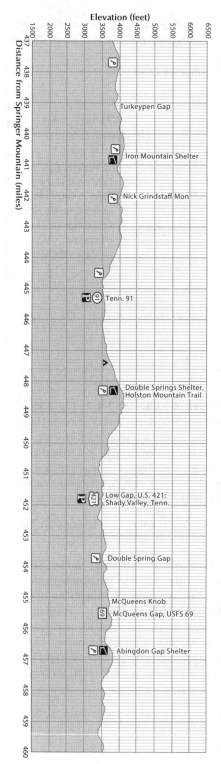

Elevation (feet)

Distance from Springer Mountain (miles)

Turkeypen Gap

Iron Mountain Shelter

Nick Grindstaff Mon.

Tenn. 91

Double Springs Shelter, Holston Mountain Trail

Low Gap, U.S. 421; Shady Valley, Tenn.

Double Spring Gap

McQueens Knob
McQueens Gap, USFS 69

Abingdon Gap Shelter

Dennis Cove Road/USFS 50—West 0.2 mile to *Hostel:* the never-closed Kincora Hiking Hostel, 1278 Dennis Cove Rd., Hampton, TN 37658; (423) 725-4409, with bunkroom, showers, tentsites, cooking facilities, laundry, fuel, shuttles to Hampton (other shuttles by arrangement), $5/night donation; owner Bob Peoples holds packages for guests ($5 nonguests). No dogs, alcohol, or drugs allowed. Plan to arrive before 10 p.m.

East 0.4 mile to *Lodging:* Black Bear Resort, 1511 Dennis Cove Road, Hampton, TN 37658; (423) 725-5988, <www.blackbearresorttn.com>. Open Mar–Oct, reservations accepted. Creekside resort with bunkroom $15 withtowel and shower; tent $10PP; rustic cabin minimum $40/$55. Courtesy phone, Internet access, movies (DVD), and free morning coffee for guests. Camp store with long-term resupply items, snacks, beer, sodas, ice cream, and food that can be prepared on-site with microwave or stove. Laundry $4. Fuel by ounce & canister. Pet-friendly, accepts credit cards. Parking free for section-hiking guests, $2/night for nonguests. Shuttles. Mail drops (nonguest fee $5) accepted.

Laurel Fork Falls—The Trail passes within sight of this waterfall, under which two hikers, father and son, drowned in 2012. Be careful if swimming or wading; the undertows are dangerous.

Laurel Fork Shelter (1977)—Sleeps 8. No privy. Constructed from native rocks, this shelter is located on the blue-blazed high-water route above the Laurel Fork. Water source is a stream found 50 yards behind the shelter.

Bear Closure Notice
The USDA Forest Service lands are closed to most recreation from north of Shook Branch (U.S. 321) to a half-mile north of Wilbur Dam Road. This includes approximately 4 miles of the A.T. around Watauga Lake. Bears are active in this area. Individuals are only permitted to hike through this area. Please continue hiking through this area without stopping. Watauga Lake Shelter is closed. No preparation or consumption of food or overnight stays allowed. This closure is effective until December 1, 2015.

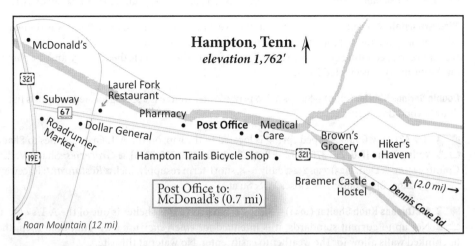

Hampton, Tenn. ↑
elevation 1,762'

McDonald's

321

Laurel Fork
Restaurant

Subway

67

Pharmacy

Roadrunner Market

Dollar General

Post Office

Medical
Care

Brown's
Grocery

Hiker's
Haven

19E

Hampton Trails Bicycle Shop

321

Braemer Castle
Hostel

(2.0 mi) →

Dennis Cove Rd

Post Office to:
McDonald's (0.7 mi)

Roan Mountain (12 mi)

U.S. 321—West 2 miles to **Hampton, Tenn.** [P.O. ZIP 37658: M–F 7:30–11:30 & 12:30–4:00, Sa 8–10; (423) 725-2177]. ■ *Lodging:* Braemar Castle Hostel and Guest House, (423) 725-2411 or 725-2262. Sutton and Beverly Brown offer hiker space, kitchen, and showers for $15PP; private rooms $25S $40D. Hikers Haven, (423) 957-2300, WiFi, Internet, hot food and snack, bunk $10/tent $5 (showers included), wash/dry $1.25/75¢, shuttles available. Iron Mountain Inn B&B, (423) 768-2446, <www.ironmountaininn.com>; private room and bath $125D, includes B. Creekside Chalet, same phone as Iron Mountain Inn, <www.creeksidechalet.net>, $50PP includes hot tub on deck, pet-friendly, call from Hampton or Tenn. 91 for pick-up, inquire about slackpacking, packages held addressed c/o Woods, 268 Moreland Dr., Butler, TN 37640. ■ *Restaurants:* McDonald's; Subway. ■ *Groceries:* Brown's Grocery, 613 U.S. 321, (423) 725-2411, long-term resupply, closed Su; check with Sutton at the grocery store for accommodations and shuttles; Coleman fuel and denatured alcohol; holds USPS and UPS packages. ■ *Other services:* Dollar General, convenience stores, health clinic, banks, and ATM. ■ *Shuttles:* Hampton Trails Bicycle Shop, (423) 725-5000, owner Brian White, <www.hamptontrails.com>, <brian@hamptontrails.com>. *Note: The best access to Hampton from the A.T. is the 0.8-mile blue-blazed trail in Laurel Gorge, two miles downstream from Laurel Falls.*

West 9 miles to **Elizabethton, Tenn.** ■ *Lodging:* Travelers Inn, (423) 543-3344, hiker's discount $49.99, B, coin laundry, pool (seasonal); Americourt Hotel, (423) 542-4466, <americourthotels.com>, located on U.S. 19E, $59 hiker rate includes B, WiFi, Internet. ■ *Groceries:* Food City, Walmart. ■ *Internet access:* library. ■ *Other services:* restaurants, convenience stores, doctor, bank, veterinarian, laundry, and ATM.

Shook Branch Recreation Area—This developed area on Watauga Lake offers picnic tables, restroom, water that is turned on after the last freeze of spring (usually by late Apr), and a beach for swimming.

Watauga Lake Shelter (1980)—*Closed until December 2015.* Water source is on A.T., south of the shelter (if dry, follow stream up to small pool).

Watauga Dam—The A.T. crosses the Watauga River on this dam at Watauga Lake. A visitors center with restroom, often closed during cold-weather months, can be reached by following Wilbur Dam Road 0.9 mile east.

Vandeventer Shelter (1961)—Sleeps 6. No privy. Water source is 0.3 mile down a steep, blue-blazed trail south of the shelter.

Iron Mountain Shelter (1960)—Sleeps 6. No privy. Water source is a spring 500 yards south on A.T.

Nick Grindstaff Monument—Nick Grindstaff traveled west to win his fortune but was robbed of all his money during the journey. He then returned to Iron Mountain, where he lived for more than 40 years, becoming one of the region's most famous hermits. He died in 1923, and the plaque on the chimney was erected in 1925.

Double Springs Shelter (1960)—Sleeps 6. No privy. Water source is a spring located 100 yards in the draw beyond the shelter.

U.S. 421/Low Gap—A piped spring is located in the gap, on the A.T. **East** 2.7 miles to **Shady Valley, Tenn. [P.O. ZIP 37688: M–F 8–12, Sa 8–10; (423) 739-2073].** ■ *Groceries:* Shady Valley Country Store & Deli, (423) 739-2325, daily 6–8, short-term resupply, fuel. ■ *Restaurant:* Raceway, (423) 739-2499, open daily 7–8, closes W & Su at 3.

McQueens Knob Shelter (1934)—Sleeps 4. No privy. This shelter is one of the A.T.'s oldest. Not up to current standards, it is intended *for emergency use only,* and, even then, the unchinked walls allow for the weather to easily enter. No water at this site.

Abingdon Gap Shelter (1959)—Sleeps 5. No privy. Water source is a spring 0.2 mile east on a steep, blue-blazed side trail, downhill behind the shelter.

Tennessee/Virginia State Line—You're entering or leaving Virginia when you see the Mt. Rogers National Recreation Area sign, which is on the state line.

Virginia—Part 1 (Southwest)

Miles from Springer	Fr Last Point	Features	Services	Miles from Katahdin	M A P
465.4	6.5	Tennessee–Virginia State Line (3,302')...*Mt. Rogers NRA sign*		1,723.8	
466.9	1.5	Spring (2,600')	w	1,722.3	
469.1	2.2	U.S. 58 (1,928') **Damascus, Va. 24236**	R, P, H, G, L, M, O, D, cl, sh, f (E–10m AFS; W–2m V; 12m all)	1,720.1	
470.1	1.0	U.S. 58 Va. 91, Virginia Creeper Trail (1,928')...*steps*	R	1,719.1	
471.2	1.1	Cockoo Knob (2,990')		1,718.0	
472.6	1.4	Iron Mountain Trail, Feathercamp Ridge (2,850')		1,716.6	
474.1	1.5	Beech Grove Trail (2,490')		1,715.1	
474.7	0.6	U.S. 58, Straight Branch Feathercamp Branch, Feathercamp Trail (2,200') ...*picnic area*	R, P, w	1,714.5	
476.1	1.4	Stream (2,490')...*footbridge*	w	1,713.1	
476.7	0.6	Taylors Valley Side Trail, Virginia Creeper Trail (2,850')	(E–0.7m on Va. Creeper M, w)	1,712.5	
478.3	1.6	Straight Mountain (3,500')		1,710.9	
478.6	0.3	**Saunders Shelter** (3,310') ...*19.9mS; 6.5mN*	W–0.2m S, w	1,710.6	
480.9	2.3	Beartree Gap Trail (3,050')...USFS Beartree Campground	(W–0.6m P, w, sh; 3.6m C,w,sh)	1,708.3	
481.1	0.2	Campsite (3,020')	C, w	1,708.1	
482.7	1.6	Va. 728, Creek Junction Station (2,720')...*old railroad bed*	R	1,706.5	
483.3	0.6	Virginia Creeper Trail, Whitetop Laurel Creek (2,690')	R, P	1,705.9	
483.9	0.6	Va. 859, Grassy Ridge Road (2,900')	R	1,705.3	
484.1	0.2	Spring (3,040')	w	1,705.1	
484.6	0.5	Lost Mountain (3,400')		1,704.6	
484.9	0.3	**Lost Mountain Shelter** (3,360') ...*6.5mS; 12.4mN*	S, w	1,704.3	
486.0	1.1	U.S. 58; Summit Cut, Va. (3,160')	R	1,703.2	
486.4	0.4	Campsites near stream (3,300')	C, w	1,702.8	
487.3	0.9	Va. 601, Beech Mountain Road (3,600')	R, P, w	1,701.9	
489.8	2.5	Buzzard Rock on Whitetop Mountain (5,080')		1,699.4	
490.6	0.8	Spring (5,100')... *piped*	w	1,698.6	
490.7	0.1	USFS 89, Whitetop Mountain Road (5,150')	R, C	1,698.5	
493.1	2.4	Va. 600, Elk Garden (4,434') **Whitetop, Va. 24292**	R, P, privy (E–2.9m PO) (W–7m L)	1,696.1	
495.1	2.0	Deep Gap (4,900')	E–0.2m w	1,694.1	

Miles from Springer	Fr Last Point	Features	Services	Miles from Katahdin	M A P
495.4	0.3	Virginia Highlands Horse Trail, Mt. Rogers Trail (5,200')...*USFS Grindstone Campground*	(W–4m C, w, sh)	1,693.8	
496.2	0.8	Brier Ridge Saddle (5,125')...*views in meadow*		1,693.0	
497.1	0.9	Spur Trail to summit of Mt. Rogers (5,490')	W–0.5m	1,692.1	
497.3	0.2	**Thomas Knob Shelter** (5,400') *...12.4mS; 5.2mN*	S, w	1,691.9	
498.3	1.0	Rhododendron Gap (5,440')	C	1,690.9	
498.9	0.6	Fatman Squeeze (5,300')...*rock tunnel*		1,690.3	
499.6	0.7	Wilburn Ridge (4,900')		1,689.6	
500.4	0.8	Park service road to Massie Gap (4,800')	(E–2m R, C, G, sh)	1,688.8	
502.5	2.1	Grayson Highlands State Park, Wilson Creek Trail, (4,460') **Wise Shelter**...*5.2mS; 6mN*	S, w (E–2m R, C, G, sh)	1,686.7	
502.6	0.1	Big Wilson Creek (4,300')	C, w	1,686.6	
502.8	0.2	Wilson Creek Trail (4,300')	E–1.3m C, w	1,686.4	
503.8	1.0	Spring (4,610')	w	1,685.4	
505.1	1.3	Stone Mountain (4,820')		1,684.1	
505.5	0.4	The Scales (4,620')...*livestock corral*		1,683.7	
506.9	1.4	Pine Mountain (5,000')		1,682.3	
508.5	1.6	**Old Orchard Shelter**...*6mS; 4.2mN*	S, C, w	1,680.7	
510.2	1.7	Va. 603, Fox Creek (3,480')...*footbridge, Fox Creek Horse Camp; USFS Grindstone Campground*	R, P, C, w (W–2.5m C, w, sh)	1,679.0	
511.5	1.3	Hurricane Mountain (4,320') Tennesse–New River Divide		1,677.7	
511.8	0.3	Iron Mountain Trail, Chestnut Flats (4,240')		1,677.4	
512.7	0.9	**Hurricane Mountain Shelter** (3,400') *...4.2mS; 9mN*	S, w	1,676.5	
513.3	0.6	Hurricane Creek Trail (3,300')		1,675.9	
514.1	0.8	Stream (3,000')	w	1,675.1	
515.8	1.7	Dickey Gap Trail (3,090')...*USFS Hurricane Campground*	(W–0.5m C,w,sh)	1,673.4	
516.6	0.8	Comers Creek, Comers Creek Falls Trail (3,100')	w	1,672.6	
517.8	1.2	Va. 650, Va. 16, Dickey Gap (3,300') **Troutdale, Va. 24378** **Sugar Grove, Va. 24374**	R, P (E–100yds to Va. 16; then E–2.6m PO, D, H; 3.6m G, M) (W–5m PO; 5.6m G, M, f, ATM)	1,671.4	
519.3	1.5	Bobby's Trail, Raccoon Branch Campground (3,570')...*spring*	E–0.2m C, w; 3.3m C, w)	1,669.9	
519.9	0.6	High Point (4,040')		1,669.3	
521.7	1.8	**Trimpi Shelter** (2,900')...*9mS; 9.8mN*	S, w	1,667.5	
522.9	1.2	Va. 672 (2,700')	R	1,666.3	

ATC Southwest Va. Map 4

ATC Southwest Va. Map 3

Miles from Springer	Fr Last Point	Features	Services	Miles from Katahdin	M A P
523.8	0.9	Va. 670, Teas Road, South Fork Holston River (2,450')...*bridge*	R, P	1,665.4	
527.6	3.8	Va. 601, Pugh Mountain Road (3,250') ...*gravel*	R, P	1,661.6	
531.5	3.9	**Partnership Shelter** (3,360') ...*9.8mS; 6.7mN*	S, w, sh	1,657.7	
531.6	0.1	Va. 16, Mt. Rogers NRA Headquarters (3,220') **Sugar Grove, Va. 24375** **Marion, Va. 24354**	R, P, w (E–3.2m PO, G, M, f, ATM) (W–6m PO, G, L, M, D, B, cl, f)	1,657.6	
532.3	0.7	Va. 622 (3,270')	R	1,656.9	
532.8	0.5	Brushy Mountain (3,600')		1,656.4	
535.0	2.2	Locust Mountain (3,900')		1,654.2	
535.4	0.4	USFS 86, Glade Mountain Road (3,650')...*spring*	R, P, C, w	1,653.8	
536.7	1.3	Glade Mountain (4,093')		1,652.5	ATC Southwest Va. Map 3
538.2	1.5	**Chatfield Shelter** (3,150') ...*6.7mS; 18.9mN*	S, w	1,651.0	
538.5	0.3	USFS 644 (3,100')	R	1,650.7	
540.0	1.5	Va. 615, Rocky Hollow Road, Settlers Museum, Lindamood Schoolhouse (2,650')	R, P	1,649.2	
540.5	0.5	Va. 729 (2,700')...*gravel*	R	1,648.7	
541.0	0.5	Kegley Trail (2,650')		1,648.2	
541.8	0.8	Middle Fork of Holston River (2,500')		1,647.4	
542.7	0.9	U.S. 11, I-81, Va. 683 (2,420') Groseclose, Va. **Atkins, Va. 24311** **Marion, Va. 24354**	R, P, G, L, M, sh, cl, f (W–3.2m PO, G, L, M cl; 10.2m PO,B,G,L,M,D,cl)	1,646.5	
543.7	1.0	Va. 617, Davis Valley Road (2,580')	R, P	1,645.5	
544.4	0.7	Spring (2,610')	E–50yds w	1,644.8	
545.5	1.1	Davis Path Campsite (2,840')	C, nw	1,643.7	
548.1	2.6	Gullion (Little Brushy) Mountain (3,300')		1,641.1	
549.2	1.1	Crawfish Valley along Reed Creek (2,600')	w on A.T. (E–0.3m C, w)	1,640.0	
551.0	1.8	Tilson Gap, Big Walker Mountain (3,500')		1,638.2	
552.5	1.5	Va. 610, Old Rich Valley Road (2,700')	R	1,636.7	
554.0	1.5	Va. 742, Shady Grove Road, North Fork of Holston River (2,460')...*bridge*	R, w	1,635.2	
554.2	0.2	Spring (2,550')	w	1,635.0	ATC Southwest Va. Map 2
555.0	0.8	Va. 42, Ceres, Va. (2,650')	R, P (E–0.2m w)	1,634.2	
555.9	0.9	Brushy Mountain (3,200')		1,633.3	
557.1	1.2	**Knot Maul Branch Shelter** (2,880') ...*18.9mS; 9.4mN*	S, nw	1,632.1	
557.6	0.5	Campsite and spring (2,810')...*water for Knot Maul Branch Shelter*	C, w	1,631.6	
558.2	0.6	Lynn Camp Creek (2,400')...*footbridge*	w	1,631.0	
559.0	0.8	Lynn Camp Mountain (3,000')		1,630.2	

Miles from Springer	Fr Last Point	Features	Services	Miles from Katahdin	M A P
560.5	1.5	Lick Creek (2,300')...*footbridge*	w	1,628.7	
561.9	1.4	USFS 222, Va. 625 (2,300')	R, P	1,627.3	
564.7	2.8	Spring-fed pond (3,800')...*water for Chestnut Knob Shelter*	w	1,624.5	
564.8	0.1	Chestnut Ridge (3,700')		1,624.4	
566.5	1.7	**Chestnut Knob Shelter** (4,409') *...9.4mS; 10.6mN* Burkes Garden Overlook	S, nw	1,622.7	
567.8	1.3	Walker Gap (3,520')...*water for Chestnut Knob Shelter*	R, P, w	1,621.4	
568.0	0.2	Spring (3,570')	E–0.2m w	1,621.2	ATC Southwest Va. Map 2
572.6	4.6	Va. 623, Burkes Garden Road, Garden Mountain (3,880')	R, P	1,616.6	
573.6	1.0	Davis Farm Campsite (3,850')	(W–0.5m C, w)	1,615.6	
576.2	2.6	Stream (3,700')	w	1,613.0	
577.1	0.9	**Jenkins Shelter** (2,470') *...10.6mS; 15.6mN*	S, w	1,612.1	
581.3	4.2	Brushy Mountain (3,080')		1,607.9	
582.3	1.0	Va. 615, Suiter Road, Laurel Creek (2,450')	R, C, w	1,606.9	
589.2	6.9	U.S. 52 (2,920') **Bland, Va.24315 Bastian, Va.24314** Bluefield, W. Va.	R (E–2.7m PO, G, M, f; 3.3m G, L, M, D) (W–2.5m PO; 3.5m D; 12.5m B)	1,600.0	
589.6	0.4	Va. 612, I–77 overpass (2,750')	R	1,599.6	
590.0	0.4	Va. 612, Kimberling Creek (2,700')	R, w	1,599.2	
592.4	2.4	**Helveys Mill Shelter** (3,090') *...15.6mS; 10mN*	E–0.3m S, w	1,596.8	
599.0	6.6	Va. 611 (2,820')	R, P	1,590.2	
600.4	1.4	Brushy Mountain (3,101')		1,588.8	
602.1	1.7	**Jenny Knob Shelter** (2,800') *...10mS; 14.5mN*	S, w	1,587.1	
603.3	1.2	Va. 608, Lickskillet Hollow (2,200')	R, P	1,585.9	
606.7	3.4	Brushy Mountain (2,800')		1,582.5	
608.5	1.8	Kimberling Creek (2,090')...*suspension bridge*	C, w	1,580.7	ATC Southwest Va. Map 1
608.6	0.1	Va. 606 (2,040')	R (W–0.5m C, G, M, cl, sh, f)	1,580.6	
610.5	1.9	Dismal Creek Falls Trail (2,320')	(W–0.3m w)	1,578.7	
612.4	1.9	Walnut Flats Campground (2,400')	(W–0.4m C, w)	1,576.8	
614.5	2.1	Ribble Trail south junction (2,400')... *USFS White Cedar Horse Campground*	(W–0.5m C, w)	1,574.7	
614.8	0.3	Stream (2,500')	w	1,574.4	
616.6	1.8	**Wapiti Shelter** (2,600')...*14.5mS; 9.5mN*	S, w	1,572.6	
619.0	2.4	Sugar Run Mountain (3,800')...*rocky outcrop*		1,570.2	
622.1	3.1	Ribble Trail north junction (3,800')	w	1,567.1	
622.2	0.1	USFS 103, Big Horse Gap (3,752')	R	1,567.0	

Miles from Springer	Fr Last Point	Features	Services	Miles from Katahdin	M A P
623.8	1.6	Va. 663, Sugar Run Gap Road, Sugar Run Gap (3,450')	R, P (E–0.5m H)	1,565.4	ATC Southwest Va. Map 1
625.2	1.4	Rock Cliff Overlook (3,850')		1,564.0	
626.1	0.9	**Doc's Knob Shelter** (3,555') ...9.5mS; 15.7mN	S, w	1,563.1	
632.0	5.9	Campsite and spring (3,750')	C, w	1,557.2	
632.5	0.5	Angels Rest on Pearis Mountain (3,555')...vista		1,556.7	
633.9	1.4	Spring (2,300')	w	1,555.3	
634.5	0.6	Va. 634 (2,200')	R	1,554.7	

The state's highest mountain, Mt. Rogers, an area of spectacular highland meadows, routinely receives snowfall from October to May, making it considerably colder, wetter, and snowier than other areas of Virginia. Northbounders may be tempted to mail home their cold-weather gear, only to see spring flavored by winter.

Caution: According to Mt. Rogers National Recreation Area officials, hikers should use caution when leaving vehicles at any local trailhead. Safer hiker parking is available at some locations in Damascus, as well as the Mt. Rogers NRA headquarters.

Mt. Rogers Appalachian Trail Club—MRATC, with maintenance responsibility for the A.T. from the Tennessee line north to Teas Road (58.4 miles), maintains trails in the Mt. Rogers NRA, Jefferson National Forest, Grayson Highlands State Park, and other areas. Send correspondence to MRATC Box 789, Damascus, VA 24236-0789; <www.mratc.org>.

U.S. 58/Damascus, Va. [P.O. ZIP 24236: M–F 8:30–1 & 2–4:30, Sa 9–11; (276) 475-3411]—Called "the friendliest town on the Trail" and the home of Trail Days (to be held this year May 15–17). First held in '87 as a commemorative event for the 50th anniversary of the A.T., the festival's activities and crowds have grown each year since. Activities include a hiker reunion and talent show, hiking-related exhibits, arts-and-crafts exhibits, street dances, live music, and the popular hiker parade through downtown. If you are unable to walk into Damascus for the weekend, rides are easy to find from all points along the Trail. Be aware that state open-container laws that restrict drinking in public places are enforced. Hiker camping during Trail Days is at the edge of town on Shady Lane. Camping is prohibited everywhere else. Please keep quiet in the late evening and early morning, and, upon departure, leave your campsite clean. Leave No Trace camping principles apply in town as well as on the Trail. You'll find all major services, except veterinary, in Damascus. ■ *Hostels:* The Place, (276) 475-3441, <www.facebook.com/theplacehostel>, opens in late Mar and closes when the pipes are in danger of freezing. Stays are limited to two days (unless sick or injured). A large house for hikers and TA cyclists only, with bunk space, showers (towels/soap), tenting, and pavilion/picnic tables. Seven-dollars-per-night donation is requested, but larger donations are appreciated in addition to cleaning chores. Seasonal caretaker. No vehicle-assisted hikers except during Trail Days. No dogs, drinking, or smoking are allowed on the property of the First United Methodist Church, its parking lot, or pavilion. Dave's Place Hostel, 110 Laurel Ave., run by Mt. Rogers Outfitters, 5 rooms with two bunks each, $21/room/night (max. 2, 2-night stay), shower without stay $3, no dogs allowed, daily parking $2/day, no alcohol/smoking on property. Crazy Larry's Hostel, 209 Douglas Dr., (276) 274-3637, bunks $20PP includes shower, B $7, laundry $5, no drugs/alcohol. Woodchuck Hostel, (406)

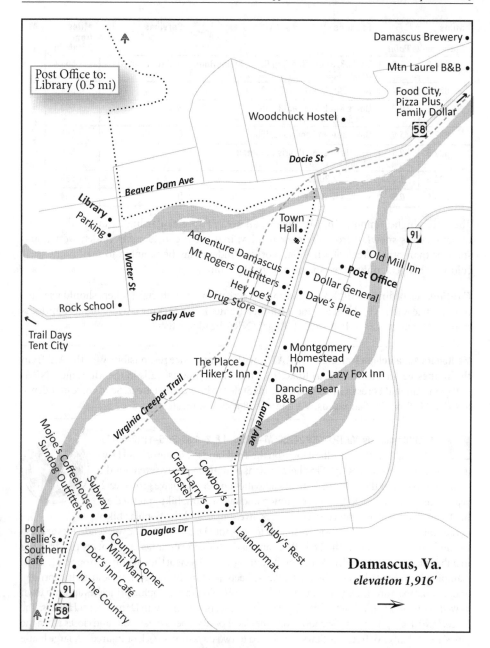

Post Office to:
Library (0.5 mi)

Damascus Brewery •

Mtn Laurel B&B •

Food City,
Pizza Plus,
Family Dollar

58

Woodchuck Hostel •

Docie St

Beaver Dam Ave

Library

Parking •

Town
Hall •

91

Water St

Adventure Damascus

Mt Rogers Outfitters

• Old Mill Inn

• **Post Office**

• Dollar General

Hey Joe's •

Drug Store •

• Dave's Place

Rock School •

Shady Ave

Trail Days
Tent City

• Montgomery
Homestead
Inn

The Place •

Hiker's Inn •

• Lazy Fox Inn

Dancing Bear
B&B •

Virginia Creeper Trail

Laurel Ave

Mojoe's Coffeehouse

Sundog Outfitter

Subway

Crazy Larry's
Hostel

Cowboy's

Pork
Bellie's •
Southern
Café

Country Corner
Mini Mart

Douglas Dr

Laundromat

• Ruby's Rest

Dot's Inn Café

In The Country

91

58

Damascus, Va.
elevation 1,916'

→

407-1272, 53 Docie St., open Mar 15–Nov 1, bed with linens $25, 1 private cabin $45–$55 s/d, teepee $20, tent/hammock $10, continental B with stay, shower without stay $3, kitchen privileges, laundry

NOTE: Because of 2014 remeasurements throughout the section, virtually all Southwest Virginia mileposts have changed by small amounts (0.1, 0.2 mile) since the profiles were made in 2012. *Consult the tables for current milepoints!*

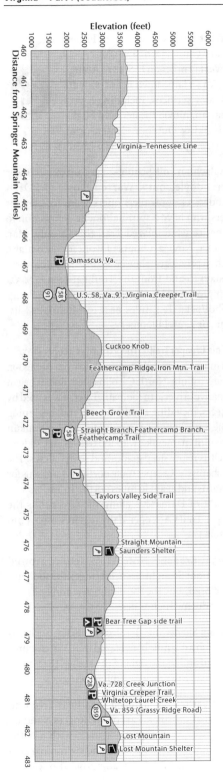

Elevation (feet)

Distance from Springer Mountain (miles)

Virginia–Tennessee Line

Damascus, Va.

U.S. 58, Va. 91, Virginia Creeper Trail

Cuckoo Knob

Feathercamp Ridge, Iron Mtn. Trail

Beech Grove Trail

Straight Branch, Feathercamp Branch, Feathercamp Trail

Taylors Valley Side Trail

Straight Mountain
Saunders Shelter

Bear Tree Gap side trail

Va. 728, Creek Junction
Virginia Creeper Trail,
Whitetop Laurel Creek
Va. 859 (Grassy Ridge Road)

Lost Mountain
Lost Mountain Shelter

$5, common area, pavilion with gas grill, large yard, dogs welcome, cold drinks and snacks available; free shuttle to Food City, others by arrangement; no drugs or alcohol. Mail drops accepted at P.O. Box 752, Damascus, VA 24236. ■ *Lodging:* Hiker's Inn, 216 E. Laurel Ave., (276) 475-3788, owned and operated by Paul (Skink of 2010) and Lee, bunks in hostel $25, private room $50, private room in house $75/night or $65/multiple nights, a/c and WiFi, laundry $5 for guests, dogs allowed only in hostel, closed in winter; Lazy Fox Inn, (276) 475-5838, no mail drops accepted; Mountain Laurel Inn, (276) 475-5956, 0.5 mile west of town on U.S. 58, 2-night minimum; Montgomery Homestead Inn, 103 Laurel Ave., (276) 492-6283, <montgomeryhomestead.com>, mail drops accepted for guests sent to Susie Montgomery Box 12, Damascus, VA 24236, no alcohol/smoking/pets; The Victorian Inn B&B, 203 N. Legion St., (276) 475-5059; Ruby's Rest, 719 E. 2nd St. (near Dairy King), (276) 475-3914, <www.rubysrest.com>, $40S/D, $10EAP, dogs free in fenced yard; Outdoors Inn, (276) 475-3611, rent the entire space for groups of 10 for $150/night including full kitchen. ■ *Groceries:* Food City (long-term resupply). ■ *Restaurants:* Pork Bellies Southern Café; Subway; Dot's Inn; Cowboy's Deli and convenience store, with ATM; In the Country; Mojoe's Trailside Coffee House, B; Hey Joe's Tacos. ■ *Outfitters:* Mt. Rogers Outfitters (MRO), 110 Laurel Ave. (P.O. Box 546), (276) 475-5416, <mtrogersoutfitters. com>, owned and operated by 1990 thru-hiker and Damascus native Dave Patrick and son Jeff, backpacking gear and supplies, stove fuel, shuttles, accepts mail drops, open M–Sa 9–6, Su 12–6; Adventure Damascus Outdoor Co., 128 W. Laurel Ave., open 7 days/week, backpacking gear and clothing, fuel, $4 shower; Sundog Outfitter, 331 Douglas Dr., (276) 475-6252, <www.sundogoutfitter.com>, backpacking gear and clothing, repairs, hiker food, denatured alcohol and other fuels, will hold USPS and UPS mail drops, call ahead for shuttles, open 7 days a week. ■ *Internet access:* Damascus Public Library & Visitors Center, WiFi/Skype, M–W–F 9–5, T–Th 11–7, Sa 9–1; long-term parking available, inquire at town hall. ■ *Other services:* Town-wide WiFi; medical clinic; pharmacy; Dollar General; two banks with ATM.

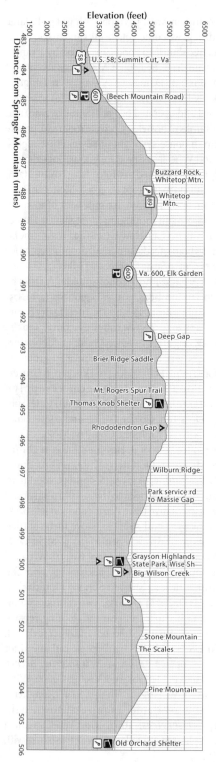

West 2 miles on U.S. 58 to Fisher Hollow Veterinary Clinic, (276) 475-5397.

West 12 miles on U.S. 58 to Abingdon, Va., a large town near I-81 with all major services, including a veterinarian, movie theater, and Highlands Ski & Outdoor Center, (276) 628-1329, open M–F 10–7, Sa 9–7, Su 12–6.

Appalachian Folk School— (423) 341-1843, <www.warrendoyle.com>. Warren Doyle (ALDHA Founder; 34,000-miler) offers work-for-stay for hikers who have a spiritual/poetic connection to the entire white-blazed Trail (M–Th only, Mar, Apr, Oct, Nov); 2-3 hours of work for each night. Kitchen privileges, shower, WiFi. Rides (for work-for-stay) to and from the Trail between U.S. 321 (Hampton) and Va. 603 (Fox Creek). No smoking/alcohol/pets. Ten miles **east** to Mountain City, Tenn., or Laurel Bloomery.

Virginia Creeper Trail—The Virginia Creeper stretches 33 miles along an old railroad bed from Abingdon to the Virginia–North Carolina state line. It began as a native-American footpath. Later, it was used by pioneers, including Daniel Boone, and, beginning in the early 1900s, by a quintessential mountain railroad, its namesake, with 100 trestles and bridges, as well as many steep grades and sharp curves. The A.T. shares the Creeper route north of Damascus for 300 yards and again 10 miles north. [In Taylors Valley, east of Damascus along the Creeper, is the Creeper Trail Café, open daily 11–5 in season, (276) 475-3918.]

Straight Branch—Note Trail detour around washed-out Straight Branch bridge. The footpath isn't closed, but the local club recommends the detour during high water.

Saunders Shelter (1987)—Sleeps 8. Privy. Shelter is located on a 0.2-mile blue-blazed trail. Water source is behind and to the right of the shelter, then down an old road to a reliable, seeping spring.

USFS Beartree Campground—*via* Bear Tree Gap Trail **West** 3.6 miles. Part of Mt. Rogers National Recreation Area, (276) 388-3642, with a bathhouse (hot showers $4), lake, and swimming area 0.6 mile from the A.T. Campground is 3 miles

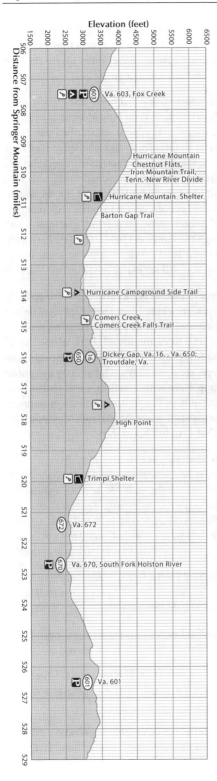

beyond swimming area, with tent sites $20 and hot showers $4. Parking $5/day. Open mid-Apr–Oct. Cash or check only.

Lost Mountain Shelter (1994)—Sleeps 8. Privy. Water source is on a trail to the left of the shelter.

Whitetop Mountain—At 5,520 feet, this is Virginia's second-highest peak, although the Trail does not go to the top. Nearby Whitetop is home to a ramp festival, held the weekend after Memorial Day. The celebration includes a ramp-eating contest thru-hikers have won in past years. Ramps emerge from the forest floor in early spring. The two-leafed greens sprout from an onion-like tuber that can be used to spice up Trail meals. Other plants have a similar look, but ramps are identified easily by their smell and taste, which are akin to onions and garlic.

Va. 600, Elk Garden—Elk Garden is named after the extinct eastern elk that once roamed throughout this area, along with timber wolves, mountain lions, and bison. Today, none of those exist here, but black bear, white-tailed deer, and wild turkey are common. **West** 7 miles to Coolgreen B&B in Konnarock, (276) 388-3902; rates start at $95D (with B), ask about possible shuttles for guests.

USFS Grindstone Campground—*via* Mt. Rogers Trail **West** 4 miles. Tent sites including shower $20; hot shower $4; partking $5/day. Open Apr 15–Nov 30.

Mt. Rogers—Virginia's highest peak, at 5,729 feet; the Trail does not go to the viewless summit, but it can be reached *via* a side trail, going west 0.5 mile. Camping is prohibited in the area from the A.T. to the summit due to fragile plant life and the endangered Wellers salamander. The Wellers, a dark blue-black salamander with gold splotches on its back, can be found only in coniferous forests above 5,000 feet. You may also see or hear northern birds, such as the hermit thrush and winter wren. Such species nest here because of the favorable altitude at the summit area.

Thomas Knob Shelter (1991)—Sleeps 16. Privy (moldering). This two-level shelter was built by the MRATC and Konnarock Crew. Water source is in an enclosed area in a pasture behind the

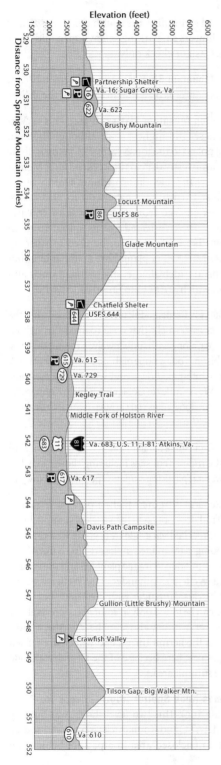

Elevation (feet)

Distance from Springer Mountain (miles)

Partnership Shelter
Va. 16; Sugar Grove, Va.

Va. 622

Brushy Mountain

Locust Mountain

USFS 86

Glade Mountain

Chatfield Shelter
USFS 644

Va. 615

Va. 729

Kegley Trail

Middle Fork of Holston River

Va. 683, U.S. 11, I-81; Atkins, Va.

Va. 617

Davis Path Campsite

Gullion (Little Brushy) Mountain

Crawfish Valley

Tilson Gap, Big Walker Mtn.

Va. 610

shelter; lock the gate leading to the water source to keep the feral ponies in the area from polluting the water. Be aware those ponies like to chew on packs and other salty items.

Rhododendron Gap—Just below the highest point on the Virginia A.T. on Pine Mountain and Wilburn Ridge. Many large, established campsites between Thomas Knob and Rhododendron Gap. This section extremely popular with weekend and day-hikers. In June, rhododendron blooms here in full force. Panoramic views of the rhododendron thickets can be seen from a rock outcropping. Watch your step from Thomas Knob through the Grayson Highlands State Park area; cattle and feral ponies roam the area. In the spring, you will see mares tending their foals.

Grayson Highlands State Park—(276) 579-7092. At Massie Gap, a blue-blaze leads **East** 0.5 mile to a parking area, then 1.5 miles farther on roads or horse trail to campground. Park is open year-round from dawn to 10 p.m. The campstore and showers are open May 1–Oct 31; may use phone at camp store with a calling card; tentsite $21, shower only $5. Camp store staffed by volunteers is usually open on weekends from Memorial Day to Labor Day, but hours vary.

Wise Shelter (1996)—Sleeps 8. Privy. Water source is a reliable spring south of the shelter on a trail east of the A.T. No tenting around the shelter or in the state park. Tentsites are in the Mt. Rogers NRA, across Wilson Creek, 0.3 mile north. Follow the Wilson Creek Trail 2 miles east to Grayson Highlands State Park (see above).

Old Orchard Shelter (1970)—Sleeps 6. Privy. Water source is 100 yards on a blue-blazed trail to the right of the shelter.

Va. 603/Fox Creek—Parking. **East** 100 yards to Fox Creek Horse Camp, $5/night, no water.

Hurricane Mountain Shelter (2004)—Sleeps 8. Privy (moldering). Water source is a nearby stream.

USFS Hurricane Campground—**West** 0.5 mile *via* side trail to Hurricane Campground, (276) 783-5196, one of nine USFS campgrounds within the

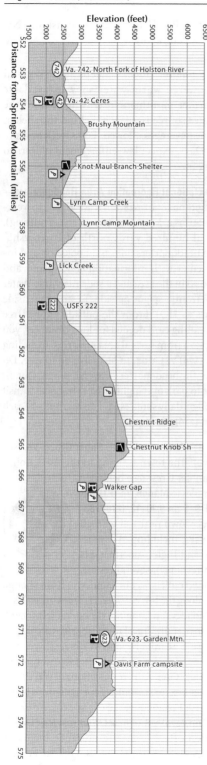

Elevation (feet)

Distance from Springer Mountain (miles)

Va. 742, North Fork of Holston River

Va. 42; Ceres

Brushy Mountain

Knot-Maul-Branch-Shelter

Lynn Camp Creek

Lynn Camp Mountain

Lick Creek

USFS 222

Chestnut Ridge

Chestnut Knob Sh

Walker Gap

Va. 623, Garden Mtn.

Davis Farm campsite

George Washington and Jefferson National Forests. The campground charges $16 per site; $2 shower 10-2; parking $3/day. Open Apr 15–Oct 31, depending on weather. Cash or check only.

Va. 650, East 100 yards to **Va. 16/Dickey Gap**— Turn right **(compass south)** 2.6 miles to Trout-dale, Va. **[P.O. ZIP 24378: M–F 8–12, Sa 8–11:30; (276) 677-3221].** ■ *Hostel:* Troutdale Baptist Church, Pastor Ken Riggins, (276) 677-4092, located at 10148 Trout-dale Hwy., offers a place to tent or use of a hiker bunkhouse, shower; pets welcome, donations accepted. ■ *Other services:* ATM, bank, dentist, medical clinic.

Continue on Va. 16 3.6 miles to Fox Creek General Store (short-term resupply), 7116 Troutdale Hwy, (276) 579-6033, open M–F 7–7, Sa 7–6; groceries, deli withsandwiches, pizza, and occasional BBQ. Deli closes 30 minutes before store.

From gap, left on Va. 16 5 miles to **Sugar Grove, Va. [P.O. ZIP 24375: M–F 8:30–12 & 2–4, Sa 8:15–10:30; (276)677-3200].** *Groceries:* Sugar Grove Food Mart (short-term resupply) on Va. 16, (276) 377-3037, M–Sa 6–9:30, Su 7–9:30, snack bar, ATM.

Trimpi Shelter (1975)—Sleeps 8. Privy. A reliable spring is in front of the shelter.

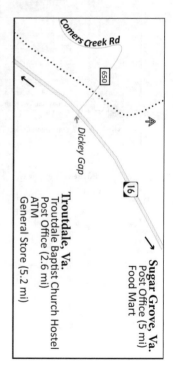

Comers Creek Rd

650

Dickey Gap

16

Troutdale, Va.
Troutdale Baptist Church Hostel
Post Office (2.6 mi)
ATM
General Store (5.2 mi)

Sugar Grove, Va.
Post Office (5 mi)
Food Mart

Piedmont Appalachian Trail Hikers (PATH)—PATH maintains the 65.4 miles between Teas Road, a mile north of Va. 670, South Fork of the Holston River, and U.S. 52 at Bland, Va. Correspondence

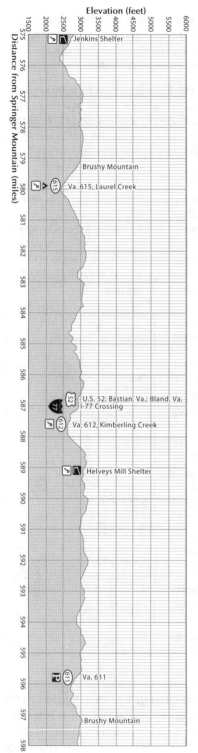

Elevation (feet)

Distance from Springer Mountain (miles)

Jenkins Shelter

Brushy Mountain

Va. 615, Laurel Creek

U.S. 52; Bastian, Va.; Bland, Va.
I-77 Crossing

Va. 612, Kimberling Creek

Helveys Mill Shelter

Va. 611

Brushy Mountain

can be sent to PATH Box 4423, Greensboro, NC 27404; <www.path-at.org>.

Partnership Shelter (1998)—Sleeps 16. Privy and propane-powered warm-water shower (available during warmer months). No tenting around the shelter. Water source is a faucet behind the shelter. No alcoholic beverages allowed. For a week or more after Trail Days, expect law-enforcement officers to be checking in.

Mt. Rogers National Recreation Area Headquarters— (276) 783-5196 or (800) 628-7202, M–F 8–4:30 year-round, Sa–Su 9–4 May–Oct (weather permitting). Only several hundred yards north of Partnership Shelter, the headquarters houses a bookshop and interpretive center with information about plants and animals found in the area and a soda machine. Water is available from a spigot outside. Restroom outside (same hours as HQ). From the outside phone (free local calls, calling card needed for long distance), you can order pizza from several area pizzerias, including Pizza Hut, (276) 783-3104, to be delivered to gate. Do not sleep on the headquarters' covered porch. Obtain free permit to park overnight or weekly. Local transit authority offers daily shuttles M–F to Marion, 50¢ each way; info at (276) 782-9300.

Va. 16—East 3.2 miles to **Sugar Grove, Va.** (see above). The town is home to the ATC Konnarock Volunteer Crew (see below).

    West 6 miles to **Marion, Va. [P.O. ZIP 24354: M–F 9–5 Sa 9:30–12; (276) 783-5051]**, a larger town near I-81 with all major services, including Walmart, Food Lion, and Ingles supermarkets (long-term resupply), several restaurants, fast-food outlets, a coin laundry, and Greyhound bus service along the I-81 corridor, (276) 783-7114 (closed Sa, Su, and holidays). ■ *Lodging:* various motels, including the hiker-friendly Travel Inn, (276) 783-5112, 1419 N. Main/U.S. 11, 0.25 mile beyond Walmart, hiker rate $37.99S, $42.99D (except during Bristol Raceway weekends), dogs $7, CATV, in-room phones, WiFi, coin laundry, hiker box (in season), accept mail drops ($5 fee for nonguests); EconoLodge, (276) 783-6031; America's Best Value Inn, (276) 378-0481. ■ *Other services:* Downtown Marion offers several restaurants, including Wolfe's BBQ, 11–8 M–Th, 11–9 F–S, 11–4 Su, and the

Army Navy Store, which stocks isobutane canisters and solid-fuel tablets, along with outdoor clothing; hospital; Greyhound bus.

Konnarock Crew—Based 1 mile from Sugar Grove post office at USFS facility. If you want part of your experience to be a week on the crew that builds and rehabilitates the Trail, call the Roanoke, Va., ATC regional office at (540) 904-4393 before your hike to make arrangements. Getting to base camp and back is your responsibility, but, once there, food and amenities are provided. Commitments include 5 days/4 nights along the Trail in the South. Be prepared to work and have a lot of fun.

Chatfield Shelter (1970s)—Sleeps 6. Privy. A creek is in front.

Va. 615, Settlers Museum—On USFS lands adjacent to the Trail, the farmstead and visitors center include exhibits of rural life at the time the valley was settled. Admission free to hikers.

Va. 683, U.S. 11, I-81—At Groseclose, Va. (no post office), this is the southernmost crossing of I-81. *See map on next page.* ■ *Restaurant:* The Barn Restaurant, 7412 Lee Hwy, Rural Retreat, VA 24368; B/L/D, M–Sa 7–8, Su 7–3 buffet, ask permission for long-term parking, (276) 686-6222, mail drops accepted (no fee). ■ *Groceries:* Village Truck Stop (Sunoco station open 24 hours), (276) 783-5775, 5–11, snack bar (7 a.m.–8 p.m.), showers $5, Heet fuel (in season), and short-term resupply; E-Z Stop (Exxon), 7 a.m.–10 p.m. daily), short-term resupply, Burrito Loco restaurant inside scheduled to open before 2015 season. ■ *Lodging:* The Relax Inn, 7253 Lee Hwy, Rural Retreat, VA 24368, (276) 783-5811, $40S, $45D, $5EAP, $10 per pet; long-term hiker parking $3/day; coin laundry; call for info on reservations and possible shuttle; will hold up to 2 packages for staying guests; please provide your ETA. No visitors after 8 p.m.

    West 3.2 miles (on U.S. 11 south) to **Atkins, Va. [P.O. ZIP 24311: M–F 8:30–12:30 & 1:45–3:45, Sa 9–10:45; (276) 783-5551].** ■ *Restaurants:* Atkins Tank (at Arnold's Exxon), M–Sa 7–8, Su 11–3; Subway (at Kangaroo Express), M–F 6–11, Sa–Su 8–11. ■ *Groceries:* Arnold's Exxon, M–F 4–10, Sa–Su 5–9, hiker-friendly, ATM, fuel, short-term resupply, craft-beer selection; Kangaroo Express, open 24 hrs., ATM, short-term resupply; Dollar General, daily 8–10, long-term resupply. ■ *Lodging:* Comfort Inn, 5558 Lee Hwy, (276) 783-2144, call for rates and services. ■ *Other services:* coin laundry, M–Sa 7:30–8, across from Dollar General.

    West 10.2 miles (on U.S. 11 south) to **Marion, Va.** (see above), a larger town.

Davis Path Campsite—Tent platform, table, and privy. Water source is a spring 0.9 mile south of the campsite. Southbounders can carry water from Crawfish Valley, 3.5 miles north.

Knot Maul Branch Shelter (1980s)—Sleeps 8. Privy. Water source is 0.2 mile north on the A.T.

Chestnut Knob Shelter (renovated 1994)—Sleeps 8. Privy. A former firewarden's cabin; plexiglass windows to let in some light. No water is available at this shelter, but water is sometimes found 0.2 mile south on the A.T., then 50 yards east on an old Jeep road. Otherwise, southbounders can find water 1.3 miles north in Walker Gap, and northbounders can find water at a spring-fed pond 1.8 miles south.

Burkes Garden—Chestnut Knob Shelter, elevation 4,410 feet, overlooks this unusual geologic feature. It is a large, crater-shaped depression surrounded on all sides by a high ridge that the A.T. follows for nearly 8 miles. From Chestnut Knob, you can see how it got its nickname, "God's Thumbprint."

Jenkins Shelter (1960s)—Sleeps 8. Privy. Water source is a stream 100 yards north on a blue-blazed trail.

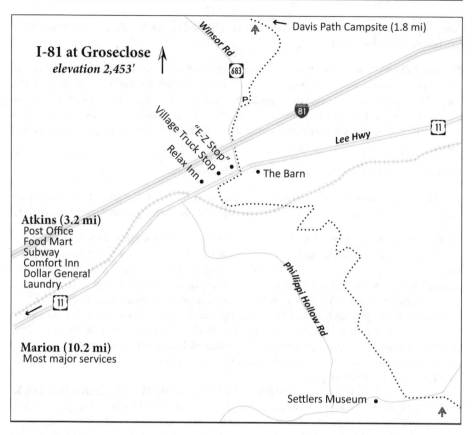

I-81 at Groseclose
elevation 2,453'

Davis Path Campsite (1.8 mi)

Winsor Rd

683

81

P

Lee Hwy

11

"E-Z Stop"
Village Truck Stop
Relax Inn

The Barn

Atkins (3.2 mi)
Post Office
Food Mart
Subway
Comfort Inn
Dollar General
Laundry

11

Phillippi Hollow Rd

Marion (10.2 mi)
Most major services

Settlers Museum

U.S. 52—East 2.7 miles to **Bland, Va. [P.O. ZIP 24315: M–F 8–11:30 & 12–4, Sa 9–11; (276) 688-3751].** ■ *Grocery*: Grant's Grocery. ■ *Restaurant*: Bland Square Grill (in Bland Square Citgo, 8870 South Scenic Hwy, first block west of Main on U.S. 52 in downtown Bland, B/L/D, 7 days. ■ *Internet access:* townwide WiFi; library, (276) 688-3737, M, W, F–Sa 10–4:30, Tu, Th 10–7:30. ■ *Other services:* Napa Auto; banks with ATM.

East 3.3 miles to ■ *Lodging:* Big Walker Motel, 70 Skyview Lane, (276) 688-3331, $57.89 1-2 persons, $62.18 3 or more, pets OK, WiFi, will hold packages for guests. Call motel or Bubba, (276) 266-6147, for shuttle possibilities. ■ *Other services:* Bland Family Clinic, (276) 688-0500, M 10–6, T 11–7, Th 9–5, F 10–2, closed W; Dairy Queen/gas station (short-term resupply) with ATM; Subway; Dollar General. *There is no place to camp in Bland.*

West 2.5 miles to **Bastian, Va. [P.O. ZIP 24314: M–F 8–12, Sa 8:15–11:15; (276) 688-4631].** P.O. is **West** 1.9 miles, left on Railroad Trail, right on Walnut Drive. Two miles farther down U.S. 52 to *Other services:* medical clinic, after hours call (276) 688-4331, M, W 8:30–6, Tu 8:30–8, Th 8:30–8, F 8:30–5; pharmacy next door, (276) 688-4204, M–F 9–5, Tu 9–8, Sa 9–12; Greyhound bus, (304) 325-9442, available for the I-77 corridor in Bluefield, W.Va., about 10 miles beyond Bastian on U.S. 52 (closed Su and holidays); Pizza Plus, (276) 688-3332, will deliver to U.S. 52 Trailhead and Bland.

Outdoor Club of Virginia Tech—OCVT maintains the 9.8 miles between U.S. 52 and Va. 611 and 18.9 miles in central Virginia between U.S. 460 and Pine Swamp Branch Shelter. Correspondence should be sent to OCVT Box 538, Blacksburg, VA 24060; <www.outdoor.org.vt.edu>.

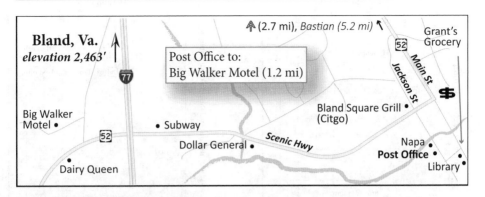

Helveys Mill Shelter (1960s)—Sleeps 6. Privy. Water source is down a switch-backed trail in front of the shelter.

Jenny Knob Shelter (1960s)—Sleeps 6. Privy. Water source, considered unreliable, is a seasonal spring near shelter.

Roanoke Appalachian Trail Club—RATC maintains the 36.5 miles between Va. 611 and U.S. 460 and 87.0 miles in the next section between Pine Swamp Branch Shelter and Black Horse Gap. Correspondence should be sent to RATC Box 12282, Roanoke, VA 24024; <www.ratc.org>.

Va. 606—West 0.5 mile to *Groceries:* Trent's Grocery, 900 Wilderness Rd., Bland, VA 24315; (276) 928-1349; with ATM, deli, and pizza; possible shuttles. Open M–Sa 7–8, Su 9–8, Coleman and denatured alcohol by the ounce, canister fuel, and soda machines. Camping, shower, and laundry $6, or shower and laundry $3. Room with 2 beds, $40–$50, includes fridge, microwave, laundry. Accepts packages.

Wapiti Shelter (1980)—Sleeps 8. Privy. Water source is Dismal Creek, just south of the turn-off to the shelter.

Sugar Run Road/Sugar Run Gap—East 0.5 mile to *Hostel:* Woodshole Hostel, 3696 Sugar Run Rd., Pearisburg, VA 24134; (540) 921-3444, <www.woodsholehostel.com>; "a slice of Heaven not to be missed." The isolated 1880s' chestnut-log cabin was discovered by the late Roy and Tillie Wood while he was studying elk in 1940. The two opened the hostel in 1986. Their granddaughter, Neville, and her husband, Michael, continue their legacy, placing an emphasis on sustainable living through farming, beekeeping, organic gardening, yoga, and massage therapy. The bunkhouse has mattresses, electricity, hot shower, and a.m. organic coffee/tea, $15PP; camping, $10PP; 3 indoor rooms $28 shared, $55 private (thru-hiker special). Guests often are invited for local/organic community D, $13; B $8. Please call to inquire or reserve. Shuttles, Internet, laundry, smoothies, home-made bread, baked goods, and cheese. Coleman fuel, denatured alcohol, fuel canisters. Credit and cash (discount). Pet-friendly. Mail drops accepted. *Directions:* Going north, at Sugar Run Gap, turn right on dirt road, bear left at fork, go 0.5 mile downhill; going south, at Sugar Run Gap, turn left and downhill 0.5 mile. Watch for signs.

Doc's Knob Shelter (1971)—Sleeps 8. Privy. A reliable spring is to left of the shelter.

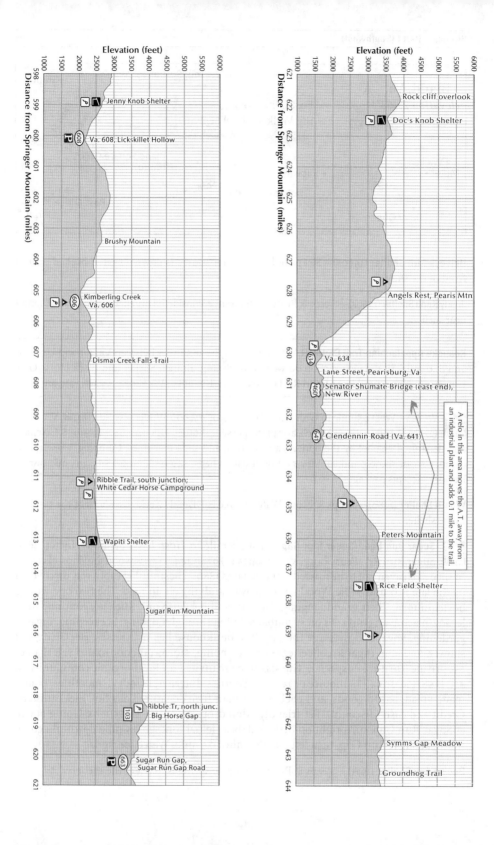

Elevation (feet)

Distance from Springer Mountain (miles)

Jenny Knob Shelter

Va. 608, Lickskillet Hollow

Brushy Mountain

Kimberling Creek
Va. 606

Dismal Creek Falls Trail

Ribble Trail, south junction;
White Cedar Horse Campground

Wapiti Shelter

Sugar Run Mountain

Ribble Tr, north junc.
Big Horse Gap

Sugar Run Gap,
Sugar Run Gap Road

Elevation (feet)

Distance from Springer Mountain (miles)

Rock cliff overlook

Doc's Knob Shelter

Angels Rest, Pearis Mtn

Va. 634
Lane Street, Pearisburg, Va.

Senator Shumate Bridge (east end),
New River

Clendennin Road (Va. 641)

A relo in this area moves the A.T. away from
an industrial plant and adds 0.1 mile to the trail.

Peters Mountain

Rice Field Shelter

Symms Gap Meadow

Groundhog Trail

Virginia—Part 2 (Central)

Miles from Springer	Fr Last Point	Features	Services	Miles from Katahdin	M A P
634.5	0.6	Va. 634 (2,200')	R	1,554.7	
634.9	0.4	Lane Street (1,650') **Pearisburg, Va. 24134** Pembroke, Va. Blacksburg, Va.	R (E–1m PO, all; 2.9m H; 6m O; 20m all)	1,554.3	
635.5	0.6	U.S. 460, Senator Shumate Bridge (east shore) over New River (1,600') **Narrows, Va. 24124**	R (W–3m PO, C, G, L, M, cl)	1,553.7	
638.9	3.4	Hemlock Ridge (2,470')		1,550.3	
639.4	0.5	Va. 641, Clendennin Road (1,750')	R	1,549.8	
640.5	1.1	Stream (2,250')	w	1,548.7	
641.6	1.1	Springs (3,250')	C, w	1,547.6	
641.8	0.2	**Rice Field Shelter** (3,400')...*15.7mS; 12.6mN*	S (E–0.3m w)	1,547.4	
643.4	1.6	Campsite and spring (3,450')	C, w	1,545.8	
646.9	3.5	Symms Gap Meadow (3,480')	C, w	1,542.3	
647.9	1.0	Groundhog Trail (3,400')		1,541.3	
649.5	1.6	Dickerson Gap (3,300')		1,539.7	
651.7	2.2	Peters Mountain Ridgecrest (3,860')		1,537.5	
651.9	0.2	Allegheny Trail Junction (3,740')		1,537.3	
654.4	2.5	**Pine Swamp Branch Shelter** (2,530') ...*12.6mS; 3.9mN*	S, C, w	1,534.8	
654.7	0.3	Va.635, Stony Creek Valley (2,370') ...*USFS parking area*	R, P	1,534.5	
655.8	1.1	Dismal Branch (2,480')	w	1,533.4	
656.8	1.0	Va. 635, Stony Creek (2,450')	R, w	1,532.4	
658.1	1.3	Spring (3,490')	w	1,531.1	
658.3	0.2	**Bailey Gap Shelter** (3,525')...*3.9mS; 8.8mN*	S, w	1,530.9	
662.0	3.7	Va. 613, Mountain Lake Road (3,950') Salt Sulphur Turnpike	R, P (E–5m L)	1,527.2	
662.2	0.2	Wind Rock (4,121')...*vista*		1,527.0	
663.4	1.2	Campsite and spring (4,000')	C, w	1,525.8	
667.1	3.7	**War Spur Shelter** (2,340')...*8.8mS; 5.8mN*	S, w	1,522.1	
667.9	0.8	USFS 156, Johns Creek Valley (2,102')	R, P, w	1,521.3	
668.9	1.0	Stream (2,700')	w	1,520.3	
669.9	1.0	Va. 601, Rocky Gap (3,250')	R, P	1,519.3	
672.9	3.0	**Laurel Creek Shelter** (2,720')...*5.8mS; 6.7mN*	S, w	1,516.3	
673.9	1.0	Spring (2,400')	w	1,515.3	
675.3	1.4	Va. 42, Sinking Creek Valley (2,200')	R	1,513.9	
676.2	0.9	Va. 630, Sinking Creek (2,100')	R, P, w	1,513.0	
676.6	0.4	Keffer Oak (2,240')		1,512.6	

Appalachian Trail Thru-Hikers' Companion–2015

Miles from Springer	Fr Last Point	Features	Services	Miles from Katahdin	M A P
677.8	1.2	Sinking Creek Mountain (south) (3,200')		1,511.4	
679.3	1.5	**Sarver Hollow Shelter** (3,000')...*6.7mS; 6.3mN*	E–0.3m S, w	1,509.9	
682.9	3.6	Sinking Creek Mountain (north) (3,490')		1,506.3	
684.6	1.7	Cabin Branch (2,490')	C, w	1,504.6	
685.3	0.7	**Niday Shelter** (1,800')...*6.3mS; 10.4mN*	S, w	1,503.9	
686.6	1.3	Va. 621, Craig Creek Valley (1,560')	R, P	1,502.6	
690.0	3.4	Brushy Mountain (3,100')		1,499.2	
690.4	0.4	Audie Murphy Monument (3,100')		1,498.8	
692.6	2.2	Brushy Mountain (2,600')...*vistas*		1,496.6	
694.2	1.6	Va. 620, Trout Creek, Miller Cove Road (1,525')	R, P, w	1,495.0	
695.4	1.2	**Pickle Branch Shelter** (1,845') ...*10.4mS; 13.9mN*	E–0.3m S, w	1,493.8	
699.6	4.2	Cove Mountain, Dragons Tooth (3,020')		1,489.6	
700.6	1.0	Lost Spectacles Gap (2,550')		1,488.6	
701.1	0.5	Rawies Rest (2,350')		1,488.1	
702.1	1.0	Va. 624, Newport Road, North Mountain Trail (1,810')	R, P (E–0.4m H) (W–0.4m C,G,M)	1,487.1	
703.7	1.6	Va. 785, Blacksburg Road (1,790')	R	1,485.5	
708.0	4.3	Va. 311, Catawba Valley Drive (1,990') **Catawba, Va. 24070**	R, P (W–1m PO, G; 1.3m M)	1,481.2	
709.0	1.0	**Johns Spring Shelter** (1,980')...*13.9mS; 1mN*	S, w	1,480.2	
710.0	1.0	**Catawba Mountain Shelter** (2,580') ...*1mS; 2.4mN*	S, w	1,479.2	
711.7	1.7	McAfee Knob (3,199')...*vista*		1,477.5	
712.3	0.6	Pig Farm Campsite (3,000')	C, w	1,476.9	
712.4	0.1	**Campbell Shelter** (2,580')...*2.4mS; 6mN*	S, w	1,476.8	
715.5	3.1	Brickey's Gap (2,250')		1,473.7	
717.3	1.8	Tinker Cliffs (3,000')		1,471.9	
717.8	0.5	Scorched Earth Gap, Andy Layne Trail (2,600')		1,471.4	
718.4	0.6	**Lamberts Meadow Shelter** (2,080') ...*6mS; 14.4mN*	S, w	1,470.8	
718.7	0.3	Lamberts Meadow Campsite, Sawmill Run (2,000')	C, w	1,470.5	
722.7	4.0	Angels Gap (1,800')		1,466.5	
723.8	1.1	Hay Rock, Tinker Ridge (1,900')		1,465.4	
727.3	3.5	Tinker Creek (1,165')...*concrete bridge*		1,461.9	
727.8	0.5	U.S. 220, Va. 816 (1,350') **Daleville, Va 24083** Roanoke, Va.	R, P, G, L, M (E–0.8m G, L, M, cl, sh; 12m O) (W–0.3m G,M,O, f; 1m PO, G, D, V)	1,461.4	
729.0	1.2	U.S. 779, I-81 underpass (1,400')	R, P	1,460.2	

ATC Central Va. Map 4

ATC Central Va. Map 3

Miles from Springer	Fr Last Point	Features	Services	Miles from Katahdin	M A P
729.3	0.3	U.S. 11, Norfolk Southern Railway (1,300') **Troutville, Va. 24175**	R (W–0.8m PO; 1.3m C, G, M)	1,459.9	
729.8	0.5	Va. 652, Mountain Pass Road (1,450')	R	1,459.4	
732.8	3.0	**Fullhardt Knob Shelter** (2,676') *...14.4mS; 6.2mN*	S, w	1,456.4	
735.6	2.8	USFS 191, Salt Pond Road (2,260')	R	1,453.6	ATC Central Va. Map 3
736.4	0.8	Curry Creek (1,680')	w	1,452.8	
738.3	1.9	Wilson Creek (1,690')	w	1,450.9	
739.0	0.7	**Wilson Creek Shelter** (1,830')*...6.2mS; 7.5mN*	S, w	1,450.2	
739.4	0.4	Spring (2,050')	w	1,449.8	
741.4	2.0	USFS 186; BRP mp 97.7 (2,402') Old Fincastle Road; Black Horse Gap	R, P	1,447.8	
742.2	0.8	BRP mp 97.0; Taylors Mountain Overlook (2,350')	R	1,447.0	
743.3	1.1	BRP mp 95.9; Montvale Overlook (2,400')	R	1,445.9	
743.9	0.6	BRP mp 95.3; Harveys Knob Overlook (2,550')	R	1,445.3	
746.3	2.4	**Bobblets Gap Shelter** (1,920')*...7.5mS; 6.7mN*	W–0.2m S, w	1,442.9	
747.0	0.7	BRP mp 92.5; Peaks of Otter Overlook (2,350')	R, P	1,442.2	
747.7	0.7	BRP mp 91.8; Mills Gap Overlook (2,450')	R, P	1,441.5	
749.4	1.7	Va. 43, Bearwallow Gap; BRP mp 90.9 (2,228') **Buchanan, Va. 24066**	R, P (E–4.4m C, L, M) (W–5m PO, G, M; 7m L, M)	1,439.8	
751.0	1.6	Cove Mountain (2,707')		1,438.2	
751.4	0.4	Little Cove Mountain Trail (2,600')		1,437.8	
752.8	1.4	**Cove Mountain Shelter** (1,925')*...6.7mS; 7mN*	S, nw	1,436.4	
754.5	1.7	Buchanan Trail (1,790')		1,434.7	
756.0	1.5	Va. 614, Jennings Creek Road (987') Jennings Creek	R, P, C, w (E–1.4m G, C, cl, sh, f) (W–4.5m L, M)	1,433.2	ATC Central Va. Map 2
757.6	1.6	Fork Mountain (2,042')		1,431.6	
759.8	2.2	**Bryant Ridge Shelter** (1,330')*...7mS; 4.9mN*	S, w	1,429.4	
764.1	4.3	Floyd Mountain (3,560')		1,425.1	
764.7	0.6	**Cornelius Creek Shelter** (3,145') *...4.9mS; 5.3mN*	S, w	1,424.5	
765.6	0.9	Black Rock (3,450')		1,423.6	
767.3	1.7	Apple Orchard Falls Trail (3,250')		1,421.9	
767.4	0.1	USFS 812, Parkers Gap Road; BRP mp 78.4 (3,410')	R, P	1,421.8	
768.8	1.4	Apple Orchard Mountain (4,206')*...FAA radar dome*		1,420.4	
769.1	0.3	The Guillotine (4,090')*...suspended boulder*		1,420.1	
769.7	0.6	Upper BRP crossing mp 76.3 (3,900')	R	1,419.5	

Miles from Springer	Fr Last Point	Features	Services	Miles from Katahdin	M A P
770.0	0.3	**Thunder Hill Shelter** (3,960')...*5.3mS; 12.4mN*	S, w	1,419.2	
771.0	1.0	Lower BRP crossing mp 74.9 (3,650')	R, P	1,418.2	
771.4	0.4	BRP mp 74.7; Thunder Hill Overlook (3,525')	R, P	1,417.8	
773.3	1.9	Harrison Ground Spring (3,200')	w	1,415.9	
774.7	1.4	BRP mp 71.0; USFS 35, Petites Gap (2,369')	R, P	1,414.5	
775.9	1.2	Highcock Knob (3,054')		1,413.3	
776.9	1.0	Marble Spring (2,290')	C, w	1,412.3	
777.4	0.5	Sulphur Spring Trail (south crossing) (2,400')		1,411.8	
779.2	1.8	Gunter Ridge Trail, Hickory Stand (2,650')		1,410.0	
779.7	0.5	Sulphur Spring Trail (north crossing) (2,588')		1,409.5	
780.5	0.8	Big Cove Branch (1,890')	w	1,408.7	
782.4	1.9	**Matts Creek Shelter** (835')...*12.4mS; 3.9mN*	S, w	1,406.8	
783.2	0.8	Campsite (700')	C, w	1,406.0	
784.4	1.2	James River Foot Bridge (678')		1,404.8	
784.6	0.2	U.S. 501, Va. 130, James River (680') **Big Island, Va. 24526** **Glasgow, Va. 24555**	R, P (E–4.8m C, g, L, cl, sh; 5.3m PO, G, M, D) (W–6.1m PO, S, G, M, D, cl, g)	1,404.6	
784.7	0.1	Lower Rocky Row Run Bridge (740')	w	1,404.5	
785.6	0.9	Rocky Row Run (760')...*campsites along creek*	C, w	1,403.6	
785.7	0.1	Va. 812, USFS 36 (825')	R	1,403.5	
786.3	0.6	**Johns Hollow Shelter** (1,020')...*3.9mS; 9mN*	S, w	1,402.9	
788.3	2.0	Rocky Row Trail (2,400')		1,400.9	
788.4	0.1	Fullers Rocks, Little Rocky Row (2,486')		1,400.8	
789.4	1.0	Big Rocky Row (2,974')		1,399.8	
790.9	1.5	Saddle Gap, Saddle Gap Trail (2,600')		1,398.3	
792.0	1.1	Saltlog Gap (south) (2,573')		1,397.2	
793.5	1.5	Bluff Mountain (3,391')...*Ottie Cline Powell Memorial*		1,395.7	
794.6	1.1	Punchbowl Mountain (2,850')		1,394.6	
795.1	0.5	**Punchbowl Shelter** (2,500') ...*9mS; 9.7mN*	W–0.2m S, w	1,394.1	
795.5	0.4	BRP mp 51.7; Punchbowl Mountain Crossing (2,170')	R, P, w	1,393.7	
795.8	0.3	Va. 607, Robinson Gap Road (2,100')	R	1,393.4	
797.7	1.9	Rice Mountain (2,169')		1,391.5	
799.6	1.9	USFS 39 (990')	R	1,389.6	
799.7	0.1	Pedlar River Bridge (970')		1,389.5	
802.6	2.9	USFS 38, Swapping Camp Road (1,000')	R, P	1,386.6	
804.6	2.0	**Brown Mountain Creek Shelter** (1,395') ...*9.7mS; 6.2mN*	S, w	1,384.6	

ATC Central Va. Map 2

Miles from Springer	Fr Last Point	Features	Services	Miles from Katahdin	M A P
806.4	1.8	U.S. 60, Lexington Turnpike (2,060') Long Mountain Wayside **Buena Vista, Va. 24416** **Lexington, Va. 24450**	R, P, C (W–9.7m PO, C, G, L, M, D, V, sh, cl, f; 16.2m PO, all)	1,382.8	
809.2	2.8	Bald Knob (4,059')		1,380.0	
810.2	1.0	Old Hotel Trail (3,428') **Cow Camp Gap Shelter**...*6.2mS; 10.8mN*	E–0.6m S, w	1,379.0	
811.4	1.2	Cole Mountain (4,022')		1,377.8	
812.7	1.3	USFS 48, Wiggins Spring Road (3,485') Hog Camp Gap	R, P, C, w (W–1.3m H)	1,376.5	
813.6	0.9	Tar Jacket Ridge (3,840')		1,375.6	
814.9	1.3	USFS 63, Va. 634, Salt Log Gap (north) (3,290')	R, P	1,374.3	
816.1	1.2	USFS 246 (3,500')	R	1,373.1	
816.6	0.5	Greasy Spring Road (3,600')	R	1,372.6	
818.5	1.9	North Fork of Piney River (3,500')	C, w	1,370.7	
819.7	1.2	Elk Pond Branch (3,750')	C, w	1,369.5	
820.4	0.7	**Seeley–Woodworth Shelter** (3,770') ...10.8mS; 6.6mN	S, w	1,368.8	
821.5	1.1	Porters Field (3,650')	C, w	1,367.7	
822.7	1.2	Spy Rock Road (3,454') **Montebello, Va. 24464**	R, C (W–2.5m PO, C, G, L, M, cl, sh, f)	1,366.5	ATC Central Va. Map 1
823.2	0.5	Spy Rock (3,680')		1,366.0	
824.0	0.8	Cash Hollow Rock (3,550')		1,365.2	
825.3	1.3	Cash Hollow Road (3,280')	R	1,363.9	
826.1	0.8	Va. 826, Crabtree Farm Road (3,350') Crabtree Falls Trail	W–0.5m C, w	1,363.1	
827.0	0.9	**The Priest Shelter** (3,840')...*6.6mS; 7.6mN*	S, w	1,362.2	
827.5	0.5	The Priest (4,063')		1,361.7	
830.5	3.0	Cripple Creek (1,800')		1,358.7	
831.8	1.3	Va. 56, Crabtree Falls Highway (997')	R, P (W–3.9m C, G, sh)	1,357.4	
831.9	0.1	Tye River (950')	C, w	1,357.3	
833.5	1.6	Mau-Har Trail (2,090')		1,355.7	
834.6	1.1	**Harpers Creek Shelter** (1,800')...*7.6mS; 6.2mN*	S, w	1,354.6	
836.6	2.0	Chimney Rocks (3,190')		1,352.6	
838.3	1.7	Three Ridges (3,970')		1,350.9	
838.8	0.5	Hanging Rock (3,750')		1,350.4	
840.8	2.0	**Maupin Field Shelter** (2,720')...*6.2mS; 15.8mN*	S, w	1,348.4	
842.5	1.7	Va. 664, Reeds Gap; BRP mp 13.6 (2,645')	R, P	1,346.7	
843.0	0.5	BRP mp 13.1; Three Ridges Parking Overlook (2,700')	R, P	1,346.2	
846.8	3.8	Cedar Cliffs (2,800')		1,342.4	

Miles from Springer	Fr Last Point	Features	Services	Miles from Katahdin	M A P
847.3	0.5	BRP mp 9.6; Dripping Rock Parking Area (2,950')	R, P, w	1,341.9	
850.1	2.8	Humpback Mountain (3,606')		1,339.1	
851.1	1.0	Trail to Humpback Rocks (3,250')		1,338.1	
852.6	1.5	Bear Spring (3,200')	w	1,336.6	
854.8	2.2	Glass Hollow Overlook (2,750')		1,334.4	
855.1	0.3	Trail to Humpback Visitors Center (2,150')	W–1.3m R, w	1,334.1	
856.6	1.5	Mill Creek (1,700') **Paul C. Wolfe Shelter**...*15.8mS; 13mN*	S, w	1,332.6	
861.6	5.0	U.S. 250, I-64, Rockfish Gap (1,902') **Waynesboro, Va. 22980**	R, P, L, M (W–1m L; 4.5m all)	1,327.6	

BRP=Blue Ridge Parkway, mp=milepost

Central Virginia's treadway is well-graded and includes several 2,000- to 3,000-foot climbs. You will traverse some of the northernmost balds on the Trail. Unusual rock formations offer up views to the valley below from the peaks of Humpback Rocks, Three Ridges, The Priest, McAfee Knob, and Dragons Tooth. This section, more rugged and remote than Shenandoah to the north, parallels the Blue Ridge Parkway for 90 miles.

U.S.460/East 1 mile to **Pearisburg, Va. [P.O. ZIP 24134: M–F 9–4:30, Sa 10–12: (540) 921-1100].** ▪ *Lodging: Motels will be heavily booked into the spring as Celanese plant construction continues; call ahead for reservations.* Plaza Motel, 415 N. Main St., (540) 921-2591, $40S plus $5EAP, stay 3 nights $25S plus $5EAP, WiFi, laundry, no pets, will hold packages whether guest or not, e-mail available in office; Holiday Motor Lodge, 401 N. Main St., (540) 921-1551, rates start at $20 (hostel with

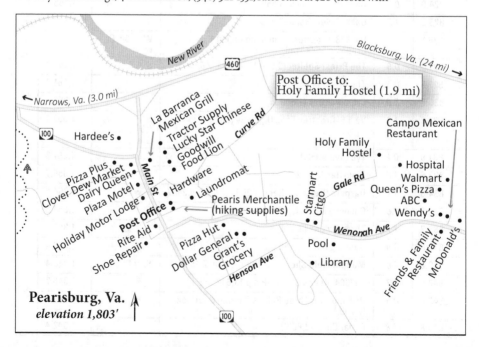

New River

460

Blacksburg, Va. (24 mi)

Post Office to:
Holy Family Hostel (1.9 mi)

← Narrows, Va. (3.0 mi)

La Barranca Mexican Grill
Tractor Supply
Lucky Star Chinese
Curve Rd
Goodwill
Food Lion

100   Hardee's

Campo Mexican Restaurant

Holy Family Hostel

Pizza Plus
Clover Dew Market
Dairy Queen
Main St
Hardware
Laundromat

Plaza Motel
Holiday Motor Lodge
Post Office
Rite Aid
Shoe Repair

Pearis Merchantile
(hiking supplies)

Starmart
Citgo
Gale Rd

Hospital
Walmart
Queen's Pizza
ABC
Wendy's

Pizza Hut
Dollar General
Grant's Grocery
Henson Ave

Wenonah Ave

Pool

Library

Friends & Family Restaurant
McDonald's

Pearisburg, Va.
elevation 1,803'

100

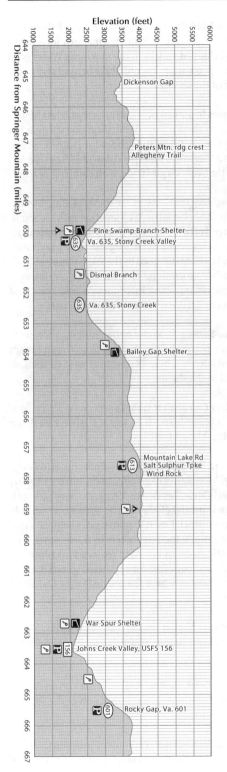

Elevation (feet)

Distance from Springer Mountain (miles)

Dickenson Gap

Peters Mtn. rdg crest
Allegheny Trail

Pine Swamp Branch Shelter
Va. 635, Stony Creek Valley

Dismal Branch

Va. 635, Stony Creek

Bailey Gap Shelter

Mountain Lake Rd
Salt Sulphur Tpke
Wind Rock

War Spur Shelter

Johns Creek Valley, USFS 156

Rocky Gap, Va. 601

shower, TV, fridge, microwave), $40D plus $10EAP, Internet access, swimming pool during the season, pet-friendly, accepts packages. ■ *Groceries:* Food Lion, Grant's Grocery, and 7-Day Market (all long-term resupply). ■ *Restaurants:* Pizza Plus, buy one pizza, get one free, AYCE salad/pizza buffet, and free delivery; Papa's Pizza Inn with subs, salads; Pizza Hut with AYCE L buffet. ■ *Internet access:* Pearisburg Public Library. ■ *Other services:* Pearis Mercantile, with hiking supplies; Rite Aid with one-hour photo service; automotive and hardware stores; Melinda's Barber Shop; Walmart; coin laundry; ATM; hospital; dentist; veterinarian; municipal swimming pool open to the public Memorial Day to Labor Day (fee). ■ *Shuttles:* Tom Hoffman, (540) 921-1184, <gopullman@aol.com>; Don Raines, (540) 921-7433, <ratface20724@aol.com>.

East 2.9 miles, follow blue-blaze to *Hostel:* Holy Family Church Hostel is located in a peaceful setting on a hill, hidden by trees beyond the church parking lot. Refrigerator, microwave, and loft with sleeping pads, $5 suggested donation per night; additional donations and cleaning appreciated. Stays are limited to two nights. Open Mar–Oct 1. Alcoholic beverages and drugs are prohibited. Pets allowed if well taken care of. Caretaker: Pat Muldoon, (540) 626-3337.

East 6 miles on U.S. 460 to *Outfitter:* Tangent Outfitters, 201 Cascade Dr., Pembroke, VA 24136; (540) 626-4567, <www.newrivertrail.com>, primarily oriented to rafters.

East 20 miles *via* U.S. 460 to Blacksburg, Va., home of Virginia Tech, with all services. ATC's Virginia regional office, (540) 953-3571, is located at 110 Southpark Dr. *Outfitter:* Back Country Ski & Sports, (800) 560-6401 or (540) 552-6400, open M–Sa 10–8, Su 1–5.

West 3 miles *via* U.S. 460 to Va. 61 to **Narrows, Va. [P.O. ZIP 24124: M–F 8:30–12 & 12:30–4, Sa 9–11, (540) 726-3272].** ■ *Lodging:* MacArthur Inn, 117 MacArthur Lane, (540) 726-7510, <www.macarthur-inn.com>; renovated hotel, 26 rooms; hiker rates start at $45, private room with shared bath, full B; shower $8; laundry; no pets; WiFi; free long-distance phone; fuel; shuttle to and from Trail $5 each way (call from Pearisburg); accepts mail drops. ■ *Other services:* town campground on river, $2; restaurant; deli; groceries; coin laundry.

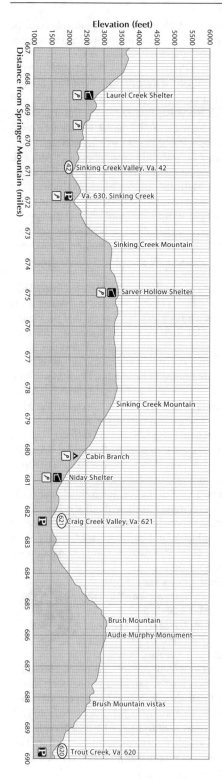

Rice Field Shelter (1995)—Sleeps 7. Privy. This shelter has an excellent viewing area for sunsets and clouded valleys in the morning. Water is on a steep, 0.3-mile downhill hike behind and to the left of the shelter.

Symms Gap Meadow—The traverse of Peters Mountain on the Virginia–West Virginia state line is a dry one. At this mountain meadow, with views into West Virginia, a small pond downhill from the A.T. on the West Virginia side, with camping nearby.

Allegheny Trail—2.5 miles south of Pine Swamp Branch Shelter is the A.T.'s junction with the southern end of the Allegheny Trail, which extends about 300 miles across West Virginia to Pennsylvania. The trail is maintained by the West Virginia Scenic Trails Association, <www.wvscenictrails.org>. Portions are being incorporated into the Great Eastern Trail, <www.greateasterntrail.net>.

Pine Swamp Branch Shelter (1980s)—Sleeps 8. Privy. Stone shelter. Water is from the stream 75 yards down a blue-blazed trail west of the side trail to the shelter.

Bailey Gap Shelter (1960s)—Sleeps 6. Privy. Water is 0.2 mile south on the A.T., then east down a blue-blazed trail.

Va. 613, Salt Sulfur Turnpike— East 5 miles to *Lodging:* Mountain Lake Lodge and Conservancy, 115 Hotel Circle, Pembroke, VA 24136; (800) 346-3334, <www.mtnlakelodge.com>; site of one of only two natural lakes in Virginia; rates begin at $129/room/night; includes access to resort amenities, shuttle from and to A.T.; reservations required. Will hold packages for registered guests. One of the locations where the movie "Dirty Dancing" was filmed.

War Spur Shelter (1960s)—Sleeps 6. Privy. Water source is a stream 80 yards north of the shelter on the A.T.

Laurel Creek Shelter (1988)—Sleeps 6. Privy. Water is west on the A.T., 45 yards south of the shelter-trail junction.

Keffer Oak—Located about 0.2 mile north of Va. 630, this is the largest oak tree on the A.T. in the

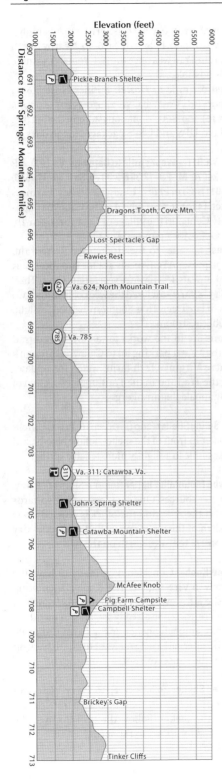

Elevation (feet)

Distance from Springer Mountain (miles)

Pickle Branch Shelter

Dragons Tooth, Cove Mtn.

Lost Spectacles Gap

Rawies Rest

Va. 624, North Mountain Trail

Va. 785

Va. 311; Catawba, Va.

Johns Spring Shelter

Catawba Mountain Shelter

McAfee Knob

Pig Farm Campsite

Campbell Shelter

Brickey's Gap

Tinker Cliffs

South. Last measured, the girth was 18 feet, 3 inches; it is estimated to be 300 years old. The Dover Oak along the A.T. in New York is slightly larger.

Sarver Hollow Shelter (2001)—Sleeps 6. Privy. Water source is a spring located on a blue-blazed trail near the shelter.

Sinking Creek Mountain—The northernmost spot where the A.T. crosses a notable "continental divide." Waters flowing down the western side of the ridge drain into Sinking Creek Valley and the Mississippi River to the Gulf of Mexico. Waters flowing on the eastern side empty into Craig Creek Valley, the James River, and the Atlantic Ocean.

Niday Shelter (1980)—Sleeps 6. Privy. Water source is 75 yards down a blue-blazed trail west of the A.T.

Audie Murphy Monument—located on a blue-blazed trail to the west on Brushy Mountain. Murphy was the most decorated American soldier of World War II, and his single-handed capture of a large number of German soldiers made him a legend. After the war, he starred in many Hollywood war and B-grade western movies. He died in a 1971 plane crash near this site. A trail leads beyond the monument to a view from a rock outcropping.

Pickle Branch Shelter (1980)—Sleeps 6. Privy. Water from stream below the shelter.

Dragons Tooth—Named by Tom Campbell, an early RATC member and prime mover in the 1930s–1950s in locating the A.T. here. He also named Lost Spectacles Gap, north of Dragons Tooth, after his glasses disappeared on a scouting/work hike.

Camping Restrictions—Between Va. 624 and U.S. 220, camping and fires are allowed only at the following designated sites of this heavily used section: Johns Spring, Catawba Mountain, Campbell, and Lamberts Meadow shelters and Pig Farm and Lamberts Meadow campsites.

 Va. 624/North Mountain Trail—West 0.3 mile to Va. 311, then left 0.1 mile to Catawba

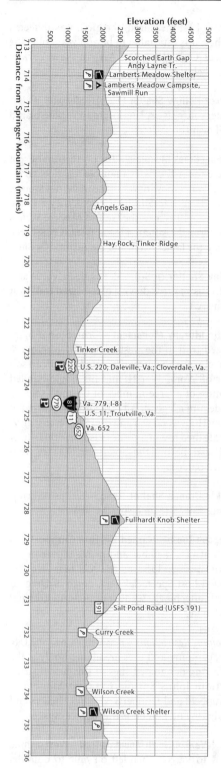

Grocery, (540) 384-8050 (short-term resupply), open M–Th 5–10, F–Sa 5–11, Su 6–10. Nearby North Mountain Trail was once the A.T. route. A 30-mile loop is possible.

East 0.4 mile to *Hostel:* 4 Pines Hostel, 6164 Newport Rd., Catawba, VA 24070; (540) 384-7599, cell (540) 309-8615; donations accepted; shuttles. Will hold UPS and USPS packages for 30 days.

Va. 311—West 1 mile to **Catawba, Va. [P.O. ZIP 24070: M–F 9–12:30 & 2:30–5, Sa 8:30–11; (540) 384-6011].** *Groceries:* Catawba Valley Farmers Market, (540) 767-6114, held at the Catawba Community Center in the village of Catawba; open Th, May–Oct, 3:30–7 p.m.

West 1.3 miles to the Homeplace Restaurant, (540) 384-7252; AYCE meals $14 for two meats, $15 for three meats, less if you're vegetarian. Open Th–F 4–8, Sa 3–8, Su 11–6 (closed the week of Jul 4 and two weeks in late Dec); Th is Southern-barbeque night. No public restroom.

Plans are in the works for a blue-blazed trail from the Va. 311 parking lot to Catawba through a 400-acre Virginia Tech farm; watch for updates along the Trail and in the Trail-updates section of <www.appalachiantrail.org>.

Johns Spring Shelter (2003)—Sleeps 6. Privy. Unreliable water in front of the shelter; follow blue-blazed trail 0.25 mile to a slightly more reliable spring.

Catawba Mountain Shelter (1984)—Sleeps 6. Privy. Two water sources: One is a piped spring 50 yards south on the A.T., and the other is crossed a few feet north of the piped spring, but often goes dry in summer. Tentsites north on the A.T.

McAfee Knob—Considered by many to have the best view in Virginia, McAfee Knob is a tempting campsite. However, it is absolutely *forbidden* to camp here; the knob already sustains tremendous impact. Campbell Shelter or Pig Farm Campsite are good alternatives if you want to climb back up to catch the sunset or sunrise from the cliff.

Campbell Shelter (1989)—Sleeps 6. Privy. Water can be found by following the blue-blazed trail left and behind the shelter. Follow the trail through the "electrified meadow" to the spring.

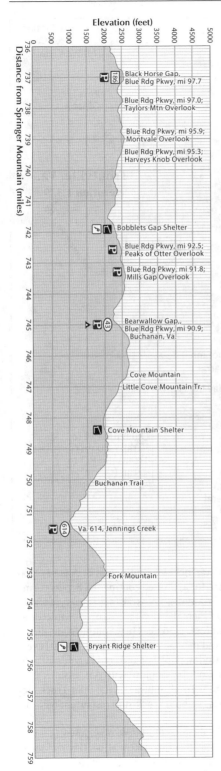

Elevation (feet)

Distance from Springer Mountain (miles)

Black Horse Gap,
Blue Rdg Pkwy, mi 97.7

Blue Rdg Pkwy, mi 97.0;
Taylors Mtn Overlook

Blue Rdg Pkwy, mi 95.9;
Montvale Overlook

Blue Rdg Pkwy, mi 95.3;
Harveys Knob Overlook

Bobblets Gap Shelter

Blue Rdg Pkwy, mi 92.5;
Peaks of Otter Overlook

Blue Rdg Pkwy, mi 91.8;
Mills Gap Overlook

Bearwallow Gap,,
Blue Rdg Pkwy, mi 90.9;
Buchanan, Va.

Cove Mountain

Little Cove Mountain Tr.

Cove Mountain Shelter

Buchanan Trail

Va. 614, Jennings Creek

Fork Mountain

Bryant Ridge Shelter

Tinker Cliffs—A cliff-walk half a mile long, with views back to McAfee Knob. Folklore says the name comes from Revolutionary War deserters who hid near here and repaired pots and pans ("tinkers").

Lamberts Meadow Shelter (1974)—Sleeps 6. Privy. Tentsites are 0.3 mile farther north. Water is 50 yards down the trail in front of the shelter; may run dry in drought years.

U.S. 220/I-81 Interchange Area—The interchange area offers all the comforts of interstate travel, with most services near the A.T.

On U.S. 220. ■ *Lodging:* Super 8, (540) 992-3000, hiker rates subject to availability, $60 up to 4 people, continental B, coin laundry, pool, no pets; Howard Johnson Express Inn, 437 Roanoke Road, Daleville, VA 24083, (540) 992-1234, hiker rate $50S/D, includes continental B, holds UPS and USPS packages for registered guests, microwave & refrigerator, coin laundry, dogs permitted, $10 per pet. Both motels fill up quickly, particularly on the weekends. If you wish to stay there, make reservations during an earlier town stop. ■ *Restaurants:* Pizza Hut with AYCE salad bar; Rancho Viejo Mexican. ■ *Other services:* Several convenience stores.

West 0.3 mile to Botetourt Commons Shopping Plaza. ■ *Restaurants:* Mill Mountain Coffee House, 3 Little Pigs BBQ, Wendy's, Bojangles, Lil Caeser's, C.L. Asian (L buffet). ■ *Groceries:* Kroger Super Store, with pharmacy (long-term resupply). ■ *Outfitter:* Outdoor Trails, Botetourt Commons, 28 Kingston Dr., Daleville, VA 24083; (540) 992-5850; M–F 10–8, Sa 10–6 (opens 9 a.m. M–Sa in May and Jun), closed Su; a full-service outfitter, sells fuel by the ounce and accepts mail drops; make reservation for shuttle or slackpacking. ■ *Internet access:* Outdoor Trails. ■ *Other services:* UPS Store, (540) 966-0220, M–F 8–6, Sa 9–5; bank with ATM.

West 1 mile to **Daleville, Va. [P.O. ZIP 24083: M–F 8–5, Sa 8–12 (540) 992-4422]**. Convenience stores, Food Lion (long-term resupply), CVS, and bank are nearby. *Other services:* Medical center fits in hikers as schedule permits; veterinarian.

East 0.8 mile to U.S. 11. ■ *Lodging:* Stay at Inn, 2619 Lee Hwy., Troutville, VA 24175, (540) 992-6700, $35D, $6EAP, pool, dogs $10, hot B; Comfort Inn, 2545 Lee Hwy, Troutville, VA 24175, (540) 992-5600, will hold UPS/USPS packages for guests,

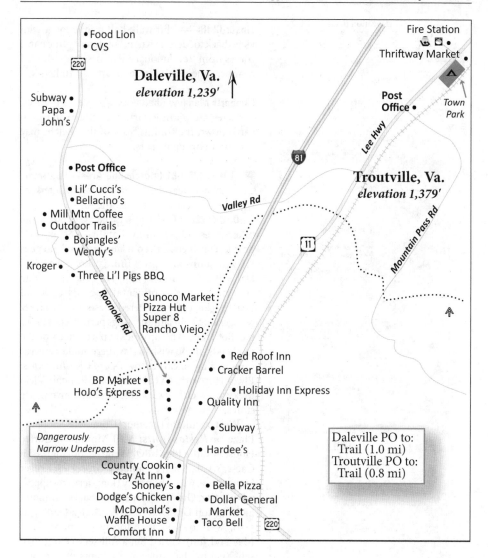

Daleville, Va.
elevation 1,239'

Troutville, Va.
elevation 1,379'

• Food Lion
• CVS

220

Fire Station

Thriftway Market •

Subway •
Papa •
John's

Post
Office •

Town
Park

Lee Hwy

81

• Post Office

• Lil' Cucci's
•Bellacino's
• Mill Mtn Coffee
• Outdoor Trails
• Bojangles'
• Wendy's
Kroger•
• Three Li'l Pigs BBQ

Valley Rd

Mountain Pass Rd

11

Roanoke Rd

Sunoco Market•
Pizza Hut
Super 8
Rancho Viejo•

• Red Roof Inn
• Cracker Barrel

BP Market •
HoJo's Express •

• Holiday Inn Express
• Quality Inn

• Subway

*Dangerously
Narrow Underpass*

• Hardee's

Country Cookin •
Stay At Inn •
Shoney's •
Dodge's Chicken •
McDonald's •
Waffle House •
Comfort Inn •

• Bella Pizza
•Dollar General
Market
• Taco Bell

220

Daleville PO to:
Trail (1.0 mi)
Troutville PO to:
Trail (0.8 mi)

ask for the "hiker-corporate" rates of $49.99S/D, $5EAP, includes continental B, pets $25, pool, and Internet access; Red Roof Inn, (540) 992-5055, $50 for 4, limited continental B, pets permitted, pool, hot tub; Quality Inn, 3139 Lee Hwy. South, Troutville, VA 24175, (540) 992-5335, $80S/D, pets permitted with one-time $25 fee, hot and cold continental B, pool, exercise room, microwave and refrigerator, accepts mail drops; Holiday Inn Express, 3200 Lee Hwy. South, Troutville, VA 24175, (540) 966-4444, $109S/D, weekends add $10 (and may be much higher on "special event" weekends), microwave and refrigerator in rooms, laundry, pool, hot and cold B, holds UPS and USPS packages for registered guests. ■ *Restaurants:* Country Cookin', with AYCE buffet $6.99; Shoney's, $7.49 B bar; Italian Bella, with AYCE $6.29 L Tu–F; Subway inside Pilot Truck Stop, which also has $10 shower; Travel Centers of America, 24-hour truck-stop restaurant with coin laundry and showers for $10.

East 12 miles to **Roanoke**. *Outfitters:* In Roanoke, Walkabout Outfitters, downtown, (540) 777-2727, and Valley View Mall, (540) 777-0990, owned by 1999 thru-hiker Kirk Miller (Flying Money), open daily. Nearby in **Salem**: Backcountry Ski and Sports, (540) 389-8602, closed Su.

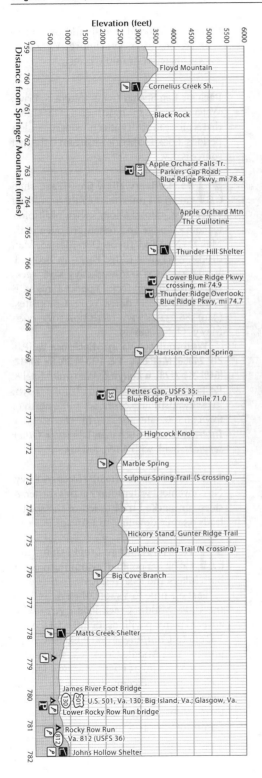

Elevation (feet)

Distance from Springer Mountain (miles)

Floyd Mountain
Cornelius Creek Sh.
Black Rock
Apple Orchard Falls Tr.
Parkers Gap Road;
Blue Rdige Pkwy, mi 78.4
Apple Orchard Mtn
The Guillotine
Thunder Hill Shelter
Lower Blue Ridge Pkwy
crossing, mi 74.9
Thunder Ridge Overlook;
Blue Ridge Pkwy, mi 74.7
Harrison Ground Spring
Petites Gap, USFS 35;
Blue Ridge Parkway, mile 71.0
Highcock Knob
Marble Spring
Sulphur Spring Trail (S crossing)
Hickory Stand, Gunter Ridge Trail
Sulphur Spring Trail (N crossing)
Big Cove Branch
Matts Creek Shelter
James River Foot Bridge
U.S. 501, Va. 130; Big Island, Va.; Glasgow, Va.
Lower Rocky Row Run bridge
Rocky Row Run
Va. 812 (USFS 36)
Johns Hollow Shelter

U.S. 11—West 0.8 mile (1.3 miles north of the interchange area) to **Troutville, Va. [P.O. ZIP 24175: M–F 9–12 & 1–5, Sa 9–11; (540) 992-1472].** Town hall, (540) 992-4401, M–F 9–11:45 and 1–5, sometimes allows hikers to camp at the city park; call or find park manager, (540) 293-4548, for permission; bathrooms and water. The town permits hikers to shower and do laundry at the fire station. ■ *Groceries:* Thriftway Market (long-term re-supply), M–Sa 8–8, closed Su. ■ *Other services:* Pomegranate Restaurant, (540) 966-6052, 106 Stoney Battery Rd, open for D Tu–Sa 5–10, casual and fine dining; banks with ATMs. ■ *Shuttles:* Del Schechterly, (540) 529-6028, <dschecht1@juno.com>, helps hikers in need and shuttles from Pearisburg to Waynesboro.

Fullhardt Knob Shelter (1960s)—Sleeps 6. Privy. The water source for this shelter is an elaborate cistern system of run-off hooked to the shelter's roof. Give the water enough time to flow through the freeze-proof valve, which is a few feet up the pipe toward the cistern. Please make sure spigot is off when you have finished getting water.

Wilson Creek Shelter (1986)—Sleeps 6. Privy. Water source is reliable stream 200 yards in front of the shelter.

Blue Ridge Parkway—Black Horse Gap is the A.T.'s southernmost encounter with the Blue Ridge Parkway (BRP). The A.T. parallels BRP, and later Skyline Drive, for approximately 200 miles. Much of the original A.T. route along the Blue Ridge south of Roanoke was displaced by the parkway when it was built. Hitchhiking is not permitted on the BRP.

Natural Bridge Appalachian Trail Club—NBATC maintains the 90.5 miles between Black Horse Gap and the Tye

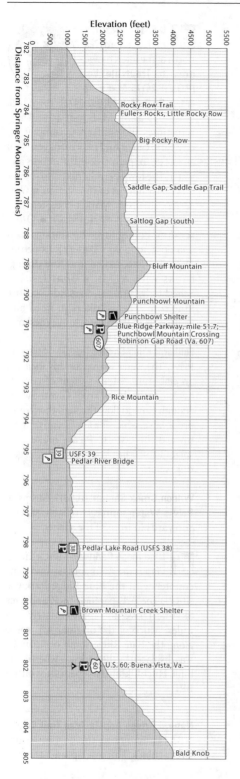

Elevation (feet)

Distance from Springer Mountain (miles)

Rocky Row Trail
Fullers Rocks, Little Rocky Row

Big Rocky Row

Saddle Gap, Saddle Gap Trail

Saltlog Gap (south)

Bluff Mountain

Punchbowl Mountain
Punchbowl Shelter
Blue Ridge Parkway, mile 51.7;
Punchbowl Mountain Crossing
Robinson Gap Road (Va. 607)

Rice Mountain

USFS 39
Pedlar River Bridge

Pedlar Lake Road (USFS 38)

Brown Mountain Creek Shelter

U.S. 60; Buena Vista, Va.

Bald Knob

River. Correspondence should be sent to NBATC Box 3012, Lynchburg, VA 24503; <www.nbatc.org/trailinfo.html>.

Bobblets Gap Shelter (1961)—Sleeps 6. Privy. Water source is a spring to the left of the shelter that is prone to go dry after prolonged rainless periods. Look farther downstream if the first source is dry.

Va. 43/Bearwallow Gap—East, then north 4.4 miles on the BRP to Peaks of Otter Area, (540) 586-1081, <www.peaksofotter.com>. Lodge and restaurant open daily Mar 27–Nov and Th–Su Dec–Mar 26. Mail drops: 85554 Blue Ridge Parkway, Bedford, VA 24523. Rates $126 weekdays, $136 weekends, $150 in Sep–Oct; D buffet F night, B buffet Su, B/L/D daily, WiFi. Campsites, (540) 586-7321, <www.recreation.gov>, open May 9–Oct 21, $16–19.

West 5 miles on Va. 43 to **Buchanan, Va. [P.O. ZIP 24066: M–F 8:30–1 & 1:30–4:30, Sa 10–12; (540) 254-2178].** ■ *Lodging:* Wattstull Motel & Restaurant, 130 Arcadia Rd., (540) 254-1551, <www.wattstullinn.com>, is 2 miles north of town on I-81, rates $68–$75, Internet access. ■ *Internet access:* Buchanan Library. ■ *Other services:* bank with ATM, restaurants.

Cove Mountain Shelter (1981)—Sleeps 6. Privy. No convenient water source at this shelter. A steep, unmarked trail to left of the shelter leads 0.5 mile downhill to a stream.

Va. 614/Jennings Creek—Jennings Creek is a popular swimming hole for both hikers and local residents.

East 0.2 mile to Va. 618, then 0.1 mile to the USFS Middle Creek Picnic Area with covered picnic pavilions; 1.1 miles farther on Va. 618 to *Camping:* Middle Creek Campground, 1164 Middle Creek Rd., Buchanan, VA 24066; (540) 254-2550, <www.middlecreekcampground.com>, tentsites for 4 with shower $26; cabins sleep 4–6, $65 for 4, $75 for 6; showers $5, leashed dogs allowed. Campstore (short-term resupply), Coleman fuel, canister and denatured alcohol by the ounce, coin laundry; mail drops accepted; when available, shuttle to the A.T.

West 4.5 miles to Wattstull Motel & Restaurant (see Buchanan entry above).

Bryant Ridge Shelter (1992)—Sleeps 20. Privy. This trilevel, timber-frame shelter is one of the A.T.'s largest. Water source is a stream 25 yards in front of the shelter, also crossed on the trail to the shelter.

Cornelius Creek Shelter (1960)—Sleeps 6. Privy. A blue-blazed trail leads to the shelter, but just north of the turn-off is a branch of Cornelius Creek where you can find water. Water can also be found on the trail to the shelter. An unmarked trail behind the shelter leads 0.1 mile to a fire road and then left 0.2 mile to the BRP, where it is then 6 miles south to the Peaks of Otter Area.

Apple Orchard Falls Trail—Located 2.6 miles north of Cornelius Creek Shelter. When the water is high, these falls are impressive, making the 3-mile round-trip worth the effort.

Apple Orchard Mountain—When you reach the top, you will be at 4,225 feet. Once an Air Force radar base, the meadows were covered with barracks and support-service buildings for 250 people. On the northern side of the mountain, the A.T. leads you under The Guillotine—an impressively large boulder stuck over the Trail between rock formations. No camping is permitted on top of the mountain, the highest point on the A.T. between Chestnut Knob and Mt. Moosilauke in New Hampshire.

Thunder Hill Shelter (1962)—Sleeps 6. Privy. Water source is a walled-in spring south of the shelter, prone to go dry by late summer. A larger, reliable spring can be found by going south on the A.T. to the BRP. At the BRP, turn left, walk 0.3 mile to a gated road on the left; 500 feet down the gated road, where the road turns left, angle right to a spring basin.

Matts Creek Shelter (1961)—Sleeps 6. Privy. Several small swimming holes are nearby. The rocks you will find in this area are 500 million years old. Tentsites north 1.0 mile, where Matts Creek flows into the James River, with river views and the sound of trains across the river. Water source is Matts Creek, in front of the shelter.

James River Foot Bridge—This bridge, the longest foot-use-only bridge on the A.T., is dedicated to the memory of Bill Foot, a 1987 thru-hiker and ALDHA honorary life member (Trail-named "The Happy Feet" with his wife, Laurie) whose efforts in securing the existing piers, applying for grants, and gaining numerous agencies' cooperation made the bridge a reality.

U.S. 501 & Va. 130/James River—The two roads diverge at a fork east of the Trail crossing. On Va. 130, **East** 4.8 miles to *Camping:* Wildwood Campground, (434) 299-5228. Owners Terry and Dona Farmer, tentsites $20 per tent for up to 2 tents (hikers only), cabins $60–$80 for 4 adults, $5EAP; camp store, showers for registered guests, laundry, pool, and snack bar.

On U.S. 501, **East** 5.3 miles to **Big Island, Va. [P.O. ZIP 24526: M–F 8:15–12 & 1–4, Sa 8–10; (434) 299-5072].** ■ *Groceries:* H&H Market, (434) 299-5153, open daily 5:30–9 (long-term resupply), short-order restaurant, B/L/D. ■ *Other services:* bank with ATM and medical center, (434) 299-5951.

West 6.1 miles to **Glasgow, Va. [P.O. ZIP 24555: M–F 8–11:30, 12:30–4:30, Sa 8:30–10:30; (540) 258-2852].** ■ *Hostel:* Glasgow Hiker's Shelter, 9th St., sleeps 6, shower and water, fire pit. ■ *Groceries:* Glasgow Grocery Express (long-term resupply), (540) 258-1818, open 6–11:30, has Coleman fuel by the ounce, denatured alcohol, and Heet. ■ *Restaurants:* Scotto's, (540) 258-2500; Petro's Stop & Go, (540) 258-2012, deli and convenience store. ■ *Internet access:* library, (540) 258-2509; M, Th

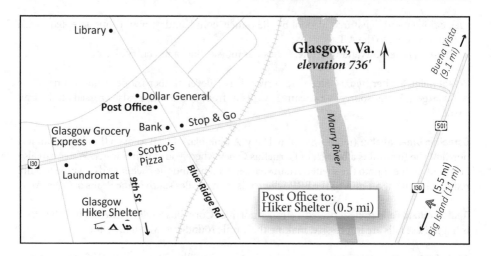

10–7; T, W 10–5:30, Sa 10–1. ■ *Other services:* Dollar General, coin laundry, doctor. ■ *Shuttles:* Ken Wallace, (434) 609-2704, between Black Horse Gap and Tye River (May–mid-Oct), sometimes farther.

Johns Hollow Shelter (1961)—Sleeps 6. Privy. Water source is a spring to the left of the shelter or a stream to right 25 yards from the shelter.

Bluff Mountain—Site of a monument to four-year-old Ottie Cline Powell. In the fall of 1890, Ottie went into the woods to gather firewood for his schoolhouse and never returned. His body was found five months later on top of this mountain. NBATC members erected a permanent gravestone for his final resting place, seven miles from the monument.

Punchbowl Shelter (1961)—Sleeps 6. Privy. Some believe this shelter is haunted by Little Ottie's ghost. Tentsites nearby if the shelter is full, which it often is. Water source is a spring by a tree next to the pond drainage in front and to the left of the shelter. An alternative water source is a spring in the ravine north 0.4 mile, shortly after crossing the BRP.

Brown Mountain Creek Valley—Community of freed slaves lived here from the Civil War until about 1918; remains of cabins and interpretive signs tell of life in the valley then.

Brown Mountain Creek Shelter (1961)—Sleeps 6. Privy. Water source is a spring in front of, and uphill from, the shelter. In dry conditions, get water from Brown Mountain Creek, crossed on the trail south of the shelter.

U.S. 60—West 9.7 miles to **Buena Vista [P.O. ZIP 24416: M–F 8:30–4:30, closed Sa; (540) 261-8959].** ■ *Hostel:* Three Springs Hostel, (434) 922-7069, accepts mail drops to 612 Wiggins Spring Road, Vesuvius, VA 24483, (near Hog Camp Gap); $54PP includes bunk, shower with towel, B/D, free shuttles from/to Trail. Other shuttles, slacking, fuel, snacks, and parking available, no dogs; reservations required; not a party place. ■ *Lodging:* Buena Vista Motel, (540) 261-2138, $49–$79; Budget Inn, (540) 261-2156, $49.95S, $59.95S/D, $10EAP, $5 charge for early check-in, pet fee (allowed in smoking rooms only), laundry, WiFi, possible shuttle to and from the Trail. ■ *Camping:* Glen Maury Campground, (540) 261-7321, hiker specials, tentsites with shower, $5+tax per tent, free shower without stay, pool $2 for guests (closes mid-Aug). ■ *Groceries:* Food Lion (long-term resupply); Sheltman's

Gas & Grocery (short-term resupply); Amish Cupboard, (540) 264-0215, bulk foods, resupply, mail drops, hiker assistance, and info. ■ *Restaurants:* Original Italian Pizza, 10% discount to hikers; Mexican, Italian, Chinese, and fast-food choices. ■ *Shuttles:* Rockbridge Taxi Service, (540) 261-7733; E's-Y Rider Taxi, (540) 461-2467; Buddy Johnson, (540) 817-9168; Gary Serra, (757) 681-2254; Aubrey Taylor, (540) 261-6998; Ken Hawkins, (540) 817-9640. An hourly fixed-rate service (Maury Express) runs between Lexington and Buena Vista M–F 8–6 and Sa 10–4 for 50¢ each way. ■ *Other services:* Regional Visitors Center, (540) 261-8004; library with Internet access; Michael Ohleger, (540) 460-0236, formerly with Uncorked wine shop, may be able to provide shuttles and other support; Bald Bear Outdoors, (540) 261-1029, limited supplies; Advanced Auto (Heet); coin laundry; banks with ATM; hardware store; doctor; dentist; pharmacy; and veterinarian. ■ *Other attractions:*

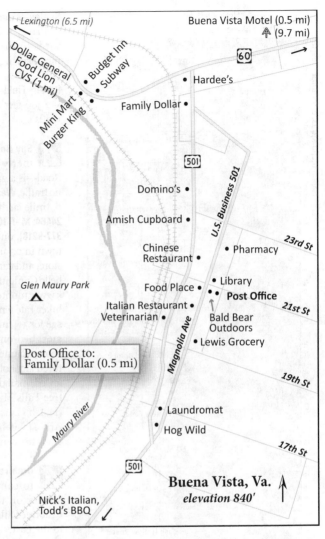

Lexington (6.5 mi)
Buena Vista Motel (0.5 mi)
(9.7 mi)
Dollar General
Food Lion
CVS (1 mi)
Budget Inn
Subway
Mini Mart
Burger King
60
Hardee's
Family Dollar
501
Domino's
U.S. Business 501
Amish Cupboard
23rd St
Chinese Restaurant
Pharmacy
Glen Maury Park
Food Place
Library
Post Office
Italian Restaurant
21st St
Veterinarian
Magnolia Ave
Bald Bear Outdoors
Post Office to: Family Dollar (0.5 mi)
Lewis Grocery
19th St
Maury River
Laundromat
Hog Wild
17th St
501
Buena Vista, Va.
elevation 840'
Nick's Italian, Todd's BBQ

The annual Maury River Fiddlers Convention, popular with hikers, is held at Glen Maury Park, the third weekend in Jun; Beach Music Festival, last Sa in Jul; Nothin' Fancy Bluegrass Festival, last weekend in Sep; annual Mountain Day street festival, second Sa in Oct.

West 16.2 miles to **Lexington [P.O. ZIP 24450: M–F 9–5, Sa 10–12; (540) 463-6449]**. A larger town with groceries, motels, doctors, vets. *Outfitter:* Walkabout Outfitter, (540) 464-HIKE, 15 W. Washington St., M–F 10–5:30, Sa 10–5, Su 11:30–3:30, owned by Kirk Miller (Flying Monkey '99), full-service outfitter, only MSR canisters.

Cow Camp Gap Shelter (1986)—Sleeps 8. Privy. Water source is on blue-blazed trail to the left of the shelter; if you have crossed a small stream, you missed the spring.

Cole Mountain—Bald Knob, south of Cole Mountain, isn't a bald, but Cole Mountain and Tar Jacket Ridge are. A mowing project was undertaken by NBATC and the Forest Service to preserve the open views and habitat for northern cottontail rabbits, various raptors, turkey, and grouse.

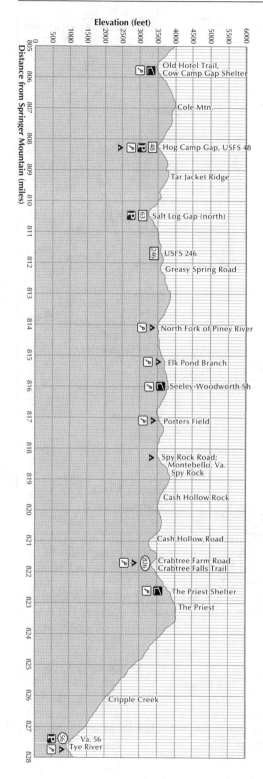

Elevation (feet)

Distance from Springer Mountain (miles)

Old Hotel Trail,
Cow Camp Gap Shelter

Cole Mtn.

Hog Camp Gap, USFS 48

Tar Jacket Ridge

Salt Log Gap (north)

USFS 246

Greasy Spring Road

North Fork of Piney River

Elk Pond Branch

Seeley-Woodworth-Sh

Porters Field

Spy Rock Road;
Montebello, Va.
Spy Rock

Cash Hollow Rock

Cash Hollow Road

Crabtree Farm Road
Crabtree Falls Trail

The Priest Shelter

The Priest

Cripple Creek

Va. 56
Tye River

Seeley–Woodworth Shelter (1984)—Sleeps 8. Privy. A blue-blazed trail leads 100 yards to shelter and 0.1 mile beyond to piped spring.

Porters Field—West to a spring and campsite 300 feet down the second of two dirt roads.

Spy Rock Road—This "road"—formerly known as Fish Hatchery Road—is a gated, one-lane dirt road with no traffic. **West** 1.5 miles to the fish hatchery, 0.7 mile farther to **Montebello, Va. [P.O. ZIP 24464: M–F 10–2 & 1:30–4:30, Sa 10–1; (540) 377-9218]**, on Va. 56. Turn left, and reach town in 0.3 mile, with post office, grocery store, and campground. *Lodging:* Montebello Camping and Fishing, (540) 377-2650, <www.montebellova.com>, special thru-hiker-rate tentsites with shower $14S, $21D, $28 for 3+, furnished efficiency cabin $90–$165, bed-only camping cabin $50–$60, shower, laundry, long-term resupply, denatured alcohol, other fuels, leashed dogs allowed, mail drops accepted at 15702 Crabtree Falls Hwy., Montebello, VA 24464. (Dutch Haus B&B: Owners Earl and Lois Arnold will be hiking in 2015 and have no plans to open the B&B.)

Crabtree Farm Road—**West** 0.5 mile to campsite and spring; 2 miles farther on the Crabtree Falls Trail to Crabtree Falls, one of the highest cascades in the East.

The Priest Shelter (1960)—Sleeps 8. Privy. Named for the massif dominating the area; near a busy access for backpackers and often full. Water source is a spring to left of the shelter.

Tidewater Appalachian Trail Club—TATC maintains the 10.6 miles between the Tye River and Reids Gap. Correspondence should be sent to P.O. Box 8246, Norfolk, VA 23503; <president@tidewateratc.com>; <www.tidewateratc.com>.

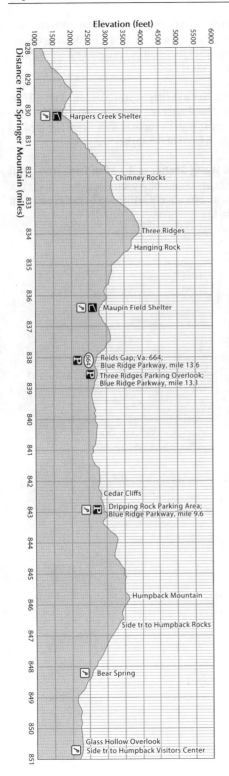

Elevation (feet)

Distance from Springer Mountain (miles)

Harpers Creek Shelter

Chimney Rocks

Three Ridges

Hanging Rock

Maupin Field Shelter

Reids Gap; Va. 664;
Blue Ridge Parkway, mile 13.6
Three Ridges Parking Overlook;
Blue Ridge Parkway, mile 13.1

Cedar Cliffs

Dripping Rock Parking Area;
Blue Ridge Parkway, mile 9.6

Humpback Mountain

Side tr to Humpback Rocks

Bear Spring

Glass Hollow Overlook
Side tr to Humpback Visitors Center

Va. 56/Tye River—West 3.9 miles to *Camping:* Crabtree Falls Campground (short-term resupply), 11039 Crabtree Falls Hwy., Tyro, VA 22976; (540) 377-2066, <www.crabtreefallscampground. com>; tentsites with shower $26D, cabins $55D; M–Th 10–5, F–Sa 9–10, Su 9–2, no charge for shower without stay. Accepts mail drops for guests. *Northbound directions:* Take Route 826 (Shoe Creek Rd.) west 0.5 mile to Crabtree Meadows parking lot, then down Crabtree Falls Trail 2.9 miles to Va. 56, then east 0.5 mile to campground. *Southbound:* Va. 56 west 2.5 miles to campground.

Mau-Har Trail—Traversing an area rich in waterfalls and good swimming holes, this steep, 3-mile blue-blaze connects with the A.T. at Maupin Field Shelter. It's shorter, but harder, than the white-blazed route.

Harpers Creek Shelter (1960)—Sleeps 6. Privy. Designated low-impact tentsites, which campers are requested to use. Water source is Harpers Creek, in front of the shelter. In extreme droughts, go upstream, and find water in the spring-fed ponds.

Maupin Field Shelter (1960)—Sleeps 6. Privy. Designated low-impact tentsites, which campers are requested to use. The Mau-Har Trail begins behind the shelter and rejoins the A.T. 3 miles south. Water source is a dependable spring behind the shelter.

Fire Road to Blue Ridge Parkway— From Maupin Field Shelter, turn left on fire road (just north of shelter), 1.2 miles to BRP.

Old Dominion Appalachian Trail Club—ODATC maintains the 19.1 miles between Reids Gap and Rockfish Gap. Correspondence should be sent to P.O. Box 25283, Richmond, VA 23260; <odatc. president@gmail.com>; <www.odatc.net>.

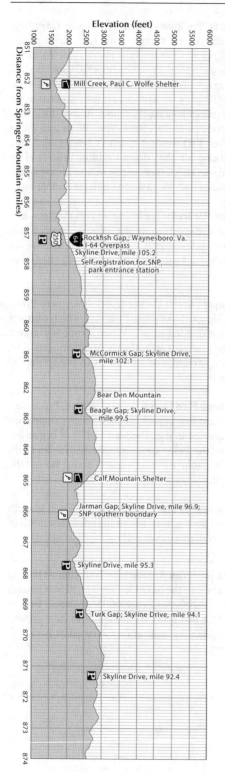

Humpback Rocks—The Trail circumvents the rocks, but, if you are seeking a bouldering opportunity, they may still be reached by a short, blue-blazed side trail.

Paul C. Wolfe Shelter (1991)—Sleeps 10. Privy. Tentsites. This shelter has windows and a porch cooking area. Water source is Mill Creek, located 50 yards in front of the shelter.

Paul Wolfe Shelter to Rockfish Gap—The Trail passes remnants of a cabin, cemetery, and rock piles, all evocative of settlement by early mountain folks.

Virginia—Part 3
(Shenandoah National Park)

Miles from Springer	Fr Last Point	Features	Services	Miles from Katahdin	MAP
861.6	5.0	U.S. 250, I-64, Rockfish Gap (1,902') **Waynesboro, Va. 22980**	R, P, L, M (W–1m L; 4.5m all)	1,327.6	
861.7	0.1	I-64 overpass (1,902')	R	1,327.5	
861.9	0.2	Skyline Drive mp 105.2 (1,902')	R, P	1,327.3	
862.4	0.5	SNP kiosk for self-registration; park entrance station (2,200')	Kiosk on Trail (W–0.2m R)	1,326.8	
865.3	2.9	Skyline Drive mp 102.1; McCormick Gap (3,450')	R, P	1,323.9	
866.6	1.3	Bear Den Mountain (2,885')...*old tractor seats, vista*		1,322.6	
867.1	0.5	Skyline Drive mp 99.5; Beagle Gap (2,550')	R, P	1,322.1	
869.3	2.2	**Calf Mountain Shelter** (2,700') ...*13mS; 13.5mN*	W–0.3m S, w	1,319.9	
869.9	0.6	Spring (2,200')	w	1,319.3	
870.3	0.4	Skyline Drive mp 96.9; SNP southern boundary; Jarman Gap (2,173')	R	1,318.9	
870.5	0.2	Spring (2,150')	w	1,318.7	
872.1	1.6	Skyline Drive mp 95.3; Sawmill Run Overlook (2,200')	R, P	1,317.1	
873.7	1.6	Skyline Drive mp 94.1; Turk Gap (2,600')	R, P	1,315.5	PATC Map 11
875.7	2.0	Skyline Drive mp 92.4 (3,100')	R, P	1,313.5	
879.8	4.1	Skyline Drive mp 88.9 (2,350')	R	1,309.4	
881.6	1.8	Skyline Drive mp 87.4; Blackrock Gap (2,321')	R, P	1,307.6	
881.8	0.2	Skyline Drive mp 87.2 (2,700')	R	1,307.4	
882.3	0.5	**Blackrock Hut** (2,645')...*13.5mS; 13.5mN*	E–0.2.m S, w	1,306.9	
882.9	0.6	Blackrock (3,100')...*open rocky summit*		1,306.3	
883.9	1.0	Skyline Drive mp 84.3 (2,800')	R, P	1,305.3	
885.2	1.3	Dundo Group Campground (2,700')	W–0.1m w	1,304.0	
885.4	0.2	Skyline Drive mp 82.9; Browns Gap (2,600')	R, P	1,303.8	
886.3	0.9	Skyline Drive mp 82.2 (2,800')	R	1,302.9	
886.7	0.4	Skyline Drive mp 81.9; Doyles River Parking Area (2,800')	R, P	1,302.5	
887.6	0.9	Skyline Drive mp 81.1; Doyles River Cabin (locked) (2,900')	R, P (E–0.3m w)	1,301.6	
889.7	2.1	+Loft Mountain Campground (3,300')	W–0.2m C, G, cl, sh; 1.2m M)	1,299.5	
890.8	1.1	Frazier Discovery Trail to Loft Mountain Wayside (2,950')	W–0.6m R, M	1,298.4	
891.5	0.7	Loft Mountain (3,200')		1,297.7	
891.8	0.3	Spring (2,950')	W–0.1m	1,297.4	

Miles from Springer	Fr Last Point	Features	Services	Miles from Katahdin	MAP
893.9	2.1	Skyline Drive mp 77.5; Ivy Creek Overlook (2,800')	R, P	1,295.3	
895.5	1.6	**Pinefield Hut** (2,430')...*13.5mS; 8.4mN*	E–0.1m S, C, w	1,293.7	
895.7	0.2	Skyline Drive mp 75.2; Pinefield Gap (2,590')	R	1,293.5	
897.6	1.9	Skyline Drive mp 73.2; Simmons Gap (2,250')	R, P (E–0.2m w)	1,291.6	
900.9	3.3	Skyline Drive mp 69.9; Powell Gap (2,294')	R	1,288.3	
901.3	0.4	Little Roundtop Mountain (2,700')		1,287.9	PATC Map 11
902.5	1.2	Skyline Drive mp 68.6; Smith Roach Gap (2,600')	R, P	1,286.7	
903.7	1.2	**Hightop Hut** (3,175')...*8.4mS; 12.6mN*	W–0.1m S; 0.2m C, w	1,285.5	
904.2	0.5	Spring (3,450')	w	1,285.0	
904.3	0.1	Hightop Mountain (3,587')		1,284.9	
905.8	1.5	Skyline Drive mp 66.7 (2,650')	R, P	1,283.4	
907.1	1.3	U.S. 33; Skyline Drive mp 65.5; Swift Run Gap, Spotswood Trail (2,367') **Elkton, Va. 22827**	R, w (W–2.9m L; 3.2m C, G, M, cl; 7.5m PO, G, M)	1,282.1	
910.1	3.0	South River Picnic Grounds (3,200')	W–0.1m w	1,279.1	
913.4	3.3	Pocosin Cabin (locked) (3,150')	W–0.1m w	1,275.8	
913.7	0.3	Spring (3,100')	w	1,275.5	
915.4	1.7	Skyline Drive mp 57.6; +Lewis Mountain Campround and Cabins (3,500')	R (W–0.1m C, G, L, cl, sh)	1,273.8	
916.1	0.7	**Bearfence Mountain Hut** (3,110') ...*12.6mS; 11.8mN*	R, P (E–0.1m S, C, w)	1,273.1	
918.7	2.6	Skyline Drive mp 55.1; Bootens Gap (3,243')	R, P	1,270.5	
919.6	0.9	Hazeltop (3,812')		1,269.6	
921.5	1.9	Skyline Drive mp 52.8; Milam Gap (3,300')	R, P	1,267.7	
922.4	0.9	Spring (3,380')	w	1,266.8	
923.2	0.8	Lewis Spring; Big Meadows Wayside; Harry F. Bird Sr. Visitor Center (3,390')	R, w (E–0.4m R, P, G, M)	1,266.0	PATC Map 10
924.1	0.9	Big Meadows Lodge; +Big Meadows Campground (3,500')	E–0.1m R, P, C, L, M, cl, sh; 0.9m G, M)	1,265.1	
924.7	0.6	David Spring (3,490')	w	1,264.5	
925.7	1.0	Skyline Drive mp 49.3; Fishers Gap (3,050')	R	1,263.5	
927.6	1.9	**Rock Spring Hut** and (locked) Cabin (3,465') ...*11.8mS; 11.1mN*	W–0.2m S, C, w	1,261.6	
927.9	0.3	Trail to Hawksbill Mountain, Byrd's Nest #2 Picnic Shelter (3,600')	E–0.9m R	1,261.3	
928.9	1.0	Skyline Drive mp 45.6; Hawksbill Gap (3,361')	R, P	1,260.3	
929.3	0.4	Skyline Drive mp 44.4; trail to Crescent Rock Overlook (3,450')		1,259.9	
931.4	2.1	Skyland Service Road (south); Horse Stables (3,550')	R, P	1,257.8	
932.2	0.8	Skyland Service Road (north) (3,790')...*best access to Skyland*	R, P (W–0.2m L, M)	1,257.0	

Miles from Springer	Fr Last Point	Features	Services	Miles from Katahdin	M A P
932.6	0.4	Trail to Stony Man Mountain summit (3,837')	R, P	1,256.6	
934.2	1.6	Skyline Drive mp 38.6; Hughes River Gap; Trail to Stony Man Mountain Overlook (3,097')	R, P, w	1,255.0	
936.4	2.2	Skyline Drive mp 36.7; Pinnacles Picnic Ground (3,390')	R, w	1,252.8	
936.5	0.1	Skyline Drive mp 36.4; Trail to Jewell Hollow Overlook (3,350')	R	1,252.7	PATC Map 10
937.5	1.0	The Pinnacle (3,730')		1,251.7	
938.5	1.0	**Byrds Nest #3 Shelter** (3,290') ...*11.1mS; 4.6mN*	S, C (E–0.3m w)	1,250.7	
939.2	0.7	Meadow Spring (3,100')	E–0.3m w	1,250.0	
939.8	0.6	Marys Rock (3,514')...*vista*		1,249.4	
941.7	1.9	U.S. 211; Skyline Drive mp 31.5 (2,307') Thornton Gap, Panorama **Luray, Va. 22835**	R, P (W–0.1m w; 4.6m L, M; 5.6m C, G, L, cl; 8m all)	1,247.5	
942.9	1.2	**Pass Mountain Hut** (2,690')...*4.6mS; 13.5mN*	E–0.2m S, w	1,246.3	
943.7	0.8	Pass Mountain (3,052')		1,245.5	
944.8	1.1	Skyline Drive mp 28.6 (2,490')	R	1,244.4	
945.1	0.3	Skyline Drive mp 28.5; Beahms Gap (2,490')	R, P	1,244.1	
945.2	0.1	Byrds Nest #4 Picnic Shelter (2,600')	E–0.5m	1,244.0	
949.8	4.6	Spring (2,600')	w	1,239.4	
950.3	0.5	Skyline Drive mp 23.9 (2,480') Elkwallow Gap; Elkwallow Wayside	R, P (E–0.1m G, M)	1,238.9	
951.1	0.8	Range View Cabin (locked) (2,950')	E–0.1m w	1,238.1	
951.8	0.7	Skyline Drive mp 21.9 (3,100') Rattlesnake Point Overlook	R, P	1,237.4	
952.4	0.6	Tuscarora Trail (southern terminus) to +Matthews Arm Campground (3,400')	W–0.9m C	1,236.8	
952.8	0.4	Skyline Drive mp 21.1 (3,350')	R, P	1,236.4	PATC Map 9
953.0	0.2	Hogback Third Peak (3,400')		1,236.2	
953.1	0.1	Skyline Drive mp 20.8 (3,350')	R, P	1,236.1	
953.3	0.2	Hogback Second Peak (3,475')		1,235.9	
953.5	0.2	Spring (3,250')	E–0.2m w	1,235.7	
953.6	0.1	Hogback First Peak (3,390')		1,235.6	
954.3	0.7	Skyline Drive mp 19.7; Little Hogback Overlook (3,000')	R	1,234.9	
954.4	0.1	Little Hogback Mountain (3,050')		1,234.8	
954.9	0.5	Skyline Drive mp 18.9 (2,850')	R	1,234.3	
956.0	1.1	**Gravel Springs Hut** (2,480') ...*13.5mS; 10.7mN*	E–0.2m S, C, w	1,233.2	
956.2	0.2	Skyline Drive mp 17.7; Gravel Springs Gap (2,666')	R, P	1,233.0	
957.3	1.1	South Marshall Mountain (3,212')		1,231.9	
957.8	0.5	Skyline Drive mp 15.9 (3,050')	R	1,231.4	
958.5	0.7	North Marshall Mountain (3,368')		1,230.7	

Miles from Springer	Fr Last Point	Features	Services	Miles from Katahdin	M A P
959.4	0.9	Hogwallow Spring (2,950')	w	1,229.8	
960.0	0.6	Skyline Drive mp 14.2; Hogwallow Gap (2,739')	R	1,229.2	
961.7	1.7	Skyline Drive mp 12.3; Jenkins Gap (2,400')	R	1,227.5	
962.6	0.9	Compton Springs (2,700')	w	1,226.6	
963.0	0.4	Compton Peak (2,909')		1,226.2	
963.8	0.8	Skyline Drive mp 10.4; Compton Gap (2,550')	R, P	1,225.4	
964.1	0.3	Indian Run Spring (2,350')	E–0.3m w	1,225.1	PATC Map 9
965.6	1.5	Compton Gap Horse Trail; Trail to Chester Gap (2,350')	N– 0.5m H, M, f	1,223.6	
965.8	0.2	Possums Rest Overlook, SNP kiosk for self-registration, SNP northern boundary (2,300')		1,223.4	
966.5	0.7	**Tom Floyd Wayside** (1,900')...*10.7mS; 8.1mN*	S, w	1,222.7	
967.5	1.0	Northern Virginia 4-H Swimming Pool (1,350')	W–0.3m	1,221.7	
968.0	0.5	Va. 602 (1,150')	R	1,221.2	
969.4	1.4	U.S. 522 (950') **Front Royal, Va. 22630**	R, P, L (W–3.2m all)	1,219.8	

+Fee charged, mp=milepost

Shenandoah National Park, with 96 miles of well-graded Appalachian Trail, is memorable for its many vistas and abundant wildlife. Skyline Drive, which you will cross 28 times, has many waysides and concessions for resupply stops. *Backcountry permits are required when camping in the park.*

U.S. 250, I-64/Rockfish Gap—Where the A.T. crosses U.S. 250, it is **West** 500 yards to the Rockfish Gap Visitors Center (on the hill next to the Inn at Afton), (540) 943-5187. Open daily 9–5, provides an information packet on the area created specifically for hikers, that notes volunteers provide free shuttles between Rockfish Gap and downtown. (See list at the visitors center, YMCA, and various other locations.) If closed, packets are in box near door and pay phone, or you can dowload it from <www.visitwaynesboro.net/outdoors-your-way/appalachian-trail>; click on "hiking guide." ■ *Lodging:* Inn at Afton, (540) 942-5201, above and behind the visitors' center, $40 hiker rate, B/L/D, pool, pets allowed, vehicles may be parked in lot; leave name, vehicle information, and date of return with desk staff. ■ *Outfitter:* Rockfish Gap Outfitters, (540) 943-1461, located on U.S. 250 on the way to town; fuel by the ounce, backpacking gear, ATC publications, large footwear selection, minor gear repairs, and warranty assistance.

West 1 mile to *Lodging:* Colony House Motel, (540) 942-4156, hiker rate $48.80 incl. tax., pets $10, pool, laundry, can shuttle back to Trail if asked and available.

West 4.5 miles to **Waynesboro, Va. [P.O. ZIP 22980: M–F 9–5, closed Sa (hikers have gotten mail by knocking on the back door); (540) 942-7320]**, a large, hiker-friendly town with most services; <www.visitwaynesboro.net>. ■ *Hostel:* Grace Evangelical Lutheran Church, 500 South Wayne Ave., open May 18–Jun 20, closed Su nights, check-in 5–9 p.m., check-out 9 a.m, but will store packs for those staying another night. Lounge with big-screen TV, a/c, Internet, showers, cots, kitchen, snacks, and continental breakfast. Members of the congregation host a Th night supper for hikers (max. 15) followed by an optional vespers service. No pets, drugs, smoking, alcohol, firearms, foul language. Maximum 15 hikers; 2-night limit. Donations accepted. Hiker Fest is Jun 15. ■ *Camping:* Waynes-

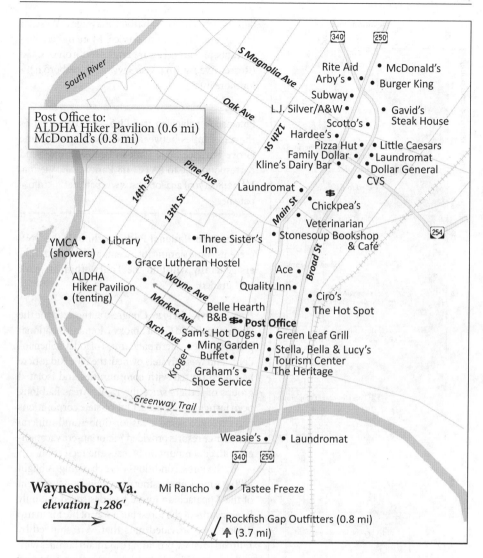

Post Office to:
ALDHA Hiker Pavilion (0.6 mi)
McDonald's (0.8 mi)

Waynesboro, Va.
elevation 1,286'

boro Parks and Recreation offers tent and hammock sites on a grassy area at the foot of 14th St. near the South River. The ALDHA Hiker Pavilion has a solar charging station for devices. The YMCA, (540) 942-5107, on South Wayne Ave., offers showers, restroom, and gym; check in at desk M–F 5:15 a.m.–10 p.m., Sa 8–5, Su 1–5; donations appreciated. ■ *Lodging:* Quality Inn, (540) 942-1171, $53.59S, $59.59D, $5EAP, pets in smoking rooms only $10; Tree Streets Inn B&B, 421 Walnut Ave., (540) 949-4484, $75S/D includes B, pool. no pets, shuttle from/to Rockfish Gap, mail drops accepted for guests; Belle Hearth B&B, (540) 943-1910, <www.bellehearth.com>, $75S $95D hiker rate with B and pick-up/drop-off, laundry, mail drops for guests. ■ *Groceries:* Kroger (long-term resupply). ■ *Restaurants:* Ming Garden, AYCE L/D; Gavid's Steaks; Scotto's Italian; Ciros Pizza; Pizza Hut, AYCE L; Chickpeas; Stone Soup; Stella, Bella & Lucy Café; Weasie's Kitchen, B/L/D with AYCE pancake B anytime, open M–Sa 5:30 a.m.–8 p.m., Su 7–2; Greenleaf Grill; Market on Main; Mi Rancho; many fast-food outlets. ■ *Internet access:* Waynesboro Public Library, M–F 9–9, Sa 9–5; Learning Tree, 421 W. Main St., during normal business hours; Grace Church during times of hostel operation (see above). ■ *Other services:* cobbler, coin laundry, pharmacy, ATM, doctor,

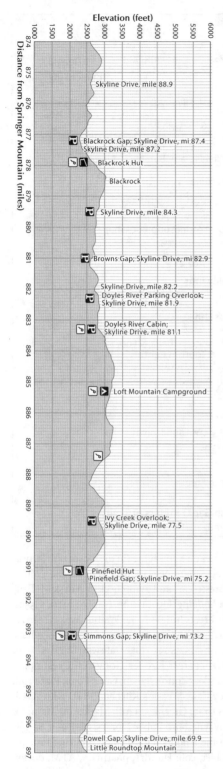

dentist, veterinarian, barber, massages, Western Union, one-hour photo service. More motels, restaurants, and groceries are 2 miles south on U.S. 340 (Rosser Ave.) at I-64; visit <www.waynesboro.net> for more information.

Potomac Appalachian Trail Club—PATC maintains the 240.5 miles between Rockfish Gap and Pine Grove Furnace State Park in Pennsylvania. Send correspondence to PATC, 118 Park St. SE, Vienna, VA 22180; (703) 242-0693; <www.patc.net>; <info@patc.net>.

Shenandoah National Park—Although the SNP presents some significant ascents and descents, hikers generally will find the Trail within the park well-graded.

Park history—In 1926, Congress authorized the the Shenandoah and Great Smoky Mountains national parks. Unlike western parks, most of today's Shenandoah land was privately owned; the Blue Ridge here had been dotted with communities and isolated groups of settlers since the 1750s. Areas had long been farmed and grazed. Out-of-state corporations had exploited some areas for timber and mineral ores. Three resorts provided Victorian-era vacationers with cool mountain breezes and recreation.

By the 1910s, conditions were changing. A blight killing American chestnut trees, some 30–40 percent of the Appalachian forest, had destroyed not only large swaths of the forest but a way of life for many. Those trees provided nuts that were shipped by railroad to cities, providing mountain families with cash income. The chestnut was strong, straight, and rot-resistant, and its wood was valuable for fence posts, railroad ties, roof shingles, siding boards, and general lumber that residents used and sold in the Shenandoah Valley and the Piedmont.

In 1927, Virginia authorized condemnation of all private property within the boundary of the proposed park. More than 4,000 tracts were surveyed, and 1,081 were purchased and given to the federal government, uprooting most of the 465 families who lived on the land. Virginia resettled the majority and evicted those unwilling to move. Approximately 45 elderly residents were allowed to spend their last years in their homes.

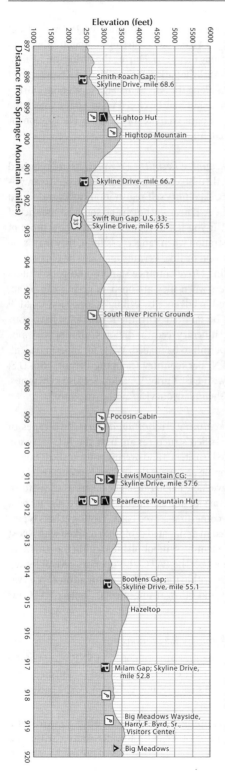

Elevation (feet)

Distance from Springer Mountain (miles)

Smith Roach Gap;
Skyline Drive, mile 68.6

Hightop Hut

Hightop Mountain

Skyline Drive, mile 66.7

Swift Run Gap, U.S. 33;
Skyline Drive, mile 65.5

South River Picnic Grounds

Pocosin Cabin

Lewis Mountain CG;
Skyline Drive, mile 57.6

Bearfence Mountain Hut

Bootens Gap;
Skyline Drive, mile 55.1

Hazeltop

Milam Gap; Skyline Drive,
mile 52.8

Big Meadows Wayside,
Harry F. Byrd, Sr.,
Visitors Center

Big Meadows

In 1931, four years before Shenandoah was established, construction of Skyline Drive began. First built as a second entrance to President Herbert Hoover's summer White House, Rapidan Camp, the road was only to go from the camp to Skyland. State leaders successfully lobbied for congressional appropriations to extend the highway north to Thornton Gap (U.S. 211), on to Front Royal, and then south to Rockfish Gap. But, until the park was established in December 1935, Skyline Drive existed only as a 100-foot right-of-way within privately held land that basically coincided with the route of the A.T. In 1933, President Franklin D. Roosevelt's CCC "boys" established camps along the route and built many of the facilities, overlooks, rock walls, and gutters seen there today. They planted hundreds of thousands of trees and shrubs, creating the landscape that draws millions of visitors to the park, and built a new route for the A.T. ATC Chair Myron Avery's acceptance of this disruption, after years of simmering disagreements, produced an open schism between the organization's leadership and founder Benton MacKaye and his allies in New York and New England.

Today, 95 percent reforested, the park is home to wild turkey, white-tailed deer, black bears, and shelter mice. Hundreds of migrating birds and butterflies summer or stop over in this central Appalachian biome. Nearly one million visitors a year come to watch wildlife, get back to nature, view the Shenandoah Valley to the west and the foothills to the east, or visit land on which their ancestors lived.

Ranger Programs—From Memorial Day through Oct, rangers present a variety of organized hikes, programs, and participatory events highlighting the natural and human history of the park. The SNP visitors' guide, available at entrance stations and visitors centers, outlines the seasonal schedule.

Forest Damage—Hurricane Isabel (2003) and fires before it damaged thousands of acres. Coupled with the floods, Tropical Storm Fran in 1996, a severe ice storm in 1998 and 2006, a 2012 derecho, and gypsy-moth and woolly adelgid infestations, the park has been hit hard in recent years. Be mindful of trees and branches that have been weakened by those events and could still fall.

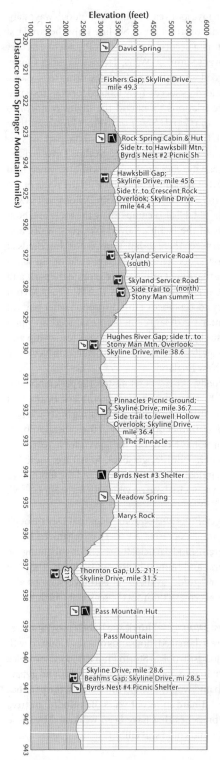

Elevation (feet)

David Spring

Fishers Gap; Skyline Drive, mile 49.3

Rock Spring Cabin & Hut
Side tr. to Hawksbill Mtn,
Byrd's Nest #2 Picnic Sh

Hawksbill Gap;
Skyline Drive, mile 45.6

Side tr. to Crescent Rock
Overlook; Skyline Drive,
mile 44.4

Skyland Service Road
(south)

Skyland Service Road
Side trail to   (north)
Stony Man summit

Hughes River Gap; side tr. to
Stony Man Mtn. Overlook;
Skyline Drive, mile 38.6

Pinnacles Picnic Ground;
Skyline Drive, mile 36.7
Side trail to Jewell Hollow
Overlook; Skyline Drive,
mile 36.4
The Pinnacle

Byrds Nest #3 Shelter

Meadow Spring

Marys Rock

Thornton Gap, U.S. 211;
Skyline Drive, mile 31.5

Pass Mountain Hut

Pass Mountain

Skyline Drive, mile 28.6
Beahms Gap; Skyline Drive, mi 28.5
Byrds Nest #4 Picnic Shelter

Fee—Hikers entering the park *via* the A.T. are not charged a fee; hikers entering at other trailheads in SNP may incur one. During the spring (mid-Feb to mid-Apr), the park occasionally conducts prescribed burns along the A.T. to manage vegetation. During burns, a hut may be closed up to 3 days. Check the ATC or park Web sites or ask at any NPS station for current information.

Backcountry Permits—Free permits are **required** of all thru-hikers and overnight backcountry travelers. Backcountry self-registration kiosks are located on the A.T. near the north and south boundaries of SNP. If you fail to register or can't show proof of registration when rangers ask for it, they may issue a citation or fine. Permits may also be obtained at Skyline Drive entrance stations and park visitors centers when they are open. A permit can be acquired in advance by calling (540) 999-3500, M–F 8–4. Be familiar with the regulations, have your exact itinerary ready, and allow 5–7 business days for the permit to be mailed. Write to: Superintendent, ATTN: Backcountry Camping Permit, 3655 U.S. Hwy. 211 East, Luray, VA 22835. See also <www.nps. gov/shen/planyourvisit/cambc_regs.htm>.

Backcountry Accommodations—Two types of three-sided structures are near the A.T.—day-use (called "shelters") and overnight-use (called "huts"). Camping at or near the shelters is prohibited. Huts are available to long-distance hikers (those with an itinerary of at least three consecutive nights) on a first-come, first-served basis. Tenting at huts is permitted in designated campsites marked with a post and a tenting symbol; all huts within the park have campsites. The PATC also operates several locked cabins within the park that require advance reservations and other arrangements. Contact PATC for details.

Backcountry Regulations

• Campfires are prohibited in SNP, except at the commercial campgrounds and established fireplaces at shelters, huts, and cabins. Use a backpacking stove.

• Camping is prohibited within 10 yards of a stream or other natural water source; within 20 yards of a park trail or unpaved fire road; within 50 yards of culturally historic sites, other campers, or no-camping signs; within 100 yards of a hut, cabin, or day-use shelter (except designated sites); within 0.25 mile of a paved road, park boundary, picnic area, visitors center, or commercial facility. Several zones have been designated "noncamping areas," including Limberlost, Hawksbill Summit, Whiteoak Canyon, Old Rag summit, Big Meadows clearing, and Rapidan Camp.

- Camping is permitted almost everywhere else. New regulations encourage hikers to seek "pre-existing campsites" in legal locations that show signs of use and are not posted with no-camping signs. Camping at those sites is limited to two consecutive nights. If necessary, dispersed camping at undisturbed sites is permissible, but they must be left in pristine condition; use such sites only one night.

- Maximum group size is 10 people.

- Food must be stored so that wildlife cannot get it—hang food from a tree branch at least ten feet from the ground and four feet away from a tree's trunk. Alternatively, overnight huts feature food-storage poles, which are to be used instead of the familiar "mouse hangers." Park-approved, bear-resistant food-storage canisters are also permissible.

- Solid human waste should be buried in accordance with Leave No Trace ethics, under 6 inches of soil, more than 200 feet from trails, water sources, or roads. In mouldering privies, add a small handful of wood chips.

- Carry out all trash from the backcountry, and dispose of it properly.

- Glass containers are discouraged.

- Pets must be leashed at all times and are prohibited on certain side trails.

Commercial Facilities—Campgrounds, restaurants, lodges, waysides, and small stores are normally open spring through fall and are located strategically near the A.T. and Skyline Drive. Long-distance hikers may be able to save pack weight by resupplying or taking meals at these facilities. Call the park for the precise dates and times of operation. More details can be found at <www.visitshenandoah.com>. Campground reservations: (877) 444-6777 or <www.recreation.gov>. Site rates range from $17 to $20.

Calf Mountain Shelter (1984)—Sleeps 6. Privy. Featuring two skylights, this shelter is not a part of the SNP hut system, so SNP rules don't apply here. Water source is a piped spring on the access trail to the shelter. From here to Blackrock Hut, the A.T. usually is without reliable water sources; plan accordingly.

Blackrock Hut (1941)—Sleeps 6. Mouldering privy. Designated tentsites nearby. Water source is a piped spring 10 yards in front of the shelter.

Loft Mountain Campground—Open mid-May to late Oct. The A.T. skirts the campground, but several short side trails lead to campsites and the camp store (short-term resupply). Campsites $16, subject to change; showers $1, laundry, restroom, and soda machine. Loft Mountain Wayside and Grill serves B/L/D, short-order menu, soda machine. From the camp store, follow the paved road 1.0 mile downhill to Skyline Drive or continue north on the A.T. 0.9 mile and take the Frazier Discovery Trail 0.5 mile west (steep descent) to Skyline Drive.

Pinefield Hut (1940)—Sleeps 6. Mouldering privy. Designated tentsites nearby. Water source is a spring behind the shelter 50 yards that tends to fail during dry seasons. Northbounders can get water from Ivy Creek or Loft Mountain Campground; southbounders, an outdoor spigot at the Simmons Gap ranger station.

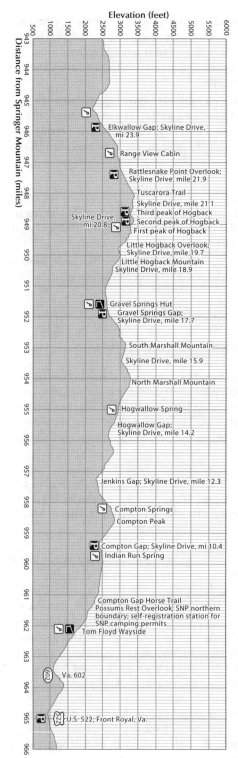

Elevation (feet)

Distance from Springer Mountain (miles)

Elkwallow Gap; Skyline Drive, mi 23.9

Range View Cabin

Rattlesnake Point Overlook; Skyline Drive, mile 21.9

Tuscarora Trail
Skyline Drive, mile 21.1
Third peak of Hogback
Skyline Drive, mi 20.8   Second peak of Hogback
First peak of Hogback

Little Hogback Overlook; Skyline Drive, mile 19.7
Little Hogback Mountain Skyline Drive, mile 18.9

Gravel Springs Hut
Gravel Springs Gap; Skyline Drive, mile 17.7

South Marshall Mountain

Skyline Drive, mile 15.9

North Marshall Mountain

Hogwallow Spring

Hogwallow Gap; Skyline Drive, mile 14.2

Jenkins Gap; Skyline Drive, mile 12.3

Compton Springs
Compton Peak

Compton Gap; Skyline Drive, mi 10.4
Indian Run Spring

Compton Gap Horse Trail
Possums Rest Overlook, SNP northern boundary; self-registration station for SNP camping permits
Tom Floyd Wayside

Va. 602

U.S. 522; Front Royal, Va.

Simmons Gap—Simmons Gap ranger station is down the paved road 0.2 mile east from where the A.T. crosses Skyline Drive. Frost-free pump.

Hightop Hut (1939)—Sleeps 6. Mouldering privy. Designated campsites nearby. Water source is a usually reliable piped spring 0.1 mile from the shelter on a side trail. An alternative water source is a boxed spring 0.5 mile north on the Trail.

U.S.33/Swift Run Gap/Spotswood Trail— West from Skyline Drive to water. Backcountry self-registration station located at SNP entrance station, north of U.S. 33 bridge.

On U.S. 33—**West** 2.9 miles to *Lodging:* Country View Motel, 19974 Spotswood Trail, Elkton, VA 22827, (540) 298-0025, $50, no pet fee, shuttle possible back to Trail and Elkton, mail drops accepted for guests; Misty Mountain Motel, (540) 298-9771, $53–$63 1–4 people, no pets, all rooms nonsmoking.

West 3.2 miles to ■ *Camping:* Swift Run Camping, (540) 298-8086, $20 campsite, laundry, pool, and snack bar. ■ *Groceries:* Bear Mountain Grocery, with a deli, daily 6–9.

West 7.5 miles to **Elkton, Va. [P.O. ZIP 22827: M–F 8:30–4:30, Sa 9–11; (540) 298-7772].** ■ *Groceries:* Food Lion, O'Dell's Grocery (both long-term resupply). ■ *Restaurants:* several fast-food places. ■ *Other services:* pharmacy, bank, and ATM.

South River Parking Area—Water, picnic benches, restrooms with sinks.

Lewis Mountain Campground and Cabins—(540) 999-2255. Open early May to Nov; reservations, (800) 999-4714. The A.T. passes in sight of the campground, and several short side trails lead to campsites and the camp store. Campsites $16; hiker special only for cabins available *via* <www.visitshenandoah.com/mvs> or by calling (877) 778-2871 (press option 2, and ask for code SHMVS). *Campground sites are not on the reservation system.* Lewis Mountain Camp Store (short-term resupply), open 9–7 in summer. Showers $1, laundry, restroom, and soda machine.

Bearfence Mountain Hut (1940)—Sleeps 6. Privy. Designated tentsites nearby. Located on a blue-blazed trail off a fire road. Water source is a piped spring in front of the shelter; prone to fail during even moderately dry spells.

Big Meadows Lodge, Campground, and Wayside—The A.T. passes within sight of the campground, and short side trails lead to the lodge, which also houses a restaurant and tap room and has Internet access. ■ *Lodging:* hiker special (includes B, taxes, B gratuity) available *via* <www.visitshenandoah.com/mvs> or by calling (877) 778-2871 (press option 2, and ask for code SHMVS); rooms available in main lodge; also cabins, suites, and motel-type accommodations. A few pet-friendly rooms. Reservations required. Lodging and restaurant open late May–late Oct. ■ *Camping:* Open early Apr–late Nov, campsites $20, reservations recommended. Walk-ins are possible, but the campground is often full; (800) 365-CAMP (use SHEN designator); showers $1, laundry. ■ *Restaurant:* Dining room open daily for L/D; tap room, with nightly entertainment and light fare, open daily from late afternoon to late evening. From the lodge, follow the paved entrance road 0.9 mile to Big Meadows Wayside and Grill, B/L/D, open late Mar–late Nov, with short-order menu. ■ *Groceries:* Wayside has a good selection (short-term resupply) and camping supplies, and soda machine. Next door is the Harry F. Byrd, Sr., Visitors Center, with exhibits and videos on the history of the area.

Rock Spring Hut (1940, updated 1980)—Sleeps 8. Privy. Designated tentsites nearby. Located on 0.2-mile blue-blazed trail. Water source, down a steep trail in front of the hut, flows from beneath a rock.

Skyland Service Road/Skyland—Skyland was originally a 19th-century mountain summer resort owned by A.T. pioneer George Freeman Pollock, who pushed hard to evict surrounding small landholders and create a national park and then, ironically, was forced to sell and give up management of the resort. Cross the road at the stables, and follow the A.T. north, passing a water tank on your right and the junction marked by a concrete post, which points to Skyland and dining room.

   West 0.2 mile to ■ *Lodging:* Skyland, (800) 999-4714, late Mar–late Nov; hiker special (includes B, taxes) available *via* <www.visitshenandoah.com/mvs> or by calling (877) 778-2871 (press option 2, and ask for code SHMVS); also motel-type accommodations and suites, reservations required. A few pet-friendly rooms. ■ *Restaurant:* Pollock Dining Room serves B/L/D; limited hours. Tap room, light fare, nightly entertainment.

Pinnacles Picnic Area—Restrooms, covered area, picnic tables, fireplaces. Uphill from picinic pavilion is a frost-free pump for year-round water.

Byrds Nest #3 Hut—Sleeps 8. Mouldering privy. A picnic shelter converted to overnight use. A spring is 0.3 mile east, down the fire road.

U.S. 211/Thornton Gap/Panorama—A short side trail, on the southern side of Thornton Gap, leads to Panorama area. The restaurant and backcountry-permit office were torn down in 2008; new restrooms, water source, and a parking area have been installed at "east" end of lot. Park entrance station is north of U.S. 211, east of where the Trail crosses Skyline Drive, with water. *Until further notice, treat or boil water from both those locations due to contamination.*

   On U.S. 211—**West** 4.6 miles to *Lodging:* Brookside Cabins, (540) 743-5698, luxury cabins $85–$195; full-menu restaurant featuring home-style foods and daily AYCE L/D buffet, weekend B buffet, open 8–8 (summer until 9). Closed early Dec–Mar.

   West 5.6 miles to ■ *Lodging:* Days Inn, (540) 743-4521, $79–$229, pets $10/night. ■ *Camping:* Yogi Bear's Jellystone Park, (540) 743-4002, <www.campluray.com>, tentsites $37–$59, cabins

$55–$190, two-night minimum on weekends, campstore (short-term resupply), pool, laundry, pets allowed (free) only at sites.

    West 8.0 miles to the town of **Luray, Va. [P.O. ZIP 22835: M–F 8:30–4:30, closed Sa; (540) 743-2100]**. Luray–Page County Chamber of Commerce, 18 Campbell St., (540) 743-3915, <www.luraypage.com>, M–Sa 9–5, Su 12–4. ■ *Lodging:* Best Value Cardinal Inn, (888) 648-4633, $70 and up, no pets; Mayne View B&B, (540) 743-7921; Mimslyn Inn, (540) 743-5105; Best Western Motel, (540) 743-6511, call for rates; Budget Inn, (540) 743-5176, $49s and up, pets $5; Luray Caverns Motels East and West, (540) 743-4531, 20% discount coupon for food/merchandise at Luray Caverns; Woodruff Inns B&B, (540) 743-1494, $109 and up. includes B. ■ *Groceries:* Farmer's Foods, Food Lion, Walmart (all long-term resupply). ■ *Restaurants:* Anthony's Pizza XII, L/D; East Wok, L/D and AYCE L; Mindi's Mexican, L/D; Gathering Grounds, espresso, sandwiches, desserts; Artisan's Grill, deli sandwiches and full meals; Uncle Buck's; The Speakeasy at the Mimslyn Inn, sandwiches and D 4–10 p.m., full bar; and several fast-food restaurants. ■ *Internet access:* Page County Library. ■ *Outfitters:* Appalachian Outdoors Adventures, 18 E. Main St., (540) 743-7400, full-service outfitter, fuel by the ounce, Th 10–6, F–Sa 10–8, Su 1–5. ■ *Other services:* veterinarian, Blue Mountain Animal Clinic, (540) 743-PETS; laundromats; hospital; ATMs; and 5-screen Page Theater.

Pass Mountain Hut (1939)—Sleeps 8. Privy. Known for the "kissing trees," the shelter is located on a blue-blazed trail. Designated campsites nearby. Water source is a piped spring 15 yards behind the shelter.

Elkwallow Wayside and Grill—Open 9–7 early Apr–early Oct. Visible from where the A.T. crosses Skyline Drive in Elkwallow Gap, the wayside includes a grill, gift shop, and restroom. Grill, B/L/D. Last chance in SNP for northbounders to get a blackberry milkshake. Gift shop offers limited groceries, camping supplies, soda machine outside. Frost-free pump at picnic area south of wayside.

Mathews Arm Campground—West 0.9 mile from the A.T., 0.3 mile south of the Hogback Parking Area *via* the Tuscarora and Traces trails. Signs lead to nearby primitive (*i.e.,* no services) campground, open mid-May–late Oct, campsites $16 per night, rate subject to change. This junction is the southern terminus of the 260-mile Tuscarora Trail. The northern is on the A.T. south of Darlington Shelter in Pennsylvania.

Gravel Springs Hut (1940)—Sleeps 8. Mouldering privy. Designated tentsites nearby on a blue-blazed trail. Water source is a boxed spring found on side trail near the shelter.

Trail to Chester Gap—At the last SNP concrete post on the Trail, labeled Va. 610/Chester Gap, the A.T. will turn left. Go straight, following the Compton Gap Trail 0.5 mile to paved road (if you come to the backcountry sign-in box, turn back 0.1 mile and then turn left). First house on left along paved road to *Hostel:* Front Royal Terrapin Station Hostel, 304 Chester Gap Rd., Chester Gap, VA 22623; (540) 539-0509; owned by Mike Evans (AT '95, PCT '98), <gratefullgg@hotmail.com>; enter in back through marked gate. Open Apr 27–Jul 6. Hikers only, picture ID required; bunk only $23/night, shower (with soap & shampoo) $3, laundry (with change of clothes). Hiker special for $30 includes bunk/shower/laundry, pizza (2), ice cream (pint), and soda (2); $50 special also includes free slackpack for 2 nights. Shuttles available. Accepts mail drops for guests.

Southbound Registration Station—1.0 mile south of Tom Floyd Wayside.

Tom Floyd Wayside (1980s)—Sleeps 6. Privy. Tentsites. Shelter has an overhanging front deck with storage space above, a railed deck with benches. Outside the SNP boundary, so SNP rules don't

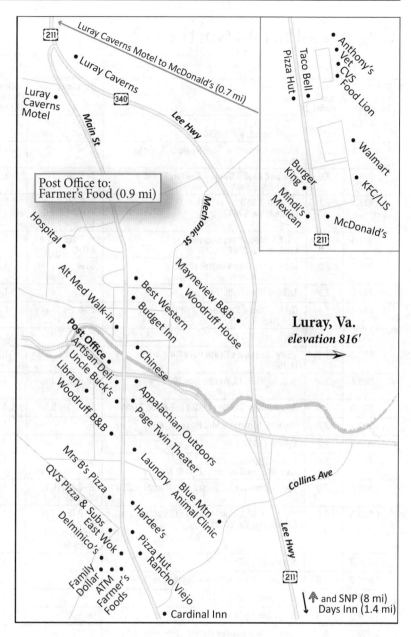

Luray, Va.
elevation 816'

apply. Water source 0.2 mile on a blue-blazed trail to the right of the shelter often stops flowing. Next closest water source is a stream crossed about 1.5 miles north on the A.T. near Va. 602.

Northern Virginia 4-H Swimming Pool—Blue-blazed side trail 0.9 mile north of Tom Floyd Wayside leads 0.3 mile **West** to the swimming pool. It is open to the public, including hikers, Su–Th 12–7, M–W 12–3 & 5:30–7, open some Fridays until 9 p.m. (Memorial Day–Labor Day), $4.50 admission ($2 after 5:30), swimsuits required. Inquire at 4-H office about multiday parking availability (advance arrangements required).

Virginia—Part 4 (Northern Virginia)

Miles from Springer	Fr Last Point	Features	Services	Miles from Katahdin	M A P
969.4	1.4	U.S. 522 (950') **Front Royal, Va. 22630**	R, P, L (W–3.2m all)	1,219.8	
972.7	3.3	Mosby Campsite, Tom Sealock Spring (1,800')	C, w	1,216.5	
974.6	1.9	**Jim and Molly Denton Shelter** (1,310') ...8.1mS; 5.5mN	S, C, w	1,214.6	
975.7	1.1	Va. 638 (1,150') **Linden, Va. 22642**	R, P (W–1.1m PO, g; 2.5m G, M; 7m all)	1,213.5	
977.6	1.9	Va. 55, Manassas Gap (800') **Linden, Va. 22642**	R, P (W–1.1m PO, G, M)	1,211.6	
980.1	2.5	**Manassas Gap Shelter** (1,655') ...5.5mS; 4.7mN	S, w	1,209.1	
982.0	1.9	Trillium Trail (1,900')		1,207.2	PATC Map 8
984.6	2.6	**Dick's Dome Shelter** (1,230') ...4.7mS; 8.8mN	E–0.2m S, w	1,204.6	
985.6	1.0	Spring (1,850')	C, w	1,203.6	
986.8	1.2	+Sky Meadows State Park Side Trail (1,780')	E–1.7m C, w	1,202.4	
989.4	2.6	U.S. 50, U.S. 17, Ashby Gap (900')	R, P (E–1.1m L, M; 18.5m O)	1,199.8	
993.0	3.6	**Rod Hollow Shelter** (840')...8.8mS; 7.1mN	W–0.2m S, w	1,196.2	
996.7	3.7	Va. 605, Morgans Mill Road (1,140')	R	1,192.5	
997.9	1.2	Spring (1,150')	w	1,191.3	
999.9	2.0	Sawmill Spring (990') **Sam Moore Shelter**...7.1mS; 11.3mN	S, w	1,189.3	
1,002.9	3.0	Bears Den Rocks, Bears Den Hostel (1,350')	E–0.2m H, L, C, g, cl, sh, f	1,186.3	
1,003.5	0.6	Va. 7, Va. 679, Snickers Gap (1,000') **Bluemont, Va. 20135**	R, P (E–1.6m G; 1.7m PO) (W–0.3m M; 0.9m M)	1,185.7	
1,005.7	2.2	Spring (1,083')	w	1,183.5	
1,006.0	0.3	Virginia–West Virginia State Line (1,140')		1,183.2	
1,006.1	0.1	Crescent Rock (1,312')		1,183.1	
1,006.7	0.6	Sand Spring (1,150')	w	1,182.5	PATC Map 7
1,006.8	0.1	Devils Racecourse (1,200')...*boulder field*		1,182.4	
1,009.7	2.9	Wilson Gap (1,380')		1,179.5	
1,010.9	1.2	**Blackburn Trail Center** (1,650') ...11.3mS; 3.6mN	E–0.1m C; 0.2m C, S, w	1,178.3	
1,014.1	3.2	**David Lesser Memorial Shelter** (1,430') ...3.6mS; 15.8mN	E–0.1m S; 0.3m C, w	1,175.1	
1,017.1	3.0	W. Va. 9, Keys Gap (935')	R, P (E–0.3m G; 5.5m H) (W– 0.3m G, M, w)	1,172.1	

+ Fee charged

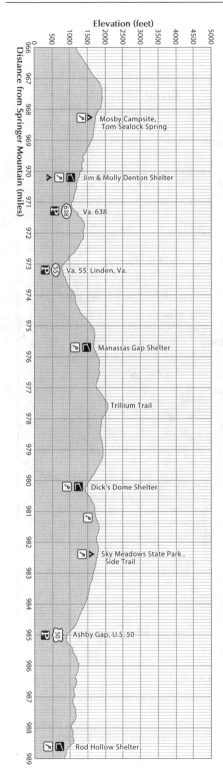

Elevation (feet)

Distance from Springer Mountain (miles)

Mosby Campsite,
Tom Sealock Spring

Jim & Molly Denton Shelter

Va. 638

Va. 55; Linden, Va.

Manassas Gap Shelter

Trillium Trail

Dick's Dome Shelter

Sky Meadows State Park,
Side Trail

Ashby Gap, U.S. 50

Rod Hollow Shelter

Higher rates of Lyme disease occur from northern Virginia into New England. Take precautions to prevent infection.

This 48-mile section follows a long, low ridge rich in American history and home to the infamous "roller-coaster" south of Snickers Gap.

U.S. 522—East 50 yards to *Lodging:* Mountain Home B&B, (540) 692-6198, $20PP with continental B, snacks, shower, outdoor kennel, cell coverage, shuttles to PO.

West 3.2 miles to **Front Royal, Va. [P.O. ZIP 22630: M–F 8:30–5, Sa 8:30–1; (540) 635-7983].** *See map on next page.* The post office is 1.0 mile farther. The large town offers all major services, but they are spread

out over a wide area. Except for the post office, most services are located near the U.S. 522 and Va. 55 intersection as you come into town from the A.T. ■ *Lodging:* Front Royal is the gateway to Shenandoah National Park, with motel rates that vary considerably according to season; be sure to specify you are a hiker, as most have special rates. Skyline Resort Motel, (540) 635-5354, office open 8:30–3:30, no dogs; newly renovated Pioneer Motel, (540) 631-1152, $50S, $55D; Scottish Inns, (540) 636-6168, dogs $10; Super 8 Motel, (540) 636-4888, dogs $10; Quality Inn, (540) 635-3161, dogs $15, Trailhead shuttle 10 a.m. M–F; Woodward House B&B, (540) 635-7010 or (800) 635-7011, no dogs, includes full B, shuttle to and from Trail, no smoking in house. ■ *Groceries:* Food Lion, Martin's, Better Thymes natural foods, Big Lots, Walmart Supercenter (all long-term resupply). ■ *Restaurants:* Happy Creek Coffee, 18 High St., (540) 660-2133, open daily, WiFi, gluten-free foods, accepts mail drops; Pizza Hut, AYCE; China Jade, AYCE L buffet; and many other food outlets. ■ *Internet access:* Samuels Public Library, M–Sa; Warren County Community Center, daily. ■ *Other services:* Visitors Center, 414 E. Main St., (800) 338-2576, open daily 9–5, hiker's box, WiFi, accepts mail drops. ■ *Shuttles:* A1 Taxi, (540) 636-8294; Yellow Cab, (540) 622-6060; Sharon's Shuttles, (703) 615-5612; Mobile Mike's Shuttles, operates through Jun (540) 539-0509.

National Zoological Park—Next to U.S. 522 is the National Zoological Park Conservation and Re-

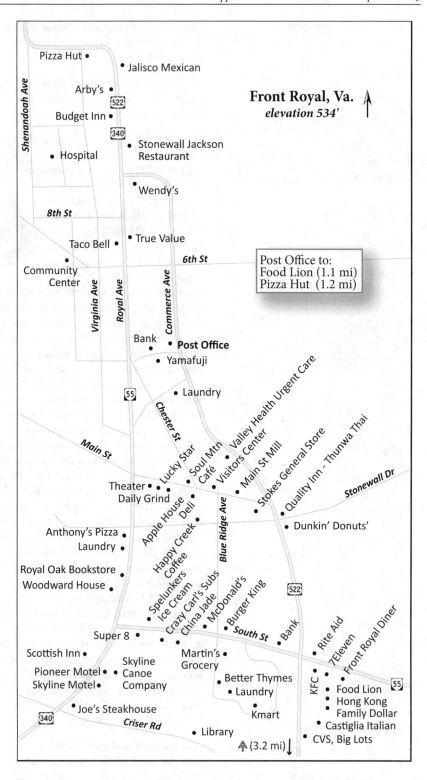

Pizza Hut •

• Jalisco Mexican

Shenandoah Ave

Arby's •

522

Budget Inn •

340

• Hospital

Front Royal, Va.
elevation 534'

• Stonewall Jackson
  Restaurant

• Wendy's

8th St

Taco Bell •   • True Value

6th St

• Community Center

Post Office to:
Food Lion (1.1 mi)
Pizza Hut (1.2 mi)

Virginia Ave

Royal Ave

Commerce Ave

Bank •   • **Post Office**

55   • Yamafuji

• Laundry

Valley Health Urgent Care

Main St

Chester St

Lucky Star •

Soul Mtn Café •   • Visitors Center

• Main St Mill

• Stokes General Store

Quality Inn - Thunwa Thai

Stonewall Dr

Theater •   •
Daily Grind

Apple House Deli •

Anthony's Pizza •
Laundry •

Happy Creek Coffee

Blue Ridge Ave

• Dunkin' Donuts'

Royal Oak Bookstore •
Woodward House •

Spelunkers Ice Cream

Crazy Carl's Subs
China Jade

McDonald's

Burger King

522

Super 8 •

South St

Bank

Scottish Inn •

Martin's Grocery •

Rite Aid
7Eleven
Front Royal Diner

Pioneer Motel •   •
Skyline Motel •

Skyline Canoe Company

• Better Thymes
• Laundry

KFC

• Food Lion   55
• Hong Kong
• Family Dollar
• Castiglia Italian

• Joe's Steakhouse

340

Criser Rd

• Kmart

• Library

🌲 (3.2 mi) ↓

• CVS, Big Lots

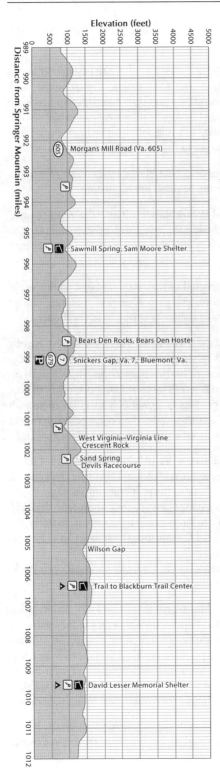

Elevation (feet)

Distance from Springer Mountain (miles)

Morgans Mill Road (Va. 605)

Sawmill Spring, Sam Moore Shelter

Bears Den Rocks, Bears Den Hostel

Snickers Gap, Va. 7,; Bluemont, Va.

West Virginia–Virginia Line
Crescent Rock

Sand Spring
Devils Racecourse

Wilson Gap

Trail to Blackburn Trail Center

David Lesser Memorial Shelter

search Center. On the north side of the highway, the Trail follows one of the center's fences. Exotic animals are sometimes visible.

Jim and Molly Denton Shelter (1991)—Sleeps 8. Privy. Enlarged front porch for extra sleepers. Water source is a spring on the A.T. near the sometimes-functional solar shower.

Va. 638—West 1.1 mile to **Linden, Va. [P.O. ZIP 22642: M–F 8–12 & 1–5, Sa 8–12; (540) 636-9936].** A small outpost on Va. 55, Linden has a post office, farm stand, and convenience store; it's an alternative to hitching into Front Royal to pick up a mail drop. *Groceries:* Monterey Service Station, M–F 4–9, Sa 7–9, Su 8–8; Giving Tree, W–M 10–6; both short-term resupply, hiker friendly, accept credit cards.

West 2.5 miles to ■ *Restaurant:* Apple House, (540) 636-6329, B, fresh-baked pies, doughnuts, sandwiches, BBQ, buffalo burgers, B, deli foods; M 7–5, Tu–Su 7–9; credit cards accepted, ATM. ■ *Groceries:* 7-Eleven (short-term resupply), (540) 635-1899, open 24 hrs., deli sandwiches, ice cream; Apple Mountain Exxon, (540) 636-2960, large store, open 24 hrs., ATM, a must stop for hungry hikers, fresh pies, deli sandwiches.

West 7 miles to Front Royal on Va. 55 (see above).

Va. 55, Manassas Gap—West 1.1 miles into Linden (see above). This is a busier road, parallel to I-66, which leads east to Washington.

Manassas Gap Shelter (1940s/2002)—Sleeps 6. Privy. Bear cables. Water source is a reliable spring near the shelter on a side trail.

Dick's Dome Shelter (1985, rebuilt 2010)—Sleeps 4. Privy. Bear cables. Water source (which hikers should treat) is Whiskey Hollow Creek in front of the shelter.

Sky Meadows State Park Side Trail—Look for the resting bench at path that leads **East** 1.7 miles to the park's visitors center in Mt. Bleak Mansion, built in the 1820s, (540) 592-3556. Now one of Virginia's finest parks, open daily 8–7:30/dusk. Cultural events are scheduled on summer weekends. Water fountain, and soda machine at the visitors center. Hike-in primitive camping (15+ sites) 1.25 mi from A.T., $15PP, on the way to the visitors center. Registration required, (800) 933-7275, and hikers must arrive before 4 p.m. or hike another 2 miles round-trip to/ from registration office.

U.S. 50, U.S. 17/Ashby Gap—**East** 0.8 mile on U.S. 50/17, then 0.3 mile south past barrier on Va. 759 to community of Paris. ■ *Lodging:* The Ashby Inn, (540) 592-3900, restaurant serves L W–Sa 12–2, Su 12–2, D W–Sa 5:30–9, Su 5–8, rooms $160 and up (10% thru-hiker discount), includes B; reservations recommended. ■ *Outfitter:* Appalachian Outdoor Readiness & Essentials, 198 North 21st St., Suite B, Purcellville, VA 20132, (540) 338-2437, <www.appalachianreadiness.com>; full-service outfitter (18.5 miles **east** from A.T.), delivery to points from Ashby Gap to Harpers Ferry.

Rod Hollow Shelter (1986)—Sleeps 8. Privy. Located on a blue-blazed trail. Water source is a spring or the streams just south of the shelter. Dining pavilion rebuilt in 2010.

The "Roller Coaster"—Northbounders leaving the Rod Hollow Shelter will enter the "roller coaster," a 13.5-mile section with ten ascents and descents. Southbounders have just completed their ride. The Virginia corridor is narrow here, leaving Trail crews very little choice other than to route the path up and over each of these viewless and rocky ridges.

Sam Moore Shelter (1990)—Sleeps 6. Privy. Constructed of materials salvaged from the old Keys Gap Shelter. Named for maintainer Sam Moore, who gave 55 years of volunteer service to the A.T. Water source is Sawmill Spring in front of shelter or spring to left of shelter.

Bears Den—Bears Den Rocks provide a fine view of the Shenandoah Valley to the west. Nearby Bears Den Hostel, 0.1 mile off the A.T., owned by ATC, is operated by PATC; 18393 Blue Ridge Mountain Rd., Bluemont, VA 20135; (540) 554-8708, <www.bearsdencenter.org>. Hiker Special includes bunk, shower, laundry, pizza, soda, pint of Ben & Jerry's ice cream for $30; bunk & shower, $17; camping $10 (with shower and indoor-cooking privileges); shower only $3. Hiker room with phone, TV, Internet, and soda is accessible all day with mileage code. The lodge, kitchen, store, and office opens at 5 p.m. daily; check-out is at 9 a.m. Mail drops accepted. Shuttles and slackpacking.

Va. 7, Va. 679/Snickers Gap—**East** 1.7 miles to **Bluemont, Va. [P.O. ZIP 20135: M–F 10–1 & 2–5, Sa 8:30–12; (540) 554-4537]**. Follow Va. 7 **East** 0.9 mile over Snickers Gap to the Snickersville Turnpike (Va. 734) sign, turn right, and continue 0.8 mile to the post office on Va. 760.
     East 1.6 mi to Bluemont General Store, 6:30 a.m.–7 p.m.; (540) 554-2054, short-term resupply, pizza by the slice, sandwiches, ice cream, pies (0.9 mile to Va. 734, turn right, 0.7 mile to store).
     West off Va. 7 on Va. 679 (Pine Grove Rd.) 0.3 mile to *Restaurant:* Horseshoe Curve Restaurant, (540) 554-8291, Tu–Su 7–9. Excellent hiker portions.
     West 0.9 mile to *Restaurant:* Pine Grove Restaurant on Va. 679, (540) 554-8126, open W–Sa 7 a.m.–8 p.m., Su–M 7 a.m.–1 p.m.

Blackburn Trail Center—**East** 0.2 mile *via* either of two blue-blazed trails. This PATC facility, (540) 338-9028, has a free bunkhouse that sleeps 8 with a wood-burning stove, a picnic pavilion with table and benches built in 2002 with ALDHA donations in memory of Edward B. Garvey. Six tentsites and a tent platform are nearby, and a camping area with privy is 0.1 mile north of the main building on the blue-blazed trail. Water available year-round from an outside spigot, and solar-heated shower on front lawn. Donations appreciated. Staffed during the summer months by a caretaker. From the porch on clear days, you might be able to glimpse the Washington Monument or National Cathedral in the distance to the east.

David Lesser Shelter (1994)—Sleeps 6. Privy. A shelter-engineering feat. Water source is a spring located 0.4 mile downhill from the shelter.

West Virginia

Miles from Springer	Fr Last Point	Features	Services	Miles from Katahdin	MAP
1,017.1	3.0	W. Va. 9, Keys Gap (935')	R, P (E–0.3m G; 5.5m H) (W–0.3m G, M, w)	1,172.1	
1,021.0	3.9	Loudoun Heights Trail, Va–W. Va. State Line (1,200')		1,168.2	
1,021.7	0.7	W. Va. 32, Chestnut Hill Road (820')	R	1,167.5	
1,022.4	0.7	U.S. 340, Shenandoah River Bridge (north end) (312') **Charles Town, W. Va. 25414**	R (W–0.1m L; 1.2m C, cl, sh; 5.6m PO, all; 20m all) (E–3.7m H, sh, cl; 20m all)	1,166.8	PATC Map 7
1,022.7	0.3	**Appalachian Trail Conservancy** Side Trail (394') **Harpers Ferry, W. Va. 25425**	W–0.2m ATC, B, w, f (see map)	1,166.5	
1,023.3	0.6	Shenandoah Street; Harpers Ferry National Historical Park (315')	R, P (W–0.1m M, O, f)	1,165.9	
1,023.4	0.1	Potomac River, Goodloe E. Bryon Memorial Footbridge, West Virginia–Maryland State Line (250')		1,165.8	

Camping and fires are prohibited one-half-mile south of Keys Gap to the powerline 1.5 miles north of the gap (W.Va. 9). An established campsite (no water) is 0.4 mile north of the powerline. Camping also is prohibited in Harpers Ferry National Historical Park, which begins on the ridgetop and extends north 3 miles to the Potomac River.

W.Va. 9/Keys Gap—East 0.3 mile to *Groceries:* Sweet Springs Country Store (short-term resupply), 34357 Charles Town Pike, Purcellville, VA 20132; (540) 668-7200, M–Sa 4–11, Su 7–11, deli, ATM, accepts hiker packages.

East 5.5 miles to Stoney Brook Organic Farm & Hostel, operated by the Twelve Tribes Spiritual Community, (540) 668-9067, 37091 Charles Town Pike, Hillsboro, VA 20132. Work for stay, meals, shower, laundry, mail drops. Pick-up and drop-off from Bears Den, Blackburn Trail Center, Keys Gap, Harpers Ferry. Grocery store and outfitter nearby in Purcellville.

West 0.3 mile on Old W.Va. 9 to ■ *Groceries:* Torlone Mini-Mart (short-term resupply), (304) 725-0916, M–Th 8–9, F–Sa 8–10, Su 8–8, shirts and shoes required. ■ *Restaurant:* Torlone Pizza, Pasta & Subs, (304) 728-4450, ATM, open M–Th 11–9, F–Sa 11–10, Su 11–8.

Harpers Ferry National Historical Park—On June 30, 1944, President Franklin D. Roosevelt signed legislation designating part of the town a national monument. Gradual land acquisition in the town and surrounding ridges led to designation as a national historical park in 1963. It saw extensive Civil War action, especially before the bloody battle at nearby Antietam, Md., but is probably best known for the raid of John Brown, an abolitionist from Kansas who attempted to capture the federal arsenal here in 1859. The arsenal was to be the staging point for a slave uprising. A U.S. colonel named Robert E. Lee crushed the raid in less than 36 hours, and historians point to the event as a steppingstone to the war, which began 16 months after Brown was hanged for treason in nearby Charles Town. But, the history of Harpers Ferry is more than one event, one date, or one individu-

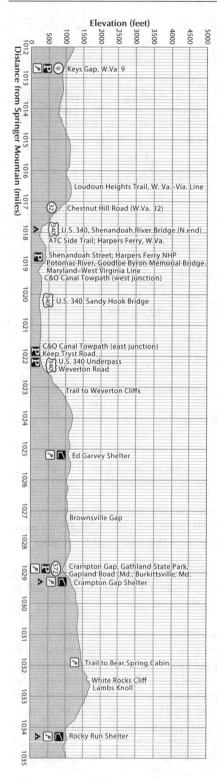

Elevation (feet)

Distance from Springer Mountain (miles)

Keys Gap, W.Va. 9

Loudoun Heights Trail, W. Va.-Via. Line

Chestnut Hill Road (W.Va. 32)

U.S. 340, Shenandoah River Bridge (N end)
ATC Side Trail; Harpers Ferry, W.Va.

Shenandoah Street; Harpers Ferry NHP
Potomac River, Goodloe Byron Memorial Bridge;
Maryland–West Virginia Line
C&O Canal Towpath (west junction)

U.S. 340; Sandy Hook Bridge

C&O Canal Towpath (east junction)
Keep Tryst Road
U.S. 340 Underpass
Weverton Road

Trail to Weverton Cliffs

Ed Garvey Shelter

Brownsville Gap

Crampton Gap, Gathland State Park,
Gapland Road (Md.; Burkittsville, Md.
Crampton Gap Shelter

Trail to Bear Spring Cabin

White Rocks Cliff
Lambs Knoll

Rocky Run Shelter

al. It is multilayered, involving a diverse number of people and events that influenced the course of American history. Harpers Ferry also witnessed the first successful application of interchangeable manufacture, the arrival of the first successful American railroad, the largest surrender of federal troops during the Civil War, the education of former slaves in one of the earliest integrated schools in the United States, and the first organized civil rights movement in the country. The park's visitors center (west of town along U.S. 340) offers parking and a free shuttle to the historic district. *Note: Hikers parking in lot must register at the visitors center, open 8–5.* Parking-lot gates open at 8, close at dusk. Entrance fee is $6 per vehicle for up to 2 weeks. Today, the Park Service runs many interpretive exhibits in renovated buildings dating back to the mid-19th century. More information on the historic town is available at ATC headquarters, (304) 535-6331, as well as the park's visitors center.

U.S. 340/Shenandoah River—East 20 miles to Frederick, Md., with all services, including Quality Shoe Service, 319 North Market St., (301) 695-9255, for boot repair, and The Trail House, an outfitter, 17 South Market St., (301) 694-8448. *Traffic can be extremely heavy at this Trailhead, and it is neither safe nor legal to hitchhike here; local police often are nearby, watching for speeders.*

Signs on U.S. 340 say "Appalachian Trail Visitor Center"—that's the ATC visitors center and headquarters.

West 0.1 mile to *Lodging:* EconoLodge, (304) 535-6391, ask for hiker rate, usually full on holiday weekends, WiFi, no pets, expanded continental B, laundry, refrigerator and microwave in rooms.

West 1.2 miles to ■ *Camping:* Harpers Ferry KOA (short-term resupply), (304) 535-6895, cabins $67–$103, tentsites $30–$41 for first 2 people and $5.50EAP, lodges $131.50–$172.50, shower only $5, laundry, campstore, snack bar, pizzeria, pool, leashed pets welcome $1.50, except Rottweillers, pit bulls, or Dobermans. Ask for hiker discount. ■ *Lodging and Restaurant:* Quality Hotel Conference Center, 4328 William L. Wilson Freeway (U.S. 340), Harpers Ferry, WV 25425, (304) 535-6302, bar and grill, call for rates, microwave and refrigerator in rooms, some rooms with Jacuzzi,

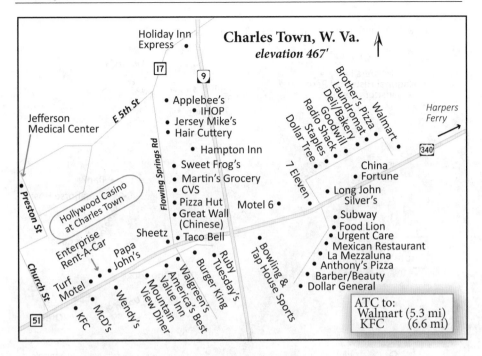

Charles Town, W. Va.
elevation 467'

Holiday Inn Express
17
9
Jefferson Medical Center
E 5th St
• Applebee's
• IHOP
• Jersey Mike's
• Hair Cuttery
• Hampton Inn
• Sweet Frog's
• Martin's Grocery
• CVS
• Pizza Hut   Motel 6 •
• Great Wall
(Chinese)
• Taco Bell

Flowing Springs Rd

Hollywood Casino at Charles Town

Preston St

Enterprise Rent-A-Car
Papa John's
Sheetz
Turf Motel •
Church St
51
KFC
McD's
Wendy's
Mountain View Diner
America's Best Value Inn
Walgreen's
Burger King
Ruby Tuesday's

Bowling & Tap House Sports

7 Eleven

Brother's Pizza
Laundromat
Deli/Bakery
Radio Shack
Goodwill
Staples
Walmart
Dollar Tree

Harpers Ferry

340

China
• Fortune
• Long John
Silver's
• Subway
• Food Lion
• Urgent Care
• Mexican Restaurant
• La Mezzaluna
• Anthony's Pizza
• Barber/Beauty
• Dollar General

ATC to:
Walmart (5.3 mi)
KFC   (6.6 mi)

WiFi with computer access for hikers, pets allowed in certain rooms, laundry, indoor pool, fitness center, FedEx and postal services available, will hold and mail out packages for guests, long-term parking for guests. Vista Tavern, L/D, Su–Th 12–1, F–Sa 12–1 a.m.

East 3.7 miles to *Hostel:* Harpers Ferry Hostel, Keep Tryst Rd., Sandy Hook/Knoxville, Md. (see next chapter for details).

West 5.6 miles to **Charles Town, W.Va. [P.O. ZIP 25414: M–F 8:30–5, Sa 9–12:30; (304) 725-2421].**
■ *Lodging:* Motel 6, (304) 725-1402, Su–Th $50–$56, F–Sa $60–$66, pets okay with prior approval and deposit; Turf Motel, (304) 725-2081, <www.turfmotel.com>, $89 weekdays, $135 weekends, $10EAP, dogs okay at $50 per day; America's Best Value Inn, (304) 725-2041, prices vary, weekdays $51–$65 weekends $65–$85, dogs $20PD ($100 deposit); Holiday Inn Express, (304) 725-1330; Hampton Inn, (304) 725-2200. ■ *Groceries:* Super Walmart; Food Lion Super Market; 7-Eleven; Sheetz; Aldi Supermarket, M–Sa 9–8, Su 10–6; Martin's, 24/7. ■ *Other services:* Jefferson Memorial Hospital, (304)-728-1600; Jefferson Urgent Care, M–F 9–7, Sa–Su & holidays 9–5, (304) 728-8533; Kams Taxi, (304) 283-5886; Community Taxi Service, LLC, (304) 725-3794.

West 20 miles (U.S. 340 to W.Va. 9) to Martinsburg, W.Va., with all services, including movie theaters, malls, as well as many restaurants. For bus service to those towns, see Harpers Ferry entry below.

Note: Hitchhiking is illegal on state-maintained roads in West Virginia. That includes U.S. 340 and the main street through Harpers Ferry and adjacent Bolivar.

Harpers Ferry, W.Va. [P.O. ZIP 25425: M–F 9–4 , Sa 9–12; (304) 535-2479]. The post office and most services are available above the old town *via* the 0.2-mile blue-blazed trail to ATC headquarters (see below). The A.T. itself leads through the historic district at the bottom of the hill along the riverfronts, with museums, stores, and restaurants. Many businesses in the

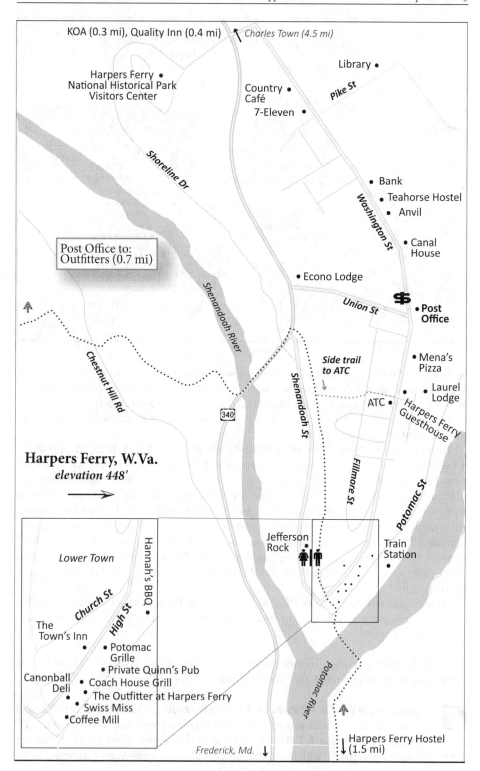

KOA (0.3 mi), Quality Inn (0.4 mi)   ↑ *Charles Town (4.5 mi)*

Library •

Harpers Ferry •
National Historical Park
Visitors Center

Country •
Café
7-Eleven •

Pike St

Shoreline Dr

• Bank
• Teahorse Hostel
• Anvil

Washington St

• Canal
House

Post Office to:
Outfitters (0.7 mi)

Shenandoah River

• Econo Lodge

Union St   💲 • **Post
Office**

Side trail
to ATC   • Mena's
Pizza

Chestnut Hill Rd

Shenandoah St

340

ATC •   • Laurel
Lodge

Harpers Ferry
Guesthouse

Harpers Ferry, W.Va.
elevation 448'

→

Fillmore St

Lower Town

Hannah's BBQ •

Jefferson
Rock

Train
Station

Potomac St

Church St

High St

The
Town's Inn

• Potomac
Grille

• Private Quinn's Pub

Canonball
Deli

• Coach House Grill

• The Outfitter at Harpers Ferry

• Swiss Miss

• Coffee Mill

Potomac River

↑

Frederick, Md. ↓   Harpers Ferry Hostel
↓ (1.5 mi)

historic district are closed in the winter or open only on weekends then. The national historical park is open 7 days a week year-round, but its visitors center closes Thanksgiving, Christmas, and New Year's Day. ■ *Hostel:* Teahorse Hostel, 1312 W. Washington St., (304) 535-6848, <www.teahorsehostel. com>, closed Nov to Feb, located 0.5 mile **west** of ATC, $33/night includes waffle B, fully equipped kitchen, WiFi, laundry $6, shuttles/slacking. *See listing in Maryland for Harpers Ferry Hostel.* ■ *Lodging:* The Town's Inn, (304) 932-0677, <info@ thetownsinn.com>, 179 High St., right in historic lower town, private rooms (ask for rates), microwave, fridge, WiFi, no pets, laundry $5, shuttles $1/mile; Laurel Lodge, 844 E. Ridge St., (304) 535-2886, <www.laurellodge.com>, $135–$165; the Ledge House B&B, (877) 468-4236, may be able to offer hiker discounts on weekdays, call for availability. Information on several other B&Bs can be found at <www.historicharpersferry.com> or at ATC. ■ *Groceries:* The Outfitter at Harpers Ferry (short-term resupply, including freeze-dried food and hiker favorites), 0.5 mile **east** of ATC, open daily 10–6 except Jan–Feb when it's F–Su only; Town's Inn, open daily 6–10, wide variety of healthy snacks, ice cream, toiletries, denatured alcohol; 7-11 convenience store (short-term resupply), 1 mile **west** of ATC; supermarkets and Walmart (long-term resupply) in Charles Town, 5 miles **west**. ■ *Restaurants.* **West** of ATC: 0.1 mile, Mena's Pizzeria & Italian Restaurant, L/D, closed M, T–Th 11–9, F–Sa 11–10, Su 12–9; 0.3 mile, Canal House Café, closed W, L/D M–F; 0.5 mile, Anvil Restaurant, W–Su 11–9; 1 mile, Country Café, B/L. **East** of ATC in lower town: The Town's Inn Restaurant, (304) 535-1860, 6 a.m.–10 p.m. daily, B/L/D; Potomac Grille, M–Th 11–6, F–Sa 11–9, Su 11–8; Cannonball Deli, hiker discounts; Hannah's Train Depot BBQ & Seafood, 20% hiker discount; many others. ■ *Outfitter:* The Outfitter at Harpers Ferry, 106 Potomac St., (304) 535-2087 or (888) 535-2087, <www.theoutfitteratharpersferry.com>, full-service outfitter, shuttle referrals, open daily 10–6, Jan–Feb F–Su only. ■ *Internet access:* Harpers Ferry/Bolivar Library, (304) 535-2301, M, Tu, F, Sa 10–5:30, W, Th 10–8; ATC. ■ *Other services:* ATC maintains a list of supporters in its A.T. Community program that provide special sercies or discounts for hikers and ATC members. Westwind Potters in lower town will store backpacks for hikers during the day, offers 10% discounts to ATC members. Banks with ATM; dentist; Caring Hands Chiropractic and Advanced Massage Therapy, Dr. Jenny Foster, a hiker (located near Middletown, Md.), (301) 371-3922, call ahead for possible pick-up (schedule permitting) at Harpers Ferry Hostel or Old South Mountain Inn; bicycle rental, repair, and supplies at The Outfitter at Harpers Ferry, (304) 535-2296. Rafting, tubing, canoeing, fishing, and horseback riding opportunities nearby; check <www.historicharpersferry.com>. ■ *Bus service:* Pan Tran bus to Charles Town or Martinsburg operates M–F; flag the bus across the street from the ATC office or anywhere along the main Washington/High St. The charge is $2.50 one-way. Bus leaves town at 6:45 a.m., 9:05 a.m., 10:40 a.m., 1:35 p.m., 3:05 p.m., 4:45 p.m., 7:30 p.m. Leaves Walmart in Charles Town for Harpers Ferry at 8:50 a.m., 10:25 a.m., 1:20 p.m., 2:50 p.m., 4:30 p.m. and 7:15 p.m. No dogs; packs OK unless driver believes one may be suspicious. Times are subject to change.

Appalachian Trail Conservancy (ATC)—Reached *via* 0.2-mile blue-blazed trail 0.3 mile north of the junction of U.S. 340 and Shenandoah Street, before northbounders reach the historic section of Harpers Ferry; at the corner of Washington Street and Storer College Place.

ATC was formed in 1925 by private citizens to make the dream of an Appalachian Trail a reality. After the initial Trail route was pieced together in 1937 (much of it on roads and across private land), ATC continued to work to identify better routes for the Trail and worked with Congress, the National Park Service, the U.S. Forest Service, states, and others to ensure a continuously protected corridor. Today, ATC is the primary organization responsible for the stewardship of the footpath and 250,000 acres of public land surrounding it. Working with more than 6,000 volunteers (mostly in 31 affiliated local clubs) and multiple public agencies, ATC leads the efforts to improve the footpath, protect the plants and animals along the Trail (and the experience of hiking it), engage communities along the A.T. to support it, and guard against encroachments. Much of the behind-the-scenes work that continues to makes the A.T. experience possible takes place out of sight in offices upstairs and the connected annex. The single largest source of ATC's funding is individual membership dues and small contributions. If you're not already an ATC member, consider joining here to help support continued protection of the Trail.

ATC publications and products are for sale at the information/visitors center. New exhibits share a room with an unique, 10-foot-long raised-relief map of the A.T. Volunteers or staffers Dave Tarasevich (Poptart of 2002) and Laurie Potteiger (Mountain Laurel of 1987) can answer your Trail questions. The office accepts donations for Coleman fuel and denatured alcohol and holds packages sent USPS to P.O. Box 807 or FedEx and UPS to 799 Washington St., Harpers Ferry, WV 25425. Thru- and section-hikers are encouraged to stop at ATC headquarters to sign the register and have their picture taken to be counted among the class of 2015. The same photo can be purchased as a postcard for $1 (postage and tax included; first one free for ATC members). Volunteers are needed periodically at headquarters and almost always at the sales-distribution center 11 miles away.

The ATC Visitors Center, (304) 535-6331, is open daily 9–5 except Thanksgiving, Christmas, and New Year's Day. Frost-free faucet is on west (Storer College Place) side of building. Drinks for sale inside. Bench and picnic tables in side yard. Phone, WiFi, and Internet access for hikers. Ask for ATC's often-updated "Guide to Harpers Ferry Hiker Services," with more details on area services. Driving directions are available at <www.appalachiantrail.org/locations>.

Jefferson Rock—The white blazes take you past this Harpers Ferry viewpoint that overlooks the confluence of the Potomac and Shenandoah rivers. Named in honor of Thomas Jefferson, who was inspired by the beautiful view in 1783. Several large slabs of shale originally rested naturally but not securely atop each other. "Jefferson Rock" now rests securely on a set of short pillars erected in the 1850s.

Trains to Washington, D.C.—Amtrak, (800) USA-RAIL, <www.amtrak.com>: Train No. 30 (Capitol Limited) is scheduled to depart Harpers Ferry at 10:55 a.m. (although it can be 2 or more hours late) and to arrive at D.C.'s Union Station at 12:40 p.m. Train No. 29 is scheduled to leave D.C. at 4:05 p.m., arriving in Harpers Ferry at 5:16 p.m. 7 days a week Coach fares are $11–$20 one way (cost may be more if coach is not available). Fares and schedules subject to change. *Harpers Ferry station is not staffed.* Reservations are required; backpacks allowed, but not bikes. Maryland Rail Commuter Service (MARC), [(800) 325-7245 outside local calling area; others call (301) 834-8360; <www.mtamaryland.com>]: Three scheduled commuter trains on the Brunswick line leave Harpers Ferry for D.C. on weekdays. They depart at 5:25 a.m., 5:50 a.m. and 6:50 a.m., arriving at 7:09 a.m., 7:35 a.m. and 8:32 a.m. Five trains leave D.C. for Harpers Ferry on weekdays. They depart at 3:30 p.m., 4:25 p.m., 5:40 p.m., 6:20 p.m., and 7:25 p.m. and arrive at 5:10 p.m., 6:05 p.m., 7:18 p.m., 7:54 p.m., and 9 p.m. Fares are $11 one way, seats are not reserved, and tickets must be purchased on board (cash only).

Maryland

Miles from Springer	Fr Last Point	Features	Services	Miles from Katahdin	M A P
1,023.4	0.1	Potomac River, Goodloe E. Bryon Memorial Footbridge, West Virginia–Maryland State Line(250')		1,165.8	
1,023.6	0.2	C & O Canal Towpath mp 60.2 (A.T. west jct.) (290')	W–2.7m C, w (C&O campsite Huckleberry Hill)	1,165.6	
1,024.7	1.1	U.S. 340, Sandy Hook Bridge above (290')	R	1,164.5	
1,026.2	1.5	C & O Canal Towpath mp 58 (A.T. east jct.) (290'), Lockhouse 38		1,163.0	
1,026.3	0.1	Keep Tryst Road; Railroad tracks (320')	R, P (E–2.5m G, M) (W–1.1m H, g, L, M,cl, sh, f)	1,162.9	
1,026.5	0.2	U.S. 340 (400')...underpass	R	1,162.7	
1,026.7	0.2	Weverton Road (420')	R, P	1,162.5	
1,027.6	0.9	Weverton Cliffs Trail (780')...Potomac River view		1,161.6	
1,029.7	2.1	**Ed Garvey Shelter** (1,100')...15.8mS; 4.5mN	E–0.1m S; 0.5m w	1,159.5	
1,031.7	2.0	Brownsville Gap (1,140')...dirt road		1,157.5	
1,033.4	1.7	Gapland Road, Md. 572 (950') Gathland State Park, Crampton Gap	R, P, w (W–0.4m C, g, f)	1,155.8	PATC Map 5-6
1,033.8	0.4	**Crampton Gap Shelter** (1,000') ...4.5mS; 5.5mN	E–0.3m S, C, w	1,155.4	
1,036.4	2.6	Trail to Bear Spring Cabin (locked) (1,480')	W–0.5mw	1,152.8	
1,037.0	0.6	White Rocks Cliff (1,500')...view		1,152.2	
1,037.2	0.2	Lamb's Knoll (1,600')...antenna tower		1,152.0	
1,038.3	1.1	Tower Road (1,300')	R	1,150.9	
1,038.8	0.5	**Rocky Run Shelter** (970')...5.5mS; 7.8mN	W–0.2m S, C, w	1,150.4	
1,039.8	1.0	Reno Monument Road (910')	R, P (E–2m M)	1,149.4	
1,040.6	0.8	Dahlgren Backpacker Campground (980')	C, sh, w	1,148.6	
1,040.8	0.2	U.S. Alt. 40, Turners Gap (1,000') **Boonsboro, Md. 21713**	R, P, M (W–2.4m PO, M, D, V, cl; 3.8m G)	1,148.4	
1,042.2	1.4	Monument Road (1,350')	R	1,147.0	
1,042.4	0.2	Washington Monument Road (1,400')	R, P, w	1,146.8	
1,042.8	0.4	Washington Monument (1,500')...view	R, P	1,146.4	
1,044.9	2.1	Boonsboro Mountain Road (1,300')	R, P	1,144.3	
1,045.2	0.3	Bartman Hill Trail to Greenbrier State Park (1,380')	W–0.6m C, sh, w	1,144.0	
1,045.7	0.5	U.S. 40, 1-70 Footbridge (northend), Blue Blaze to Greenbrier State Park (1,200')	R, P (W–1.4m C, w)	1,143.5	
1,046.3	0.6	**Pine Knob Shelter** (1,360')...7.8mS; 8.3mN	W–0.1m S, C, w	1,142.9	

Miles from Springer	Fr Last Point	Features	Services	Miles from Katahdin	M A P
1,047.9	1.6	Trail to Annapolis Rock (1,820')	W–0.2m C; 0.4m w	1,141.3	
1,048.9	1.0	Black Rock Cliffs (1,800')		1,140.3	
1,049.5	0.6	Pogo Memorial Campsite (1,500')	C, w (W–0.9m P)	1,139.7	
1,054.3	4.8	Md. 17, Wolfsville Road (1,400') **Smithsburg, Md. 21783**	R, P (W–1.8m G, D, V; 2.4m PO, G, M, D, cl; 2.7m G, M, f)	1,134.9	
1,054.5	0.2	**Ensign Cowall Shelter** (1,430')...*8.3mS; 5.1mN*	S, C, w	1,134.7	
1,055.8	1.3	Md. 77, Foxville Road (1,450')	R	1,133.4	
1,057.0	1.2	Spring (1,300')	w	1,132.2	
1,057.6	0.6	Warner Gap Road (1,150')	R, P, w	1,131.6	
1,058.4	0.8	Md. 491, Raven Rock Hollow (1,190')	R	1,130.8	
1,059.4	1.0	**Raven Rock Shelter** (1,480')...*5.1mS; 9.8mN*	(E–0.1m w) (W–0.2m S, C)	1,129.8	
1,061.2	1.8	Trail to High Rock (1,950')...*view*	R, P	1,128.0	
1,064.1	2.9	Pen Mar County Park (1,300')...*picnic area* **Cascade, Md. 21719 Rouzerville, Pa. 17250**	R, w (E–1.4m PO, G, L, M, f) (W–1.8m PO, G, M, f)	1,125.1	
1,064.3	0.2	Mason–Dixon Line (1,250') Maryland–Pennsylvania State Line	R	1,124.9	

PATC Map 5-6

Overnight camping in Maryland is allowed only at designated campsites: Ed Garvey Shelter, Crampton Gap Shelter, Rocky Run Shelters, Dahlgren Back Pack Campground, Pine Knob Shelter, Annapolis Rocks, Pogo Memorial Campsite, Ensign Cowall Shelter, and Raven Rocks Shelter. Please obey camping regulations in this heavily used section. Alcoholic beverages are prohibited on all Appalachian Trail lands in Maryland. Illegal activity should be reported to Park Watch, (800) 825-7275.

This section boasts easy terrain, the C & O Canal towpath along the Potomac River, a free on-trail hot-water shower, Civil War history, the War Correspondents Monument, the first monument to George Washington, and the Mason-Dixon line.

C&O Canal Towpath—The southernmost 2.8 miles of the Trail in Maryland follow this path from which until 1924 mules towed barges, between what's left of the canal on one side and the Potomac River on the other. Stretching 185 miles from Washington, D.C., to Cumberland, Md., it was rescued from highway development by a protest hike led by Supreme Court Justice William O. Douglas, an A.T. 2,000-miler. Now, it is part of a national historical park, accessible to both hikers and bicyclists. Blazes are scarce, but the points at which the Trail enters and leaves it are hard to miss. The Maryland state line is the southern shore of the Potomac, which you cross above when leaving Harpers Ferry National Historical Park.

Keep Tryst Road—East 2.5 mile to Brunswick, Md., via U.S. 340 and Md. 478 at Knoxville exit or stay on towpath. ■ *Groceries:* Super Fresh, (301) 834-9895. ■ *Restaurants:* Beans in the Belfry, (301) 834-7178; Potomac Grill, (301)969-0548; A Better Choice Bakery, (301) 969-0341; Kings Pizza, (301) 834-9999; El Sloppy Tacos, (301) 834-3311; Pacific Café, (301)

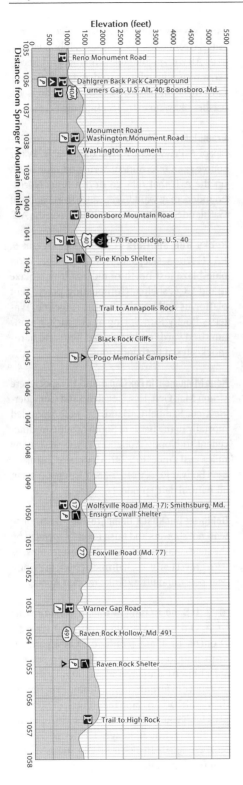

Elevation (feet)

Distance from Springer Mountain (miles)

Reno Monument Road

Dahlgren Back Pack Campground
Turners Gap, U.S. Alt. 40; Boonsboro, Md.

Monument Road
Washington Monument Road
Washington Monument

Boonsboro Mountain Road

I-70 Footbridge, U.S. 40

Pine Knob Shelter

Trail to Annapolis Rock

Black Rock Cliffs

Pogo Memorial Campsite

Wolfsville Road (Md. 17); Smithsburg, Md.
Ensign Cowall Shelter

Foxville Road (Md. 77)

Warner Gap Road

Raven Rock Hollow, Md. 491

Raven Rock Shelter

Trail to High Rock

834-3338. ■ *Internet access:* library, 915 N.
Maple Ave., (301) 600-7250, open M–Th
10:30–8, Sa 10–5, closed F.

West 1.1 mile to (left on Sandy Hook Road)
Hostel: Harpers Ferry Hostel (Hostelling International), 19123 Sandy Hook Rd., Knoxville,
MD 21758-1330; (301) 834-7652; open Apr 15–Dec
1; bunks start at $18PP, private rooms $55, includes make-your-own pancake B, Internet/
WiFi, small store w/snacks, coin-op laundry;
tenting $6PP if thru-hiking ($10 otherwise);
parking $5 per day w/o stay. Vending machine
on porch. Mail drops for hikers. ■ *Lodging:*
Knight's Inn, (301) 660-3580, $60S, $70D, continental B. ■ *Groceries:* Hillside Station, (301)
834-5300; deli hot food, pizza, ice cream, hot
wings; ATM; M–F 5 a.m.–9 p.m., Sa 6–9, Su 7–9.
■ *Other services:* River and Trails Outfitters,
(888) 446-7529 or (301) 695-5177, <www.river-
trail.com>, 604 Valley Rd., Knoxville; canoe,
kayak, tube, and bike rentals, shuttles for C&O
Canal, A.T., and Potomac and Shenandoah
rivers. ■ *Shuttles:* Hostelhiker.com, (202) 670-
6323, from Thornton Gap, Va., in SNP to Pen
Mar Park at Pa. line; also to D.C., Baltimore, *etc.*

Ed Garvey Shelter (2001)—Sleeps 12. Composting privy. Two tentsites north and south of
shelter. Water source is found at the end of a
0.5-mile, steep side trail in front of the shelter.

Gathland State Park—Located in Crampton
Gap, the state-run facility has water (frost-free
faucet), restroom (with electrical outlet), covered picnic pavilion, parking. No camping.
Two museums—Civil War and War Correspondent—are open weekdays 9–5 Jun–Sep
and weekends in Oct. The War Correspondents Monument is the only one of its kind in
the country. Constructed in 1896, it stands 50
feet high, 40 feet broad, with plaques relating
Battle of South Mountain history. Southbounders may want to pick up water here
before heading to Ed Garvey Shelter.

Gapland Road—West 0.4 mile on Gapland Rd., right on Townsend Rd. to
Camping: Maple Tree Campground, 20716
Townsend Rd., Gapland, MD 21779, (301) 432-

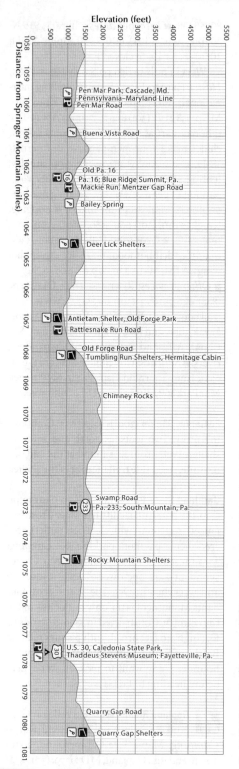

Elevation (feet)

Distance from Springer Mountain (miles)

Pen Mar Park; Cascade, Md.
Pennsylvania–Maryland Line
Pen Mar Road

Buena Vista Road

Old Pa. 16
Pa. 16; Blue Ridge Summit, Pa.
Mackie Run; Mentzer Gap Road

Bailey Spring

Deer Lick Shelters

Antietam Shelter, Old Forge Park
Rattlesnake Run Road

Old Forge Road
Tumbling Run Shelters, Hermitage Cabin

Chimney Rocks

Swamp Road
Pa. 233; South Mountain, Pa.

Rocky Mountain Shelters

U.S. 30, Caledonia State Park,
Thaddeus Stevens Museum; Fayetteville, Pa.

Quarry Gap Road

Quarry Gap Shelters

5585, <www.thetreehousecamp.com>; tentsites, treehouses, ask for rates; Hobbit House, $138. All with picnic table, fire ring, grill. Short-term resupply; white gas, denatured alcohol, canisters; mail drops accepted; dogs on leashes okay, no extra fee; Internet access.

Crampton Gap Shelter (built by CCC, 1941)—Sleeps 6. Privy, deck with cooking table. Water source is an intermittent spring 0.1 mile south on the A.T. that may go dry in June. North-bounders may want to get water from faucet at Gathland State Park, 0.25 mile south on the A.T.

Rocky Run Shelters (CCC–1941, sleeps 6; PATC–2008. sleeps 16)—Newer shelter is on blue-blaze just north of old-road/blue-blaze to old CCC shelter. Composting privy. Tent platforms and benches on the ridgeline. Water is Rocky Run Spring at old shelter a few hundred yards on blue-blaze. Tent and hammock sites at both locations.

Reno Monument in Fox Gap marks the spot where Union Maj. Gen. Jesse Lee Reno and Confederate Gen. Samuel Garland, Jr., were wounded mortally in the Battle of South Mountain, antecedent to bloody Antietam to the west a few miles. **East** 2 miles to South Mountain Creamery, 8305 Bolivar Rd., (301) 371-8665, ice cream, fresh all-natural dairy products.

Dahlgren Backpack Campground—Bathhouse with hot showers and flush toilets. Operated by the state at no charge, the bathhouse, campsites with gravel tentpads, hammock sites, fire rings, bear poles, and utility sink are open Apr–Oct.

U.S. 40-A/Turners Gap. ■ *Restaurant:* Old South Mountain Inn, (301) 432-6155, D opens Tu–F at 5 p.m. and Sa at 4 p.m., Su brunch 10:30–2, Su D 2–close. Hikers staying at Dahlgren Campground can literally shower and shave before an elegant dining experience, then walk back to camp in minutes. (Take your pack with you.) ■ *Other services:* chiropractic and therapeutic massage, Dr. Jenny Foster, (301) 371-3922, can pick up at Old South Mountain Inn, schedule permitting.

West 2.4 miles to **Boonsboro, Md. [P.O. ZIP 21713: M–F 9–1 & 2–5, Sa 9–12; (301) 432-6861].**
■ *Groceries:* Cronise Market Place (short-term resupply), (301) 432-7377, M–F 10–7, Sa 9–7, Su 10–6. ■ *Restaurants:* Crawford Confectionery (candy & sweets); Subway; Mountainside Deli, (301) 432-6700; Vesta Pizzera & Restaurant, (301) 432-6166, will deliver to parking lot at South Mountain Inn; Potomac Street Creamery ice-cream shop; Kristi's Bakery and Café, (301) 799-7111, WiFi, hot and cold food; Dan's Tap House Restaurant. ■ *Internet access:* library, (301) 432-5723, M–F 10–7, Sa 10–2; Turn the Page Bookstore Café, (301) 432-4588, with A.T. books and maps and expresso coffee bar. ■ *Other services:* Marcy's Laundry, (301) 491-5849, 6 a.m–9:30 p.m. daily; banks with ATM; barber shop; doctor; dentist; veterinarian; and pharmacy.

West 3.8 miles to *Groceries:* Weis Supermarket & Pharmacy (long-term resupply), (301) 432-3950.

Washington Monument State Park—A state park built around the first monument to George Washington. The bottle-shaped structure is more modest than the big one in Washington, D.C., but impressive for small-town Marylanders in 1827. When open, the observation deck on top provides views of the surrounding countryside. South of the monument, on the A.T., are park facilities with picnic shelters, and restroom near the museum. Museum is open 9 a.m–5 p.m. daily May–Sept, weekends only Apr and Oct. No camping permitted in the park. Frost-free faucet on trail above main parking lot. Overnight parking permitted after registration at kiosk.

 U.S. 40/Greenbrier State Park—North of the I-70 footbridge, the A.T. crosses U.S. 40. **West** 0.4 mile to the park entrance.

West 1.4 miles to *Camping:* Greenbrier State Park, (301) 791-4767, open Apr–Oct, pets on leash allowed on some sites. Visitors center, restroom with showers, concession stand, paddle-boat rental and swimming in Greenbrier Lake. Tentsites with hot showers $26. Reservations recommended on the weekends; two-night minimum. Walk-in hikers may be allowed a one-night stay if a site is available; day-use-only fee may apply; access *via* Bartman Hill Trail

Pine Knob Shelter (1939)—Sleeps 5. Privy. Shelter is located on a blue-blazed trail. Tent and hammock sites. Water source is a piped spring beside the shelter.

Annapolis Rock Campsite—13 tentsites and two privies at this popular area; caretaker on site. Tentsites are near an outstanding overlook popular with climbers. No fires. Spring location is marked.

Pogo Memorial Campsite—The campsite is immediately east of the Trail, with a spring 30 yards on a blue-blazed trail to the west.

 Md. 17/Wolfsville Road—**West** 1.7 miles on Wolfsville Road and then left 0.1 mile on Md. 64 to a small shopping center. ■ *Groceries:* Phil & Jerry's Meats & More (short-term resupply), (301) 824-3750, M–Th 8–6, F–Sa 8–8; Dollar General Store. ■ *Other services:* veterinarian, (301) 416-0888; medical clinic, (301) 824-3343; pharmacy, (301) 824-3900; two banks with ATM, near shopping center.

West 2.0 miles *via* Wolfsville Road and Md. 77 to **Smithsburg, Md. [P.O. ZIP 21783: M–F 8:30–1 & 2–4:30, Sa 8:30–12; (301) 824-2828].** ■ *Groceries:* Smithsburg Market, (303) 824-2171, M–Sa 8–8, Su 10–8. ■ *Restaurants:* Vince's New York Pizza, (301) 824-3939; Dixie Eatery, (301) 824-5224, WiFi; The Wolfe's Den. ■ *Internet access:* library, Tu 12–9, M, W, Th–F 10–7, Sa 10–2. ■ *Other services:* coin laundry; dentist; and banks with ATM.

West 1.7 miles *via* Wolfsville Road and south on Md. 64 1.0 mile to ■ *Groceries:* Food Lion, (301) 824-7011; Mountain Valley Orchard, (301) 824-7902. ■ *Restaurants:* Carmine's Italian Restaurant; China 88; Subway; Debbie's Soft Serve; Rocky's New York Pizza. ■ *Other services:* Rite Aid, (301) 824-2211; Ace Hardware, fuel and camping supplies.

Ensign Cowall Shelter (1999)—Sleeps 8. Privy. Five tent pads, hammock sites, picnic table, fire ring with grill, bear pole. Water source is a boxed spring south of the shelter 0.2 mile on the A.T.

Raven Rock Shelter (2010)— Sleeps 16. Composting privy. Bear cables. Tent and hammock sites, picnic table. Water source is a spring 200 feet east of the A.T. (on trail to former Devils Racecourse Shelter).

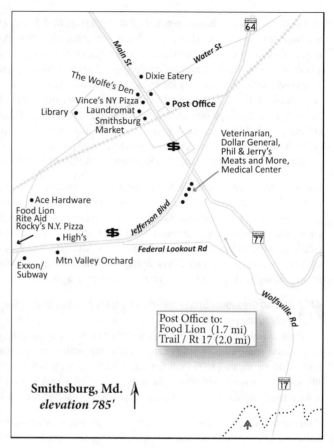

Pen Mar County Park— Open from the first Su in May to the last Su in Oct. No camping in the park (campsite at Falls Creek 0.9 mile north). Dogs must be leashed and are allowed only on the A.T. proper (pack out poop). The pavilion provides views of the countryside to the west. Seasonal snack bar. Museum (pay phone inside) open Sa and Su. Restroom locked in the evening. No alcohol permitted in the park. Bobby D's, (717) 762-0388; Rocky's New York Pizza, (301) 241-3470; and Brother's Pizza, (717) 765-8808, will deliver food from menus to park.

    East 1.4 miles to the small community of **Cascade, Md. [P.O. ZIP 21719: M–F 8–1 & 2–5, Sa 8–12; (301) 241-3403].** *See map.* To reach town from the park entrance, turn left on High Rock Road to Pen-Mar Road, go straight at intersection, pass under a railroad trestle, turn right at the stop sign onto Md. 550. To reach the post office, continue 0.1 mile, and turn left on Ft. Ritchie Road across from entrance to former Ft. Ritchie. ■ *Lodging:* Sunflower Cottage AirBnB, 25210 Elhuff Ct.; (240) 469-7609, <www.airbnb.com/rooms/423854>; cottage-style home with rooms to rent, $25PP/night includes B; call for pick-up from nearby Trailheads; accepts mail drops. Nostalgic Dreams B&B, (717) 816-5699, call for pick-up; $25PP/night, laundry, WiFi. ■ *Groceries:* GT's Handimart (short-term resupply), (301) 241-3434, 4 a.m–11 p.m. daily, ice cream, sandwiches, hot bar, ATM, ask about lodging; Sanders Market (long-term resupply), (301) 241-3612, open M, W, Tu, F 8:30–9, Tu, Sa 8:30–8.

Mason-Dixon Line—This site—with a new stone monument, register, and mailbox constructed by Boy Scouts—signifies the historical survey line, important again in the Civil War, that separates Maryland from Pennsylvania. When Mason and Dixon surveyed this line in 1763–67, they placed at one-mile intervals limestone blocks 3 to 5 feet long, weighing between 300 and 600 pounds, from an English quarry. Every fifth mile, a "Crown" stone was laid with the Penn coat of arms on the Pennsylvania side and the Calvert coat of arms on the Maryland side.

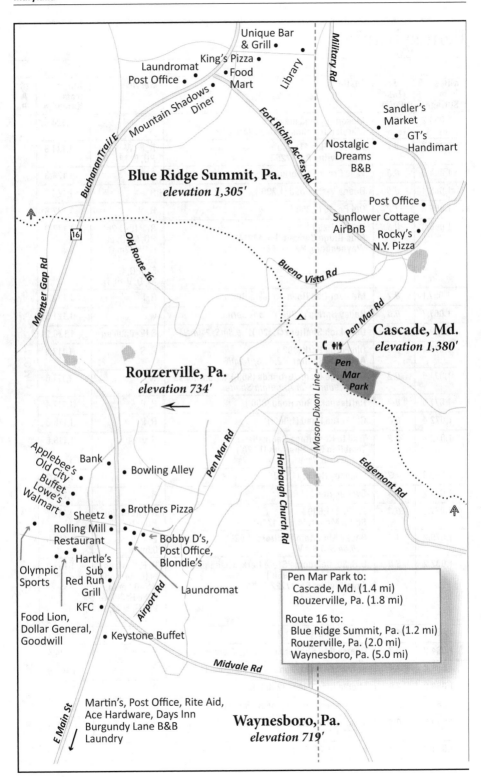

Unique Bar & Grill •

King's Pizza •

Laundromat
Post Office • • Food Mart

Library

Military Rd

Mountain Shadows Diner

Buchanan Trail/E

Fort Richie Access Rd

Sandler's Market

GT's Handimart •

Nostalgic Dreams B&B •

Blue Ridge Summit, Pa.
elevation 1,305'

Post Office •

Sunflower Cottage
AirBnB

Rocky's N.Y. Pizza •

16

Old Route 16

Menter Gap Rd

Buena Vista Rd

Pen Mar Rd

Cascade, Md.
elevation 1,380'

C ♦↟♦

Rouzerville, Pa.
elevation 734'

←

Pen Mar Park

Mason-Dixon Line

Edgemont Rd

Applebee's
Old City Buffet,
Lowe's,
Walmart •

Bank •

• Bowling Alley

Pen Mar Rd

Harbaugh Church Rd

• Brothers Pizza

Sheetz •

Rolling Mill Restaurant •

• Bobby D's,
Post Office,
Blondie's

Olympic Sports •

Hartle's Sub •
Red Run Grill •

Laundromat

Airport Rd

KFC •

Food Lion,
Dollar General,
Goodwill

• Keystone Buffet

Midvale Rd

Pen Mar Park to:
Cascade, Md. (1.4 mi)
Rouzerville, Pa. (1.8 mi)

Route 16 to:
Blue Ridge Summit, Pa. (1.2 mi)
Rouzerville, Pa. (2.0 mi)
Waynesboro, Pa. (5.0 mi)

E Main St

Martin's, Post Office, Rite Aid,
Ace Hardware, Days Inn
Burgundy Lane B&B
Laundry

↓

Waynesboro, Pa.
elevation 719'

Pennsylvania

Miles from Springer	Fr Last Point	Features	Services	Miles from Katahdin	M A P
1,064.3	0.2	Mason–Dixon Line (1,250') Maryland–Pennsylvania State Line	R	1,124.9	
1,064.4	0.1	Pen Mar Road (1,240') **Rouzerville, Pa. 17250**	R, P (W–1.5m PO, G, M, cl)	1,124.8	
1,064.9	0.5	Falls Creek Footbridge (1,100')	C, w	1,124.3	
1,065.4	0.5	Buena Vista Road (1,290')	R	1,123.8	
1,066.6	1.2	Old Pa. 16 (1,350')	R	1,122.6	
1,066.9	0.3	Pa. 16 (1,200') **Blue Ridge Summit, Pa. 17214 Waynesboro, Pa. 17268**	R, P (E–1.2m PO, M, D, cl, f) (W–2m G, M; 2.3m G; 5m PO, G, L, M, D, V, cl, f)	1,122.3	
1,067.1	0.2	Mentzer Gap Road, Mackie Run v	R, P	1,122.1	
1,067.7	0.6	Bailey Spring (1,300')...box spring	w	1,121.5	
1,069.0	1.3	**Deer Lick Shelters** (1,420')...9.8mS; 2.4mN	S (E–0.2m w)	1,120.2	
1,071.4	2.4	Old Forge Park (890') **Antietam Shelter**...2.4mS; 1.2mN	R, S	1,117.8	PATC Map 4
1,071.6	0.2	Old Forge Picnic Grounds (900')...well-house water source for Antietam Shelter	w	1,117.6	
1,071.8	0.2	Rattlesnake Run Road (900')	R, P	1,117.4	
1,072.4	0.6	Old Forge Road (1,000')	R, P	1,116.8	
1,072.6	0.2	Trail to Hermitage Cabin (locked) **Tumbling Run Shelters** (1,120') ...1.2mS; 6.8mN	S, w	1,116.6	
1,073.9	1.3	Chimney Rocks (1,900')		1,115.3	
1,077.2	3.3	Swamp Road (1,560')	R	1,112.0	
1,077.5	0.3	Pa. 233 (1,600') **South Mountain, Pa. 17261**	R, P (E–1.2m PO, M)	1,111.7	
1,079.2	1.7	**Rocky Mountain Shelters** (1,520') ...6.8mS; 5.8mN	E–0.2mS; 0.5m w	1,110.0	
1,082.2	3.0	U.S. 30, Caledonia State Park, Thaddeus Stevens Museum (960') **Fayetteville, Pa. 17222**	R, P, C, M, sh, w (E–14m all) (W–0.3m M; 0.8m H; 3.5m PO, G, L, M, D, cl)	1,107.0	
1,084.1	1.9	Quarry Gap Road (1,250')	R	1,105.1	
1,084.8	0.7	**Quarry Gap Shelters** (1,455')...5.8mS; 7.4mN	S, w	1,104.4	PATC Map 2-3
1,086.3	1.5	Stillhouse Road, Sandy Sod Junction (1,980')	R	1,102.9	
1,088.9	2.6	Middle Ridge Road (2,050')	R	1,100.3	
1,089.4	0.5	Ridge Road, Means Hollow Road (1,800')	R	1,099.8	
1,089.8	0.4	Milesburn Road, Milesburn Cabin (locked) (1,600')	R, w	1,099.4	
1,092.2	2.4	**Birch Run Shelter** (1,795')...7.4mS; 6.2mN	S, C, w	1,097.0	

Miles from Springer	Fr Last Point	Features	Services	Miles from Katahdin	M A P
1,093.5	1.3	Shippensburg Road, Big Flat Fire Tower (2,040')	R, P	1,095.7	
1,094.6	1.1	Midpoint 2015 (2,000')		1,094.6	
1,095.4	0.8	Michener Cabin (locked) (1,850')	E–0.3m w	1,093.8	
1,097.3	1.9	Woodrow Road (1,850')	R	1,091.9	
1,098.4	1.1	**Toms Run Shelter** (1,300')...*6.2mS; 11.1mN*	S, C, w	1,090.8	
1,100.2	1.8	Halfway Spring (1,100')...*signed*	w	1,089.0	
1,101.8	1.6	Pa. 233 (900')	R, P	1,087.4	
1,102.1	0.3	Pine Grove Furnace State Park, Ironmasters Mansion, **Appalachian Trail Museum** (850')	R, P, H, C, g, w, sh	1,087.1	
1,102.3	0.2	Fuller Lake (850')...*beach, swimming*		1,086.9	PATC Map 2-3
1,104.6	2.3	Pole Steeple side trail (1,300')		1,084.6	
1,107.9	3.3	Lime Kiln Road (1,080')	R	1,081.3	
1,108.1	0.2	Trail to Mountain Creek Campground (1,050')...*on Pine Grove Road*	W–0.7m C, G, w, sh, f	1,081.1	
1,108.9	0.8	Spring (signed) (750')	W–0.1m w	1,080.3	
1,109.3	0.4	**James Fry (Tagg Run) Shelter** (805') ...*11.1mS; 8.5mN*	E–0.2m S, w	1,079.9	
1,109.8	0.5	Pine Grove Road (750')	R (W–0.4m C, M)	1,079.4	
1,110.7	0.9	Pa. 34, Hunters Run Road, Gardners, Pa. (670')	R, P (E–0.2m G, f)	1,078.5	
1,111.1	0.4	Sheet Iron Roof Road (680')	R (W–0.4m C, M, L, g, sh, cl, f)	1,078.1	
1,112.5	1.4	Pa. 94 (880') **Mt. Holly Springs, Pa. 17065**	R, P (W–2.5m PO, G, L, M, D, cl)	1,076.7	
1,115.3	2.8	Whiskey Spring Road, Whiskey Spring (830')	R, P, w	1,073.9	
1,117.4	2.1	**Alec Kennedy Shelter** (850')...*8.5mS; 18.4mN*	E–0.2m S, C, w	1,071.8	
1,118.3	0.9	Center Point Knob (1,060')		1,070.9	
1,120.8	2.5	Backpackers' Campsite (500')	C, w	1,068.4	
1,121.0	0.2	Yellow Breeches Creek (500')	R	1,068.2	
1,121.3	0.3	Pa. 174, ATC Mid-Atlantic Office (500') **Boiling Springs, Pa. 17007**	R, P, PO, w, sh, f (E–0.8m L, M) (W–0.1m G, L, M; 1m G, D, V; 2.5m L)	1,067.9	PATC Map 1
1,123.3	2.0	Pa. 74, York Road (580')	R, P	1,065.9	
1,125.4	2.1	Pa. 641, Trindle Road (540')	R, P	1,063.8	
1,128.1	2.7	I-76 Pennsylvania Turnpike (495')...*overpass*	R	1,061.1	
1,129.3	1.2	U.S. 11 (490')...*pedestrian footbridge* Carlisle, Pa.; New Kingston, Pa	R (W–0.5m G, L, M, sh; 5m all)	1,059.9	
1,130.2	0.9	I-81 (485')...*overpass on Bernhisel Road*	R	1,059.0	
1,131.6	1.4	Conodoguinet Creek Bridge, ATC Scott Farm Trail Work Center (480')	R, w	1,057.6	

Miles from Springer	Fr Last Point	Features	Services	Miles from Katahdin	M A P
1,133.6	2.0	Pa. 944 (480')...*pedestrian tunnel*	R	1,055.6	
1,134.6	1.0	Spring at Wolf Trail Junction (650')	w	1,054.6	
1,135.5	0.9	Tuscarora Trail (northern terminus) (1,390') Darlington Trail		1,053.7	
1,135.6	0.1	**Darlington Shelter** (1,250')...*18.4mS; 7.3mN*	S, w	1,053.6	
1,137.9	2.3	Pa. 850 (650')	R, P	1,051.3	
1,142.9	5.0	**Cove Mountain Shelter** (1,200') ...*7.3mS; 8.3mN*	S, w	1,046.3	PATC Map 1
1,144.8	1.9	Hawk Rock (1,140')...*view of Duncannon*		1,044.4	
1,146.5	1.7	U.S. 11 & 15, Pa. 274 (385')	R, P (W–0.5m G; E–8m O)	1,042.7	
1,147.0	0.5	Market St. (385') **Duncannon, Pa. 17020**	R, PO, G, L, M, D, cl, f	1,042.2	
1,148.0	1.0	Pa. 849, Juniata River (380')	R, C, sh	1,041.2	
1,148.2	0.2	Susquehanna River (380') Clarks Ferry Bridge (west end)	R (W–0.1m G, M, sh; 2m L; 3.6m L)	1,041.0	
1,148.8	0.6	U.S. 22 & 322, Norfolk Southern Railway (400')	R (E–16m Harrisburg)	1,040.4	
1,151.0	2.2	Campsite (1,160')	C, w	1,038.2	
1,151.2	0.2	**Clarks Ferry Shelter** (1,260')...*8.3mS; 6.7mN*	S, w	1,038.0	
1,155.1	3.9	Pa. 225 (1,250')...*footbridge*	R, P	1,034.1	
1,157.1	2.0	Table Rock View (1,200')		1,032.1	
1,157.9	0.8	**Peters Mountain Shelter** (970') ...*6.7mS; 18.3mN*	S, w	1,031.3	
1,158.9	1.0	Victoria Trail (1,300')		1,030.3	KTA Map: Sections 7-8
1,160.6	1.7	Kinter View (1,320')		1,028.6	
1,162.0	1.4	Shikellimy Trail (1,250')		1,027.2	
1,164.3	2.3	Spring (700')	w	1,024.9	
1,164.6	0.3	Pa. 325, Clark's Valley (550')	R, P, w	1,024.6	
1,167.9	3.3	Stony Mountain; Horse-Shoe Trail (1,650')		1,021.3	
1,171.3	3.4	Yellow Springs Village Site (1,450')		1,017.9	
1,173.6	2.3	Cold Spring Trail (1,400')		1,015.6	
1,175.9	2.3	**Rausch Gap Shelter** (980')...*18.3mS; 13.7mN*	P (E–0.3m S, w)	1,013.3	
1,180.6	4.7	Pa. 443, Green Point, Pa. (550')	R, P (W–2.6m C, M, cl, sh)	1,008.6	
1,182.0	1.4	Pa. 72, Swatara Gap, Iron Bridge (480') Swatara Rail Trail to Lickdale, Pa.	R, P (E–2.4m C, G, L, M, sh)	1,007.2	
1,182.4	0.4	I-81 (450')...*underpass*	R	1,006.8	KTA Map: Sections 1-6
1,189.3	6.9	Blue Mountain Spring (1,300') **William Penn Shelter**...*13.7mS; 4.2mN*	S, w	999.9	
1,191.5	2.2	Pa. 645 (1,250')	R, P	997.7	
1,193.4	1.9	Pa. 501 (1,460') **501 Shelter**...*4.2mS; 15.5mN* **Bethel, Pa. 19507** **Pine Grove, Pa. 17963**	R, P (E–2m PO, V) (W–0.1m S, w; 3.7m PO, G, L, M, D, V, cl)	995.8	

Miles from Springer	Fr Last Point	Features	Services	Miles from Katahdin	M A P
1,193.9	0.5	Pilger Ruh Spring Trail, Applebee Campsite (1,450')	E–w; W–C	995.3	
1,196.5	2.6	Round Head, Shower Steps (1,500')	w	992.7	
1,199.0	2.5	Hertlein Campsite (1,200')	C, w	990.2	
1,199.1	0.1	Shuberts Gap (1,200')		990.1	
1,202.4	3.3	Fort Dietrich Snyder Marker (1,440')	W–0.2m w	986.8	
1,202.7	0.3	Pa. 183, Rentschler Marker (1,440')	R, P (E–4m D)	986.5	
1,204.0	1.3	Black Swatara Spring (1,510')	W–0.3m w	985.2	
1,207.8	3.8	Sand Spring Trail (1,510')...*walled spring*	E–0.2m w	981.4	
1,208.5	0.7	**Eagle's Nest Shelter** (1,510')...*15.5mS; 15mN*	W–0.3m S, w	980.7	
1,210.4	1.9	Shartlesville Cross–Mountain Road (1,450') Shartlesville, Pa.	R	978.8	
1,213.1	2.7	Phillip's Canyon Spring (1,500')	w	976.1	
1,217.1	4.0	**Port Clinton, Pa. 19549** (400')	R, P, PO, L, M (W–0.3m S,C,sh)	972.1	
1,217.8	0.7	Pa. 61 (490') **Hamburg, Pa. 19526**	R, P (E–1.5m G, L, M, O, B, f; 3.5m PO, G, L, M, D, V, B, cl)	971.4	
1,220.4	2.6	Pocahontas Spring (1,200')	w	968.8	
1,223.0	2.6	Windsor Furnace, Hamburg Reservoir (900')	E–0.5m P, C, w	966.2	
1,223.2	0.2	**Windsor Furnace Shelter** (940') ...*15mS; 9.3mN*	S, w	966.0	
1,224.8	1.6	Pulpit Rock (1,582')		964.4	
1,226.6	1.8	Trail to Blue Rocks Campground (1,150')	E–1.5m S, C, G, cl, sh, f	962.6	
1,227.0	0.4	The Pinnacle (1,615')...*overlook*		962.2	
1,232.3	5.3	Hawk Mountain Road (600') **Eckville Shelter**...*9.3mS; 7.6mN*	R, P (E–0.2m S, w, sh)	956.9	
1,235.1	2.8	Dans Pulpit (1,600')		954.1	
1,238.4	3.3	Tri-County Corner (1,560')		950.8	
1,239.7	1.3	**Allentown Hiking Club Shelter** (1,350') ...*7.6mS; 10mN*	S, w	949.5	
1,241.6	1.9	Fort Franklin Road (1,350')	R, P	947.6	
1,243.8	2.2	Pa. 309, Blue Mountain Summit (1,360')	R, P, L, M, w	945.4	
1,245.6	1.8	New Tripoli Campsite (1,400')	W–0.2m C, w	943.6	
1,246.6	1.0	Knife Edge (1,525')		942.6	
1,247.3	0.7	Bear Rocks (1,604')		941.9	
1,248.7	1.4	Bake Oven Knob Road (1,450')	R, P	940.5	
1,249.1	0.4	Bake Oven Knob (1,560')		940.1	
1,249.7	0.6	**Bake Oven Knob Shelter** (1,380') ...*10mS; 6.8mN*	S, w	939.5	
1,252.1	2.4	Ashfield Road, Lehigh Furnace Gap, Ashfield, Pa. (1,320')	R, P (E–0.7m w)	937.1	
1,256.5	4.4	**George W. Outerbridge Shelter** (1,000') ...*6.8mS; 16.8mN*	S	932.7	

Miles from Springer	Fr Last Point	Features	Services	Miles from Katahdin	M A P
1,257.1	0.6	Pa. 873, Lehigh Gap (380') **Slatington, Pa. 18080**	R (E–2m PO, G, M, D, B, cl, f)	932.1	
1,257.2	0.1	Pa. 873, Lehigh River Bridge (east end) (380')	R, P	932.0	
1,257.4	0.2	Pa. 145 (380') **Walnutport, Pa. 18088**	R (E–2m PO G, M, D, V, B)	931.8	
1,257.4	0.0	Pa. 248 (380') **Palmerton, Pa. 18071**	R (W–2m PO, H, G, L, M, D, cl, f)	931.8	
1,262.4	5.0	Blue Mountain Road, Little Gap (1,100') **Danielsville, Pa. 18038**	R, P (E–1.5m PO, G, L, M) (W–2.5m M)	926.8	
1,267.2	4.8	Delps Trail (1,580')...*unreliable spring*	E–0.25m w	922.0	
1,269.0	1.8	Stempa Spring (1,510')	E–0.6m w	920.2	
1,269.7	0.7	Smith Gap Road (1,540')	R, P (W–1m w, sh)	919.5	
1,273.2	3.5	**Leroy A. Smith Shelter** (1,410') ...*16.8mS; 13.9mN*	E–0.1m S; 0.2m, 0.4m, 0.6m w)	916.0	
1,276.8	3.6	Hahns Lookout (1,450')		912.4	
1,277.8	1.0	Pa. 33 (980') **Wind Gap, Pa. 18091**	R, P (E–1m PO, G, L, M, D, V, cl)	911.4	
1,284.2	6.4	Wolf Rocks Bypass Trail (south jct.) (1,550')		905.0	
1,284.8	0.6	Wolf Rocks (1,620')		904.4	
1,285.3	0.5	Wolf Rocks Bypass Trail (north jct.) (1,510')		903.9	
1,286.4	1.1	Pa. 191, Fox Gap (1,400')	R, P	902.8	
1,287.0	0.6	**Kirkridge Shelter** (1,500')...*13.9mS; 31.4mN*	S	902.2	
1,288.9	1.9	Totts Gap (1,300')		900.3	
1,290.9	2.0	Mt. Minsi (1,461')		898.3	
1,291.9	1.0	Lookout Rock (800')		897.3	
1,292.7	0.8	Council Rock (600')		896.5	
1,293.4	0.7	Pa. 611 (400') **Delaware Water Gap, Pa. 18327**	R, P (W–0.1m PO, H, M; 0.4m B, G, L, M, O, f; 5m G, L, M, O, D)	895.8	
1,293.6	0.2	Delaware River Bridge (west end) (350') Pennsylvania–New Jersey State Line		895.6	

Camping regulations vary depending on the type of public land. Be aware of posted notices, and check maps for boundaries. Most water sources are unreliable in summer.

Pa. 16—East 1.2 miles to **Blue Ridge Summit, Pa. [P.O. ZIP 17214: M–F 8–12 & 1–4:00, Sa 9–11:30; (717) 794-2335].** ■ *Restaurants:* Mountain Shadows, daily, B/L/D; Chapin Gray's Grill; King's Pizza; Unique Bar and Grill; and fast-food options. ■ *Internet access:* library, M–Th 3–8, Sa 10–12. ■ *Other services:* hardware store, denatured alcohol; bank with ATM; JJ's Coin laundry; barber; and Blue Ridge Summit Medical Center, M, Tu, Th 8–5, W, F 8–1.

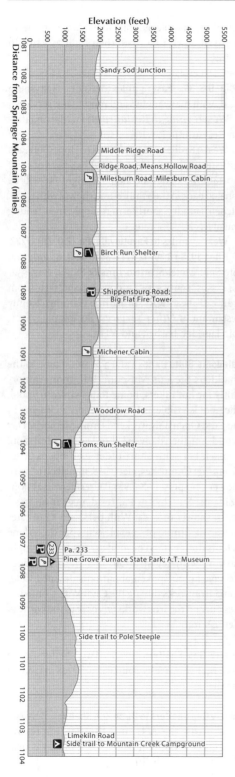

Elevation (feet)

Distance from Springer Mountain (miles)

Sandy Sod Junction

Middle Ridge Road

Ridge Road, Means Hollow Road

Milesburn Road, Milesburn Cabin

Birch Run Shelter

Shippensburg Road;
Big Flat Fire Tower

Michener Cabin

Woodrow Road

Toms Run Shelter

Pa. 233
Pine Grove Furnace State Park; A.T. Museum

Side trail to Pole Steeple

Limekiln Road
Side trail to Mountain Creek Campground

West 2 miles to **Rouzerville, Pa. [P.O. ZIP 17250: M–F 8:30–1 & 2–4:30, Sa 8:30–11:30; (717) 762-7050]**, with most major services (*see map on page 121*). *Lodging:* Cobblestone Hotel, (888) 693-8262.

West 2.3 miles to *Groceries:* Food Lion (long-term resupply).

West 5 miles to **Waynesboro, Pa. [P.O. ZIP 17268: M–F 8:30–5, Sa 9–12; (717) 762-1513; pick-up window only, M–F 6–5, Sa 6–12:15]**, with all major services. ■ *Lodging:* Burgundy Lane B&B, (717) 762-8112, phone for shuttle from Trailhead, Internet access, laundry, local shuttles, and slackpacks; Days Inn, (717) 762-9113, call for current rates. ■ *Groceries:* Martin's (long-term resupply); 7–11 (short-term resupply). ■ *Internet access:* library, M–F 9:30–8, Sa 9–4. ■ *Other services:* YMCA; hospital; Radio Shack; pharmacies; veterinarian; dentist; and UPS Store.

Deer Lick Shelters (1940s)—Two shelters, each sleeps 4. Privy. Water source is a spring 0.2 mile on a blue-blazed trail to the east of the shelter area (seasonal) or stream 50 feet north of shelter.

Antietam Shelter (1940)—Sleeps 6. Privy. Water source is 0.2 mile north on the A.T. to a springhouse with spigot by the ballfield in Old Forge Park. Southbounders should get their water before reaching the shelter.

Tumbling Run Shelters (1940s)—Two shelters, each sleeps 4. Privy. Located on a short, blue-blazed trail. Water source is 100 yards to the west of the shelter.

Pa. 233—**East** 1.2 miles to **South Mountain, Pa. [P.O. ZIP 17261: M–F 12–4, Sa 8:30–11:30; (717) 749-5833]**. *Restaurant:* South Mountain Bar and Restaurant; (717) 749-3845, grill-type menu (no lodging), M–Sa 9 a.m.–2 a.m., Su 11 a.m.–midnight, with patio and outside shower.

Rocky Mountain Shelters (1989)—Two shelters, each sleeps 4. Privy. Located 0.2 mile on a steep,

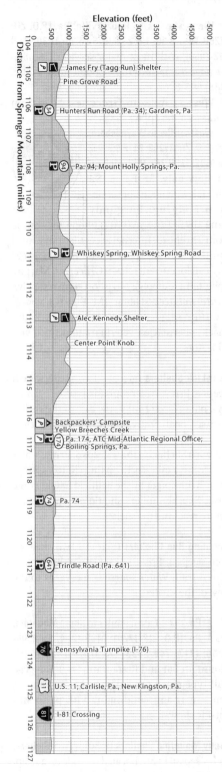

downhill, blue-blazed trail; for water, continue on side trail down to a road, then right 75 yards to spring.

U.S. 30—East 14 miles to historic Gettysburg with many motels and most major services.

West 0.3 mile to *Restaurant:* La Mattina Italian Restaurant, (717) 352-8503.

West 0.8 mile to *Hostel:* Trail of Hope Outreach Ministries Church Hostel, (717) 658-7971 or (717) 360-1481, no drugs/alcohol, $22/night ($1 will be donated back to the Trail), bunk, shower with towel, kitchen, laundry, short-term resupply, fuel. Tenting available; check for rate.

West 3.5 miles to **Fayetteville, Pa. [P.O. ZIP 17222: M–F 8–4:30, Sa 8:30–12; (717) 352-2022].** ■ *Lodging:* Rite Spot Motel/Scottish Inns & Suites, (717) 352-2144, $59S, $69D, $20EAP, dogs $15; shuttle to/from Trail, call ahead. ■ *Restaurants:* Flamingo Family Restaurant. ■ *Other services:* doctor, pharmacy, coin laundry, barber, and ATM.

Caledonia State Park—(717) 352-2161, home to the Thaddeus Stevens Museum, but, more importantly for hot hikers, home to a swimming pool. The pool is visible as the A.T. enters a clearing in the park. Open only weekends from Memorial Day to mid-Jun, then daily to Labor Day; $4 admission. A snack bar with short-order grill opens at 10. *Camping:* Campsites, electric & nonelectric, with showers, no pets: F–Sa, $23 Pa. residents/$25 nonresidents; Su–Th, $19 Pa. residents/$21 nonresidents; shower only $3. With pets, add $2 to rates above. Maximum of 5 people/tents per site as long as tents don't extend beyond campsite. Overnight parking with registration. U.S. Sen. Thaddeus Stevens, an outspoken abolitionist, owned Caledonia Ironworks during the Civil War. Confederates burned the ironworks *en route* to the battle of Gettysburg..

Quarry Gap Shelters (1935)—Two shelters, each sleeps 4. Privy. Water source is 10 yards in front of the shelter.

Quarry Gap Shelters to Birch Run Shelter—Between these areas, the A.T. runs through impressive thickets of mountain laurel. Peak bloom is usually late May–early Jun.

Birch Run Shelter (2003)—Sleeps 8. Privy. Shelter located on the east side of the A.T. Water source is a spring 30 yards in front of the shelter.

Midpoint Marker—A new wooden sign with a register marks the 2011 midpoint of the Trail. The old one has been retired to the nearby A.T. Museum. ALDHA honorary life member Chuck Wood, a.k.a. "Woodchuck" of 1985, built and erected both markers.

Toms Run Shelter(s) (1936)—One burned in 2013; remaining shelter sleeps 4. Privy. Water source is a spring near old chimney.

Pa. 233/Pine Grove Furnace State Park—(717) 486-7174. *Appalachian Trail Museum,* (717) 486-8126, <www.atmuseum.org>, in an old grist mill on the Trail, well worth the visit; free, open Mar 28–May 3 weekends 12–4, May 9–Jul 19 daily 9–4, Jul 20–Aug 9 daily 12–4, Aug 10–Nov 1 W–Su 12–4; hiker festival on Jun 6; parking for up to a week but register at park office. ■ *Hostel:* Ironmasters Mansion, <www.ironmastersmansion.com>, south of the entrance to Pine Grove Furnace State Park, an Egnlish Tudor brick residence built by the ironmaster for his family in 1829 and renovated in 2010; $25/person with B; check-in 5–9 p.m., check-out 9 a.m., closed daily 9–5 p.m. and Tu nights; call for reservations, (717) 486-4108, or e-mail <ironmasterspinegrove@gmail.com>. ■ *Groceries:* Pine Grove General Store (short-term resupply), open Apr 15–mid-Nov, weekends only, hours may be limited. The first opportunity for northbounders to join the traditional "half-gallon club." To belong, you have to eat a half-gallon of ice cream to mark your halfway point. ■ *Camping:* Campground open Mar 27–Dec 12, electric & nonelectric sites, $19–$34 (resident and nonresident rates), swimming in Laurel and Fuller lakes; heated restrooms with hot showers, electric outlets, and flush toilets. Alcohol prohibited. ■ *Shuttles:* Mike, (717) 437-6022; Freeman, (717) 352-2513; Jim, (717) 701-2324 or (717) 343-8955; Bill, (570) 997-2701; Gary, (717) 706-2578.

Mountain Club of Maryland—MCM maintains the 16.2 miles from Pine Grove Furnace State Park to Center Point Knob and the 12.6 miles from the Darlington/Tuscarora Trail junction to the Susquehanna River. Correspondence should be sent to 7923 Galloping Circle, Baltimore, MD 21244; <paulives2@aol.com>.

Mountain Creek Campground—**West** 0.7 mile; 349 Pine Grove Rd., Gardners, PA 17324; (717) 486-7681, <www.mtncreekcg.com>; mid-Apr–Oct, tenting, cabin, hot showers, call for rates; pool, camp store, camp supplies, snack shack; pets must be kept on a leash.

James Fry Shelter at Tagg Run (1998)—Sleeps 9. Tentsites. Privy (composting). Called "Tagg Run" in some sources, after the 1930s-vintage shelters it replaced. Water source is 0.4 mile east of the A.T. on a blue-blazed trail; may run dry in drought times.

Pine Grove Road—**West** 0.4 mile to Cherokee Family Restaurant and Campground, (717) 486-8000; tentsites with shower $16D, $5EAP.

Sheet Iron Roof Road—**West** 0.4 mile to Deer Run Camping Resort, (717) 486-8168, $10 tent camping, short-term resupply, laundry, showers, WiFi, pool, fishing pond, snack bar on weekends, cabins with hiker discount.

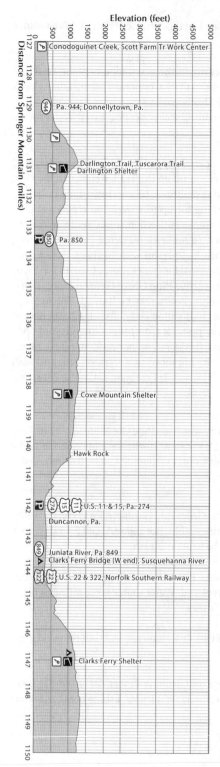

Elevation (feet)

Distance from Springer Mountain (miles)

- 1127 — Conodoguinet Creek, Scott Farm Tr Work Center
- 1128
- 1129 — (944) Pa. 944; Donnellytown, Pa.
- 1130
- 1131 — Darlington Trail, Tuscarora Trail / Darlington Shelter
- 1132
- 1133 — (850) Pa. 850
- 1134
- 1135
- 1136
- 1137
- 1138 — Cove Mountain Shelter
- 1139
- 1140 — Hawk Rock
- 1141
- 1142 — (274) U.S. 11 & 15; Pa. 274 / Duncannon, Pa.
- 1143
- 1144 — (849) Juniata River, Pa. 849 / Clarks Ferry Bridge (W end), Susquehanna River / (322) U.S. 22 & 322, Norfolk Southern Railway
- 1145
- 1146
- 1147 — Clarks Ferry Shelter
- 1148
- 1149
- 1150

 Pa. 34—East 0.2 mile to the Green Mountain Store and Deli (short-term resupply), M–Sa 7–8, Su 9–6, Coleman fuel by the pint. For southbounders, the first opportunity to join the Half-Gallon Club.

Pa. 94—West 2.5 miles to **Mt. Holly Springs, Pa. [P.O. ZIP 17065: M–F 8–4:30, Sa 9–12; (717) 486-3468].** ■ *Lodging:* Holly Inn and Restaurant, 31 S. Baltimore St., Mt. Holly Springs, PA 17065, (717) 486-3823, call for pick-up; <www.hollyinn.com>; $55S/D $10EAP includes continental B and ride back to the Trail; L/D M–Th Su 11:30–9, F-Sa 11:30–10; Internet; mail drops accepted. ■ *Restaurants:* Cassell's Grill, 5 West Pine St., (717) 486-8800, Tu–Su 11–9; Laura's Family Restaurant; Sicilia Pizza and Subs. ■ *Internet access:* library. ■ *Other services:* Uni-Mart, Dollar General, and Family Dollar (short-term resupply); coin laundry; pharmacy; dentist; optometrist; and bank with ATM.

Alec Kennedy Shelter (1991)—Sleeps 7. Privy (composting). Built by the MCM and Tressler Wilderness School. The shelter is 0.2 mile east on a blue-blazed trail. Water source is a spring located on a side trail behind the shelter; prone to go dry during the summer. A second source is a small stream 0.5 mile south of the shelter on the A.T.

Center Point Knob—In 2012, the Mountain Club of Maryland replaced the missing Center Point Knob bronze plaque with a replica on the original boulder along the Trail.

Cumberland Valley Appalachian Trail Club—CVATC maintains the 17.2 miles between Center Point Knob and the Darlington/Tuscarora Trail junction. Correspondence should be sent to P.O. Box 395, Boiling Springs, Pa. 17007; <www.cvatclub. org>; <wbohn@paonline.com>.

No fires in the valley—Between Alec Kennedy and Darlington shelters, the Boiling Springs campsite (see next entry) is the only place where camping is allowed.

Boiling Springs, Pa. [P.O. ZIP 17007: M–F 9–12, 1–4:30, Sa 9–12; (717) 258-6668]—Home to

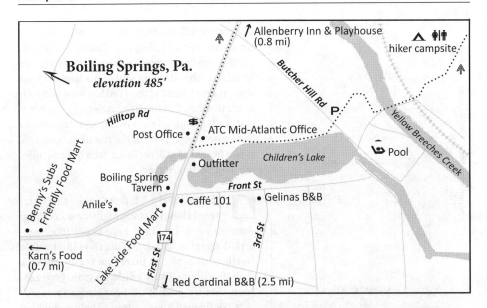

Boiling Springs, Pa.
elevation 485'

Allenberry Inn & Playhouse (0.8 mi)
hiker campsite
Butcher Hill Rd
Yellow Breeches Creek
Hilltop Rd
Post Office • ATC Mid-Atlantic Office
Pool
• Outfitter   Children's Lake
Boiling Springs
Tavern •   **Front St**
Anile's •   • Caffé 101   • Gelinas B&B
Benny's Subs
Friendly Food Mart
174
3rd St
First St
Lake Side Food Mart
Karn's Food (0.7 mi)
↓ Red Cardinal B&B (2.5 mi)

ATC's mid-Atlantic regional office, (717) 258-5771. Open weekdays 8–5. Staff members and volunteers can provide information on Trail conditions, weather forecasts, and water availability. Coleman fuel and denatured alcohol are available for a donation; A.T. maps and books for sale. Picnic table and hiker bulletin board are located on the porch. Bursting-at-seams office cannot accommodate packages sent to hikers; please use P.O. across street. *No camping at the office.* Limited parking at opposite end of lake in township parking lot; obtain permit from ATC office during regular office hours (overnight parking is only allowed with permit that you display on your dashboard; call ahead if arriving late). Lodging is limited in Boiling Springs, but a year-round campsite with a portable toilet in season is south of town, before the railroad tracks (toilet Memorial Day–Labor Day). The trains do run past here all night long. The water source for the campsite is a spigot behind the ATC office, next to the oil tank, and might not be available during winter months. Check the hiker-information board for postings of additional camping possibilities in the area. ■ *Lodging:* Gelinas Manor B&B, 219 Front St., Boiling Springs, PA 17007 , (717) 258-6584, $69 (one room only) to $129 includes full B, no pets, no packs inside, $5 laundry service, mail drops for registered guests accepted. ■ *Restaurants:* Anile's Ristorante & Pizzeria, (717) 258-5070, L/D; Boiling Springs Tavern, L/D; Caffe 101, B/L/D; Benny's Subs, (717) 258-6522. ■ *Outfitter:* Yellow Breeches Outfitter, (717) 258-6752, closed M, limited hiker supplies, socks, clothing, rain gear, first aid, A.T. maps of Pa., bug spray, water-purification tablets. ■ *Groceries:* Karn's Store (long-term resupply), open daily 7–10; Getty Mart and Friendly Food Mart (both short-term resupply). ■ *Other services:* bank with ATM next to post office; doctor; dentist; veterinarian; Boiling Springs pool, (717) 258-4121, open Memorial–Labor Day, $12 admission, $7 seniors or evenings, $1 hot shower, check ATC hiker bulletin board for coupons; barber; Jumpers Shoe Service, (717) 766-3422, in nearby Mechanicsburg. ■ *Shuttles:* Mike Gelinas, (717) 497-6022.

East 0.8 mile on Pa. 174—Allenberry Inn & Playhouse, 1559 Boiling Springs Rd., (717) 258-3211; hikers' special $40/room, no reservations, first-come/first-served; bar and lounge; seasonal pool; B/D buffet extra: dinner-and-theater package W–Su, $25PP. Mail drops accepted ($5/box).

West 2.5 miles on Pa. 174—*Lodging:* Red Cardinal B&B, (717) 245-0823, <redcardinalbandb@aol.com>, call for reservations and a ride.

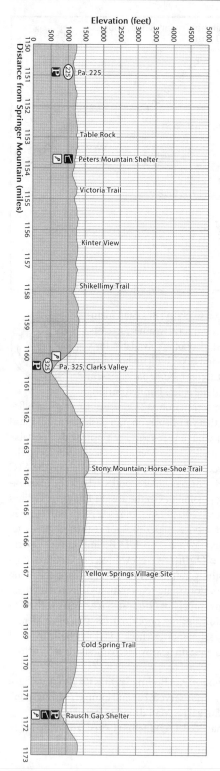

Elevation (feet)

Distance from Springer Mountain (miles)

- P 225 Pa. 225
- Table Rock
- Peters Mountain Shelter
- Victoria Trail
- Kinter View
- Shikellimy Trail
- 325 Pa. 325, Clarks Valley
- Stony Mountain; Horse-Shoe Trail
- Yellow Springs Village Site
- Cold Spring Trail
- Rausch Gap Shelter

Cumberland Valley—Water is scarce between Boiling Springs and Darlington Shelter, as the A.T. winds along hedgerows and through Pennsylvania farmland. Thanks to an ambitious land-acquisition program, most of the Trail has been taken off roads through this heavily developed area, but it is still a hot walk on steamy summer days. Water can be obtained at one of the restaurants on U.S. 11 (see below) or at Scott Farm, which is 10.3 miles north of Boiling Springs.

U.S. 11—West 0.5 mile to various facilities spread along this busy highway. ■ *Lodging:* America's Best Inn, (717) 245-2242 or (800) 445-6715, dogs extra, laundry, WiFi; Days Inn Carlisle North, (717) 245-2242, hiker rate $54.99; Super 8, 1800 Harrisburg Pike, Carlisle, PA 17013, (717) 249-7000, laundry, pool, WiFi; Econolodge, (717) 249-7775, continental B, pets extra and only in smoking rooms, laundry, pool, WiFi; Holiday Inn, (717) 245-2400, pets okay ($10 nonrefundable fee), laundry, pool, Duffy's Restaurant and Pub, WiFi; Pheasant Field B&B, (717) 258-0717, Su–Th $88D, F–Sa $105–$185D, pet-friendly room may be available, laundry, free phone, shuttle to and from Trail with stay; Hotel Carlisle, (717) 243-1717, heated indoor pool, sauna, hot tub, WiFi. Other options beyond I-81: Travel Lodge, Rodeway Inn, Howard Johnson, Quality Inn. ■ *Restaurants:* Trailside Restaurant (limited hours), 24-hour Middlesex Diner, Bob Evans, Dunkin' Donuts, and fast-food restaurants on the other side of I-81. ■ *Other services:* The Flying J Travel Plaza has a restaurant, showers $11.50 (includes refundable $5 towel deposit), laundry, and a store (short-term resupply).

West—5 miles to Carlisle, a large town with all major services.

Conodoguinet Creek Bridge—An old ATC-managed farmhouse, known as the Scott Farm, is located next to the bridge where the Trail U-turns, passes under the bridge, and heads north. Open May–Oct, the farm has a privy, water, and a picnic table. *No camping.*

Wolf Trail—Spring water where the A.T crosses an overgrown dirt road.

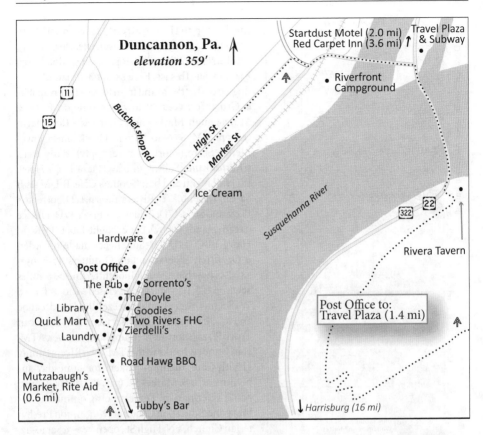

Duncannon, Pa.
elevation 359'

Startdust Motel (2.0 mi)
Red Carpet Inn (3.6 mi)
Travel Plaza & Subway

Riverfront Campground

11
15

Butcher shop Rd

High St

Market St

Ice Cream

Susquehanna River

322 22

Rivera Tavern

Hardware

Post Office

The Pub Sorrento's
The Doyle
Library Goodies
Quick Mart Two Rivers FHC
Laundry Zierdelli's

Post Office to:
Travel Plaza (1.4 mi)

Road Hawg BBQ

Mutzabaugh's
Market, Rite Aid
(0.6 mi)

Tubby's Bar

Harrisburg (16 mi)

Tuscarora Trail—The northern terminus of the blue-blazed Tuscarora Trail, a 260-mile route to its southern terminus on the A.T. in Shenandoah National Park in Virginia near Matthews Arm Campground. It was blazed when maintainers feared that the A.T. route would be closed by private landowners.

Darlington Shelter (2005)—Sleeps 8. Privy. Campsites. Water source, an intermittent spring 0.2 mile on a blue-blazed trail in front of the shelter, regularly dries up early in the hiker season. It is recommended that northbounders bring water to the shelter from the Wolf Trail spring at the base of North Mountain; southbounders, from Cove Mountain.

Cove Mountain Shelter (2000)—Sleeps 8. Privy. Built with the help of the Timber Framers Guild using timber salvaged from a barn, some pieces more than 100 years old. Water source is a spring 125 yards away on a steeply graded trail near the shelter.

U.S. 11/Duncannon, Pa. [P.O. ZIP 17020: M–F 8–11, 12–4:30, Sa 8:30–12:30; (717) 834-3332.] *ID required for mail drops.*—The A.T. passes through the center of town, and all services are within a short walk. ■ *Camping:* Riverfront Campground (south of the Clarks Ferry Bridge), (717) 834-5252, tentsites and shower $3.50PP in designated hiker area, shuttle service, canoe and kayak rentals. ■ *Lodging:* Doyle Hotel, 7 North Market St., Duncannon, PA 17020, (717) 834-6789, one of the original Anheuser-Busch hotels, more than 100 years old, $25S, $7.50EAP, laundry, free Internet, pets allowed, shower only $7.50 (includes towel), fuels (denatured, white gas, canister), will hold

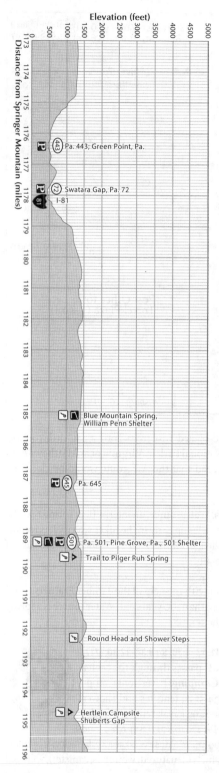

Elevation (feet)

Distance from Springer Mountain (miles)

Pa. 443; Green Point, Pa.

Swatara Gap, Pa. 72

I-81

Blue Mountain Spring,
William Penn Shelter

Pa. 645

Pa. 501; Pine Grove, Pa., 501 Shelter

Trail to Pilger Ruh Spring

Round Head and Shower Steps

Hertlein Campsite
Shuberts Gap

mail drops (ID required), free shuttles to Mutzabaugh's, other shuttles available. On U.S. 11/15, 2 miles **North** of the truck stop, Stardust Motel, (717) 834-3191, Su–Th $45S, F–Sa $53S, $5EAP, laundry, no dogs, free shuttles to and from town when available. ■ *Groceries:* **West** of town 0.5 mile on Pa. 274, Mutzabaugh Market and pharmacy (long-term resupply), M–Sa 6–10, Su 7–10; Quick Mart Convenience Store (short-term resupply), daily 6–11. ■ *Restaurants:* Subway in Travel Plaza; Doyle Hotel, L/D full menu and bar; Goodie's Café, B/L M–F, B Sa–Su; The Pub, L/D; Riviera Tavern, L/D; Sorrento's Pizza and Subs, L/D; Zeiderelli's Pizza, L/D, 3 B's Ice Cream Stand; Tubby's Bar & Nightclub, L/D; Road Hawg BBQ, L/D Th–Su; Sheetz made-to-order. ■ *Outfitter:* Blue Mountain Outfitters, (717) 957-2413, <www.bluemountainoutfitters.net>, 8 miles **south** on U.S. 11 in Marysville, closed M, 10–8 T, 10–6 W–Su; fuel, water bottles, freeze-dried food, canoe and kayak rentals. ■ *Other services:* All-American Truck Plaza (short-term resupply), $8 shower, ATM; coin laundry; banks with ATM; Two Rivers Family Health Care, mention "hiker" for same-day appointment, 4 S. Market St., (717) 834-3900; dentist; bank; veterinarian; Duncannon Community Library and Education Center at Duncannon Presbyterian Church, 3 N. High St., open W 1–3, Sat 10–12, Internet, a/c, cold drinks & snacks, hiker box, all hikers welcome; Mary Parry (Trail Angel Mary), (717) 834-4706, can tell you about services.

York Hiking Club—YHC maintains the 6.9 miles from the Susquehanna River to Pa. 225. Correspondence should be sent to YHC, 2684 Forest Rd., York, PA 17402; (717) 244-6769; <president@yorkhikingclub.com>.

Earl V. Shaffer—Almost all hikers recognize Earl "Crazy One" Shaffer (1918–2002) from York, Pa., as the first A.T. thru-hiker. In 1948, he completed a northbound thru-hike; in 1965, he did a southbound thru-hike, becoming the first to record both northbound and southbound hikes. To celebrate the 50th anniversary in 1998 of his first hike, Earl did a northbound thru-hike at the young age of 79. ATC's first "corresponding secretary," he was active in Trail work and promoting trails for the YHC and Susquehanna Appalachian Trail Club for many years.

Clarks Ferry Shelter (1993)—Sleeps 8. Privy. A blue-blazed trail leads 100 yards to the shelter and 100 yards farther to a reliable piped spring.

Susquehanna Appalachian Trail Club—SATC maintains the 20.8 miles from Pa. 225 to Rausch Creek. Correspondence should be sent to <hike-hbg@satc-hike.org> or SATC Box 61001, Harrisburg, PA 17106-1001.

Peters Mountain Shelter (1994)—Sleeps 20. Privy. The little shelter that Earl Shaffer built years earlier was removed in 2008 for inclusion in the A.T. Museum. Water source for shelter is down a steep, blue-blazed trail of almost 300 rock steps in front of shelter on north side of the mountain.

Blue Mountain Eagle Climbing Club—BMECC maintains the 62.5 miles from Rausch Creek to Tri-County Corner and the 3 miles from Bake Oven Knob to Lehigh Furnace Gap. Correspondence can be sent to P.O. Box 14982, Reading, PA 19612; (610) 326-1656; <www.bmecc.org>; <info@bmecc.org>.

Rausch Gap Shelter (1972, rebuilt in 2012)—Sleeps 12. Privy. Tenting along side trail. Water source is a reliable spring next to the shelter.

 Pa. 443—West 2.6 miles to *Camping:* Twin Grove KOA, (800) 562-5471, <www.twingrove. com>, $45 tentsite, laundry, restaurant, ice-cream parlor, Internet, pool, nonguest shower $5.

 Pa. 72/Swatara Gap—East 2.4 miles to Lickdale, adjacent to I-81 Exit 90. ■ *Restaurants:* Wendy's, Dairy Queen, McDonald's, Chester's Chicken, Sbarro Italian, Subway, Godfather's Pizza. ■ *Lodging:* Best Western, (717) 865-4234, $109D, continental B, laundry, pool, Internet; Days Inn, (717) 865-4064, $50–$99, pets $10, laundry, hot tub, continental B, Internet access; Comfort Inn, (717) 865-8080, $65–$109, continental B, Internet access, laundry, pool. ■ *Camping:* Lickdale Campground and General Store (short-term resupply), (877) 865-6411, $26–$30/tentsite, laundry, ATM, store with rotisserie chicken, pizza. ■ *Other services:* Love's (showers $9, ATM), BP, and Exxon all have stores (short-term resupply).

William Penn Shelter (1993)—Sleeps 16. Privy. With second-floor loft and windows, 0.1 mile east of the A.T, often visited by summer camping groups. Water source is 200 yards on a blue-blazed trail to the west of the A.T.

 Pa. 501—East 2 miles to Bethel, Pa. [P.O. ZIP 19507: M–F 8–12 & 1:15–4:30, Sa 8:30–10:30; (717) 933-8305]. ■ *Other services:* Bethel Animal Clinic, (717) 933-4916. ■ *Internet access:* Bethel Library, M–Th 10–8, F 10–5, Sa 9–4. ■ *Shuttle:* Joyce and Lance Carlin, (570) 345-0474 or cell (570) 51-3447, <smtownqn@yahoo.com>; 8 a.m.–10 p.m.; call for rates.

West 3.7 miles to Pine Grove, Pa. [P.O. ZIP 17963: M–F 8:30–4:30, Sa 9–12; (570) 345-4955]. Most major services but spread out over three miles. ■ *Lodging:* Hampton Inn, (570) 345-4505, indoor pool, laundry, WiFi, continental B; Econo Lodge, (570) 345-4099, weekdays $45–$60, dogs $10 (in smoking rooms), continental B; Comfort Inn, (570) 345-8031, $60–$109D, pets $10, includes continental B, pool, Internet access; Colony Lodge, (570) 345-8095, $40–$55D, pets $5. ■ *Groceries:* Turkey Hill Market with ATM (short-term resupply); BG's Market (long-term resupply), daily 7–9. ■ *Restaurants:* O'Neals Pub, L/D W–Su; McDonald's; Arby's; the Original Italian Pizza Place,

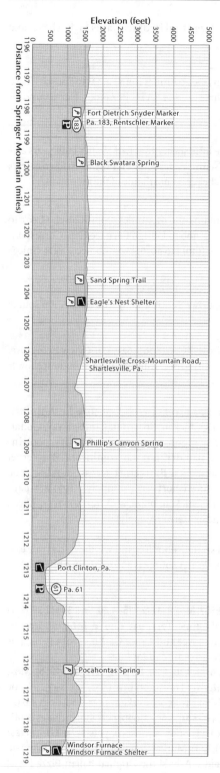

L/D; Do's Pizza, L/D, closed Su; Dominick's Pizza, L/D, closed M; Buddy's Log Cabin Restaurant; Burke's Dairy Bar; Gooseberry Farms Family Restaurant; Subway; Dairy Queen; Blimpie. ■ *Other services:* coin laundry (7 a.m.–10 p.m.), barber, bank with ATM, doctor, podiatrist, dentist, veterinarian, pharmacy (closed Su), movie theater, and community pool ($9.50).

501 Shelter (1980s)—Immediately north of paved Pa. 501, go west on the blue-blaze 0.1 mile; always open, no fee. Shelter is fully enclosed, with 12 bunks, table, chairs, skylight (a potter once had her wheel underneath), privy, and solar shower. Tentsites off woods road uphill, beyond fire ring. Water from faucet at adjacent house of BMECC caretaker. No smoking inside shelter; no alcoholic beverages allowed. Pets allowed (on leash only) if other shelter guests are willing to share and owner takes care of sanitary needs. Shuttles and motoring visitors park in public lot on paved 501 and walk in *via* blue-blaze.

Eagles Nest Shelter (1988)—Sleeps 8. Privy. Shelter is 0.3 mile from the A.T. on a blue-blazed trail. Intermittent Yeich Spring is crossed *en route* to the shelter.

Port Clinton, Pa. [P.O. ZIP 19549: M–F 7:30–12:30 & 2–5, Sa 8–11; (610) 562-3787]—Port Clinton allows hikers to camp free under the roof of its pavilion. The pavilion, with outhouse, located 0.3 mile west of the A.T. on Penn Street, is a drug- and alcohol-free area. Permission is required for a stay of more than two nights [call LaVerne Sterner, (570) 366-0489]. No car camping. Water can be obtained from a spigot outside the Port Clinton Hotel. ■ *Lodging:* Port Clinton Hotel, (610) 562-3354, <www.portclintonhotel.net>, $49PP, $10 deposit for room key and towel, shower only $5, closed M, limited rooms available, laundry, no reservations, WiFi; Union House Bed & Bath, (610) 562-4076, (610) 562-3155, bedroom, bath, and sitting room for hikers $65S, call to ask about double rooms and pets. ■ *Restaurants:* Port Clinton Hotel, L/D, closed M; 3-C's Restaurant, B/L, M–F 5–3, Sa–Su 6–2; Union House B&B, D. ■ *Other services:* The Port Clinton Peanut Shop, open M–Th 10–7, F–Sa 10–8, Su 10–6, with home-

Port Clinton ↑
elevation 417'

3C's
Restaurant (0.6 mi.)

🚹🚺 Pavilion

Little Schuylkill River

Penn St

61

Port Clinton
Hotel •
Peanut •
Shop

Post Office •
Union House
•B&B

made goodies and snacks, cold drinks, ATM.

East on Pa. 61 1.5 miles to ■ *Lodging:* Microtel Inn, <www.microtelinn.com>, (610) 562-4234, $84–$159D, continental B, pet-friendly ($10 nonrefundable fee), free long-distance phone, laundry, WiFi. ■ *Restaurants:* Cabela's Restaurant, B/L/D; Wendy's; Burger King; Cracker Barrel; Pappy T's in Microtel Inn, L/D; Dunkin' Donuts–Baskin Robbins; Shell with food mart (short-term resupply); Subway; Taco Bell/Long John Silver's; McDonald's; Pizza Hut/Wings Street, (610) 562-3619. ■ *Outfitter:* Cabela's Superstore, <www.cabelas.com>, (610) 929-7000, M–Sa 8–9, Su 9–8, camping department, fuel (Esbit, propane/butane, Coleman Powermax), A.T. maps, ATM. ■ *Other services:* Walmart, next to Cabela's. ■ *Bus service:* M–Sa from Cabela's to Hamburg to Reading with connections to Philadelphia; (610) 921-0601, <www.bartabus.com>.

East on Pa. 61 3 miles, then left (0.5 mile) on State Street to **Hamburg, Pa. [P.O. ZIP 19526; M–F 9–5, Sa 9–12; (610) 562-7812]**. ■ *Lodging:* American House Hotel near center of town, (610) 562-4683. ■ *Groceries:* Weis Supermarket, open daily 6–11, one block east of the town center. ■ *Other services:* coin laundry, pharmacy, movie theater, doctor, dentist, bakery, medical center, veterinarian, banks with ATM. Near Pa. 61 are Redner's Market Warehouse (open 24 hrs., long-term resupply), Dollar General, Family Dollar, Rite Aid, Arby's, Xiang Shan (Chinese food), Loue's Pizza, Subway.

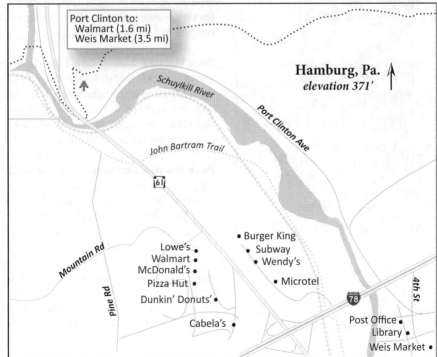

Port Clinton to:
Walmart (1.6 mi)
Weis Market (3.5 mi)

Schuylkill River

Hamburg, Pa. ↑
elevation 371'

Port Clinton Ave

John Bartram Trail

61

Mountain Rd

pine Rd

Lowe's •
Walmart •
McDonald's •
Pizza Hut •
Dunkin' Donuts' •

Cabela's •

• Burger King
• Subway
• Wendy's

• Microtel

78

4th St

Post Office •
Library •
Weis Market •

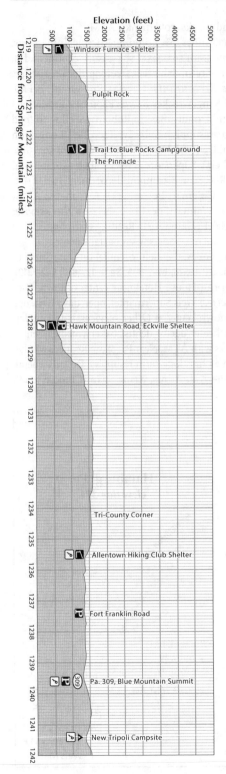

Hamburg Reservoir—A parking area 0.3 mile **East** of the A.T. requires free permits for overnight parking. Call the Borough of Hamburg, (610) 562-7821, for permission.

Windsor Furnace Shelter (1970s)—Sleeps 8. Privy. Tentsites. Shelter is located on a blue-blazed trail near the reservoir. Water source is the creek south of the shelter. *No campfires except at shelter. No swimming in streams or reservoir.*

Blue Rocks Campground— **East** 1.5 miles to campground, 341 Sousley Rd., Lenhartsville, PA 19534; (866) 478-5267, <www.bluerockscampground.com>; *via* a blue-blazed trail from Pulpit Rock and a yellow-blazed trail from The Pinnacle. Tentsites $32 M–F, 50% discount for thru-hikers M–Th, showers, swimming (nonguest) $4, laundry, WiFi. Camp store (short-term resupply), M–Th 9–7, F 9–11, Sa 8–11, Su 8–7, with Coleman fuel and limited hiker supplies. Mail drops accepted. Hiker-friendly.

The Pinnacle—A panoramic view of Pennsylvania farmland from an elevation of 1,635 feet, said to be the best view on the A.T. in the state. Below the viewpoint lies a sheer cliff and a few caves. *No camping or fires are permitted.*

Hawk Mountain Road—**East** 0.2 mile to Eckville Shelter, an enclosed bunkroom that offers space for 6. No fee. Water from a spigot at the back of the caretaker's house. Solar shower, flush toilet, tent platforms, picnic table. Open year-round; privy and shower are winterized.

Hawk Mountain Sanctuary—Atop the Kittatinny Ridge sits the Hawk Mountain Visitors Center, <www.hawkmountain.org>, accessible *via* a 2.5-mile blue-blazed trail from the A.T. Located within the visitors center are a bookstore, gift shop, and interpretive exhibits on raptors that fly by the mountain during the migratory seasons. Several species other than raptors can be seen; 16 species of hawks, falcons, and eagles have been spotted over the mountain. Entrance fee $6 adults, $5 seniors, $3 children, except in autumn, when it rises to adults $8, children $4.

Allentown Hiking Club—AHC maintains the 10.7 miles from Tri-County Corner to Bake Oven Knob. Correspondence should be sent to P.O. Box 1542, Allentown, PA 18105; <www.allentown-hikingclub.org>; <info@allentownhikingclub.org>.

Allentown Hiking Club Shelter (1997)—Sleeps 8. Privy. Tentsites. First water source is a spring 0.2 mile downhill in front of shelter; if dry, continue downhill 0.1 mile to second spring.

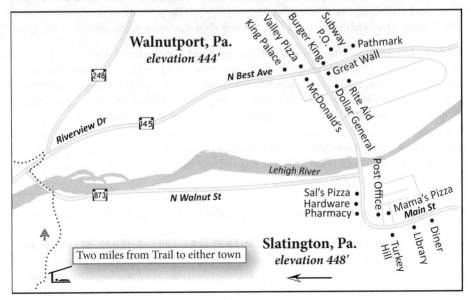

Pa. 309—*Lodging:* Blue Mountain B&B, (570) 386-2003, <www.bluemountainsummit. com>, $95–$125/ night. Restaurant open Th–Sa 11–10, Su 11–8; live music all year on F 7–10, on Su Jun–Sep Su 5–8 on the patio; hiker register. Possible camping near restaurant if you ask first. Water available from outside spigot.

Bake Oven Knob Shelter (1937)—Sleeps 6. No privy. One of the original Pennsylvania shelters. The first water source on the blue-blazed trail is often dry; continue 200 yards to the second, more dependable spring, although both may be intermittent.

Philadelphia Trail Club—PTC maintains the 10.3 miles from Lehigh Furnace Gap to Little Gap. Correspondence should be sent to 741 Golf Rd., Warrington, PA 18976; <pauls@deperjico.com>.

George W. Outerbridge Shelter (1965)—Sleeps 6. No privy. The surrounding area suffers from heavy-metal contamination from the zinc plant at Palmerton (see Superfund entry below). Water source is a piped spring north 150 yards on the A.T.

Pa. 873/Lehigh Gap—**East** 2 miles on Pa. 873 to **Slatington, Pa. [P.O. ZIP 18080: M–F 8:30–5, Sa 8:30–12; (610) 767-2182].** ■ *Restaurants:* The Shack, L/D; Mama's Pizza; Sal's Pizza; Slatington Diner B/L/D. ■ *Internet access:* Slatington Library, M, W 9–7, Tu 9–3, F 9–5, Sa 8–2. ■ *Other services:* coin laundry, ATM, convenience stores, A.F. Boyer Hardware store, doctor, dentist, pharmacy, bowling alley, and bus service to Walnutport and Allentown.
　East 2 miles on Pa. 145 to **Walnutport, Pa. [P.O. ZIP 18088: M–F 8:30–5, Sa 8:30–12; (610) 767-5191].** *See map on page 139.* ■ *Groceries:* Super Fresh Supermarket (long-term resupply). ■ *Restaurants:*

Walnutport, Pa.
elevation 444'

King Palace · Valley Pizza · Burger King · P.O. · Subway · Pathmark
248
N Best Ave · Great Wall
McDonald's · Rite Aid · Dollar General
Riverview Dr
145
Lehigh River
Post Office
873
N Walnut St
Sal's Pizza ·
Hardware ·
Pharmacy ·
Mama's Pizza · Main St
Diner · Library · Turkey Hill

Slatington, Pa.
elevation 448'

Two miles from Trail to either town

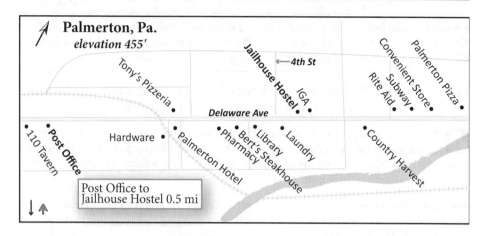

Palmerton, Pa.
elevation 455'

Tony's Pizzeria
Jailhouse Hostel
←4th St
IGA
Convenient Store
Subway
Rite Aid
Palmerton Pizza
Delaware Ave
Post Office
110 Tavern
Hardware
Palmerton Hotel
Pharmacy
Bert's Steakhouse
Library
Laundry
Country Harvest

Post Office to
Jailhouse Hostel 0.5 mi

Valley Restaurant and Pizza, $5.75 AYCE L; King Palace Chinese, $4.95 AYCE L; Great Wall Chinese; d'Sopranos Pizza; fast-food options. ■ *Other services:* ATM, doctor, dentist, pharmacy, veterinarian, Kmart.

West 2 miles on Pa. 248 or 2-mile blue-blaze to **Palmerton, Pa. [P.O. ZIP 18071: M–F 8:30–5, Sa 8:30–12; (610) 826-2286]**. *Blue-blaze directions:* **West** 1.5 miles from the gravel lot on the northwest side of the Lehigh River over the Aquashicola Creek Bridge to the back road leading to Delaware Ave. in Palmerton. ■ *Hostel:* The city allows hikers to sleep in the basement of the borough hall, 443 Delaware Ave., (610) 826-2505; showers. Hikers (unassisted-by-vehicles only) should check in before 4:30; the town police (located at 401 Delaware Ave.) admit hikers after 4:30 weekdays and Sa–Su. You will need to provide an ID, name, address, and Trail name. No pets. *No alcoholic beverages or intoxicated persons permitted.* ■ *Lodging:* The Palmerton Hotel, (610) 826-5454, $55S, $65 efficiency unit. ■ *Groceries:* IGA, Country Harvest (both long-term resupply). ■ *Restaurants:* Bert's Steakhouse, B/L/D; One Ten Tavern, L/D, closed M; Simply Something Café, B/L/D; Tony's Pizzeria; Joe's Place, deli sandwiches; Palmerton Pizza and Restaurant; Subway; Hunan House Chinese. ■ *Internet access:* library M 10–8, T–F 10–5, Sa 9–4 (Sa Jul–Aug 9–1). ■ *Other services:* coin laundry; ATM; shuttle back to the Trail, Duane Masonheimer, (610) 767-7969; Shea's Hardware and Sporting Goods, Heet, Coleman fuel, and denatured alcohol; bowling alley; pharmacy; doctor; dentist; and hospital.

Palmerton EPA Superfund Site—The devastation along Blue Mountain near Lehigh Gap is the result of nearly a century of zinc smelting in Palmerton. In 1980, the Environmental Protection Agency shut down the furnaces and, in 1982, put the affected area on the Superfund clean-up list. Revegetation efforts are underway, and the mountain is slowly coming back to life. The scramble up the denuded rocks is among the most challenging on the A.T. south of New Hampshire.

Appalachian Mountain Club–Delaware Valley Chapter—AMC–Delaware Valley maintains the 15.4 miles from Little Gap to Wind Gap. Correspondence should be sent to 1180 Greenleaf Dr., Bethlehem, PA 18017; <www.amcdv.org>.

 Little Gap, Blue Mountain Drive—**West** 2.5 miles to Little Gap and *Restaurant:* Covered Bridge Inn.

East 1.5 miles to **Danielsville, Pa. [P.O. 18038: M–F 8:30–12 & 2–4:30, Sa 8–12; (610) 767-6822]**. ■ *Lodging:* Filbert B&B, (610) 428-3300, <www.filbertbnb.com>, starting at $100D, reservations required; full, hearty, country B; pay laundry; will pick up and drop off hikers and possibly shuttle; mail drops accepted, but call first; deliveries by local restaurants, use of dining room. ■ *Restaurants:* Blue

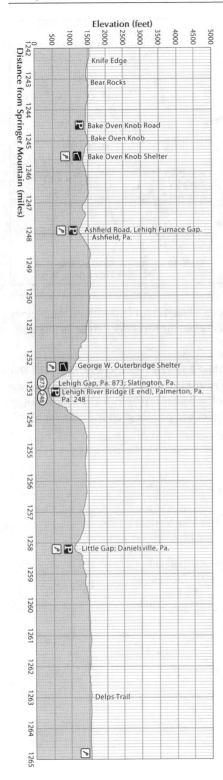

Elevation (feet)

Distance from Springer Mountain (miles)

Knife Edge

Bear Rocks

Bake Oven Knob Road
Bake Oven Knob

Bake Oven Knob Shelter

Ashfield Road, Lehigh Furnace Gap,
Ashfield, Pa.

George W. Outerbridge Shelter

Lehigh Gap, Pa. 873; Slatington, Pa.
Lehigh River Bridge (E end), Palmerton, Pa.
Pa. 248

Little Gap; Danielsville, Pa.

Delps Trail

Mountain Family Restaurant, Chinese restaurant, Mama's Pizza and Como Pizza (both deliver). ■ *Groceries:* Millers Market.

Smith Gap Road—For northbounders, it is the first road after the Stempa Spring side trail, on which it's **West** 1 mile to a water spigot at the rear of the house of Linda "Crayon Lady" and John "Mechanical Man" Stempa, (610) 381-4606. Free cold shower; hiker register; pets welcome; homemade alcohol stoves, windscreens, and methyl fuel available. Shuttles to area Trailheads by arrangement. Ask about safe parking.

Leroy A. Smith Shelter (1972)—Sleeps 8. Privy (composting). Shelter is 0.2 mile down a blue-blazed trail. Water sources are said to be reliable; the first, 0.2 mile down the blue-blazed trail; a second, on a yellow-blazed trail 0.2 mile farther; a third, even farther, may be running when the first two are not. *Note: Water is out at Kirkridge Shelter.*

Batona Hiking Club—BHC maintains the 8.6 miles from Wind Gap to Fox Gap (Pa. 191). Correspondence can be sent to BHC, 6651 Eastwood St., Philadelphia, Pa. 19149; <www.batonahikingclub.org>.

Pa. 33—**East** 1 mile to **Wind Gap, Pa. [P.O. ZIP 18091: M–F 8:30–5, Sa 8:30–12; (610) 863-6206].** *See map on next page.* ■ *Lodging:* About 2 miles from the Trail: Red Carpet Inn, (610) 863-7782, $65S, $75D, 2 to a room. ■ *Groceries:* Giant Food Store located in Kmart Plaza (long-term resupply, 24 hrs.); Turkey Hill Mini Market, Sunoco Mini Mart (both short-term resupply). ■ *Restaurants:* Sal's Pizza; Beer Stein; Hong Kong Restaurant; diners serving B/L/D; Rita's Ices; other fast-food options. ■ *Other services:* coin laundry, Kmart, hardware store, doctor (24-hour clinic), dentist, pharmacy, veterinarian, bank with ATM, and movie theater.

Wilmington Trail Club—WTC maintains the 7.2 miles from Fox Gap to the Delaware River Bridge. Correspondence should be sent to P.O. Box 1184, Wilmington, DE 19899; <www.wilmingtontrailclub.org>.

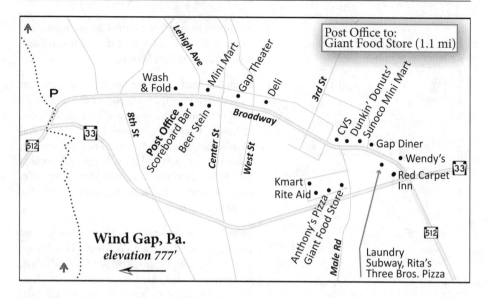

Kirkridge Shelter (1948)—Sleeps 8. Privy. Shelter is on a blue-blazed trail with excellent views south. Water source, an outside tap to rear of shelter before the Kirkridge Retreat facility parking lot, was *out of order at publication time.*

Pa. 611/Delaware Water Gap, Pa. [P.O. ZIP 18327: M–F 8:30–12 & 1–4:45, Sa 8:30–11:30; (570) 476-0304]—The A.T. doesn't go through the town center, but services are within a mile of where it crosses Pa. 611. ■ *Hostel:* The Presbyterian Church of the Mountain Hostel, with overflow lean-to in backyard, has Th hiker feeds in summer at 6 p.m.; please respect the good-will of Pastor Sherry

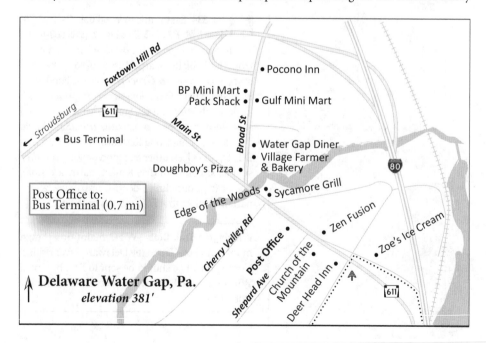

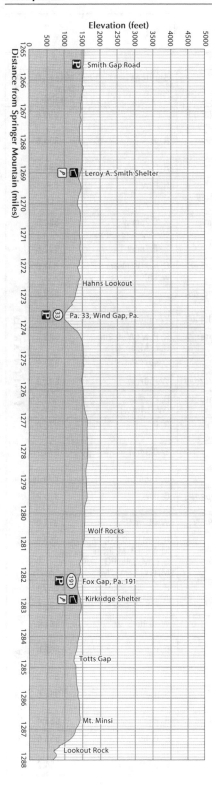

Elevation (feet)

Distance from Springer Mountain (miles)

Smith Gap Road

Leroy A. Smith Shelter

Hahns Lookout

Pa. 33, Wind Gap, Pa.

Wolf Rocks

Fox Gap, Pa. 191

Kirkridge Shelter

Totts Gap

Mt. Minsi

Lookout Rock

Blackman and parishioners. Space with shower limited to long-distance hikers—no car or van parking or support vehicles permitted in parking lot. Two-night limit, donations suggested, *absolutely no drugs or alcohol.* ■ *Lodging:* Deer Head Inn, (570) 424-2000, restaurant and upscale rooms; Pocono Inn, (570) 476-0000, 101 Broad St., $55 (4 max), $65 on weekends, no pets, coin laundry, hiker-friendly. ■ *Restaurants:* DWG Diner, (570) 476-0132, B/L/D; Doughboy Pizza; Deer Head Inn for fine dining F–Su, pizza, and live entertainment, notably jazz; Sycamore Grille, L/D, closed Su–M, D by reservation; Castle Inn, near Trail at Mountain Road, old-fashioned ice cream. ■ *Groceries:* Fuel On Mini Mart with ATM, Gulf Mini Mart (both short-term resupply); Farmer's Market with fruits, vegetables, baked goods, and ice cream. ■ *Outfitters:* The Pack Shack, (570) 424-8530, Leki repair, limited hiker gear, some fuels, shuttles; Edge of the Woods Outfitters, 110 Main St. (Rt. 611), (570) 421-6681, maps, bike rentals, outerwear, activewear, footwear, all brands, will hold UPS packages for thru-hikers, shuttle $1.50/mi, very hiker-friendly. ■ *Other services:* hair salon, run by Paulette, (570) 421-8218, Tu–F 10–7, Sa 10–3. ■ *Bus service:* Martz Trailways, (570) 421-4451 or (570) 421-3040, to New York, Philadelphia, and Scranton, and local service on "Pocono Pony" to Stroudsburg and Delaware Water Gap National Recreation Area.

West 5 miles to East Stroudsburg and Stroudsburg, Pa., full-service towns. ■ *Outfitter:* Dunkelberger's Sports Outfitter, (570) 421-7950, with backpacking equipment, supplies, and clothing, is located at 6th and Main streets. ■ *Other services:* 7-day walk-in clinic at hospital.

New Jersey

Miles from Springer	Fr Last Point	Features	Services	Miles from Katahdin	M A P
1,293.6	0.2	Delaware River Bridge (west end) (350') Pennsylvania–New Jersey State Line		895.6	
1,294.6	1.0	Delaware Water Gap NRA Kittatinny Point Visitors Center (350')	R, w	894.6	
1,295.0	0.4	I-80 (350')...underpass	R	894.2	
1,295.1	0.1	Dunnfield Creek Natural Area (350')... water pump at northern end of parking area	R, P, w	894.1	
1,295.2	0.1	Dunnfield Hollow Trail to Dunnfield Creek Falls (350')	E–0.25m w	894.0	
1,296.6	1.4	Holly Springs Trail (950')	E–0.2m w	892.6	
1,298.2	1.6	Blue-blazed Douglas Trail, Backpacker Campsite (1,300')	C, nw (W–1.8m C, w, sh)	891.0	
1,299.5	1.3	Sunfish Pond (1,382')...glacial pond, no camping		889.7	
1,299.6	0.1	Orange-blazed Garvey Spring Trail (1,400')	W–600 ft w	889.6	ATC N.Y.–N.J. Map 4
1,303.9	4.3	Camp Road; Mohican Outdoor Center (1,150')	R, P, w (W–0.3m C, L, M, sh, f)	885.3	
1,306.3	2.4	Catfish Fire Tower (1,565')	C, nw	882.9	
1,306.9	0.6	Rattlesnake Spring (1,260')...on dirt road	W–50ft w	882.3	
1,307.3	0.4	Millbrook–Blairstown Road–County Road 602 (1,260')	R, P (W–1.1m w)	881.9	
1,311.2	3.9	Blue Mountain Lakes Road (1,350') (Flatbrookville Stillwater Road)	R, P	878.0	
1,313.0	1.8	Crater Lake Trail (1,560') ...view 150 ft. east	E–0.3m w	876.2	
1,314.1	1.1	Buttermilk Falls Trail (1,560')	E–1.5m w	875.1	
1,316.0	1.9	Rattlesnake Mountain (1,492')...open ledges	C, nw	873.2	
1,318.2	2.2	**Brink Shelter** (1,110')...31.4mS; 6.9mN	W–0.2m S, w	871.0	
1,321.8	3.6	U.S. 206, Culvers Gap (935') **Branchville, N.J. 07826**	R, P, M (E–0.8 G; 1m M; 1.6m G, M; 2.5m G, L, M; 3.4m PO, M) (W–1.8m L, M)	867.4	
1,322.1	0.3	Sunrise Mountain Road (970')	R	867.1	
1,323.7	1.6	Culver Fire Tower (1,550')		865.5	
1,324.8	1.1	**Gren Anderson Shelter** (1,320')...6.9mS; 5.9mN	W–0.1m S, w	864.4	ATC N.Y.–N.J. Map 3
1,327.2	2.4	Sunrise Mountain (1,653')...picnic pavilion	R, P, nw	862.0	
1,328.0	0.8	Crigger Road (1,400')...dirt	R	861.2	
1,330.6	2.6	**Mashipacong Shelter** (1,425') ...5.9mS; 3mN	S, nw	858.6	
1,330.8	0.2	Deckertown Turnpike (1,320')...paved	R, P	858.4	
1,333.2	2.4	**Rutherford Shelter** (1,345') ...3mS; 5.1mN	E–0.4m S, w	856.0	
1,335.0	1.8	Blue Dot Trail (1,600')	W 0.4m C, w	854.2	

Miles from Springer	Fr Last Point	Features	Services	Miles from Katahdin	MAP
1,336.1	1.1	N.J. 23; High Point State Park HQ (1,500') **Port Jervis, N.Y. 12771**	R, w (E–1.5m L; 2.9m M) (W–0.7m sh; 4.4m G, L, M; 7.1m PO, G, L, M, D, T)	853.1	
1,337.1	1.0	Observation Platform (1,680')		852.1	
1,337.3	0.2	Side Trail to High Point Monument (1,600')		851.9	
1,337.8	0.5	**High Point Shelter** (1,280') *...5.1mS; 12.5mN*	E–0.1m S, w	851.4	
1,339.1	1.3	County Road 519 (1,100')	R, P (E–2.5m L)	850.1	
1,339.9	0.8	Courtwright Road (1,000')	R	849.3	
1,341.1	1.2	Ferguson Road (900')	R	848.1	
1,341.7	0.6	Gemmer Road (740')	R	847.5	
1,342.4	0.7	Stream (710')	w	846.8	
1,342.7	0.3	Goodrich Road (610')	R	846.5	
1,342.9	0.2	Concrete Dam (outlet of pond) (700')		846.3	
1,343.1	0.2	Trail to Jim Murray property (660')	W–0.2m S, C, w, sh	846.1	
1,343.2	0.1	Goldsmith Road (600')	R	846.0	
1,343.4	0.2	Vernie Swamp (northern end) (590')... *puncheon*		845.8	
1,344.0	0.6	Unionville Road, County Road 651 (610')	R, P	845.2	
1,344.9	0.9	Lott Road (590') **Unionville, N.Y. 10988**	R (W–0.4m PO, C, G, M)	844.3	
1,345.9	1.0	N.J. 284 (420')	R, P (W–0.4m G, M)	843.3	
1,346.4	0.5	Oil City Road (400')	R	842.8	
1,347.4	1.0	Wallkill River (410')	R	841.8	
1,347.7	0.3	Wallkill National Wildlife Perserve (410')		841.5	
1,349.7	2.0	Lake Wallkill Road (Liberty Corners Road) (440')	R	839.5	
1,350.2	0.5	**Pochuck Mountain Shelter** (840') *...12.5mS; 11.6mN*	S, nw	839.0	
1,351.7	1.5	Pochuck Mountain (1,200')		837.5	
1,352.9	1.2	County Road 565 (720') **Glenwood, N.J. 07418**	R, P (W–1.1m PO, C, G, L, w)	836.3	
1,354.4	1.5	County Road 517 (440') **Glenwood, N.J. 07418**	R (W–1.1m PO, C, G, L, w)	834.8	
1,355.1	0.7	Pochuck Creek (410')...*boardwalk, bridge*		834.1	
1,355.8	0.7	Canal Road (410')	R, P	833.4	
1,356.7	0.9	N.J. 94 (450') **Vernon, N.J. 07462**	R, P (E–1.4 L; 2.4m PO, H, G, M, D, V, cl, f; 5.2 D) (W–0.1m G, M, w; 2.5m M; 6.1m Warwick, N.Y. below)	832.5	
1,358.1	1.4	Wawayanda Mountain (1,340')		831.1	
1,359.8	1.7	Barrett Road, New Milford, N.Y. (1,140')	R, P	829.4	
1,360.9	1.1	Iron Mountain Road (1,060')...*bridge*	R (E–1.6m M, w)	828.3	

ATC N.Y.–N.J. Map 3

Miles from Springer	Fr Last Point	Features	Services	Miles from Katahdin	M A P
1,361.5	0.6	Wawayanda Road (1,150')	R	827.7	ATC N.Y.–N.J. Map 3
1,361.7	0.2	**Wawayanda Shelter** (1,200') ...11.6mS; 12.2mN	W–0.1m S	827.5	
1,361.8	0.1	Hoeferlin Trail (1,200')...*water for Wawayanda Shelter*	E–0.2m w	827.4	
1,362.2	0.4	Warwick Turnpike (1,140')	R, P (W–2.7m G, M)	827.0	
1,363.6	1.4	Long House Road (Brady Road) (1,080')	R, P	825.6	
1,364.7	1.1	Long House Creek (1,085')		824.5	
1,365.8	1.1	New Jersey–NewYork State Line (1,385') State Line Trail; Hewitt, N.J.		823.4	

Bear boxes are provided at several New Jersey shelters; please use them! Bears are extremely active in this area. One pair destroyed a hiker's tent. Never feed bears or leave food unattended. Do not bury or scatter excess food; avoid eating or preparing food in your tent.

Campfires are prohibited in New Jersey. Camping in areas other than those designated by signs also is prohibited in New Jersey. Hitchhiking is illegal in New Jersey.

Venomous snakes are active throughout the area during warmer months. Be cautious when hiking at night, and pay attention near rocky ledges.

New Jersey has the highest population of bears per square mile. Southbounders are at the end of their deli-to-deli hike, whereas northbounders hungrily look forward to theirs. Thru-hiker legs are operating at machine level by now, which is good, because you may have to walk farther to find water.

New York–New Jersey Trail Conference—The NY–NJ TC maintains the 162.2 miles from Delaware Water Gap to the New York–Connecticut state line. Correspondence should be sent to NY–NJ TC, 156 Ramapo Valley Rd., Mahwah, NJ 07430; (201) 512-9348; <www.nynjtc.org>; <info@nynjtc.org>.

Delaware Water Gap National Recreation Area—The Kittatinny Point Visitors Center, (908) 496-4458, visible from the Trail, has restrooms and a picnic area. Open daily Memorial Day weekend—Labor Day and 3 days a week in early fall. Water is available from a spigot to the left of the building. The Trail on Kittatinny Ridge runs through the NRA and state parks and forests, where regulations are different. The history of the recreation area is linked to a controversial 1960s plan to dam the Delaware, defeated by local opponents and the Trail community. Thru-hikers (defined by DWG as those hiking for two or more consecutive days) are permitted to camp along the Trail in the NRA with the following restrictions: one night per campsite, no more than ten persons per site, hiker camping allowed only within 100 feet of the A.T., no camping within 0.5 mile of an established roadway, no camping within 200 feet of another party, no camping from 0.5 mile south of Blue Mountain Lakes Road to a point roughly 3 miles north, no camping within 100 feet of any water source. Ground fires and charcoal stoves and grills are prohibited.

Holly Spring Trail—Holly Spring is 0.2 mile east of the A.T.; may faily during dry weather.

Worthington State Forest—Camping in Worthington State Forest is only permitted at Backpacker Campsite 2 at the junction with the Douglas Trail 4.6 miles north of I-80 on the A.T. and at the

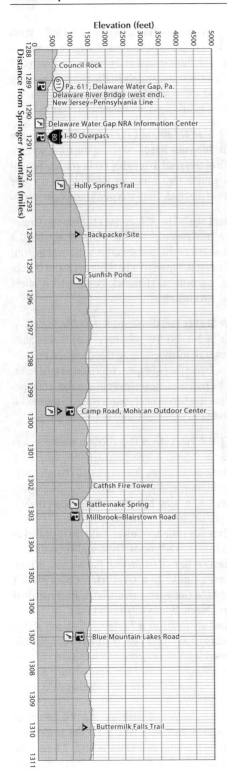

Elevation (feet)

Distance from Springer Mountain (miles)

- Council Rock
- Pa. 611, Delaware Water Gap, Pa. Delaware River Bridge (west end), New Jersey–Pennsylvania Line
- Delaware Water Gap NRA Information Center
- I-80 Overpass
- Holly Springs Trail
- Backpacker Site
- Sunfish Pond
- Camp Road, Mohican Outdoor Center
- Catfish Fire Tower
- Rattlesnake Spring
- Millbrook–Blairstown Road
- Blue Mountain Lakes Road
- Buttermilk Falls Trail

state-forest campground on Old Mine Road (see below). Rangers patrol the area and issue fines for those violating camping restrictions. Worthington State Forest Campground, (908) 841-9575, offers riverside camping and showers. From the A.T., take the blue Douglas Trail west 1.1 mile, then turn left onto the green Rock Cores Trail for another 0.7 mile to forest office; $25/site + $5 walk-in fee, max. 6 people; no pets or alcohol.

Sunfish Pond—The southernmost glacial pond on the A.T. and one of seven protected natural areas in the state of New Jersey, the pond also has several unique man-made features and is a beauty to behold. *No camping or swimming is allowed at the pond.*

Garvey Spring Trail—A seasonal spring is located 600 feet west of the A.T.

Herbert Hiller plaque—The 23rd A.T. 2,000-miler and a longtime Trail booster in New Jersey is memorialized on a plaque off the A.T. on Kittatinny Mountain.

AMC Mohican Outdoor Center—West, on a dirt road, 0.3 mile; 50 Camp Mohican Rd., Blairstown, NJ 07825; (908) 362-5670, operated by the Appalachian Mountain Club (AMC). Thru-hikers can stay overnight for $35–$40PP in a shared cabin with bunk, stove, and shower. Tent-camping $12 to thru-hikers; showers w/towel $5. Ask if meal option is available. Camp store with deli (Memorial to Labor Day), sodas, candy, and limited hiker supplies, including Coleman and denatured alcohol by the ounce. The center accepts packages marked "Hold for A.T. Hiker" (with name) and sent *via* USPS, UPS, or FedEx; it cannot send packages. Check in at the visitors center, entrance on the left. Water available there or from a seasonal spigot near the garage across the road.

Catfish Fire Tower—Several campsites are located just south of the tower, along the east side of the A.T. with good views across the valley. Get water at Rattlesnake Spring (below).

Rattlesnake Spring—Located 0.6 mile north of the Catfish Fire Tower on a dirt road about 50 feet west of the A.T. Spring may fail during drought times.

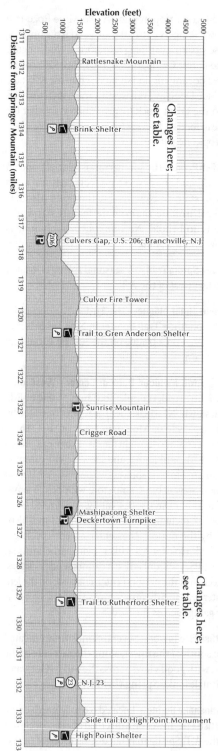

Elevation (feet)

Distance from Springer Mountain (miles)

Rattlesnake Mountain

Changes here; see table.

Brink Shelter

Culvers Gap, U.S. 206; Branchville, N.J.

Culver Fire Tower

Trail to Gren Anderson Shelter

Sunrise Mountain

Crigger Road

Mashipacong Shelter
Deckertown Turnpike

Changes here; see table.

Trail to Rutherford Shelter

N.J. 23

Side trail to High Point Monument

High Point Shelter

Millbrook–Blairstown Road, CR 602—West 1.1 miles to Millbrook Village, a historical park with flush toilets and picnic area. From Oct to May, the water supply in the picnic area is cut off, and the restrooms are closed except for a unisex, handicap-accessible bathroom.

Blue Mountain Lakes Road/Flatbrookville Stillwater Road—No camping from 0.5 mile south of this road to roughly 3 miles north. Several grassy areas for tenting are available 0.5–0.7 mile south of the road. The water pump no longer works.

Crater Lake—The A.T. crosses the orange Crater Lake Trail twice. From the second junction (0.4 mile north of the first junction), the orange trail leads east 0.3 mile to a parking area and beach; west, 0.5 mile to Hemlock Pond, which offers good swimming..

Brink Shelter (2013)—Sleeps 8. Mouldering privy. Built by NY–NJ TC volunteers and Stokes State Forest staff members using trees downed by Hurricane Irene; the old shelter, which developed leaks, will be removed. Bears and rattlesnakes are especially active here. Water source is across the road at a spring 100 yards northeast of the shelter.

U.S. 206/Culvers Gap—*Restaurants:* Stoke's Steakhouse & Pub, (973) 948-3007, open W–F 4–10, Sa–Su 11:30–10, free WiFi and charging stations, hiker-friendly; Gyp's Tavern, (973) 948-5013, located on nearby Kittatinny Lake, open daily 9 a.m.–1 a.m., serves L/D (cash only).

East 0.8 mile to Culver Lake Farm Market with fresh baked goods, fruit, and vegetables.

East 1 mile to *Restaurant:* Jumboland, B/L/D.

East 1.6 miles to ■ *Groceries:* Dale's Market with ATM (long-term resupply). ■ *Restaurants:* Dairy Queen, Jimmy's Pasta and Pizza.

East 2.5 miles to ■ *Lodging:* Cobmin Ridge Motel, (973) 948-3459, $55S, $65D, EAP's not allowed. ■ *Groceries:* Yellow Cottage Deli & Bakery (short-term resupply), closed M. ■ *Restaurants:* Riviera Mexican, open daily, L/D; Firehouse bagel Co., open daily, B/L.

East 3.4 miles to **Branchville, N.J. [P.O. ZIP 07826: M–F 8:30–5, Sa 8:30–1; (973) 948-3580].** ■ *Restaurants:* All within one block of P.O.: China One (take-out), (973) 948-8882; A&G Pizza; Victoria

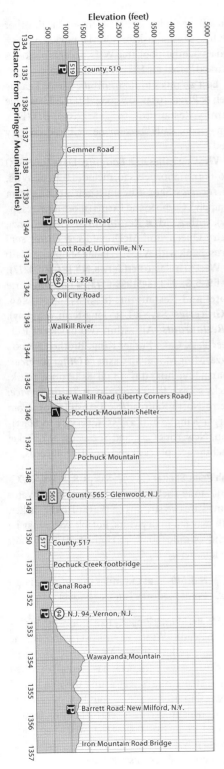

Elevation (feet)

Distance from Springer Mountain (miles)

County 519

Gemmer Road

Unionville Road

Lott Road; Unionville, N.Y.

N.J. 284

Oil City Road

Wallkill River

Lake Wallkill Road (Liberty Corners Road)

Pochuck Mountain Shelter

Pochuck Mountain

County 565; Glenwood, N.J.

County 517

Pochuck Creek footbridge

Canal Road

N.J. 94, Vernon, N.J.

Wawayanda Mountain

Barrett Road; New Milford, N.Y.

Iron Mountain Road Bridge

Diner; Third Base Pub. ■ *Shuttle:* George Lightcap, (973) 300-5127, <beatnikhiker@yahoo.com>. ■ *Other services:* bank, ATM, drugstore.

West 1.8 miles to ■ *Lodging:* Forest Motel, (973) 948-5456, $45S, $55D + tax, pets $20, call for possible pick-up from Trail. ■ *Restaurant:* Fratelli's Italian Restaurant.

Gren Anderson Shelter (1958)—Sleeps 8. Privy. Built by the now disbanded New York section of the Green Mountain Club. Water source is a spring downhill to left of the shelter.

Sunrise Mountain—*No camping allowed at pavilion.* Nearby parking lot for day-use visitors. No water.

Mashipacong Shelter (1936)—Sleeps 8. Privy. High bear activity in this area. A stone shelter with wooden floor. No water is available at this shelter.

Rutherford Shelter (1967)—Sleeps 6. Privy. High bear activity in this area. Blue access trail has been relocated 0.5 mile south of the old intersection with A.T. to avoid a steep rock scramble. Water source is an intermittent spring located 100 yards before the shelter on the connecting trail. Spring may fail during drought times.

Blue Dot Trail—West 0.4 mile to *Camping.* Steep descent from the A.T. to Sawmill Lake Campground, (973) 875-4800, open Apr 1–Oct 31, flush toilets and potable water, no showers, $25/night + $5 walk-in fee, 6/site, no pets or alcohol.

N.J. 23—High Point State Park Headquarters, 1480 State Route 23, Sussex, NJ 07461; (973) 875-4800 On the A.T., has indoor restrooms and a seasonal outdoor water spigot. Offices are open year-round; mail drops accepted. Day-use area 0.7 mile west of the A.T. on Kuser Road has swimming at spring-fed Lake Marcia, a concession stand, grill, and no charge to walk-ins for hot showers; open Memorial Day–Labor Day, 10–6. High Point Monument, on a short side trail from the A.T., marks the highest point in the state, 1,803 feet. *Camping:* See Blue Dot Trail above.

East 1.5 miles to *Lodging:* High Point Country Inn; Lee and Mike Hauck, 1328 Route 23, Wantage, NJ 07461, (973) 702-1860, <www.highpointcountryinn.com>, $80D, $10EAP, pets $5 (call

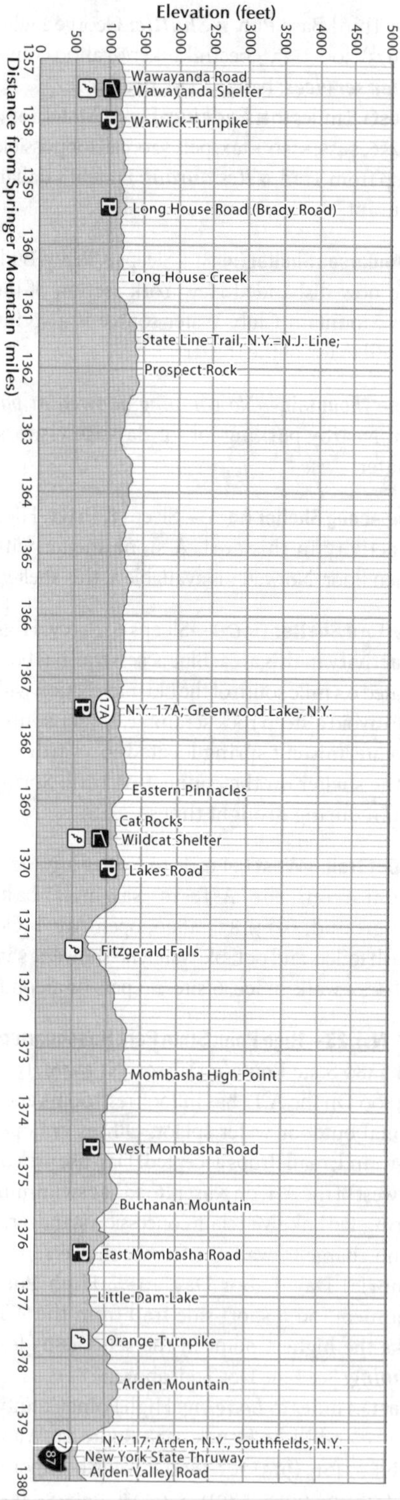
Elevation (feet)
0
500
1000
1500
2000
2500
3000
3500
4000
4500
5000
Distance from Springer Mountain (miles)
1357
1358
1359
1360
1361
1362
1363
1364
1365
1366
1367
1368
1369
1370
1371
1372
1373
1374
1375
1376
1377
1378
1379
1380
Wawayanda Road
Wawayanda Shelter
Warwick Turnpike
Long House Road (Brady Road)
Long House Creek
State Line Trail, N.Y.–N.J. Line;
Prospect Rock
17A
N.Y. 17A; Greenwood Lake, N.Y.
Eastern Pinnacles
Cat Rocks
Wildcat Shelter
Lakes Road
Fitzgerald Falls
Mombasha High Point
West Mombasha Road
Buchanan Mountain
East Mombasha Road
Little Dam Lake
Orange Turnpike
Arden Mountain
17
87
N.Y. 17; Arden, N.Y., Southfields, N.Y.
New York State Thruway
Arden Valley Road

ahead), includes shuttle to/from Trail, other shuttles $2/mile (ask for Ron), laundry service $7, soda machine, pool, free WiFi, accepts packages marked "Hold for Hiker" (with name).

East 2.9 miles to ***Restaurants:*** Major League Deli & Pizza, (973) 702-9684, B/L/D; Elias Cole Family Restaurant, (973) 875-3550, B/L/D, 7 a.m.–8 p.m., daily home-made pie, bread, country food.

West 4.4 miles to ■ ***Lodging:*** Days Inn, (845) 856-6611, $120D, pets $20, includes B, pool, WiFi. ■ ***Groceries:*** Shop-Rite supermarket (long-term resupply); Cumberland Farms (short-term resupply), with ATM. ■ ***Restaurants:*** Village Pizza, Dairy Queen, and McDonald's. ■ ***Other services:*** bank with ATM, TriState Shopping Mall.

West 7.1 miles to **Port Jervis, N.Y. [P.O. ZIP 12771: M–F 9–5, Sa 9–3; (845) 858-8173].** ■ ***Lodging:*** Erie Hotel and Restaurant, (845) 858-4100, $69. ■ ***Groceries:*** Save-a-Lot (long-term resupply). ■ ***Restaurants:*** All within two blocks of P.O.: Deer Park Café, Burger King, Brother Bruno's Pizza, Ming Moon, Mi Casita. ■ ***Other services:*** pharmacy; hospital, (845) 858-7000; bank; Bucky's Taxi, (845) 856-2220. ■ ***Train Service:*** Metro-North Railroad/NJ Transit (across from Burger King), (973) 275-5555, service to Harriman, New York City, and Secaucus, N.J. Ticket machine accepts cash and credit/debit cards.

High Point Shelter (1936)—Sleeps 8. Privy. CCC-built stone shelter with wooden floor. Water sources are two streams on the trail to the shelter; both may fail in dry years. Potable water may be found 1.5 miles south at High Point State Park headquarters.

N.J. 519—**East** 2.5 miles to ***Lodging:*** High Point Country Inn (see above).

Trail to Jim Murray Property (0.4 mile north of Goodrich Road)—**West** 0.2 mile to well water. For the past 20 years, Jim Murray (AT '89), (845) 986-0942, <backpack@warwick.net>, has cordially allowed long-distance hikers year-round use of a heated hiker cabin (sleeps 4), with outdoor shower and privy, on his property adjacent to the Trail. Tenting allowed; no groups. Follow the "well water" sign. This is a privately owned cabin. Be responsible, and please do not abuse this privilege.

Lott Road—West 0.4 mile to the town of Unionville, N.Y. [P.O. ZIP 10988: M–F 8–11:30 & 1–5, Sa 9–12; (845) 726-3535]. Lott Road is also known as Jersey Avenue. ■ *Camping:* Hikers are allowed to use Unionville Memorial Park for tenting, with water and toilet facility. ■ *Groceries:* Horler's Store with ATM (long-term resupply), (845) 726-3110, M–Sa 6–9, Su 7–7. ■ *Restaurants:* Wit's End Tavern, (845) 726-3956, Su–Th 12–12, F–Sa noon–4 a.m.; Annabel's Pizza & Italian Restaurant, (973) 940-8807, open daily 11–10.

N.J. 284—West 0.4 mile to *Groceries:* End of the Line Grocery (short-term resupply), M–F 6–8, Sa 7–8, Su 7–6, with deli sandwiches, bake shop, ATM.

Pochuck Mountain Shelter (1989)—Sleeps 6. Privy. Water is available 0.6 mile (steeply downhill) south of the shelter from a spigot (off in winter) on the north side of a vacant white house at the foot of Pochuck Mountain. No camping is allowed at the house (owned by the N.J. Department of Environmental Protection). A side trail 150 feet north of the Liberty Corners Road crossing leads 200 feet to that source. Southbounders can find water at a stream south of Sussex County Route 565.

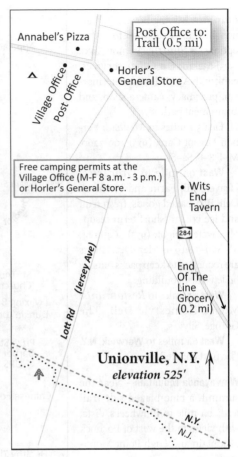

N.J. 517—West 1.1 miles to **Glenwood, N.J.** [P.O. ZIP 07418: M–F 7:30–5, Sa 10–2; (973) 764-2616]. ■ *Lodging:* Apple Valley Inn and B&B, (973) 764-3735, M–Th $135–$140, F–Su $145–$160, $25EAP, includes full B. ■ *Groceries:* Pochuck Valley Farm Market & Deli (short-term resupply), (973) 764-4732, with outside water spigot, ATM, and restroom. Open M–F 5–6, Sa–Su 6–5. ■ *Camping:* Pochuck Valley Farm Market allows limited camping for customers only; ask permission, be responsible, and please respect this privilege.

N.J. 94—East 1.4 miles to *Lodging:* Appalachian Motel, 67 Vernon–Warwick Rd., Vernon, NJ 07462; (973) 764-6070, Su–Th $75D, F–Sa $100D, $10EAP, $20 pets, recently renovated, laundry $10, call for possible pick-up from Trail or Heaven Hill Farm (see below). Accepts packages for customers only.

East 2.4 miles to **Vernon, N.J.** [P.O. ZIP 07462: M–F 8:30–5, Sa 9:30–12:30; (973) 764-9056]. ■ *Hostel:* St. Thomas Episcopal Church Hiker Hostel, (973) 764-7506, <www.st-thomas-vernon.org>, open May 15–Sep 1, but call for offseason options. Space inside for first 12, more space outside for tenting with use of indoor facilities; $10PP donation requested, includes Internet, laundry, shower, towels, refrigerator, microwave, and cooking in kitchen by permission. Coleman, denatured alcohol, and butane canisters available for purchase. Stay limited to one night; alcohol, or smoking permitted; dogs only allowed outside with tenters. Hikers may have to share space with other groups, are expected to pitch in and keep the hostel clean, and must be out of the hostel by 9 a.m. on Sunday. ■ *Groceries:* A&P Supermarket and Healthy Thymes Market (both long-term resupply). ■ *Res-*

taurants: Mixing Bowl, B/L; Vernon Inn, L/D; see map for other options. ■ *Shuttle:* Vernon Taxi, (973) 632-2005. ■ *Other services:* bank with ATM; dentist; veterinarian; pharmacy; camera shop; and amusement park.

East 5.2 miles to *Medical:* Vernon Urgent Care, (973) 209-2260, M–F 8–8, Sa–Su 9–5.

West 0.1 mile to *Groceries:* Heaven Hill Farm and Pitchfork Deli, B/L, baked goods, fresh fruit and ice cream (short-term resupply), water spigot, (973) 764-5144, M–Sa 9–7 Su 9–6, Mar–Dec. Hikers are requested to keep packs outside on left side of building.

West 2.5 miles to *Restaurants:* Mom's Homestyle Deli, The Grange, Silvio's.

West 6.1 miles to **Warwick, N.Y.** (see next chapter).

Wawayanda Mountain—Near the summit, a blue-blazed side trail leads 0.1 mile to Pinwheel's Vista, with views to the west of Pochuck Mountain and High Point Monument.

Iron Mountain Road—East 1.6 miles on blue trail to Wawayanda Lake. From Memorial Weekend to Labor Day, visitors can swim 10–6. Restrooms, first-aid station, food concession (ice cream, burgers, soda), and boat rental.

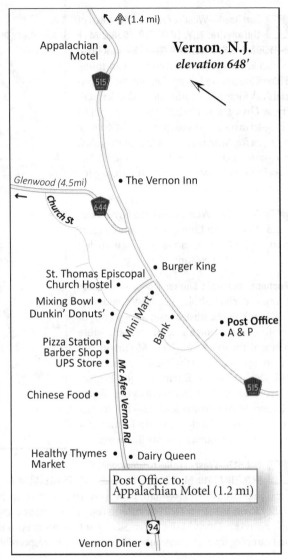

↖ 🏔 (1.4 mi)

Appalachian • Motel

Vernon, N.J.
elevation 648'

515

Glenwood (4.5mi)

← Church St

644

• The Vernon Inn

• Burger King

St. Thomas Episcopal Church Hostel •

Mixing Bowl •
Dunkin' Donuts' •

Mini Mart

Bank

• Post Office
• A & P

Pizza Station •
Barber Shop •
UPS Store •

Mc Afee Vernon Rd

515

Chinese Food •

Healthy Thymes • Market

• Dairy Queen

Post Office to:
Appalachian Motel (1.2 mi)

94

Vernon Diner •

Wawayanda Shelter (1990)—Sleeps 6. Privy. Water is available at the park office, reached by going north on the A.T. 0.1 mile, then east on the blue-blazed Hoeferlien Trail 0.2 mile; pay phone outside. Southbounders should get water at the office before reaching the shelter. Water source is the restroom faucet or a seasonal spigot on the maintenance building near the entrance to the fenced-in work yard.

Warwick Turnpike—West 2.7 miles to Shop-Rite (long-term resupply); Pennings Orchard & Farm Market (short-term resupply), (845) 986-1059, with fresh fruit, vegetables, ice cream, bakery; grill and brew pub.

New York

Miles from Springer	Fr Last Point	Features	Services	Miles from Katahdin	M A P
1,365.8	1.1	New Jersey–New York State Line (1,385') State Line Trail; Hewitt, N.J.		823.4	ATC N.Y.–N.J. Map 3
1,366.2	0.4	Prospect Rock (1,433')		823.0	
1,369.7	3.5	Greenwood Lake (Village) Vista Trail (1,180') **Greenwood Lake, N.Y. 10925**	E–0.9m (see below)	819.5	
1,371.7	2.0	N.Y. 17A (1,180') **Greenwood Lake, N.Y. 10925** **Warwick, N.Y. 10990**	R, P (E–2m PO, G, L, M, f) (W–0.1 M, w; 4.6m PO, B, G, L, M, D, cl)	817.5	
1,373.0	1.3	Eastern Pinnacles (1,294')		816.2	
1,373.5	0.5	Cat Rocks (1,080')		815.7	
1,373.8	0.3	**Wildcat Shelter** (1,180')...*12.2mS; 14.3m N*	S, w	815.4	
1,375.3	1.5	Lakes Road (680')	R, P	813.9	
1,375.6	0.3	Fitzgerald Falls (800')	w	813.6	
1,377.6	2.0	Mombasha High Point (1,280')		811.6	
1,378.8	1.2	West Mombasha Road (980')	R, P	810.4	
1,379.7	0.9	Buchanan Mountain (1,142')		809.5	
1,380.5	0.8	East Mombasha Road (840')	R, P	808.7	
1,381.2	0.7	Little Dam Lake (720')		808.0	
1,381.9	0.7	Orange Turnpike (780')	R (E–0.5m w)	807.3	
1,382.6	0.7	Arden Mountain, Agony Grind (1,180')		806.6	
1,383.7	1.1	N.Y. 17, Arden Valley Road (550') **Southfields, N.Y. 10975** Harriman, N.Y.	R (E–2.1m PO, G, L, M, B) (W–3.7m G, L, M, cl)	805.5	ATC N.Y.–N.J. Map 2
1,383.9	0.2	I-87 N.Y. State Thruway (560')...*overpass*		805.3	
1,384.1	0.2	Arden Valley Road (680')	R	805.1	
1,385.4	1.3	Island Pond Outlet (1,350')	w	803.8	
1,386.0	0.6	Lemon Squeezer (1,150')		803.2	
1,386.6	0.6	Long Path Trail Junction (1,160')		802.6	
1,387.1	0.5	Surebridge Mountain (1,200')		802.1	
1,388.1	1.0	**Fingerboard Shelter** (1,300') ...*14.3mS; 5.3mN*	S, nw	801.1	
1,389.2	1.1	Arden Valley Road (1,196')...*to Lake Tiorati Circle*	R (E–0.3m w, sh)	800.0	
1,391.4	2.2	Seven Lakes Drive (850')	R	797.8	
1,392.2	0.8	Goshen Mountain (1,180')		797.0	
1,393.4	1.2	**William Brien Memorial Shelter** (1,070') ...*5.3mS; 3.8mN*	S, nw	795.8	
1,394.8	1.4	Black Mountain (1,160')		794.4	
1,395.5	0.7	Palisade Interstate Parkway (680')... *divided highway*	R (W–0.4m w)	793.7	
1,395.7	0.2	Beechy Bottom Brook (660')	w	793.5	

Miles from Springer	Fr Last Point	Features	Services	Miles from Katahdin	M A P
1,396.6	0.9	**West Mountain Shelter** (1,240') ...*3.8mS; 32.8mN*	E–0.4m w; 0.6m S, nw	792.6	
1,398.4	1.8	Seven Lakes Drive (610')	R	790.8	
1,398.9	0.5	Perkins Drive (950')	R	790.3	
1,400.8	1.9	Bear Mountain, Perkins Tower (1,305')		788.4	
1,402.8	2.0	Bear Mountain Inn, Hessian Lake (155') **Bear Mountain, N.Y. 10911**	R, P, PO, B, L, M, w	786.4	
1,403.5	0.7	Bear Mountain Museum and Zoo (124')		785.7	
1,403.6	0.1	U.S. 9W, Bear Mountain Circle (150') Bear Mountain Bridge, Hudson River **Ft. Montgomery, N.Y. 10922**	R (W–0.9m PO, B, G, L, M)	785.6	
1,404.3	0.7	N.Y. 9D (230')	R, P	784.9	ATC N.Y.–N.J. Map 2
1,404.8	0.5	Camp Smith Trail to Anthony's Nose (700')	E–0.6m	784.4	
1,405.8	1.0	Hemlock Springs Campsite (550')	C, w	783.4	
1,406.0	0.2	Manitou Road, South Mountain Pass (460')	R, P	783.2	
1,409.4	3.4	U.S. 9, N.Y. 403 (400') **Peekskill, N.Y. 10566** Cold Spring, N.Y	R, G, M (E–4.5m PO, G, L, M, D, V, T, cl) (W–6.3m G, L, M, O, T)	779.8	
1,410.0	0.6	Old Westpoint Road; Graymoor Spiritual Life Center–Franciscan Way (550')	R, C, sh, w	779.2	
1,411.9	1.9	Denning Hill (900')		777.3	
1,412.7	0.8	Old Albany Post Road–Chapman Road (607')	R	776.5	
1,414.4	1.7	Canopus Hill Road (420')	R (E–1.6m G, M)	774.8	
1,415.4	1.0	South Highland Road (570')	R, P	773.8	
1,418.1	2.7	Dennytown Road (860')...*water faucet on building*	R, P, C, w	771.1	
1,419.7	1.6	Sunk Mine Road (800')	R	769.5	
1,421.8	2.1	N.Y. 301, Canopus Lake, Clarence Fahnestock State Park (920')	R, P (E–1m C, sh, w) (W–7.2m G, L, M, O, T)	767.4	
1,426.0	4.2	Shenandoah Mountain (1,282')		763.2	
1,426.4	0.4	Long Hill Road (1,100')	R, P	762.8	
1,427.5	1.1	Shenandoah Tenting Area (900')	C, w	761.7	
1,428.8	1.3	Hortontown Road **RPH Shelter** (350')...*32.8mS; 9mN*	R, S, w	760.4	ATC N.Y.–N.J. Map 1
1,429.1	0.3	Taconic State Parkway (650')...*underpass*	R	760.1	
1,432.3	3.2	Hosner Mountain Road (500')	R, P	756.9	
1,433.9	1.6	N.Y. 52 (800') **Stormville, N.Y. 12582**	R, P (E–0.3m G, M, w) (W–1.8m PO, G, M)	755.3	
1,435.3	1.4	I-84 overpass; Stormville Mountain Road (950')	R, P	753.9	
1,437.7	2.4	Mt. Egbert (1,329')		751.5	
1,437.8	0.1	**Morgan Stewart Shelter** (1,285') ...*9mS; 7.8mN*	S, w	751.4	
1,438.9	1.1	Depot Hill Road (1,230')	R, P	750.3	
1,440.8	1.9	Old Route 55 (750')	R, P	748.4	

Miles from Springer	Fr Last Point	Features	Services	Miles from Katahdin	MAP
1,441.1	0.3	N.Y. 55 (720') **Poughquag, N.Y. 12570**	R, P (W–1.5m M; 2.1m PO, G, M, V; 3.3m G, M)	748.1	
1,442.3	1.2	Nuclear Lake outlet (750')		746.9	
1,445.3	3.0	West Mountain (1,200')		743.9	
1,445.6	0.3	**Telephone Pioneers Shelter** (910') ...7.8mS; 8.8mN	S, w	743.6	
1,446.3	0.7	County Road 20, West Dover Road, Dover Oak (650') **Pawling, N.Y. 12564**	R, P, w (E–3.1m PO, C, G, M, D, O, T, cl; 5m G)	742.9	ATC N.Y.–N.J. Map 1
1,448.7	2.4	N.Y. 22, Appalachian Trail Metro–North Train Station (480')	R, P, C, M, T, sh, w (E–0.6m G, M) (W–2.6m G, L, M; 4m Wingdale, N.Y. below)	740.5	
1,448.9	0.2	Hurds Corners Road (480')	R	740.3	
1,449.5	0.6	Pawling Nature Preserve (675')...trail register		739.7	
1,454.0	4.5	Leather Hill Road (750')...dirt	R	735.2	
1,454.4	0.4	**Wiley Shelter** (740')...8.8mS; 4mN	S, w	734.8	
1,454.6	0.2	Duell Hollow Road (620')	R, P	734.6	
1,455.6	1.0	NewYork–Connecticut State Line (400') Hoyt Road **Wingdale, N.Y. 12594**	R, P (W–3.3m PO, G, M, L, T, f)	733.6	

In New York, campfires are prohibited except in designated fire rings and fireplaces at established campsites and shelters. Camping itself is limited to designated sites.

The first miles specifically intended for the A.T. were built here through Harriman–Bear Mountain state parks in 1922–23. With many parks, roads, and a railroad station right on the Trail, many hikers are thinking, you may find this stretch to be a uniquely multicultural experience. The Trail drops to its lowest elevation point—124 feet—after, or just before, you pass through the Trailside Museum and Zoo at Bear Mountain. Hydration becomes an issue in this area. Don't pass up an opportunity for water.

Prospect Rock—At 1,433 feet, this is the highest point on the A.T. in New York (Bear Mountain is 1,305 feet). This and other rock faces along this ridge provide views of Greenwood Lake to the east.

Greenwood Lake Vista Trail—This blue-blazed trail leads **East** 0.9 mile to Greenwood Lake without the fast traffic of N.Y. 17A; from the vista, you can see Lion's Field below, the terminus of the trail. A water fountain on the outside of the little green building next to the softball field can be used by hikers. **Greenwood Lake, N.Y. [P.O. ZIP 10925: M–F 8–5, Sa 9–12; (845) 477-7328].** ▪ *Lodging:* Breezy Point, (845) 477-8100, rates begin at $85 plus tax, ATM; Lake Lodging, (845) 477-0700, no pets or credit cards, possible pick-up/return; Linden Motel, (845) 477-0851, $90; Anton's on the Lake, 7 Waterstone Rd., (845) 477-0010, no smoking, no pets, call for rates. ▪ *Groceries:* Delicious Deli; Country Grocery; Kwik Mark; and Cumberland Farms, with deli sandwiches (all short-term resupply). ▪ *Restaurants:* Planet Pizza; Murphy's Tavern, L/D weekdays, B Sa–Su; Village Buzz Café; Huckleberry's BBQ, B/L/D; The Grill, B/L; Sing Loong Kitchen; Irish Whisper Pub; Subway. ▪ *Other services:* True Value, fuel; CVS pharmacy; Long Pond Marina, with boat rentals; Night

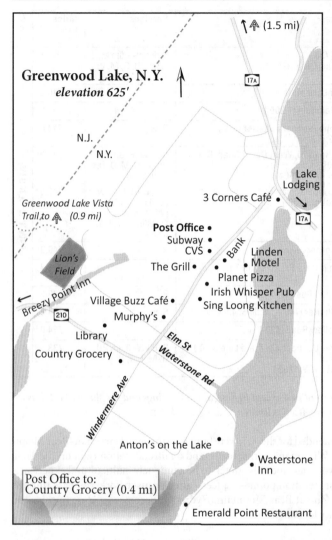

Greenwood Lake, N.Y.
elevation 625'

↑⛺ (1.5 mi)

17A

N.J.
N.Y.

Lake
Lodging

3 Corners Café •

Greenwood Lake Vista
Trail to ⛺ *(0.9 mi)*

17A

Post Office •
Subway •
CVS •

Bank

Linden
Motel

Lion's
Field

The Grill •

Planet Pizza
Irish Whisper Pub
Sing Loong Kitchen

Village Buzz Café •
Murphy's •

Breezy Point Inn

210

Library
Country Grocery

Elm St

Waterstone Rd

Windermere Ave

Anton's on the Lake •

Waterstone
Inn

Post Office to:
Country Grocery (0.4 mi)

Emerald Point Restaurant

Owl Taxi, (845) 662-0359, and Greenwood Lake Taxi, M–Th, (845) 477-3291 (call ahead).

🛣 **N.Y. 17A**—Hot Dogs Plus, cash only. **East** 2 miles to **Greenwood Lake** (see above).

West 0.1 mile to Bellvale Creamery, daily 12–9, ice cream and water.

West 4.6 miles to the larger town of **Warwick, N.Y. [P.O. ZIP 10990: M–F 8:30–5, Sa 9–4; (845) 986-0271]**. Hitchhikers have been cited leaving Warwick on N.Y. 17A. ■ *Lodging:* Warwick Motel, (845) 986-4822, $80 weekdays, $86 weekends; ask about hiker discount. ■ *Groceries:* Price Chopper, open 24 hours, is 1.7 miles south of town on N.Y. 94; ShopRite is 1.9 miles south of town on N.Y. 94 (both long-term resupply). ■ *Other services:* NJ Transit buses run frequently in the area from Warwick to New York City; hospital; restaurants; drug store; coin laundry; bank/ATM; and hardware store. ■ *Shuttle:* Josie's Taxi, (845) 820-4405.

Wildcat Shelter (1992)—Sleeps 8. Privy. Water source is a spring in front of the shelter.

Mombasha High Point—On a clear day, you can see the New York City skyline, including the Empire State Building.

Sterling Forest—Between Greenwood Lake and Arden, 6 miles of the A.T. pass through the northern portion of a 20,000-acre tract called Sterling Forest. It was the center of a decade-long struggle between a corporate private landowner and a coalition of conservation groups, state agencies in New York and New Jersey, and such organizations as the NY–NJ TC and ATC. All told, more than 30 environmental groups, along with foundations, individuals, states, and Congress, combined to contribute more than $55 million toward the purchase and protection of 14,500 acres. Efforts are underway to block a possible casino on the inholding.

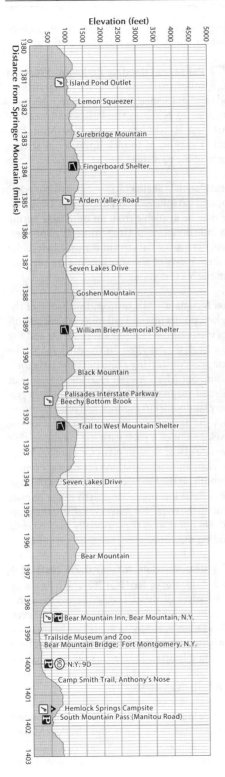

Elevation (feet)

0
500
1000
1500
2000
2500
3000
3500
4000
4500
5000

Distance from Springer Mountain (miles)

1380
1381 — Island Pond Outlet
1382 — Lemon Squeezer
1383 — Surebridge Mountain
1384 — Fingerboard Shelter
1385 — Arden Valley Road
1386
1387 — Seven Lakes Drive
1388 — Goshen Mountain
1389 — William Brien Memorial Shelter
1390 — Black Mountain
1391 — Palisades Interstate Parkway / Beechy Bottom Brook
1392 — Trail to West Mountain Shelter
1393
1394 — Seven Lakes Drive
1395
1396
1397 — Bear Mountain
1398
1399 — Bear Mountain Inn, Bear Mountain, N.Y.
1400 — Trailside Museum and Zoo / Bear Mountain Bridge; Fort Montgomery, N.Y. / N.Y. 9D
1401 — Camp Smith Trail, Anthony's Nose
1402 — Hemlock Springs Campsite / South Mountain Pass (Manitou Road)
1403

N.Y. 17—East 2.1 miles to **Southfields, N.Y.** [P.O. ZIP 10975: M–F 8:30–12 & 1–5, Sa 8:30–11:30; (845) 351-2628]. ■ *Lodging:* Tuxedo Motel, (845) 351-4747, $45.50S, $54.50D, $10EAP, WiFi available, no pets, mail drops to 985 N.Y. 17S, Southfields, NY 10975. ■ *Restaurant:* Take-out Chinese delivered to Tuxedo Motel, (845) 351-4428. ■ *Groceries:* Valero (short-term resupply), snack bar closes at 3 p.m., ATM. ■ *Other services:* ShortLine (Coach USA) buses from New York/Tuxedo/Southfields to Harriman with a flag stop at the A.T. crossing of N.Y. 17 and from New York to Fort Montgomery with a regular stop at Bear Mountain Inn.

West 3.7 miles to the town of **Harriman,** for lodgings, groceries, restaurants, and coin laundries.

Bear Mountain/Harriman State Parks—Home to the first completed section of the A.T. Dry conditions and forest fires have forced the closure of the A.T. in the park for days or even weeks in the summer. In 1994, Harriman State Park instituted a policy under which, even if other trails in the park are closed, the A.T. remains open to thru-hikers.

Fingerboard Shelter (1928)—Sleeps 8. No privy. A stone structure. The closest dependable water is the spigot at Lake Tiorati, 0.5 mile east on the blue-blazed Hurst Trail. Southbounders can get their water at Tiorati Circle, 1.1 miles north of the shelter.

Arden Valley Road—East 0.3 mile to Tiorati Circle at the intersection of Seven Lakes Drive. Near the traffic circle are a public beach on Lake Tiorati and a picnic area. Restroom; free showers in bath house for walk-ins; open Memorial Day to Labor Day, M–F 10–5:45, Sa–Su 9–7; vending machines, ice-cream sandwiches, candy, water.

William Brien Memorial Shelter (1933)—Sleeps 8. No privy. A stone shelter built by the CCC. Water source is a spring-fed well that is prone to go dry. This spring is 80 yards down a blue-blazed trail to the right of the shelter. An alternative for northbounders is to stop at Tiorati Circle, cook at one of the picnic tables, and hike to the shelter for the evening. Southbounders

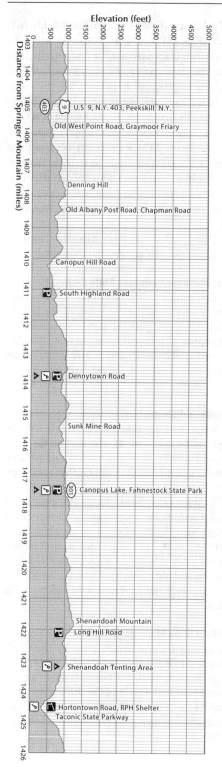

Elevation (feet)

Distance from Springer Mountain (miles)

- U.S. 9, N.Y. 403, Peekskill, N.Y.
- Old West Point Road, Graymoor Friary
- Denning Hill
- Old Albany Post Road, Chapman Road
- Canopus Hill Road
- South Highland Road
- Dennytown Road
- Sunk Mine Road
- Canopus Lake, Fahnestock State Park
- Shenandoah Mountain
- Long Hill Road
- Shenandoah Tenting Area
- Hortontown Road, RPH Shelter
- Taconic State Parkway

can get water at the park visitors center 0.4 mile west, on the Palisades Interstate Parkway.

Palisades Interstate Parkway—West 0.4 mile to park visitors center with restroom, soda and snack machines. From here, it is a mere 34 miles to NYC on the Palisades Interstate Parkway. Hikers heading to West Mountain Shelter may want to pick up water at stream north of the parkway.

West Mountain Shelter (1928)—Sleeps 8. No privy. Located 0.6 mile east on Timp-Torne Trail. Water may be available from an unreliable spring 0.4 mile down steep Timp-Torne Trail or alternately at a seasonal stream 0.2 mile before the shelter. Views of the surrounding countryside and the NYC skyline.

Bear Mountain—At 1,305 feet, this is one of the highest points on the Trail in New York and offers views of the Hudson River Valley and the New York City skyline. In the early 1900s, the state was considering a site near the base for a prison, but Mary Averell Harriman, widow of railroad magnate Edward Harriman and primary landholder in the area, had other plans. In 1910, she agreed to donate 10,000 acres for the development of a park with the condition that the state discontinue its plans for a prison. What was then known as Sing Sing Prison was eventually built on the Hudson River 20 miles south of the A.T., its location giving birth to the phrase, "sent up the river." No water available at the summit. Do not rely on the seasonally stocked soda vending machine.

Bear Mountain, N.Y.—[P.O. ZIP 10911: M–F 8–10, closed Sa; (845) 786-3747]. P.O. may close early; call ahead. Located across the street from the park administration building on Seven Lakes Drive. Fort Montgomery (see below) may be a better option. *Lodging & Restaurant:* Bear Mountain Inn, (845) 786-2731; $139–$249, ask for hiker rate; 1915 Café, M–W 10:30–7, Th–Su 11–7, with B Th–Su 7–10:30.

Trailside Museums and Zoo—North of the inn and south of Bear Mountain Bridge, the Bear Mountain Zoo contains many native species, including black bears, and offers a unique, and sometimes

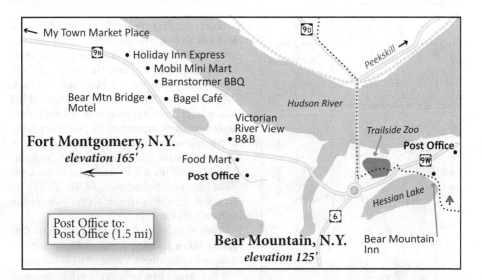

Fort Montgomery, N.Y. elevation 165'

Bear Mountain, N.Y. elevation 125'

Post Office to: Post Office (1.5 mi)

emotional, experience for thru-hikers. Within the park is also a much-photographed statue of Walt Whitman. Admission $1; A.T. hikers admitted free. The portion of the A.T. leading through the zoo to the bridge—an original section from 1923—descends to 124 feet above sea level; it's the Trail's lowest elevation between Maine and Georgia. *Dogs are not allowed in the museum/ zoo section.* The southern gate opens at 10:30 a.m.; at 4:30 p.m., the gate is closed. If you arrive when the gate is closed or are hiking with a dog, hike around on U.S. 9W, which becomes the official route for the time period/circumstances.

 Bear Mountain Circle—West 0.9 mile to **Ft. Montgomery, N.Y. [P.O. ZIP 10922: M–F 8–1 & 2:30–5, Sa 9–12; (845) 446-8459].** ■ *Lodging:* Bear Mountain Bridge Motel, (845) 446-2472, $69–$75 weekdays, higher on weekends, with shuttle to/from the Trail; Holiday Inn Express, (845) 446-4277, thru-hiker rate $120 for 1 or 2 people, Internet and computer/office for guests, laundry, indoor pool, continental B; Victorian River View B&B, (845) 446-5479, $110–$160; Econo Lodge, (845) 446-9400. ■ *Groceries:* Chestnut Mini Mart (short-term resupply). MyTown Marketplace (long-term resupply) is two miles north in Highland Falls. ■ *Restaurants:* Bagel Café with ATM, open M–F 5–3, Sa 6–2, B/L; Foodies Pizza; Barnstormer BBQ & Pub; Richies Restaurant & Pub.

Bear Mountain Bridge—Built at a cost of $5 million in 1923–24 by a private company run by the Harriman family. When Earl Shaffer arrived at the bridge in 1948, he had to pay a nickel to cross. Today, only vehicles must pay.

Anthony's Nose—Where the A.T. turns west on a dirt road, 0.5 mile north of N.Y. 9D, a turn east on this road, blazed as the Camp Smith Trail, leads 0.6 mile to the top of the mountain known as Anthony's Nose. This rock outcropping, 900 feet above the river, offers outstanding views of the Hudson River Valley. The state Office of Parks, Recreation, and Historic Preservation now owns the property; please stay on the trail. Originally, the A.T. climbed steeply to the summit but was re-routed when World War II broke out. The Nose remained closed until 1993, when the New York State Division of Military and Naval Affairs, managers of the adjacent National Guard camp, gave permission for hikers to once again walk to the summit.

U.S. 9—*Groceries:* Appalachian Equities, Shell station/convenience store just to west at U.S. 9/N.Y. 403 junction, full-service, food-to-go, 24 hours, (845) 424-6241.

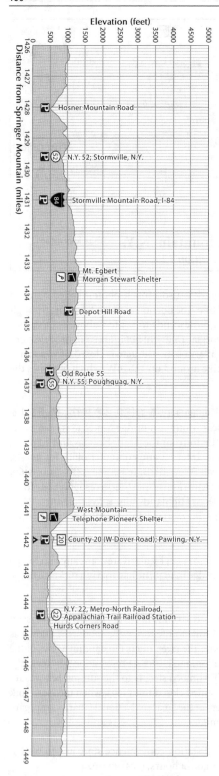

Elevation (feet)

Distance from Springer Mountain (miles)

Hosner Mountain Road

N.Y. 52; Stormville, N.Y.

Stormville Mountain Road; I-84

Mt. Egbert
Morgan Stewart Shelter

Depot Hill Road

Old Route 55
N.Y. 55; Poughquag, N.Y.

West Mountain
Telephone Pioneers Shelter

County-20 (W-Dover Road); Pawling, N.Y.

N.Y. 22, Metro-North Railroad,
Appalachian Trail Railroad Station
Hurds Corners Road

East 4.5 miles to **Peekskill, N.Y. [P.O. ZIP 10566: M–F 9–5, Sa 9–4; (914) 737-6437]**. If you plan to go into Peekskill, take Highland Avenue into town, rather than U.S. 9, where the two roads fork about 3 miles from the A.T. Highland Ave. leads directly to downtown. Services are spread out over a large, bustling area, with several motels and restaurants, supermarkets, pharmacy, laundry, banks with ATM, hospital, doctor, dentist, and veterinarian. The post office is on South St., 4.5 miles from the A.T. Free Internet access at the Field Library, 4 Nelson Ave., M, Tu, Th 9–9, W 11–9, F 9–5, Sa 10–2. *Train:* Metro–North train to New York City.

West 6.3 miles *via* Route 403 to N.Y. 9D to **Cold Spring, N.Y.** ■ *Lodging:* Countryside Motel, 3577 Route 9, Cold Spring, NY 10516, (845) 265-2090, $75 one bed, $81.28 two beds, WiFi, will receive mail drops for guests; Pig Hill Inn, (845) 265-9247, $130 and up. ■ *Restaurants:* McGuires on Main, Cold Spring Pizza, Whistling Willies. ■ *Groceries:* Food Town Supermarket (long-term resupply). ■ *Outfitter:* Old Souls Outfitter, (845) 809-5886, <www.oldsouls.com>, W–M 10–6, closed Tu; small outfitter with boots, tents, packs, fuel, *etc.* ■ *Shuttle:* Highland Transit Taxi, (845) 265-8294. ■ *Train:* Daily service to NYC.

Graymoor Spiritual Life Center—Hikers are permitted to sleep at the monastery's ball-field picnic shelter, which has water, a cold-water shower during warm months, and a privy. The shelter is open all season. *Directions:* North of U.S. 9, the A.T. climbs uphill and crosses a second paved road leading to the center. Here, northbounders should follow the blue blazes: Turn east on Franciscan Way, left on St. Anthony Way, and left on St. Joseph Drive to the ballfield. Southbounders will cross unpaved Old West Point Road onto the Graymoor driveway; continue straight on driveway, then north where the driveway forks. Pizza and deli food may be ordered for delivery to the picnic shelter.

Canopus Hill Road—**East** 1.6 miles to the Putnam Valley Market (short-term resupply), (845) 528-8626, with pizza, hot food from the grill, ATM. Open daily 6:30–9 (closes at 7 on Su). *Directions:* east on Canopus Hill Road 0.3 mile to intersection with Canopus Hollow Road.

Continue 0.1 mile south on Canopus Hollow Road, turn west on Sunset Hill Road 1.2 miles to store. Sunset Hill Road, a steep, winding road, climbs 400 feet from Canopus Hill Road.

Dennytown Road—Water available from spigot on the side of the pump building. Opens third F of Apr, closes last Su of Oct. Camping area located 500 feet west on Dennytown Road, then south onto a dirt road to top of hill.

N.Y. 301/Clarence Fahnestock State Park—East 1 mile to the park's campground, (845) 225-7207. The beach area can be reached from the A.T. 2.3 miles north of N.Y. 301 *via* an unmarked downhill gully trail that begins a quarter of a mile south of the viewpoint on the A.T. at the northern end of Canopus Lake. The beach area is visible from the overlook. Campground open Apr–second week of Dec, tentsites Su–Th $17.75, F–Sa $21.75. A free tenting area provided for thru-hikers with hot showers, flush toilets, and water; inquire at the park entrance. The beach-area concession stand, (845) 225-3998, and grill (open Memorial Day–Labor Day, Su–F 9–5, Sa 9–6, grill closes one hour earlier) has grilled sandwiches, soda, ice cream, supplies. The beach area closes Labor Day.

> **West** 7.2 miles to Cold Spring (see above).

Shenandoah Tenting Area—0.1 mile west. Group camping is permitted. Water is available from a hand pump.

RPH Shelter (1982)—Sleeps 6. Privy. Formerly a closed cabin, it was renovated as a three-sided shelter with a front porch. Water source is a hand pump.

N.Y. 52—East 0.3 mile to ■ *Groceries:* Mountain Top Market Deli, (845) 221-0928, (short-term resupply), daily 6 a.m.–8 p.m., daily specials and hot sandwiches, water for hikers on faucet at side of building. ■ *Restaurant:* Danny's Pizzeria, open at 11:30 T–F, noon Sa–M, hikers might have to wait/eat outside.

> **West** 1.8 miles to **Stormville, N.Y. [P.O. ZIP 12582: M–F 8:30–5, Sa 9–12; (845) 226-2627].** ■ *Groceries:* Citgo Mini Mart (short-term resupply). ■ *Restaurant:* Stormville Pizza, M–Sa 11–9:30, Su 12–9.

Morgan Stewart Shelter (1984)—Sleeps 6. Privy. Water source is a well with a pump located downhill and in front of the shelter.

N.Y. 55—West 1.5 miles to ■ *Restaurant:* Pleasant Ridge Pizza, L/D, closed M. ■ *Other services:* Pleasant Ridge Shopping Center, pharmacy, and deli.

> **West** 2.1 miles to **Poughquag, N.Y. [P.O. ZIP 12570: M–F 8:30–5, Sa 8:30–12:30; (845) 724-4763].** ■ *Groceries:* Beekman Corner's ShopRite & Cumberland Farms, Shell Mini-Mart, Clove Valley Deli. ■ *Restaurants:* Beekman Square Diner, Tailgates Grill, The Square, Brothers Trattoria, Via 55 Restaurant, Great Wall Chinese, Ramblers Roost Irish Bar & Restaurant. ■ *Other services:* Beekman Animal Hospital, (845) 724-8387.

> **West** 3.3 miles to Verona Pizzeria and Restaurant, Karl Ehmer East Fishkill Pork Store, and Cheers Wine and Liquor.

Nuclear Lake—The site of a nuclear fuels-processing research facility until 1972. After the Park Service acquired the lands, the buildings were razed, and the area was tested extensively and given a clean bill of health, allowing the Trail to be rerouted along the shore.

Telephone Pioneers Shelter (1988)—Sleeps 6. Privy. Built with the assistance of the White Plains Council of the Telephone Pioneers of America. Water source is the stream crossed by the side trail leading to the shelter. Alternative water source is 0.7 mile north at the Champion residence (see next entry).

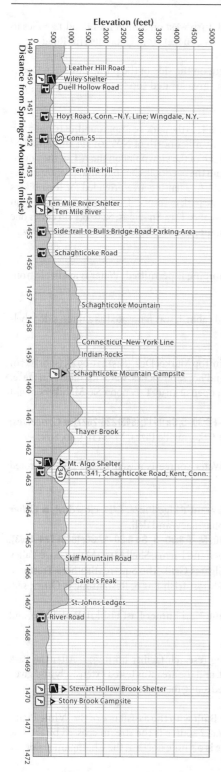

Elevation (feet)

Distance from Springer Mountain (miles)

- 1449
- 1450 — Leather Hill Road
- Wiley Shelter
- Duell Hollow Road
- 1451 — Hoyt Road, Conn.–N.Y. Line; Wingdale, N.Y.
- 1452 — Conn.-55
- 1453 — Ten Mile Hill
- 1454 — Ten Mile River Shelter / Ten Mile River
- 1455 — Side trail to Bulls Bridge Road Parking Area
- 1456 — Schaghticoke Road
- 1457
- 1458 — Schaghticoke Mountain
- 1459 — Connecticut–New York Line / Indian Rocks
- 1460 — Schaghticoke Mountain Campsite
- 1461
- 1462 — Thayer Brook
- 1463 — Mt. Algo Shelter / Conn. 341, Schaghticoke Road, Kent, Conn.
- 1464
- 1465
- 1466 — Skiff Mountain Road
- 1467 — Caleb's Peak
- St. Johns Ledges
- River Road
- 1468
- 1469 — Stewart Hollow Brook Shelter
- 1470 — Stony Brook Campsite
- 1471
- 1472

County 20/West Dover Road—Ron and Holly Champion live in the purple house east of the Trail; water is available from a tap at the end of their lower walk. *Please do not knock at door.*

East 3.1 miles to **Pawling, N.Y. [P.O. ZIP 12564: M–F 8:30–5, Sa 9–12; (845) 855-2669].** Northbounders might want to hike 2.4 miles more to N.Y. 22 for easier access. ■ *Camping:* The town allows hikers to camp in its Edward R. Murrow Memorial Park, 1 mile from the town center on West Main. The park offers lake swimming, restroom. No dogs permitted. Two-night maximum. ■ *Groceries:* Hannaford, 2 miles south from town center on Rt. 22 (long-term resupply); CVS (short-term resupply); La Guadalupana Mini-Mart. ■ *Restaurants:* Vinny's Deli & Pasta, Mama's Pizza, Gaudino Pizzeria, Great Wall Chinese, Pawling Tavern, McKeene's Restaurant, McKinney & Doyle, Pawling Café, Julia's Deli, Gaudino's Pizza, Corner Bakery, Little Red Bakeshop. ■ *Outfitter:* Gear to Go Outfitters, (917) 301-8238, <www.geartogooutfitters. com>, will deliver to Trail in N.Y. ■ *Other services:* doctor, dentist, coin laundry, banks with ATM, pharmacy, and Metro-North station with service to NYC [call (800) METRO-INFO for fare and schedule]. ■ *Internet access:* Pawling Free Library, 11 Broad St., Tu–Th 12–8, F 12–5, Sa 10–4, Su 12–4 (except Jul–Aug). *Please leave packs and poles outside or in the hallway.*

Dover Oak—Located on the north side of West Dover Road, is reportedly the largest oak tree on the A.T. Its girth four feet from the ground is more than 20 feet, 4 inches, and it is estimated to be more than 300 years old.

N.Y. 22/Appalachian Trail Railroad Station. *Other services:* Native Landscapes & Garden Center; 991 Route 22, Pawling, NY 12564; owner Pete Muroski, a hiker, is very hiker-friendly. Allows camping on site, use of restrooms, shower $5. Mail drops accepted.

East 0.6 mile to ■ *Groceries:* Tony's Deli (short-term resupply), open daily 5 a.m.–midnight. ■ *Restaurants:* Strada's Italian Restaurant, Pizza Express.

West 2.6 miles to ■ *Restaurant:* Big W's Roadside BBQ. ■ *Lodging:* Dutchess Motor Lodge, (845)

832-6400, Rt. 22, Wingdale, N.Y., $78D including weekends, $7 laundry, no pets, Internet access, shuttles. ■ *Groceries:* Village Deli & Market, Ben's Store (both short-term resupply).

West 4 miles to the village of Wingdale (see Hoyt Road below).

Commuter Train—On the south side of N.Y. 22, the Trail passes the A.T. station of a New York City commuter train (Metro-North). Trains leave the platform every Sa and Su at 2:44 p.m., 4:44 p.m., and 6:39 p.m. and arrive at Grand Central Terminal at 4:41 p.m., 6:41 p.m., and 8:40 p.m. Trains leave Grand Central at 7:48 a.m. and 9:48 a.m. on Sa and Su and arrive at the A.T. platform at 9:41 a.m. and 11:38 a.m. Fares are one-way $20 off-peak, $25 peak, and round-trip $28 off-peak, $37.50 peak. Weekday and additional weekend services are available to New York from stations in nearby Pawling and Wingdale.

Wiley Shelter (1940)—Sleeps 6. Privy. Water source is a pump 0.1 mile north of the shelter on the A.T. beyond tent platform; treat the water.

Hoyt Road—**West** 3.3 miles *via* Hoyt and Webatuck roads to **Wingdale, N.Y. [P.O. ZIP 12594: M–F 8–5, Sa 8–12:30; (845) 832-6147].** To reach Wingdale Metro-North Station, continue south on N.Y. 22 for about one mile. ■ *Lodging:* Dutchess Motor Lodge (see above). ■ *Groceries:* Wingdale Super Market with ATM and Food Market (both long-term resupply). ■ *Restaurants:* Ben's Deli; Pizza Express; Cousin's Pizza; Peking Kitchen; Cousin's Café; Riverview Café. ■ *Other services:* Dover Plains Library, M–F 10–8, Sa 10–4, Internet access; Wingdale Hardware.

Connecticut

Miles from Springer	Fr Last Point	Features	Services	Miles from Katahdin	M A P
1,455.6	1.0	New York–Connecticut State Line (400') Hoyt Road **Wingdale, N.Y. 12594**	R, P (W–3.3m PO, G, M, L, T, f)	733.6	
1,456.3	0.7	Conn. 55 (580') **Gaylordsville, Conn. 06755**	R, P (E–2.5m PO, G, M)	732.9	
1,457.4	1.1	Ten Mile Hill (1,000')		731.8	
1,458.4	1.0	**Ten Mile River Shelter** (290')...*4mS; 8.4mN*	S, w	730.8	
1,458.6	0.2	Ten Mile River (280')...*footbridge*	C, w	730.6	
1,459.3	0.7	Bulls Bridge Road (450') Trail to Bulls Bridge Parking Area	R (E–0.2m P; 0.5m G)	729.9	
1,460.0	0.7	Schaghticoke Road (320')	R, P	729.2	
1,461.7	1.7	Schaghticoke Mountain (1,331')		727.5	
1,462.9	1.2	Connecticut–New York State Line (1,250')		726.3	ATC Mass.–Conn. Map 4
1,463.3	0.4	Indian Rocks (1,290')		725.9	
1,463.9	0.6	Schaghticoke Mountain Campsite (950')	C, w	725.3	
1,465.8	1.9	Thayer Brook (900')	w	723.4	
1,466.8	1.0	**Mt. Algo Shelter** (655')...*8.4mS; 7.3mN*	S, C, w	722.4	
1,467.1	0.3	Conn. 341, Schaghticoke Road (350') **Kent, Conn. 06757**	R, P (E–0.8m PO, G, L, M, O, D, f; 3.3m L)	722.1	
1,469.9	2.8	Skiff Mountain Road (850')	R	719.3	
1,470.6	0.7	Caleb's Peak (1,160')		718.6	
1,471.3	0.7	St. Johns Ledges (900')		717.9	
1,471.8	0.5	River Road (480')	R, P	717.4	
1,474.1	2.3	**Stewart Hollow Brook Shelter** (400') ...*7.3mS; 10mN*	S, C, w	715.1	
1,474.5	0.4	Stony Brook Campsite (440')	C, w	714.7	
1,476.5	2.0	River Road (460')	R, P	712.7	
1,477.3	0.8	Silver Hill Campsite (1,000')	C, w	711.9	
1,478.2	0.9	Conn. 4 (700') **Cornwall Bridge, Conn. 06754**	R (E–0.9m PO, G, L, O, V, f; 1.9m C, sh)	711.0	
1,478.3	0.1	Guinea Brook (650')...*road bypass in highwater*		710.9	
1,478.4	0.1	Old Sharon Road (750')	R	710.8	ATC Mass.–Conn. Map 3
1,479.6	1.2	Hatch Brook (880')		709.6	
1,480.3	0.7	Pine Knob Loop Trail (1,150')...*to Housatonic Meadows State Park*	E–0.9m C, sh	708.9	
1,480.7	0.4	Caesar Road, Caesar Brook Campsite (760')	R, C, w	708.5	
1,482.9	2.2	Carse Brook (810')	w	706.3	
1,483.0	0.1	West Cornwall Road (800') **West Cornwall, Conn. 06796** **Sharon, Conn. 06069**	R, P, H (E–2.2m PO, G, L, M, O) (W–4.7m PO, G, L, M, D, cl)	706.2	

Miles from Springer	Fr Last Point	Features	Services	Miles from Katahdin	MAP
1,484.1	1.1	**Pine Swamp Brook Shelter** (1,075') ...*10mS; 11.9mN*	S, C, w	705.1	
1,485.0	0.9	Sharon Mountain Road (1,150')	R	704.2	
1,485.3	0.3	Mt. Easter (1,350')		703.9	
1,486.5	1.2	Sharon Mountain Campsite (1,200')	C, w	702.7	
1,489.3	2.8	Belter's Campsite (770')	C, w	699.9	
1,489.7	0.4	U.S. 7, Conn. 112 (520')	R, P	699.5	
1,490.3	0.6	U.S. 7, Housatonic River Bridge (500')	R, P (E–0.2m M)	698.9	
1,490.4	0.1	Mohawk Trail Junction (500')	E–0.2m M	698.8	
1,492.2	1.8	Water Street, Hydroelectric Plant (530') **Falls Village, Conn. 06031**	R, H, C, w, sh (E–0.5m PO, C, M)	697.0	
1,492.3	0.1	Iron Bridge (510')...*Housatonic River, picnic area*	R, P	696.9	
1,492.9	0.6	Housatonic River Road (650')...*Great Falls*	R, P	696.3	ATC Mass.-Conn. Map 3
1,493.4	0.5	Spring (750')	w	695.8	
1,494.8	1.4	Prospect Mountain (1,475')		694.4	
1,495.5	0.7	**Limestone Spring Shelter** (980')...*11.9mS; 8mN*	W–0.5m S, C, w	693.7	
1,495.6	0.1	Rand's View (1,250')		693.6	
1,496.1	0.5	Giant's Thumb (1,220')...*rock formation*		693.1	
1,496.4	0.3	Billy's View (1,150')		692.8	
1,498.9	2.5	U.S. 44 (700') **Salisbury, Conn. 06088** Lakeville, Conn.	R, H (W–0.4m PO, G, L, M, f; 2.4m L, M, cl, f)	690.3	
1,499.6	0.7	Conn. 41, Under Mountain Road (720') **Salisbury, Conn. 06088**	R, P, H (see above)	689.6	
1,502.3	2.7	Lions Head (1,738')		686.9	
1,503.0	0.7	**Riga Shelter** (1,610')...*8mS; 1.2mN*	S, C, w	686.2	
1,503.6	0.6	Ball Brook Campsite (1,650')	C, w	685.6	
1,504.2	0.6	Brassie Brook (south branch) (1,705') **Brassie Brook Shelter**...*1.2mS; 8.8mN*	S, C, w	685.0	
1,504.7	0.5	Undermountain Trail, Riga Junction (1,820')		684.5	
1,504.9	0.2	Bear Mountain Road (1,920')	R	684.3	
1,505.6	0.7	Bear Mountain (2,316')...*rock observation tower*		683.6	
1,506.3	0.7	Connecticut–Massachusetts State Line (1,800')		682.9	

Campfires are prohibited on the Trail in Connecticut, and camping is permitted only at designated sites. Ridgerunners patrol the state's 52 A.T. miles and serve as caretakers at Sages Ravine campsite.

Southbounders and northbounders pass each other regularly now. Southbounders should consider the hunting seasons and the need to wear bright "blaze" orange. If hiking with a four-footed friend, keep its safety in mind, too.

AMC–Connecticut Chapter—The Trails Committee of the AMC–Connecticut Chapter maintains the 51.4 miles from the New York–Connecticut state line to Sages Ravine, just across the Massachusetts line. The club can be reached at (413) 528-6333; <www.ct-amc.org>.

Conn. 55—East 2.5 miles to **Gaylordsville, Conn. [P.O. ZIP 06755: M–F 8–1 & 2–5, Sa 8–12; (860) 354-9727].** ■ *Groceries:* Gaylordsville Country Store, (860) 350-3802 (short-term resupply), M–F 6–8, Sa 6–6, Su 6–3, with deli, ATM. ■ *Restaurants:* Burgerittoville Bar and Grill Family Restaurant, Alfredo's Restaurant and Pizza, Gaylordsville Diner.

Ten Mile River Shelter (1996)—Sleeps 6. Privy. Tentsites at nearby campsite. Water source is a hand pump 100 feet south and west of the shelter.

Bulls Bridge Road—East 0.5 mile to Country Market (short-term resupply) with ATM and Internet access.

Indian Rocks—Half a mile north of the only place along the entire A.T. where the Trail (for a short piece) crosses an Indian reservation. Most of the land from here down to the river is claimed by the Schaghticoke tribe, recognized by the state and briefly by the federal government. The tribe, actually the remnants of several tribes, played a unique communications role during the Revolutionary War by transmitting signals along the ridges between Long Island Sound in N.Y. and Stockbridge, Mass., a distance of nearly 100 miles, in about 2 hours.

Mt. Algo Shelter (1986)—Sleeps 6. Privy. Water source is on blue-blaze leading to shelter, 15 yards in front of shelter.

Conn. 341—East 0.8 mile to **Kent, Conn. [P.O. ZIP 06757: M–F 8–1 & 2–5, Sa 8:30–12:30; (860) 927-3435].** ■ *Lodging:* Fife 'n Drum Inn & Restaurant, (860) 927-3509, <www.fifendrum.com>, restaurant M–Th (closed Tu) 11:30–9:30, F–Sa 11:30–10, Su 11:30–8:30, $133.40D with tax weekdays, $161D weekends, $25EAP, tax not included, no dogs, call for reservations; Starbuck Inn, (860) 927-1788, <www.starbuckinn.com>, $189-$250D plus tax, includes full B, check-in 4 p.m., check-out 11 a.m. ■ *Groceries:* Davis IGA (long-term resupply); Kent Market (short-term resupply), with deli sandwiches, M–Sa 6–8, Su 7–7. ■ *Restaurants:* Kent Pizza Garden, L/D, 11–10; Panini Café, closed T, open W–M 9:30–5. ■ *Outfitters:* Backcountry Outfitters, 5 Bridge St., (860) 927-3377, <info@bcoutfitters.com>; open M–Sa 9–6, Su 10–4; summer hours Su–Th until 8 p.m., F–Sa until 9; limited backpacking gear and supplies; white gas, Esbit, canisters, denatured alcohol by the ounce; mail drops accepted; shuttles; Annie Bananie ice cream inside. Sundog Shoe and Leather, <sundogshoe@aol.com>, (860) 927-0009, boots, socks, insoles, M–Sa 10–5, Su 12–5. ■ *Internet access:* Kent Memorial Library, M–F 10–5:30, Sa 10–4. ■ *Other services:* banks with ATM; doctor; dentist; pharmacy;

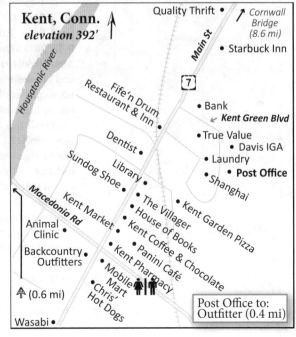

Kent, Conn.
elevation 392'

Quality Thrift • ↗ Cornwall Bridge (8.6 mi)
Main St
• Starbuck Inn
7
Housatonic River
Fife'n Drum Restaurant & Inn •
• Bank
↙ Kent Green Blvd
Dentist •
• True Value
• Davis IGA
Library
• Laundry
Sundog Shoe •
Macedonia Rd
Kent Market •
• The Villager
• Shanghai
• Post Office
• House of Books
• Kent Garden Pizza
Animal Clinic •
Backcountry • Outfitters
• Kent Coffee & Chocolate
• Kent Pharmacy
• Panini Café
• Mobile Mart
🚹🚺
⚑ (0.6 mi)
• Chris' Hot Dogs
Wasabi •

Post Office to:
Outfitter (0.4 mi)

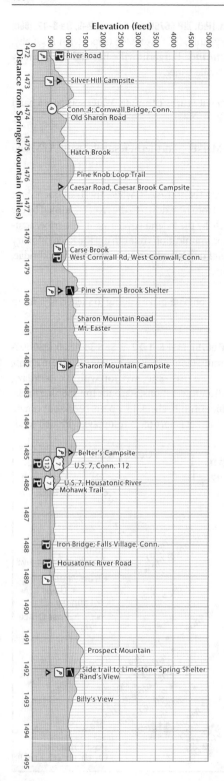

Elevation (feet)

Distance from Springer Mountain (miles)

River Road
Silver Hill Campsite
Conn. 4; Cornwall Bridge, Conn.
Old Sharon Road
Hatch Brook
Pine Knob Loop Trail
Caesar Road, Caesar Brook Campsite
Carse Brook
West Cornwall Rd, West Cornwall, Conn.
Pine Swamp Brook Shelter
Sharon Mountain Road
Mt. Easter
Sharon Mountain Campsite
Belter's Campsite
U.S. 7, Conn. 112
U.S. 7, Housatonic River
Mohawk Trail
Iron Bridge; Falls Village, Conn.
Housatonic River Road
Prospect Mountain
Side trail to Limestone Spring Shelter
Rand's View
Billy's View

House of Books, open daily, with guides, maps, fax, UPS and FedEx services.

North 2.5 miles *via* U.S. 7 to *Lodging:* Cooper Creek B&B, (860) 927-4334, <mtbotway@yahoo.com>. Hiker rate Su–Th $95, includes shuttle to Kent and B. No mail drops, no pets; check in at 3 p.m.; shuttle to and from Kent; slackpacking for guests; out-of-area shuttles (Wassaic, N.Y., train station, airports) with advance notice.

Red-pine plantation—The pines along the "river walk" north of Kent have seen hard times due to an insect blight. Most of the trees are now dead. The Connecticut Chapter of AMC harvested some of the dying trees to build new shelters, including the one at Ten Mile River.

Stewart Hollow Brook Shelter (1980s)—Sleeps 6. Privy. Water source is reliable Stony Brook, 0.4 mile north of the shelter on the A.T.

Silver Hill Campsite—Campsite, privy, swing, and pavilion sheltering two picnic tables. Water pump.

Mohawk Trail—The former A.T. route starts north of Guinea Brook on the A.T., passes through Cornwall Bridge, and returns near Falls Village.

Conn. 4—East 0.9 mile to **Cornwall Bridge, Conn.** [P.O. ZIP 06754: M–F 8:30–1 & 2–5, Sa 9–12; (860) 672-6710]. ■ *Lodging:* Hitching Post Motel, (860) 672-6219, $65D and up weekdays, $85D and up weekends, $15EAP, laundry service $5 and up, shuttle available depending on staffing; Housatonic Meadows Lodge B&B, (860) 672-6067, $110; Cornwall Inn & Restaurant, open year-round, (800) 786-6884, <www.cornwall-inn.com>, hiker rate $125D, $150 for 4 in room with 2 queen beds, includes continental B, pool, hot tub, Internet access, restaurant and lounge open Th–Su, L/D $8–$30; The Amselhaus, (860) 248-3155, <www.theamselhaus.com>, $85S, $100D, $50EAP TO 6, includes laundry and local shuttles, longer shuttles available. ■ *Groceries:* Cornwall General Store (short-term resupply). ■ *Outfitter:* Housatonic River Outfitters, 24 Kent Rd., (860) 672-1010, <hflyshop@aol.com>, open 7 days 9–5, limited hiker gear, canister fuel and fuel by ounce, will accept UPS and FedEx but not responsible for packages.

Shuttle by appointment only, $20 and up depending on distance. ■ *Other services:* hardware store; Housatonic Veterinary Care, (860) 672-4948. ■ *Camping:* Housatonic Meadows State Park, (860) 672-6772, 1 mile north of town on U.S. 7. Campsite $36 per night, up to 6 per site; open mid-Apr to Jan 1, water shut off Oct 15. The park may be self-service in midweek; registration information at the main cabin by the gate. Showers free but check with registration desk; no pets, no alcoholic beverages allowed. Accessible from the A.T. *via* Pine Knob Loop Trail (see below).

Guinea Brook—The AMC Connecticut Chapter installed stepping stones in the brook. In heavy rain, you may want to take the bypass: Northbounders should turn east on Conn. 4 and go downhill to unpaved Old Sharon Road on the north, which hikers rejoins the A.T. on the other side of the stream. Southbounders should turn east on the dirt road that the Trail crosses before the brook, then follow it to Conn. 4, and turn south.

Pine Knob Loop Trail—Housatonic Meadows State Park (see above) can be reached from the A.T. by taking the blue-blazed Pine Knob Loop Trail 0.5 mile to U.S. 7, then following the highway north for 0.4 mile. You can return to the A.T. *via* the Pine Knob Loop Trail.

West Cornwall Road—East 2.2 miles to **West Cornwall, Conn. [P.O. ZIP 06796: M–F 8–1 & 2–4:30, Sa 9–12; (860) 672-6791]**, site of a historical covered bridge over a whitewater section of the Housatonic River. ■ *Lodging:* Bearded Woods "One-of-a-Kind" Bunk & Dine, (860) 480-2966, call or text for pick-up from West Cornwall, Falls Village, or Salisbury. Hudson and Big Lu offer in-home accommodations, $50PP: bunk with linens, showere, laundry, shuttle to/from Trail and PO. Cash only. Call in advance for shuttle; last one at 5:30 p.m.; longer shuttles for a fee. All guest provided family-style D and B. smoking outside. Some supplies, including stove fuel. Limited services after Sep 1. ■ *Restaurant:* Wandering Moose Café, (860) 672-0178, 7 days, B/L/D. ■ *Groceries:* West Cornwall Market (short-term resupply), M–Th 6–7, F–Sa 6–8. ■ *Other services:* restaurants and gift shops. ■ *Outfitter:* Clarke Outdoors, (860) 672-6365, <www.clarkeoutdoors.com>, is located on U.S. 7 south of the village, with tube, canoe, and kayak rentals; limited outdoor gear and sportswear.

West 4.7 miles to **Sharon, Conn. [P.O. ZIP 06069: M–F 9:30–4:30, Sa 9:30–12:30; (860) 364-5306]**, with a supermarket, restaurant serving B/L/D, laundry, motel, bank with ATM, pharmacy, and hospital.

Pine Swamp Brook Shelter (1989)—Sleeps 6. Privy. Water is available on the blue-blazed trail.

U.S. 7/Warren Turnpike—*Restaurant:* Mountainside Café, (860) 824-7876, M–Th 7 a.m.–3 p.m., F–Sa 7–9:30, Su 7–5. After crossing Housatonic River and before Trail turns left on Warren Turnpike at high school, cross bridge over railroad tracks, then continue 0.2 mile.

Wheelchair-accessible trail—South of Falls Village, the A.T. hooks up with the River Trail, converted to create a handicap-accessible loop trail using part of the A.T. and an old racetrack.

Water Street—East 0.5 mile to **Falls Village, Conn. [P.O. ZIP 06031: M–F 8:30–1 & 2–5, Sa 8:30–12; (860) 824-7781]**. *See map on next page.* ■ *Restaurants:* Toymakers Café, (860) 824-8168, B/L, Th–Su 6:30–2:30, free tentsites; Fall Village Inn, upscale but hiker-friendly. ■ *Other services:* Falls Village Package Store, (860) 824-7971, open M–Sa 9–8, Su noon–5, owned by Pat Miller; has sodas and hiker snacks, allows hikers to charge phones, get water, and use phone to call area restaurants; Jacob's Garage has snack machines, but please remove your pack so that the dog won't be alarmed; bank with ATM at corner of Rtes. 7 & 126. Hikers may tent and shower at power plant.

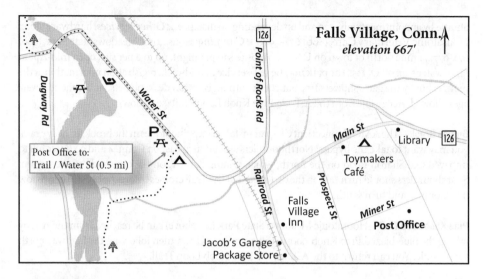

Hydroelectric Plant—Cold shower and water are available outside the small, vine-covered building past the transformer. Look for silver shower head poking through ivy, with a small concrete pad below. Water faucet is below shower head.

Iron Bridge over Housatonic—Renovations underway; when bridge is closed to pedestrian traffic, the A.T. detours along Conn. 112 west in Lime Rock to Dugway Rd., then north to rejoin the Trail at the iron bridge. The original bridge was built by the Berlin Construction Co. of Connecticut in 1903. The same company built the iron bridge that now takes hikers over Swatara Creek in Pennsylvania.

Picnic Area—North of bridge along the river, opposite the power plant, are picnic tables (no water), fire pits, a privy, trash cans, and parking area.

Limestone Spring Shelter (1986)—Sleeps 6. Privy is uphill to the right. Follow the stream to where a spring comes out of a small limestone cave.

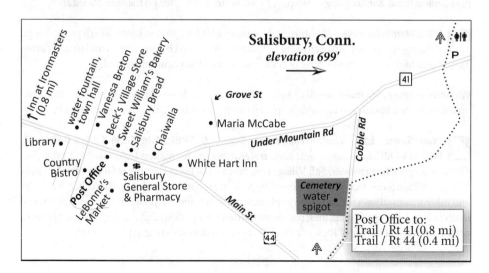

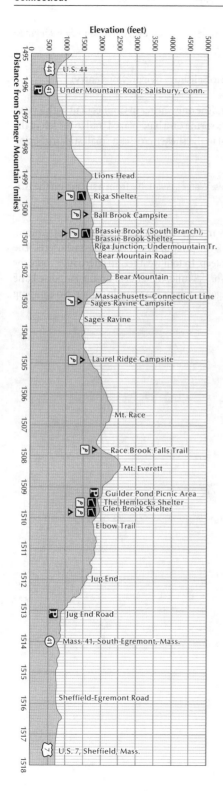

Elevation (feet)

Distance from Springer Mountain (miles)

U.S. 44

Under Mountain Road; Salisbury, Conn.

Lions Head

Riga Shelter

Ball Brook Campsite

Brassie Brook (South Branch),
Brassie Brook Shelter
Riga Junction, Undermountain Tr.
Bear Mountain Road

Bear Mountain

Massachusetts–Connecticut Line
Sages Ravine Campsite

Sages Ravine

Laurel Ridge Campsite

Mt. Race

Race Brook Falls Trail

Mt. Everett

Guilder Pond Picnic Area
The Hemlocks Shelter
Glen Brook Shelter

Elbow Trail

Jug End

Jug End Road

Mass. 41, South Egremont, Mass.

Sheffield-Egremont Road

U.S. 7, Sheffield, Mass.

Rand's View—The A.T. passes this vista, with views of the Taconic Range from Lion's Head to Mt. Everett and Jug End. *No camping allowed.*

U.S. 44—West 0.4 mile to **Salisbury, Conn. [P.O. ZIP 06068: M–F 8–1 & 2–5, Sa 9–12; (860) 435-5072].** For northbounders, turn west on U.S. 44 to town. For southbounders, it is best to follow Conn. 41, Under Mountain Road, 0.8 mile into town. Water is available from a fountain at town hall and also from a spigot in the cemetery on Cobble Road (located behind a large cement cross about 200 feet right of the maintenance shed). ■ *Lodging:* Maria McCabe offers rooms to hikers in her home, 4 Grove St., (860) 435-0593, $35PP, includes shower, use of living room, cooking outside, pets outside (no fee), no visitors in home, cash only, shuttle to laundry, mail drops accepted for guests; Vanessa Breton, 7 The Lockup Rd., (860) 435-9577, offers 3 rooms in her home for up to 5 hikers, $40PP, includes shower, laundry $5, use of living room, cooking outside, pets outside (no fee), no visitors in home, cash only, mail drops accepted for guests. Several other inns and B&Bs in the area. ■ *Groceries:* LaBonne's Epicure Market, (860) 435-2559 (long-term resupply), M–Sa, open 8–7, Su until 6. ■ *Restaurants:* Country Bistro, (860) 435-9420, appetizers, baked goods, B/L M–Th 8–5, B/L F–Su 8 a.m.–9 p.m. B/L/D, WiFi, live music F&Sa; Sweet William's Bakery, (860) 435-8889, baked goods, coffee, closed M, Tu–Th 7:30–4:30, F–Sa 7:30–6, Su 8:30–4. ■ *Internet access:* Scoville Memorial Library, Tu–F 10–6, Sa 10–4, Su 1–4. ■ *Other services:* Peter Beck's Village Store, (860) 596-4217, M–Sa 10–6, Su 10–4; Salisbury General Store and Pharmacy, (860) 435-9388, M–F 8–6, Sa 8–5, closed Su; bank with ATM; The Auto Shop, Coleman fuel and denatured alcohol. When open, town hall offers restroom and phone inside.

West 2.4 miles to **Lakeville.** ■ *Lodging:* Inn at Ironmasters, (860) 435-9844, <www.innatironmasters.com>, Mar–mid-Nov, $134S, $144D weekdays, $206 weekends, $15EAP, continental B, dogs allowed in certain rooms without fee, pool. ■ *Restaurants:* The Black Rabbit Bar and Grille, (860) 596-4227, L M W–Su 11:30–4:30, D 4:30–9:30, closed T; Mizza's Restaurant and Pizza, (860) 435-

6266, free delivery; On the Run Coffee Shop, (860) 435-2007, open every day. ■ *Other services:* hardware store, coin laundry, bank with ATM.

 Conn. 41 (Under Mountain Road)—**West** 0.8 mile to Salisbury (see previous entry).

Riga Shelter (1990)—Sleeps 6. Privy, tentsites, platform. The only shelter in Connecticut with a view. It opens to the east, providing sunrise views. Water is a spring on a blue-blazed trail to the left of the clearing at the A.T. A second source is where the trail to the shelter crosses a small stream. Spring may not run in dry years.

Brassie Brook Shelter (1980s)—Sleeps 6. Privy. Tentsites. Water is available from a stream on the A.T. 50 feet north of the side trail to the shelter.

Bear Mountain—At 2,316 feet, this is the highest peak in Connecticut but not the highest ground, which instead falls on the flank of nearby Mt. Frissel, the peak of which is in Massachusetts. The northbound descent into Sages Ravine is rocky and steep. In foul weather, an alternative route for northbounders is east on the Undermountain Trail for 0.8 mile, then north on the Paradise Lane Trail for 2.1 miles, reconnecting with the A.T. near Sages Ravine, a net 1.7-mile detour. No camping on summit.

Massachusetts

Miles from Springer	Fr Last Point	Features	Services	Miles from Katahdin	M A P
1,506.3	0.7	Connecticut–Massachusetts State Line (1,800')		682.9	
1,506.4	0.1	Sages Ravine Campsite (1,360')	C, w	682.8	
1,507.0	0.6	Sages Ravine (1,340')	w	682.2	
1,508.3	1.3	Laurel Ridge Campsite (1,750')	C, w	680.9	
1,510.1	1.8	Mt. Race (2,365')...*open ledges*		679.1	
1,511.2	1.1	Race Brook Falls Trail (1,950')	E–0.2m C; 0.4m w	678.0	
1,511.9	0.7	Mt. Everett (2,602')		677.3	ATC Mass.–Conn. Map 3
1,512.6	0.7	Guilder Pond Picnic Area (2,050')	R, P	676.6	
1,513.0	0.4	**The Hemlocks Shelter** (1,880')...*8.8mS; 0.1mN*	S, w	676.2	
1,513.1	0.1	**Glen Brook Shelter** (1,885')...*0.1mS; 14.3mN*	S, C, w	676.1	
1,513.7	0.6	Elbow Trail (1,750')		675.5	
1,515.4	1.7	Jug End (1,750')		673.8	
1,516.5	1.1	Jug End Road (890')	R, P (E–0.25m w)	672.7	
1,517.4	0.9	Mass. 41; Undermountain Road (810') ATC Kellogg Conservation Center **South Egremont, Mass. 01258**	R (W–0.1m A.T.C.; 1.2m PO, M)	671.8	
1,519.2	1.8	Sheffield–Egremont Road (700') Shay's Rebellion Monument	R	670.0	
1,521.0	1.8	U.S. 7 (700') **Sheffield, Mass. 01257** **Great Barrington, Mass. 01230**	R (E–3.2m PO, B, G, L, M) (W–0.3m M; 1.5m G; 1.8m PO, all)	668.2	
1,521.9	0.9	Kellogg Road, Housatonic River Bridge (720')	R, P	667.3	
1,523.9	2.0	Home Road (1,150')	R, P	665.3	
1,525.3	1.4	East Mountain (1,800')	w	663.9	
1,527.4	2.1	Ice Gulch (1,540') **Tom Leonard Shelter**...*14.3mS; 5.3mN*	S (E–0.2m w)	661.8	
1,528.5	1.1	Lake Buel Road (1,150')	R, P	660.7	
1,529.4	0.9	Mass. 23 (1,050') **Monterey, Mass. 01245** **Great Barrington, Mass. 01230**	R, P (E–4.3m PO) (W–1.6m H; 2.7m M; 4m PO, all)	659.8	ATC Mass.–Conn. Map 2
1,530.6	1.2	Blue Hill Road (Stony Brook Road) (1,550')	R, P	658.6	
1,531.4	0.8	Benedict Pond (1,620')	W–0.5m C, w	657.8	
1,532.0	0.6	The Ledges (1,820')		657.2	
1,532.7	0.7	**Mt. Wilcox South Shelter** (1,720') ...*5.3mS; 2.1mN*	S, w	656.5	
1,534.5	1.8	**Mt. Wilcox North Shelter** (2,100') ...*2.1mS; 14.8mN*	E–0.3m S, w	654.7	
1,535.1	0.6	Beartown Mountain Road (1,800')	R, w	654.1	
1,538.3	3.2	Fernside Road (1,200')	R, P (W–0.2m w)	650.9	

Miles from Springer	Fr Last Point	Features	Services	Miles from Katahdin	M A P
1,538.6	0.3	Shaker Campsite (1,000')	C, w	650.6	
1,540.4	1.8	Jerusalem Road (930')...*spring* **Tyringham, Mass. 01264**	R, P, w (W–0.6m PO, L)	648.8	
1,541.5	1.1	Tyringham Main Road (930')	R, P	647.7	
1,543.4	1.9	Webster Road (1,800')	R, P, w	645.8	
1,545.8	2.4	Goose Pond Road (1,650')	R, P	643.4	
1,547.7	1.9	Upper Goose Pond (1,500')	w	641.5	
1,548.2	0.5	Old Chimney and Plaque (1,520')		641.0	
1,548.5	0.3	**Upper Goose Pond Cabin** (1,480') ...*14.8mS; 9.3mN*	W–0.5m S, C, w	640.7	
1,549.7	1.2	I-90 Mass. Turnpike (1,400')...*pedestrian bridge*	R	639.5	
1,549.8	0.1	Greenwater Brook (1,400')	w	639.4	ATC Mass.—Conn. Map 2
1,550.1	0.3	U.S. 20 (1,400') **Lee, Mass. 01238**	R, P (E–0.1m L) (W–5m PO, all)	639.1	
1,550.9	0.8	Tyne Road (1,750')	R, P	638.3	
1,551.4	0.5	Becket Mountain (2,180')		637.8	
1,553.2	1.8	Finerty Pond (1,900')	w	636.0	
1,555.5	2.3	County Road (1,850')	R, P	633.7	
1,555.7	0.2	Bald Top (2,040')		633.5	
1,557.3	1.6	**October Mountain Shelter** (1,950') ...*9.3mS; 9mN*	S, C, w	631.9	
1,558.0	0.7	West Branch Road (1,960')	R, P	631.2	
1,559.5	1.5	Washington Mountain Road, Pittsfield Road (2,000') **Becket, Mass. 01223**	R, P (E–0.1m C, w; 5m PO, L, D, V)	629.7	
1,561.5	2.0	Stream (1,950')	w	627.7	
1,562.7	1.2	Blotz Road (1,850')	R, P	626.5	
1,563.4	0.7	Warner Hill (2,050')		625.8	
1,566.1	2.7	**Kay Wood Shelter** (1,860')...*9mS; 17.3mN*	E–0.2m S, w	623.1	
1,566.4	0.3	Grange Hall Road (1,650')	R, P	622.8	
1,568.5	2.1	CSX Railroad crossing (1,250')		620.7	
1,568.6	0.1	**Depot St.** (1,240')...*water at 83 Depot St.*	R, H, w	620.6	
1,569.1	0.5	Mass. 8, Mass. 9 (1,200') **Dalton, Mass. 01226**	R, PO, B, C, G, L, M, D, cl, f	620.1	ATC Mass.—Conn. Map 1
1,570.1	1.0	Gulf Road (1,180')	R, P	619.1	
1,573.8	3.7	Crystal Mountain Campsite (2,100')	E–0.2m C, w	615.4	
1,574.2	0.4	Gore Pond (2,050')		615.0	
1,576.7	2.5	The Cobbles (1,850')...*views*		612.5	
1,577.5	0.8	Furnace Hill Road (960')	R	611.7	
1,578.0	0.5	Church St., Hoosic River, Ashwillticook Rail Trail (950')	R, M	611.2	
1,578.1	0.1	Church St., School St., Hiker Kiosk (970') **Cheshire, Mass. 01225**	R, PO, B, G, M, w (W–0.1m L)	611.1	

Miles from Springer	Fr Last Point	Features	Services	Miles from Katahdin	M A P
1,578.6	0.5	Mass. 8 (1,000') **Adams, Mass. 01220**	R (E–0.8m L; 2.4m O, f; 4m PO, B, G, L, M, D, V, cl) (W–0.2m G)	610.6	
1,579.4	0.8	Outlook Ave. (1,350')	R	609.8	
1,582.1	2.7	Old Adams Road (2,350')	R	607.1	
1,583.0	0.9	**Mark Noepel Shelter** (2,750')...*17.3mS; 7.1mN*	E–0.2m S, C, w	606.2	
1,583.6	0.6	Jones Nose Trail, Saddle Ball Mountain (3,150')		605.6	
1,585.8	2.2	Notch Road; Rockwell Road (3,290')...*pond*	R	603.4	
1,586.3	0.5	Mt. Greylock, Summit Road (3,491') Bascom Lodge, War Memorial	R, P, L, M, w	602.9	ATC Mass.–Conn. Map 1
1,589.5	3.2	Notch Road (2,400')	R, P (E–0.25 w)	599.7	
1,589.6	0.1	**Wilbur Clearing Shelter** (2,300') ...*7.1mS; 10.4mN*	W–0.3m S, C, w	599.6	
1,591.7	2.1	Pattison Road (900')	R, P, w	597.5	
1,592.2	0.5	Catherine St.-Phelps Road Intersection (670')	R	597.0	
1,592.6	0.4	Mass. 2 (650') **North Adams, Mass. 01247** **Williamstown, Mass. P.O. 01267**	R, B (E–0.6m G, M, cl; 1m sh; 2.5m PO, B, G, L, M, D, V, cl) (W–0.4m G, L, M; 1.4m G, L, M, cl, f; 2.6m PO, B, G, L, M, D, V, sh)	596.6	
1,594.4	1.8	Shermon Brook Primitive Campsite (1,300')	w (W–0.1m C)	594.8	
1,595.4	1.0	Pine Cobble Trail (2,010')		593.8	
1,595.9	0.5	Eph's Lookout (2,254')		593.3	
1,596.7	0.8	Massachusetts–Vermont State Line (2,330') Long Trail (southern terminus)...*sign*		592.5	

The state line is south of Sages Ravine, near the junction with Paradise Lane Trail. The painted state abbreviations on a tree are so faded they're almost invisible.

From the peaks of Mt. Greylock to Mt. Everett, over hills and valleys, through towns and hamlets of the Berkshires, one is reminded of the cultural mecca of New England's famous writers, artists, and performers. Juicy, sweet blueberries abound in season. Water and mosquitoes seem to be everywhere—be warned!

Sages Ravine—Two tent platforms and campsites with group site, privy. Staffed by ridgerunners who take turns as caretakers. No fires permitted. No fees charged.

Berkshire Chapter of the Appalachian Mountain Club—The A.T. Committee of the AMC–Berkshire Chapter maintains 89.7 miles from the Sages Ravine area to the Massachusetts–Vermont state line. Correspondence should be sent to Berkshire A.T. Committee Box 2281, Pittsfield, MA 02102; <www.amcberkshire.org>; (413) 454-4773.

Berkshire Bus Service—The Berkshire Regional Transit Authority, (413) 499-2782 or (800) 292-2782, <www.berkshirerta.com>, serves the Trail towns of Great Barrington, Lee, Dalton, Cheshire, Adams,

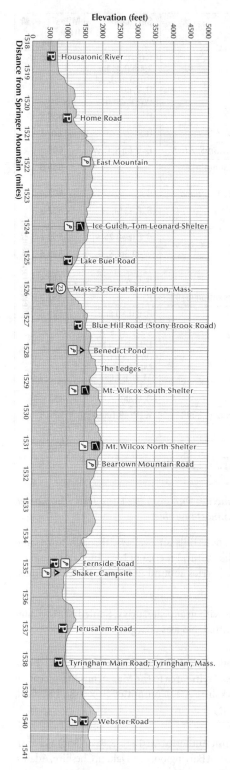

North Adams, and Williamstown. The buses run M–F 5:45 a.m.–7:20 p.m. and Sa 7:15 a.m.–7 p.m.; no service Su or holidays. Call for accurate, up-to-date information. The buses can be flagged down anywhere along Mass. 2 or 8 or U.S. 7, but there are designated bus stops. Popular trips for hikers include rides from Dalton west into Pittsfield, the region's hub with all major services, and from Cheshire south to the Berkshire Mall, with 103 shops and a 10-screen cinema. Maximum fare one way is $5 ($1.25 per community crossed; cash; drivers cannot make change); ask for free transfers. Senior rates available.

Peter Pan Bus Lines—(800) 343-9999, <www.peterpanbus.com>. Buses run daily each way between NYC and Williamstown, Mass., stopping at towns near the A.T., including Canaan and Danbury in Connecticut and Sheffield, Great Barrington, Lee, Pittsfield, and Williamstown in Massachusetts. Call for schedules and rates.

Laurel Ridge Campsite—0.1 mile south of Bear Rock Falls, 4 campsites with 5 single-tent platforms and one group site with 3-tent platform. Privy. Bear box. Water source is a spring off a short side trail south of campsites. *No fires permitted in this area.*

Race Mountain—A spectacular walk on a clear day; spooky when foggy. It's a steep drop-off to the east.

Race Brook Falls Campsite—0.2 mile east on the Race Brook Falls Trail. Group camping area, 4 tent platforms, privy, bear box. Water source is stream east of the campsite.

Mt. Everett—This range is the second-highest on the A.T. in Massachusetts.

Guilder Pond—At 2,042 feet, the short side trail to the west leads to this highest body of water in Massachusetts. Picnic table and privy. For conservation reasons, please, no camping or swimming.

The Hemlocks Shelter (1999)—Sleeps 10; has a group site. Privy. Nestled in a hemlock grove, the shelter offers a sleeping loft with overhang. Water source is on the blue-blazed access trail. If you cannot find water here, Glen Brook crosses the A.T. 50 yards north of the access trail to the shelter.

Glen Brook Shelter (1960s)—Sleeps 6. Privy. Two tent platforms and large tenting area. Water source is a reliable stream in front of, and downhill from, the shelter.

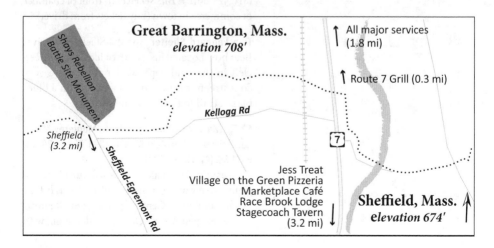

Mass. 41 (Undermountain Road)—West 0.1 mile to the Appalachian Trail Conservancy's Kellogg Conservation Center (KCC) at the old (1742) April Hill farm. Initially an office for one ATC and one Appalachian Mountain Club staff member, both of whom are frequently in the field, it became the New England regional office of ATC (formerly in Lyme, N.H.). No public parking is available yet. Trailhead parking is available on Sheffield–Egremont Road, 1.8 Trail miles north. For more information, contact Adam Brown at (413) 528-8002 or <abrown@appalachiantrail.org>.

West 1.2 miles to **South Egremont, Mass. [P.O. ZIP 01258: M–F 8:15–12 & 12:30–4, Sa 9–11:30; (413) 528-1571].** ■ *Restaurant:* Mom's Country Café, B/L, M–Su 6:30–3, D F–Su 5–9, water available from outdoor spigot. ■ *Internet access:* library, M, T & Th 10–6, Sa 9–noon. ■ *Other services:* bank with ATM.

Shays' Rebellion Monument—Stone marker commemorates the last skirmish of a bloody farmers' revolt led by Revolutionary War veteran Daniel Shays against government taxes and tactics in 1787. The incident assisted Federalists in making their case for a strong central government with powers to tax and maintain a standing army.

U.S. 7—East 3.2 miles to **Sheffield, Mass. [P.O. ZIP 01257: M–F 9–4:30, Sa 9–12; (413) 229-8772].** ■ *Lodging:* Jess Treat, (860) 248-5710, <jesstreat@gmail.com>, offers 2 rooms in her home for up to 4–5 hikers, $40PP ($60 shared bed) cash only, includes clean bed, shower, full B, WiFi, $5 laundry, no pets inside, not a party place, reservations essential, tent site for $15PP with shower and B, shuttles usually available; Race Brook Lodge, 864 South Undermountain Rd., (413) 229-2916, <www.rblodge.com>, a restored 1790s barn, summer rates Su–Th $120–$260, F–Sa $155–$335, $20EAP, pets allowed in same room $15, no mail drops. ■ *Restaurants: In town:* Village on the Green Restaurant and Pizzeria, Su–Th 11–9, F–Sa 11–10; Sheffield Pub; The Marketplace Café, (413) 248-5040, open M–Sa 7–7, Su 9–4. *Along Rt. 7 toward town:* The Bridge Restaurant, closed M, D Tu–Su, opens at 4:30; Stagecoach Tavern (at Race Brook Lodge), open for D Th–Su. ■ *Other services:* bank, ATM, and bus service.

West 0.3 mile to Route 7 Grille, L Sa–Su 11:30–3; D M–Th 5–9, F–Sa 5–10, Su 3–9.

West 1.5 miles to Guido's, with organic produce and deli.

West 1.8 miles to **Great Barrington, Mass. [P.O. ZIP 01230: M–F 8:30–4:30, Sa 8:30–12:30; (413) 528-3670].** ■ *Lodging:* Days Inn, (413) 528-3150, rates $89 and up, $10EAP, max 4/room, no pets, conti-

Great Barrington, Mass.
elevation 708′

Shays Rebellion Battle Site Monument

↑ All major services (1.8 mi)

↑ Route 7 Grill (0.3 mi)

Kellogg Rd

Sheffield (3.2 mi) ↓

Sheffield-Egremont Rd

7

Jess Treat
Village on the Green Pizzeria
Marketplace Café
Race Brook Lodge
Stagecoach Tavern
(3.2 mi) ↓

Sheffield, Mass. ↗
elevation 674′ ↑

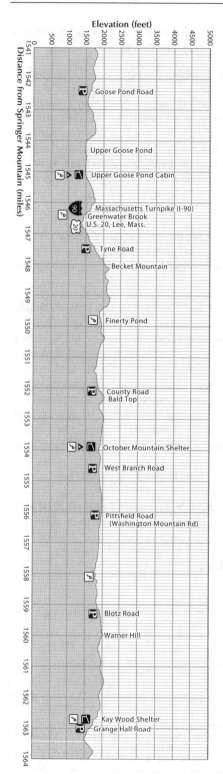

Elevation (feet) — Distance from Springer Mountain (miles)

- 1542 — Goose Pond Road
- 1544 — Upper Goose Pond
- 1545 — Upper Goose Pond Cabin
- 1546 — Massachusetts Turnpike (I-90)
- Greenwater Brook
- U.S. 20, Lee, Mass.
- 1547 — Tyne Road
- 1548 — Becket Mountain
- 1550 — Finerty Pond
- 1552 — County Road / Bald Top
- 1554 — October Mountain Shelter
- 1555 — West Branch Road
- 1556 — Pittsfield Road (Washington Mountain Rd)
- 1559 — Blotz Road
- 1560 — Warner Hill
- 1563 — Kay Wood Shelter / Grange Hall Road

nental B, WiFi; Lantern House Motel, (413) 528-2350, $75 and up, higher on weekends, $10EAP, outdoor saltwater pool, call for reservations, WiFi, continental B, no pets; Travelodge, (413) 528-2340, $55S, $69 and up, higher on weekends and during special events, $10EAP, max 2/room, pets allowed in some rooms for $10 fee, laundry, WiFi, continental B, outdoor pool; Mountain View Motel, (413) 528-0250, $65 and up, no pets, free WiFi, CATV, phone, refrigerator, microwave, continental B; Holiday Inn Express, (413) 528-1810, 20% discount on current rates, extended continental B, no pets, WiFi, computer available for guests; Berkshire Marriott Fairfield Inn, (413) 644-3200, <www.berkshiremarriott.com>, call for rates, full hot B, laundry, no pets, indoor and outdoor pools, WiFi and guest's computer; The Briarcliff Motel, (413) 528-3000, <thebriarcliffmotel.com>, $175 and up in summer, continental B, WiFi; Monument Mountain Motel, U.S. 7, 247 Stockbridge Rd., (413) 528-3272, <www.monumentmountainmotel.com>, $75 and up, higher on weekends and during special events, no pets, laundry, pool, coffee and tea when office is open, mail drops accepted for guests. ■ *Groceries:* Big Y Foods, open M–Th Sa-Su 7–9, F 7-10; and Price Chopper, M–Sa 6–midnight, Su 7–midnight (both long-term resupply). ■ *Restaurants:* numerous, in town center and north along U.S. 7. ■ *Other services:* All major services available; shopping center 1.8 miles **west** of Trail has pharmacy, coin laundry, hardware store; taxi, (413) 528-0911. ■ *Bus service:* In front of chamber of commerce in town (buy tickets from driver).

Tom Leonard Shelter (1970)—Sleeps 10. Privy. Bear box. Located just south of Ice Gulch, a deep cleft in the landscape. Water source is a very cold stream 0.2 mile down a ravine on a blue-blazed trail to the left of the shelter.

Mass. 23—East 4.3 miles to **Monterey, Mass.** **[P.O. ZIP 01245: M–F 8:30–1 & 2–4:30, Sa 9–11:30; (413) 528-4670].**

West 1 mile to Lake Buel Road, turn left, first right driveway, 0.6 mile uphill to *Hostel:* East Mountain Retreat Center, (413) 528-6617, <emrc@bcn.net>, open Apr 15–Oct 15, $10 donation, with shower; laundry $3; use of the cooking facilities and library; 10 p.m. quiet curfew and prompt 8:30 a.m. checkout; will hold UPS/FedEx packages (c/o East Mountain Retreat, 8 Lake Buel Rd., Great Barrington, MA 01230, or P.O. Box 195). Local pizza delivery.

West 4 miles to Great Barrington (see above).

Benedict Pond—West 0.5 mile on a blue-blazed side trail to a sandy beach with picnic tables, tentsites $10.

Mt. Wilcox South Shelter (1930/2007)—Old shelter sleeps 6. Privy. Bear box. Built as a CCC project; approach trail was part of the original A.T. in Massachusetts. Shelter completed in 2007 is just beyond old one. Water source is the spring crossed *en route* to the shelter.

Mt. Wilcox North Shelter (1930s)—Sleeps 10. Privy. Shelter is on a 0.3-mile blue-blazed trail. Water source, in front of the shelter, may go dry in late summer.

Shaker Campsite—Two tent platforms, privy. Bear box. Water is located north on the A.T. at stream crossing.

Tyringham Cobble—Formed by a geological event that separated this hill from the mountain behind it, the cobble rises 400 feet above the village below. The hill and nearly 200 acres around it are owned by a conservation trust.

Jerusalem Road—West 0.6 mile to **Tyringham, Mass. [P.O. ZIP 01264: M–F 9–12:30 & 4–5:30, Sa 8:30–12:30; (413) 243-1225]**. May also be reached from Tyringham Main Road 1.1 mile north on A.T. Water fountain outside post office. Library open T 3–5, Sa 10–12; WiFi and computer available. ■ *Lodging:* Cobble View B&B, (413) 243-2463, call for rates; <www.cobbleviewbandb.com>, call for rates; no pets, no visitors; across from P.O.; drinks and snacks.

Jerusalem Road Spring—West several yards to short path on left that leads to a piped spring (if you pass the first house on the right, you've gone too far).

Upper Goose Pond Cabin—AMC–Berkshire Chapter A.T. Committee maintains this cabin on a 0.5-mile side trail north of the pond. The cabin offers bunks, fireplace, covered porch, privy, bear box, swimming, and tent platforms. Open daily Memorial Day–Labor Day, then weekends through Columbus Day. During the summer, the resident volunteer caretaker brings water by canoe from a spring across the pond; otherwise, the pond is the water source. When the caretaker is not in residence or the cabin is closed for the season, hikers may camp on the porch or tent platforms. Privy behind the cabin and near tentsites. No fee is charged for staying at this site; donations appreciated.

U.S. 20—East 0.1 mile to *Lodging:* Berkshire Lakeside Lodge, 3949 Jacob's Ladder Road, Becket, MA 01223; (413) 243-9907, <www.berkshirelakesidelodge.com>, $65–$165 (call for reservations), use of outside grill, canoes, and kayaks; continental B, WiFi, minifridge and coffee pot in each room; food delivery available; mail drops accepted for nonguests, no fee but call ahead.

West 5 miles to **Lee, Mass. [P.O. ZIP 01238: M–F 8:30–4:30, Sa 9–12; (413) 243-1392]**. Nearby Lenox is home of the famous Tanglewood Performing Arts Center and the summer residence of the Boston Symphony Orchestra. "Tanglewood" also offers other types of concerts in an outdoors setting and spectacular July Fourth fireworks. ■ *Lodging:* Rodeway Inn, (413) 243-0813, Su–Th $49–$79s/D, F–Sa $89–$169, WiFi, continental B, no pets; Pilgrim Inn, (413) 243-1328, Su–Th $79–$95, F–Sa $95–$195, $10 EAP, continental B, coffee in room, pool, WiFi, microwave, fridge, laundry; Super 8, 170 Housatonic St., (413) 243-0143, $59–$205, $10EAP, continental B, WiFi, no pets, accepts mail drops (if staying more than one night); EconoLodge, (413) 243-0501, $79s/D weekdays, $190 weekends,

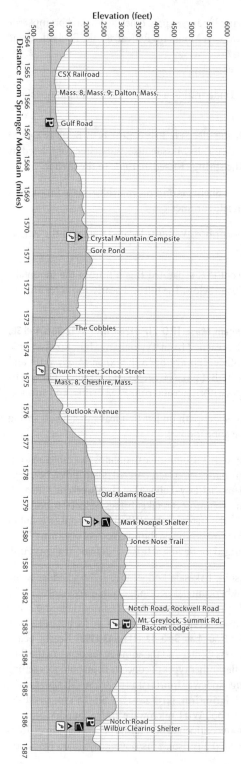

Elevation (feet)

Distance from Springer Mountain (miles)

- CSX Railroad
- Mass. 8, Mass. 9; Dalton, Mass.
- Gulf Road
- Crystal Mountain Campsite
- Gore Pond
- The Cobbles
- Church Street, School Street
- Mass. 8, Cheshire, Mass.
- Outlook Avenue
- Old Adams Road
- Mark Noepel Shelter
- Jones Nose Trail
- Notch Road, Rockwell Road
- Mt. Greylock, Summit Rd, Bascom Lodge
- Notch Road
- Wilbur Clearing Shelter

WiFi, microwave, fridge, continental B. ■ *Groceries:* Price Chopper and Big Y supermarkets (long-term resupply). ■ *Restaurants:* Joe's Diner, Athena's Pizza House, Rose's Restaurant (B/L 7–2), and several fast-food chains. ■ *Other services:* All major services available.

October Mountain Shelter (1980s)—Sleeps 12. Tentsites. Privy. Bear box. Loft overhangs picnic table. Water source is a stream just south of the shelter on the A.T.

Washington Mountain Road—East 0.1 mile to the "Cookie Lady," Marilyn Wiley, (413) 623-5859, who lives on a blueberry farm on the left of Washington Mountain Road. Water spigot near the garage door is for hikers. A.T. signs are posted; please sign register on the steps. Homemade cookies are often available to munch on as you watch hummingbirds buzz her feeder; pick your own blueberries at reasonable rates during season. Camping is allowed on the property in exchange for work. Will also hold packages and provide shuttles. Roy and Marilyn Wiley, 47 Washington Mountain Rd., Becket, MA 01223.

East 5 miles to **Becket, Mass. [P.O. ZIP 01223: M–F 8–4, Sa 9–11:30; (413) 623-8845]**, where the A.T. ironically is listed as a historical site in a town settled more than 300 years ago. ■ *Lodging:* Becket Motel, 29 Chester Rd., Becket, MA 01223, (413) 623-8888, $70–$127, coin laundry, free shuttles to/from Trail, WiFi, mail drops accepted for guests only. ■ *Groceries:* Becket General Store, (413) 623-5700, M–Sa 7-8, Su 8-5, small grocery, deli counter. ■ *Other services:* doctor, veterinarian.

Kay Wood Shelter (1980s)—Sleeps 10. Privy. Bear box. Shelter is named for Kay Wood, an early Trail angel, long-time Trail maintainer, and 1988–89 thru-hiker who died in 2010 at age 91. Water source is the stream in front of the shelter.

Dalton, Mass. [P.O. ZIP 01226: M–F 8:30– 4:30, Sᴀ 9–12; (413) 684-0364]—The A.T. goes through the eastern side of town, where most services are available; see map. Depot Street, which the A.T. follows into town from the south, offers a pharmacy and restaurants.

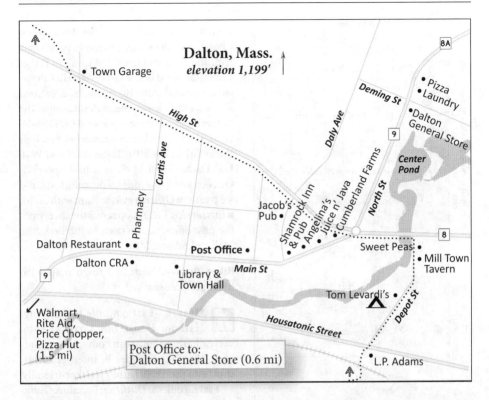

Dalton, Mass.
elevation 1,199'

Town Garage

Pizza
Laundry

Deming St

Dalton General Store

High St

Daly Ave

9

Curtis Ave

Cumberland Farms

North St

Center Pond

Pharmacy

Jacob's Pub

Shamrock Inn
Shamrock & Pub
Angelina's
Juice n' Java

8

Dalton Restaurant
Post Office
Sweet Peas

Dalton CRA

Mill Town Tavern

9

Library & Town Hall

Main St

Tom Levardi's

Walmart, Rite Aid, Price Chopper, Pizza Hut (1.5 mi)

Housatonic Street

Depot St

Post Office to: Dalton General Store (0.6 mi)

L.P. Adams

Other services are within 0.5 mile of the A.T. ■ *Lodging:* Thomas Levardi, 83 Depot St., (413) 684-3359, cell (413) 212-9691, allows hikers to use a water spigot outside his home and provides the hospitality of his front porch and back yard for tenting (limited space, get permission first); Shamrock Village Inn, (413) 684-0860, S–Th 2 doubles or 1 queen $80, 1 double $74, 1 king $90, F–Sa $104, $95, $110 respectively, F–Sa includes continental B, pets $75 deposit, hiker box, WiFi, laundry, ask about 10% hiker discount. ■ *Groceries:* Cumberland Farms with ATM, Dalton General Store with deli (both short-term resupply). ■ *Restaurants:* Jacob's Pub, 51 Daly Ave., (413) 684-9766, L/D M–Sa 11:30–1, Su 12–8, *great* Reubens, very hiker-friendly, hiker box; Mill Tavern, L/D; Dalton Diner; Angelina's Subs with veggie burgers; Juice 'n' Java, 661 Main St., specialty coffee and sandwiches, M–F 6:30–8, Sa–Su 7–7; Dalton Restaurant, serves D daily, Th–Sa with live entertainment; Shamrocks Restaurant and Pub, L/D, Tu–Sa 11:30–9, Su 11:30–8, closed M, WiFi. ■ *Internet access:* library, 1-hour limit. ■ *Other services:* Dalton CRA, 400 Main St., free showers with towel and soap to hikers; Dalton Laundry, M–F 8:30–6, Sa 8:30–4, Su 8:30–12; banks; L.P. Adams provides free denatured alcohol and Coleman fuel outside front entrance 24/7; doctor; dentist; pharmacy. ■ *Bus service:* BRTA connections to Pittsfield, with all major services.

Crystal Mountain Campsite—0.2 mile east. Privy. Bear box. Water is north on Trail; may go dry in summer.

The Cobbles—These outcroppings of marble overlook the Hoosic River Valley and offer views of Cheshire and Mt. Greylock. The Hoosic River, which is crossed south of Cheshire, flows north and empties into the Hudson River in New York.

 Cheshire, Mass. [P.O. ZIP 01225: M–F 7:30–1 & 2–4:30, Sa 8:30–11:30; (413) 743-3184]—The Trail skirts the center of town to the east and crosses Mass. 8 0.4 mile east of the main stoplight at

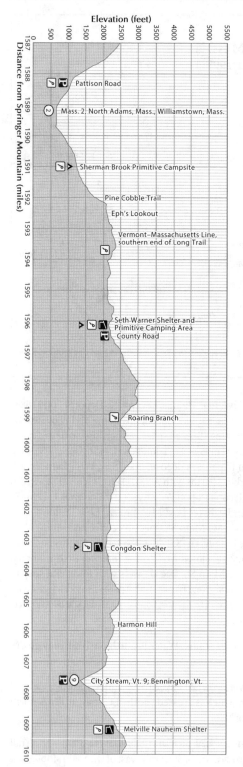

Elevation (feet)

Distance from Springer Mountain (miles)

Pattison Road

Mass. 2; North Adams, Mass.; Williamstown, Mass.

Sherman Brook Primitive Campsite

Pine Cobble Trail

Eph's Lookout

Vermont–Massachusetts Line, southern end of Long Trail

Seth Warner Shelter and Primitive Camping Area County Road

Roaring Branch

Congdon Shelter

Harmon Hill

City Stream, Vt. 9; Bennington, Vt.

Melville Nauheim Shelter

Church Street. St. Mary of the Assumption Church may allow hikers to stay in parish hall, tent, and use parking lot, but speak to Father David Raymond first. ■ *Groceries:* H.D. Reynolds, a general store, hiker snacks, denatured alcohol, and Coleman fuel. ■ *Restaurants:* The Gathering Pub & Pizzeria, closed M, L/D Su–W 11–10, Th–Sa 11–11, bar, pizza, sandwiches; Bass Water Grill, closed Tu, Sa–Su B/L/D, M W–F L/D; Diane's Twist, M–Su 11–6, mid-Apr–mid-Oct, outdoor spigot, deli sandwiches, soda, and ice cream. ■ *Other services:* bank with ATM. ■ *Bus service:* BRTA stop across the street from the post office, connections to the Berkshire Mall and Adams, Mass.

Hiker kiosk—A detailed town map with hiker services marked.

Mass. 8—**East** 0.8 mile to *Lodging:* Harbour House Inn, (413) 743-8959, <www.harbourhouseinn.com>, rooms midweek $85. Rate includes B, Internet access, shuttle to the Trail; laundry. Hiker-friendly.

East 2.4 miles to *Outfitter:* Berkshire Outfitters, (413) 743-5900, <www.berkshireoutfitters. com>, M–Sa 10–6, Th 'til 7, Su 11–4; hiker supplies, Coleman fuel, minor equipment repairs.

East 4 miles to **Adams, Mass. [P.O. ZIP 01220: M–F 8:30–4:30, Sa 10–12; (413) 743-5177]**, an alternative to the smaller town of Cheshire. Adams is accessible by the BRTA bus service. ■ *Lodging:* Mount Greylock Inn, (413) 743-2665, <mountgreylockinn.com>, $129–$199, includes B. ■ *Groceries:* Big Y Foods supermarket (long-term resupply). ■ *Restaurants:* Pizza Jim's, (413) 743-9161, will deliver; CJ's Pub and Daily Grind Coffee; many fast-food outlets. ■ *Other services:* Thrifty Bundle Coin laundry, banks, hardware store, doctor, dentist, Rite Aid, veterinarian, and Western Union.

West 0.2 mile to *Groceries:* Convenience store (short-term resupply), deli sandwiches.

Mark Noepel Shelter (1985)—Sleeps 10. Tentsites and platform. Privy. Bear box. Porcupines make regular appearances at this shelter. Water source is a stream on a blue-blazed trail to the right of the shelter.

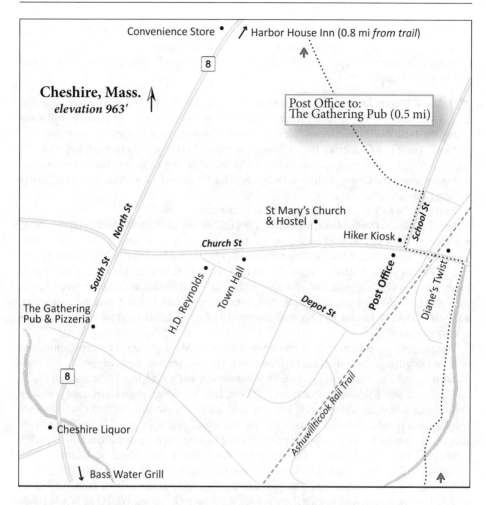

Convenience Store • ↗ Harbor House Inn (0.8 mi *from trail*)

8

Cheshire, Mass. ↑
elevation 963'

Post Office to:
The Gathering Pub (0.5 mi)

North St

St Mary's Church
& Hostel •
Hiker Kiosk •

School St

Church St

South St

H.D. Reynolds •

Town Hall •

Depot St

Post Office •

Diane's Twist •

The Gathering
Pub & Pizzeria •

8

• Cheshire Liquor

Ashuwillticook Rail Trail

↓ Bass Water Grill

Saddle Ball Mountain—At 3,238 feet and located at the A.T. junction with the Jones Nose Trail, Saddle Ball is the A.T.'s first 3,000-footer north of North Marshall in Shenandoah National Park.

Mt. Greylock—Topped by a war memorial, paved road, and Bascom Lodge, Greylock is Massachusetts' highest peak (3,491 feet). A stone tower, crowned by a globe lit at night, is a tribute to the state's war dead. You can climb the 89 steps to the top for views of the Green, Catskill, and Taconic mountains and surrounding towns. The mountain has inspired literary giants from Melville to Thoreau to Hawthorne. *Thunderbolt Shelter on Mt. Greylock is an emergency-only warming hut. No camping or fires on the summit.*

 Bascom Lodge—Operated by Bascom Lodge Group, (413) 743-1591, <www.bascomlodge.net>, open 7 days, B (8–10)/L(11–4:30)/D(7, $30), showers and towel $5, bunk $36, private rooms $125–$190D, $20EAP, open Jun–Oct.

Wilbur Clearing Shelter (1970)—Sleeps 8. Tentsites and platforms. Privy. Bear box. Located 0.3 mile down the Money Brook Trail; very popular during the summer months. Water source is a stream to the right of the shelter that might go dry in late summer.

Catherine Street/Phelps Road—Joshua Moran of 138 Catherine St., North Adams, provides three mountain bicycles for hikers to use to ride to nearby services. Hikers can leave their packs at Moran's property while using the bikes (west on Catherine Street, third house on the left, see map).

Mass. 2/North Adams—BRTA hourly bus service is available on this road (see page 176-176). *Note: The city of North Adams extends more than one mile west and several miles east of the Trail; the Williamstown line is 1.4 miles west of the Trail. See map on next page.*
East 0.6 mile to ■ *Groceries:* Price Chopper Supermarket (long-term resupply), open M–Sa 6 a.m.–midnight, Su 6–10, with deli, Western Union, ATM; West's Variety (short-term resupply). ■ *Restaurants:* Oriental Chinese Buffet, AYCE L/D; Friendly's. ■ *Other services:* Thrifty Bundle Coin laundry.
East 1.0 mile to YMCA, free showers, hiker-friendly.
East 2.5 miles to **North Adams, Mass. [P.O. ZIP 01247: M–F 8:30–4:30, Sa 10–12; (413) 664-4554]**.
■ *Lodging:* Holiday Inn Berkshires, 40 Main St., (413) 663-6500, $129–$220, pool, fitness center. ■ *Groceries:* Big Y Foods (long-term resupply); Cumberland Farms (short-term resupply). ■ *Restaurants:* Boston Seafood Restaurant, Freight Yard Pub, The Hub, Desperado's Fresh Mexican Grill, Brewhaha coffee shop, other fast-food chains. ■ *Other services:* banks with ATM, hardware store, doctor, dentist, veterinarian, Radio Shack, and movie theater. ■ *Shuttles:* Dave Ackerson, 82 Cherry St., North Adams, MA 01247, (413) 346-1033, <daveackerson@yahoo.com>.
West 0.4 mile to ■ *Groceries:* Super Shop & Stop, ATM, pharmacy, Western Union, and bank. ■ *Lodging:* Redwood Motel, (413) 664-4351, $55–$99, reservations suggested.
West 1.4 miles to municipal border with **Williamstown** and ■ *Lodging:* Williamstown Motel, (413) 458-5202, $59–$89S, $10EAP, continental B, WiFi, Internet, fridge, microwave, call for pick-up from Mass. 2 and Phelps Rd.; Howard Johnson, (413) 458-8158, <www.hojowt.com>, $59–$149 rate based on season and day of week, no pets, continental B, pool, pick-up/drop-off at Trail when available; Maple Terrace Motel, (413) 458-9677, <www.mapleterrace.com>, $75–$160 includes B, WiFi, heated pool, two rooms for pets, all rooms nonsmoking; The Willows Motel, 480 Main St., Williamstown, MA 01267, (413) 458-5768, <www.willowsmotel.com>, Su–Th $69–$119, F–Sa $89–$129, includes continental B, microwave, Internet, free laundry, and shuttles to/from Trail, mail drops accepted for guests only (call first). ■ *Restaurants: See map.* ■ *Groceries:* Wild Oats Whole Foods Market (long-term resupply). ■ *Other services:* Williamstown Wash & WiFi, M–F 7:30–9, Sa 9–9, Su 10–9; American Cab & Livery, (413) 662-2000.
West 2.6 miles to **Williamstown, Mass. [P.O. ZIP 01267: M–F 8:30–4:30, Sa 9–12; (413) 458-3707]**, home of Williams College. ■ *Lodging:* Cozy Corner Motel, (413) 458-8006, <www.cozycornermotel.com>, $49–$89, $10EAP, continental B, microwave/fridge, WiFi, pet-friendly, will pick up and drop off; Northside Motel, (413) 458-8107, <www.nothsidemotel.com>, $69–$159, continental B, fridge, WiFi, pool; Williams Inn, (413) 458-9371, $180–$295 and up, but $7 gets a towel, shower, swim, and sauna, WiFi, parking $2/day. ■ *Restaurants: See map.* ■ *Other services:* banks with ATM; doctor; dentist; pharmacy; veterinarian; movie theater; bookstore; Nature's Closet, (413) 458-7909, <www.naturescloset.net>, M–Sa 10–6, Su 11–5, includes the Gear Den of used outdoor clothing and gear on consignment; American Cab & Livery, (413) 662-2000; Bonanza Peter Pan bus line, (800) 343-9999, <www.peterpanbus.com>; Green Mountain Express bus to Bennington, Vt., M–F, (802) 447-0477.

Sherman Brook Campsite—Three tent platforms. Privy. Bear box. Water at Pete's Spring just east of the Trail and south of the 0.1-mile blue-blazed trail to the campsite. A blue-blaze west of the Trail, north of the campsite, lets you bypass a boulder field in bad weather.

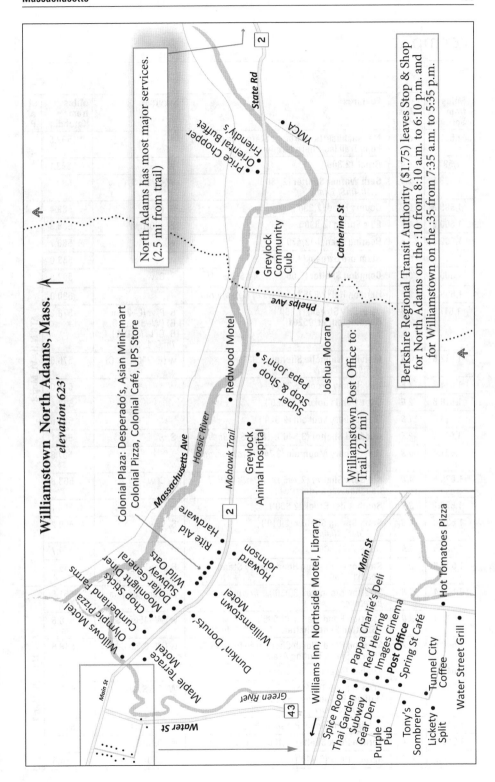

Williamstown North Adams, Mass.
elevation 623'

North Adams has most major services. (2.5 mi from trail)

Berkshire Regional Transit Authority ($1.75) leaves Stop & Shop for North Adams on the :10 from 8:10 a.m. to 6:10 p.m. and for Williamstown on the :35 from 7:35 a.m. to 5:35 p.m.

Williamstown Post Office to: Trail (2.7 mi)

State Rd

2

Price Chopper
Oriental Buffet
Friendly's

YMCA

Catherine St

Greylock
Community
Club

Phelps Ave

Colonial Plaza: Desperado's, Asian Mini-mart
Colonial Pizza, Colonial Café, UPS Store

Redwood Motel

Super
Stop & Shop
papa john's

Joshua Moran

Massachusetts Ave

Hoosic River

Mohawk Trail

Greylock
Animal Hospital

2

Rite Aid
Hardware

Howard
Johnson

Wild Oats
Subway
Dollar General
Moonlight Diner
Chop Sticks
Cumberland Farms
Olympic Pizza
Willows Motel

Williamstown
Motel

Dunkin' Donuts

Maple Terrace
Motel

Green River

Water St

43

Main St

Williams Inn, Northside Motel, Library

Main St

Spice Root
Thai Garden
Subway
Gear Den
Purple
Pub

Pappa Charlie's Deli
Red Herring
Images Cinema
Post Office
Spring St Café

Tony's
Sombrero

Lickety
Split

Tunnel City
Coffee

Water Street Grill

Hot Tomatoes Pizza

Vermont

Miles from Springer	Fr Last Point	Features	Services	Miles from Katahdin	MAP
1,596.7	0.8	Massachusetts–Vermont State Line (2,330') Long Trail (southern terminus)...*sign*		592.5	
1,597.1	0.4	Brook (2,300')	w	592.1	
1,599.5	2.4	**Seth Warner Shelter** (2,180') ...*10.4mS; 7.4mN*	W–0.2m S, C, w	589.7	
1,599.8	0.3	County Road (2,290')	R, P	589.4	
1,600.9	1.1	Ed's Spring (2,890')	E–100ft. W	588.3	
1,602.5	1.6	Roaring Branch (2,470')	w	586.7	
1,606.2	3.7	Stamford Stream (2,040')	w	583.0	
1,606.7	0.5	**Congdon Shelter** (2,060')...*7.4mS; 5.9mN*	S, C, w	582.5	
1,609.2	2.5	Harmon Hill (2,325')...*views of Bennington*		580.0	
1,611.0	1.8	Vt. 9, City Stream (1,360') **Bennington, Vt. 05201**	R, P, w (E–2.5m G) (W–5.1m PO, B, G, L, M, D, cl, f; 7m G, L, M)	578.2	ATC N.H.–Vt. Map 8
1,612.6	1.6	**Melville Nauheim Shelter** (2,330') ...*5.9mS; 8.5mN*	w (E–250ft. S, C)	576.6	
1,614.2	1.6	Hell Hollow Brook (2,350')	w	575.0	
1,616.8	2.6	Little Pond Lookout (3,060')		572.4	
1,618.6	1.8	Glastenbury Lookout (2,920')		570.6	
1,621.1	2.5	**Goddard Shelter** (3,540')...*8.5mS; 4.3mN*	S, w	568.1	
1,621.4	0.3	Glastenbury Mountain (3,748')...*observation tower*		567.8	
1,625.4	4.0	**Kid Gore Shelter** (2,795')...*4.3mS; 4.6mN* Caughnawaga Tentsites	S, C, w	563.8	
1,629.1	3.7	South Alder Brook (2,600')	w	560.1	
1,630.0	0.9	**Story Spring Shelter** (2,810') ...*4.6mS; 10.4mN*	S, C, w	559.2	
1,631.5	1.5	USFS 71 (2,500')	R	557.7	
1,633.6	2.1	Stratton–Arlington Road (Kelley Stand Road) (2,230')	R, P, w	555.6	
1,637.4	3.8	Stratton Mountain (3,936')...*firetower, caretaker cabin*	E–0.8m gondola	551.8	ATC N.H.–Vt. Map 7
1,640.4	3.0	Stratton Pond Trail to (2,565') +**Stratton Pond Shelter**...*10.4mS; 5.4mN*	w (W–450ft. S)	548.8	
1,640.6	0.2	Stratton Pond, North Shore Trail to (2,555') +North Shore Tenting Area	w (W–0.5m C, w)	548.6	
1,642.5	1.9	Winhall River (2,175')...*bridge*	w	546.7	
1,645.3	2.8	Branch Pond Trail to **William B. Douglas Shelter** (2,210') ...*5.4mS; 3.6mN*	W–0.5 S, w	543.9	
1,646.2	0.9	Old Rootville Road, Prospect Rock (2,150')	R (W–150ft. w)	543.0	
1,648.3	2.1	**Spruce Peak Shelter** (2,180')...*3.6mS; 5mN*	W–0.1m S, C, w	540.9	
1,648.7	0.4	Spruce Peak (2,040')	W–300ft.	540.5	

Miles from Springer	Fr Last Point	Features	Services	Miles from Katahdin	M A P
1,651.1	2.4	Vt. 11 & 30 (1,840') **Manchester Center, Vt. 05255**	R, P, w (E–0.5m M; 2.1m L, M; 2.5m G; 2.7m L, M; 3m L) (W–5.5m PO, B, H, G, L, M, O, D, V, cl, f)	538.1	
1,653.1	2.0	**Bromley Shelter** (2,560')...*5mS; 8.2mN*	E–0.1m S, C, w	536.1	
1,654.1	1.0	Bromley Mountain (3,260')...*ski patrol hut*		535.1	
1,656.6	2.5	USFS 21, Mad Tom Notch; Peru, Vt. (2,446')	R, P, w	532.6	
1,658.2	1.6	Styles Peak (3,394')		531.0	
1,659.9	1.7	Peru Peak (3,429')		529.3	
1,661.2	1.3	+**Peru Peak Shelter** (2,605')...*8.2mS; 4.7mN*	S, C, w	528.0	
1,661.7	0.5	Griffith Lake, +Griffith Lake Tenting Area (2,600')	C, w	527.5	
1,661.9	0.2	Griffith Lake (north end) (2,600')	w	527.3	ATC N.H.–Vt. Map 7
1,663.9	2.0	Baker Peak (2,850')		525.3	
1,665.9	2.0	**Lost Pond Shelter** (2,150')...*4.7mS; 2.5mN*	W–100ft. S, C, w	523.3	
1,667.4	1.5	Old Job Trail to (1,525') **Old Job Shelter**...*2..5mS; 1.2mN*	E–1m S, C, w	521.8	
1,667.6	0.2	**Big Branch Shelter** (1,460')...*1.2mS; 3.3mN*	S, C, w	521.6	
1,668.9	1.3	USFS 10, Danby–Landgrove Road (1,500') Black Branch **Danby, Vt. 05739**	R, P, w (W–3.5m PO, B, G, L, M, f; 5.5m C)	520.3	
1,670.9	2.0	+**Little Rock Pond Shelter** and Tenting Area (1,920') ...*3.3mS; 5mN*	S, C, w	518.3	
1,671.0	0.1	Spring (1,854')...*water for LRP Shelter*	w	518.2	
1,671.2	0.2	Green Mountain Trail to Homer Stone Brook Trail (1,854')		518.0	
1,675.2	4.0	Trail to White Rocks Cliffs (2,400')...*vista*	W–0.2m	514.0	
1,675.7	0.5	**Greenwall Shelter** (2,025')...*5mS; 5.3mN*	E–0.2m S, C, w	513.5	
1,676.3	0.6	Bully Brook (1,760')	w	512.9	
1,677.1	0.8	Sugar Hill Road (1,260')	R	512.1	
1,677.2	0.1	Vt. 140, Roaring Brook (1,160') **Wallingford, Vt. 05773**	R, P, w (W–2.8m PO, B, G, L, M)	512.0	
1,679.3	2.1	Bear Mountain (2,240')		509.9	
1,680.8	1.5	**Minerva Hinchey Shelter** (1,605') ...*5.3mS; 3.8mN*	E–200ft. S, C, w	508.4	
1,683.4	2.6	Clarendon Gorge WMA (800') Mill River Suspension Bridge	w	505.8	ATC N.H.–Vt. Map 6
1,683.5	0.1	Vt. 103 (860')...*railroad tracks*	R, P, B (W–0.5m M, V; 1m G, M)	505.7	
1,684.5	1.0	**Clarendon Shelter** (1,190')...*3.8mS; 5.9mN*	E–0.1m S, C, w	504.7	
1,685.0	0.5	Beacon Hill (1,740')		504.2	
1,685.4	0.4	Lottery Road (1,720')	R	503.8	
1,687.4	2.0	Cold River Road (1,400')	R, P (E–3m G, M)	501.8	
1,688.2	0.8	Gould Brook (1,480')...*ford*	w	501.0	
1,688.9	0.7	Upper Cold River Road (1,630')	R, w	500.3	

Miles from Springer	Fr Last Point	Features	Services	Miles from Katahdin	M A P
1,690.3	1.4	**Governor Clement Shelter** (1,900') ...*5.9mS; 4.3mN*	S, C, w	498.9	
1,694.6	4.3	Blue Blaze Trail to Killington Peak (3,900')	E–0.2m	494.6	
1,694.6	0.0	**Cooper Lodge** (3,900')...*4.3mS; 3mN*	S, C, w	494.6	
1,697.1	2.5	Jungle Jct.; Sherburne Pass Trail to (3,480') **Pico Camp**...*3mS; 2.5mN*	E–0.5m S, w	492.1	
1,699.0	1.9	**Churchill Scott Shelter** (2,560') ...*2.5mS; 12.1mN*	W–0.1m S, C, w	490.2	
1,700.9	1.9	U.S. 4 (1,880') **Rutland, Vt. 05701**	R, P, w (E–0.9m B, L, M) (W–8.6m PO, all)	488.3	
1,701.9	1.0	Maine Junction at Willard Gap, Long Trail to Tucker Johnson Tenting Area (2,250')	W–0.4m C, w	487.3	
1,702.8	0.9	Sherburne Pass Trail (2,440')...*to Inn at Long Trail*	E–0.5m L, M	486.4	
1,703.9	1.1	Kent Brook Trail Junction (1,700')	E–0.4m (see below)	485.3	ATC N.H.–Vt. Map 6
1,704.2	0.3	Vt. 100, Gifford Woods State Park (1,660') **Killington, Vt. 05751**	R, P, S, C, sh, w (E–0.6m PO, B, G, L, M, O) (W–0.3m L)	485.0	
1,704.9	0.7	Kent Pond, Trail to B.C.O.,Thundering Brook Road (1,450')	R, L, M (E–0.3m O, B)	484.3	
1,706.1	1.2	Thundering Brook Road (1,280')	R, P	483.1	
1,706.3	0.2	Thundering Falls (1,226')...*900ft. boardwalk*		482.9	
1,706.6	0.3	River Road (1,214')	R, P (E–0.5 pool)	482.6	
1,707.1	0.5	Quimby Mountain (2,550')		482.1	
1,710.9	3.8	**Stony Brook Shelter** (1,760') ...*12.1mS; 10.2mN*	E–0.1m S, C, w	478.3	
1,711.7	0.8	Stony Brook Road, Stony Brook (1,360')	R, w	477.5	
1,715.6	3.9	Chateauguay Road (2,000')	R	473.6	
1,716.3	0.7	Lakota Lake Lookout (2,640')		472.9	
1,718.4	2.1	Trail to the Lookout (2,320')...*observation deck*	W–0.2m	470.8	
1,720.8	2.4	**Winturri Shelter** (1,910')...*10.2mS; 11.9mN*	W–0.2m S, w	468.4	
1,724.6	3.8	Vt. 12, Gulf Stream Bridge (882') **Woodstock, Vt. 05091**	R, P, w (E–4.4m PO, G, L, M, D) (W–0.2m G)	464.6	
1,725.7	1.1	Dana Hill (1,530')		463.5	ATC N.H.–Vt. Map 5
1,726.1	0.4	Woodstock Stage Road, Barnard Creek (820') **South Pomfret, Vt. 05067**	R, P, w (E–0.9m PO, G, M)	463.1	
1,728.3	2.2	Pomfret–South Pomfret Road, Pomfret Brook (980')	R, P, w	460.9	
1,730.1	1.8	Cloudland Road (1,370')	R, P (W–0.2m G, M)	459.1	
1,732.1	2.0	Thistle Hill (1,800')		457.1	
1,732.4	0.3	**Thistle Hill Shelter** (1,480')...*11.9mS; 9mN*	E–0.1m S, w	456.8	
1,733.9	1.5	Joe Ranger Road (1,280')	R, P	455.3	
1,737.2	3.3	Vt. 14, Patriots Bridge over White River (390') **Hartford, Vt. 05047**	R, P, C, w (E–7m PO, B; 8m H, all)	452.0	
1,737.8	0.6	Tigertown Road, Podunk Road (540')	R, P	451.4	

Miles from Springer	Fr Last Point	Features	Services	Miles from Katahdin	M A P
1,738.6	0.8	Podunk Road, Podunk Brook (860')	R, w	450.6	
1,740.7	2.1	Griggs Mountain (1,570')		448.5	
1,741.2	0.5	**Happy Hill Shelter** (1,460')...*9mS; 7.6mN*	E–0.1m S, C, w	448.0	ATC N.H.–Vt. Map 5
1,744.7	3.5	Elm St. Trailhead (750')	R	444.5	
1,745.5	0.8	U.S. 5 (537') **Norwich, Vt. 05055**	R (E–0.25m PO, B, G, L, M)	443.7	
1,746.1	0.6	I-91; Vt. 10A (450')...*A.T. on sidewalk*	R	443.1	
1,746.5	0.4	Connecticut River (380') Vermont–New Hampshire State Line	R	442.7	

+ Fee charged

Avoid Vermont trails in "mud season," mid-Apr to Memorial Day. Hiking there in wet, sloppy conditions leads to serious Trail erosion.

Green Mountain Club—GMC maintains the 149.8 miles from the Massachusetts–Vermont border to the Connecticut River on the Vermont–New Hampshire border. Correspondence should be sent to GMC at 4711 Waterbury–Stowe Rd., Waterbury Center, VT 05677; (802) 244-7037; fax, (802) 244-5867; <gmc@greenmountainclub.org>, <www.greenmountainclub.org>.

Public transportation—Amtrak to Rutland and White River Junction, (800) 872-7245. Green Mountain Express community bus from Bennington to Manchester and Bennington to Williamstown, (802) 447-0477, M–F 8–5. Marble Valley Regional Transit community bus serves Manchester, Danby, Wallingford, North Clarendon, Rutland, and Killington; (802) 773-3244; no Sunday bus service between Rutland and Manchester; local taxi service is also available. Advance Transit bus, (802) 295-1824, free Upper Valley service goes to Hartford, White River Junction, and Norwich with connections to West Lebanon and Hanover, N.H., M–F. Vermont Translines, (844) VTTRANS (888-7267), <vttranslines.com>, runs between the Burlington, Vt., and Albany, N.Y., airports and Greyhound/Trailways terminal, with stops in Rutland, Wallingford, Manchester, and Bennington, and along the U.S. 4 corridor between Rutland and White River Junction; (802) 295-3011. Greyhound also has terminals in West Lebanon and Hanover. The Rutland Airport has daily flights to Boston.

GMC Shelter Fees—Fees are collected at high-use campsites to help defray the costs of field programs and shelter and Trail maintenance along the A.T. in Vermont. The fee is $5PP per night. This fee applies to anyone camping within 0.5 mile of a fee site. In addition, all hikers who pay the $5 fee in cash at either southern-pond fee site (Stratton Pond or Little Rock Pond—see chart for details) will receive a dated receipt that they can then use for one free night at the other fee site. The receipt must be used within 7 days. No receipt, no free nights, no exceptions. This offer does not extend north of Maine Junction on the Long Trail. This deal only works if you pay cash; it does not apply to folks who promise to pay later.

Fee Site	Includes (listed S to N)
Stratton Pond	Stratton Pond Shelter North Shore Tenting Area
Griffith Lake	Peru Peak Shelter Griffith Lake Tenting Area
Little Rock Pond	Little Rock Pond Shelter & Tenting Area

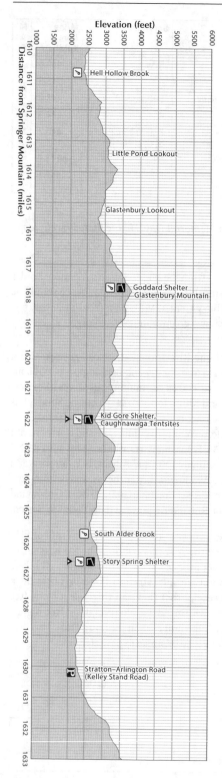

Caretakers are present throughout the season, May–Oct, at several locations. Through conversation and example, caretakers educate hikers about Leave No Trace practices and perform Trail and shelter maintenance. Most importantly, caretakers compost sewage at high-use fee sites and a few no-fee shelter sites in southern Vermont.

A ridgerunner may be found along the Coolidge Range at the following locations, although a fee is not charged: Clarendon Shelter, Governor Clement Shelter, Cooper Lodge, Pico Camp, and Churchill Scott Shelter.

Bears—To prevent future problems and costly interventions, please hang all food from tree limbs at least 12 feet off the ground, and practice Leave No Trace camping.

Long Trail—At the Vermont–Massachusetts state line, the A.T. joins the Long Trail (L.T.) for 105.2 miles, to "Maine Junction" at Willard Gap. At Maine Junction, the A.T. leads toward Maine, and the L.T. continues north, reaching the Canadian border in another 167.8 miles. Completed in 1930, the L.T. served as one inspiration for the A.T. The L.T. and A.T. are seeing increased traffic in Vermont. Please use only designated shelters and campsites, and make use of privies and wash pits to protect water quality and greatly reduce the visible and permanent impact of greater use of the Trail.

Seth Warner Shelter (1965)—Sleeps 8. Privy. Bear box. Tentsites. Water source, a brook 150 yards to the left of the shelter, is known to fail in dry years.

Congdon Shelter (1967)—Sleeps 8. Privy. Tentsites behind the shelter on the ridge. Water source is a brook in front of the shelter. If the brook is dry, follow downstream to larger Stamford Stream.

Vt. 9—East 2.5 miles to *Groceries:* Woodford Mountain General Store (short-term resupply), (802) 442-5222, daily 7–7, deli, Heet.
    West 5.1 miles to **Bennington, Vt. [P.O. ZIP 05201: M–F 8–5, Sa 9–2; (802) 442-2421].** ■ *Lodging:* Cata-

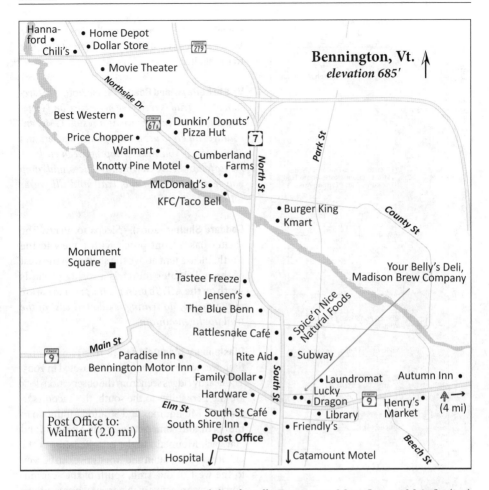

Hanna-ford •
Chili's •
• Home Depot
• Dollar Store
[279]
• Movie Theater

Bennington, Vt.
elevation 685'

Northside Dr

Best Western •
[67A]
• Dunkin' Donuts'
• Pizza Hut
[7]
Price Chopper •
Walmart •
Knotty Pine Motel •
Cumberland Farms
McDonald's •
KFC/Taco Bell

North St
Park St

• Burger King
• Kmart
County St

Monument Square ■

Tastee Freeze •
Jensen's •
The Blue Benn •
Rattlesnake Café •

Your Belly's Deli, Madison Brew Company

Spice'n Nice Natural Foods

[9]
Main St
Paradise Inn •
Bennington Motor Inn •
Family Dollar •
Hardware •
Elm St South St Café •
South Shire Inn •
Rite Aid •
• Subway
South St
• Laundromat
Autumn Inn •
• Lucky Dragon
[9]
Henry's Market •
↑→ (4 mi)
• Library
• Friendly's
Post Office

Post Office to: Walmart (2.0 mi)

Beech St

Hospital ↓
↓ Catamount Motel

mount Motel, (802) 442-5977, $50S, $60D, hiker-friendly; Bennington Motor Inn, 143 Main St., (802) 442-5479; Paradise Motor Inn, 141 West Main St., (802) 442-8351; Autumn Inn, 924 Main St., (802) 447-7625, $75D, $10 pick-up at Vt. 9 Trailhead, WiFi, laundry, dogs $10, will hold packages for guests. ■ *Groceries:* Henry's Market; Spice and Nice Natural Foods. ■ *Restaurants:* Rattlesnake Café, open Tu–Su, L/D, Mexican fare; Izabella's B/L; Blue Benn Diner, B/L/D; South Street Café, B/L, WiFi. ■ *Internet access:* Downtown is a free public WiFi zone; library. ■ *Other services:* Family Dollar; coin laundry; banks with ATM; hospital; shoe repair; doctor; dentist; pharmacy; veterinarian; hardware store; and free showers available at Town Recreation Center on Gage Street. ■ *Shuttles:* Bennington Taxi, (802) 442-9052; Green Mountain Express, (802) 447-0477, <www.greenmtncn. org>, M–F, 7:30–5:30, call to arrange $3 shuttle to Route 9 Trailhead and, M–F, $2 service between Bennington and Manchester and $1 service from Bennington to Williamstown, Mass. Bus service to Albany, N.Y. (see above under "Public transportation").

West 7 miles to **North Bennington, Vt.**, Routes 67 and 7A, and ■ *Lodging:* Knotty Pine Motel, 130 Northside Dr., (802) 442-5487, <kpine@knottypinemotel.com>, 130 Northside Dr., $80–$96D, $8EAP, pets accepted on limited basis, continental B, WiFi, pool, holds packages only for guests; Best Western, 200 Northside Dr., (802) 442-6311; Hampton Inn, 51 Hannaford Square, (802) 440-9862. ■ *Groceries:* Price Chopper, Hannaford, ALDI supermarkets (long-term resupply). ■ *Restaurants:* See map. ■ *Other services:* Walmart, movie theater.

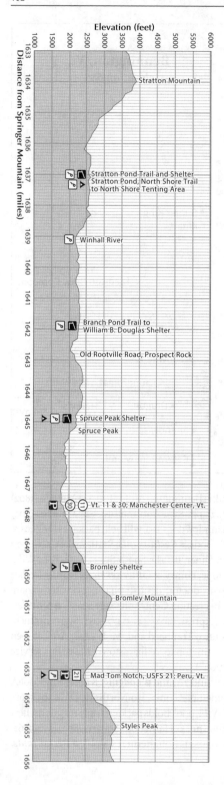

Melville Nauheim Shelter (1977)—Sleeps 8. Privy. Water source is a stream just north of the spur to the shelter.

Vt. 9 to Kelley Stand Road—Please note: *This section of the Trail is receiving heavy use and experiencing resource damage as a result. GMC encourages hikers to use the designated shelters and campsites. If you must camp between shelters, please follow Leave No Trace practices, and camp 200 feet away from the Trail and all water sources.*

Goddard Shelter (2005)—Sleeps 10. Privy. The shelter has a front porch with a view to the south. Please tent above the shelter, to the west of the A.T. Water source is a spring 50 yards south on the A.T. *To preserve the pristine nature of the spring, no tenting is allowed east of the trail up the mountain.*

Glastenbury Mountain (3,748 ft.). The original firetower was built in 1927 and renovated in 2005. The nearby ridges seen from the observation deck are the Berkshires to the south, the Taconics to the west, Mt. Equinox and Stratton Mountain to the north, and Somerset Reservoir, Mt. Snow, and Haystack Mountain to the east. Remains of the old firewarden's cabin and woodstove can be seen to the west of the Trail, south of the summit. Porcupines are active in this area; take precautions with your gear.

Kid Gore Shelter (1971)—Sleeps 8. Privy. Ecologically fragile area. Tentsites located north on Trail at the former Caughnawaga Shelter site. Water source is a brook near Caughnawaga. An unreliable spring is north of Kid Gore Shelter.

Caughnawaga Tentsites—Tenting only. A 1930s shelter was torn down in July 2008.

Story Spring Shelter (1963)—Sleeps 8. Privy. Tentsites. Water source is a spring north on the A.T. 50 yards.

 Stratton Mountain—Although he offered a number of variations on the story about how he first thought of the A.T., many believe it was on the slopes of Stratton Mountain that Benton MacKaye first imagined a long-distance trail that would link the high peaks of the Appalachian Mountains. A firetower tops the summit and is open to hikers. *No camping or fires on the summit.* A side trail at the summit leads east 0.8 mile to a ski gondola at the top of Stratton Ski Area; this hut is not available for hiker use. The gondola has operated in past years, allowing hikers to ride down to Stratton Village, which has an outfitter, grocery store, and restaurants. Please check with the GMC summit caretakers or Stratton Mountain staff to see if the gondola is available for hiker use.

Stratton Pond Shelter (1999)—Sleeps 16. Privy. Overnight fee. Go 0.2 mile west *via* Stratton Pond Trail. No tenting at this shelter, but you may tent on platforms at the nearby North Shore Tenting Area; otherwise, within 0.5 mile of the pond, camping is permitted only at designated sites. Shelter has an open first floor, table, bunks, and an enclosed loft. Water source is Bigelow Spring at Stratton Pond about 0.1 mile down the Lye Brook Trail. *No fires at this shelter.*

William B. Douglas Shelter (1956, renovated 2005)—Sleeps 10. Privy. Go 0.5 mile west *via* the Branch Pond Trail. Water source is a spring located south of the shelter.

Spruce Peak Shelter (1983)—Sleeps 14. Privy. This shelter with a covered front porch is 0.1 mile west on a spur trail. Water source is a boxed spring 35 yards to the right of the shelter.

Vt. 11 & 30—East 2.1 miles to *Lodging:* Lodge at Bromley, 4216 Vt. 11, Peru, VT 05152; (802) 824-6941, $99S/D (includes B and laundry), WiFi, Rt. 11 & 30 Trailhead shuttle, and mail drops accepted (nonguest mail-drop fee, $5).
   East 0.5 mile to Cilantro Burrito: ice cream, drinks, snacks, 11:30–6, Jun–Sep.
   East 2.5 miles *via* Vt. 11 to *Groceries:* Bromley Market, 3776 Vt. 11, Peru, VT 05152; (802) 824-4444, fresh foods, deli open 7–7 7 days, some hiker supplies, mail drops accepted.
   East 3.0 miles *via* Vt. 30 to *Lodging:* Bromley View Inn, 522 Vermont 30, Bondville, VT 05340; (802) 297-1459, <www.bromleyviewinn.com>, $85D weekends higher, includes B, pet-friendly, WiFi, call for shuttle to and from Rt. 11 & 30 Trailhead only, mail drops accepted.
   West 5.5 miles to **Manchester Center, Vt. [P.O. ZIP 05255: M–F 8:30–4:30, Sa 9–12; (802) 362-3070].** *See map on next page.* Pick up mail at the post office on the way into town to avoid an extra walk. The Mountain Goat and EMS are good resources for hiker services in town. *Note:* During the Manchester horse shows, mid-Jul–mid-Aug, affordable lodging will be difficult to find in the area. ■ *Hostel:* Green Mountain House, (330) 388-6478, <www.greenmountainhouse.net>; owners Jeff and Regina Taussig, open Jun 15–Sep 1. Space is limited, and reservations are essential. Bed, shower, free laundry, Internet, WiFi, phone, and hiker kitchen, $30PP/night + tax. Visa/MC. Breakfast supplies available. Private room for couples. Check in between 1 and 7 p.m. Free shuttle for guests back to the Trail in the morning. Not a party place; no drugs or alcohol. ■ *Lodging:* Sutton's Place, (802) 362-1165, <www.suttonsplacevermont.com>, $70S, $80D, $99T plus tax, a/c, WiFi, within walking distance of all services; Carriage House Motel, (802) 362-1706, <www.carriagehousemotel.com>, $78D weekdays, $105D weekends, $10EAP, no pets, opens end of May, 1 mile east of town; Red Sled Motel, (802) 362-2161, call for pick-up, <redsled@myfairpoint.net>, host John Hullican, smoke-free facility, $70S, $77D, WiFi; Toll Road Inn, (802) 362-1711; EconoLodge Motel, (802) 362-3333, $89D, $10EAP, higher on weekends. ■ *Groceries:* Price Chopper, Shaw's supermarkets (both long-term resupply). ■ *Restaurants:* Bob's Diner (B/L/D), Manchester Pizza House, Firefly Bar & Grill, Mrs. Murphy's Doughnuts and Coffee Shop, Cilantro's Burrito, Up For Breakfast (7–12:30), Christo's Pizza, Ben & Jerry's Scoop Shop, Zoey's Deli, and several fast-food outlets. ■ *Internet access:* library,

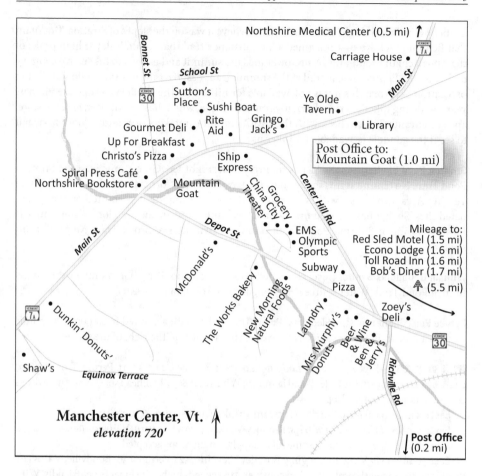

Northshire Medical Center (0.5 mi) ↑

Carriage House •

VERMONT 7A

Bonnet St

Main St

School St

VERMONT 30

Sutton's
Place • Sushi Boat

Ye Olde
Tavern •

Gourmet Deli •   Rite   Gringo
          Aid • Jack's •

• Library

Up For Breakfast •

Christo's Pizza •   iShip •
                  Express

Post Office to:
Mountain Goat (1.0 mi)

Spiral Press Café •
Northshire Bookstore •   • Mountain
                Goat

Grocery
China City
Theater

Center Hill Rd

Main St

Depot St

• • • EMS
• Olympic
  Sports

Mileage to:
Red Sled Motel (1.5 mi)
Econo Lodge (1.6 mi)
Toll Road Inn (1.6 mi)
Bob's Diner (1.7 mi)

Subway •

• McDonald's

The Works Bakery

New Morning
Natural Foods

Pizza •

🌲 (5.5 mi)

Laundry

Mrs. Murphy's
Donuts

Beer
& Wine

Ben &
Jerry's

Zoey's
Deli •

VERMONT 30

VERMONT 7A

• *Dunkin' Donuts'*

Richville Rd

•
Shaw's   *Equinox Terrace*

Manchester Center, Vt. ⋏
elevation 720' ↑

Post Office
(0.2 mi)

M–F 10–6, Sa 10–4; I Ship Express (below). ■ *Outfitters:* The Mountain Goat, 4886 Main St., (802) 362-5159, open M–Sa 10–6, Su 10–5, full-service outfitter, fuel by the ounce, custom footbeds and orthotics, mail drops (USPS, UPS & FedEx) accepted; Eastern Mountain Sports (EMS), (802) 366-8082, open Su–Th 10–6, F–Sa 10–7, Coleman and alcohol fuel by the ounce. Both are authorized Leki repair firms. ■ *Other services:* coin laundry; bank with ATM; doctor; dentist; pharmacy; veterinarian; movie theater; Manchester Taxi, (802) 362-4118 and (802) 688-6426; Leonard's Taxi, (802) 379-5332; Green Mountain Express, (802) 447-0477, <www.greenmtncn.org>, $2 bus service between Manchester and Bennington, flag stop across from RiteAid and Shaw's; I Ship Express, 5018 Main St., (802) 362-1652, M–F 9:30–5, Sa 9:30–noon, packing and shipping services; Marble Valley Regional Transportation, $2 bus service between Manchester and Rutland/Killington, with stops along the U.S. 7 corridor (Danby, Wallingford, North Clarendon).

Bromley Shelter (2003)—Sleeps 12. Privy (composting). Tent platforms and campsite are north 0.1 mile. Brook at the terminus of the spur trail.

Bromley Mountain—An observation tower recently was torn down but the spot stilloffers an outstanding view. Ski trails lead to Bromley Base Lodge area. Funds are needed to rebuild the tower.

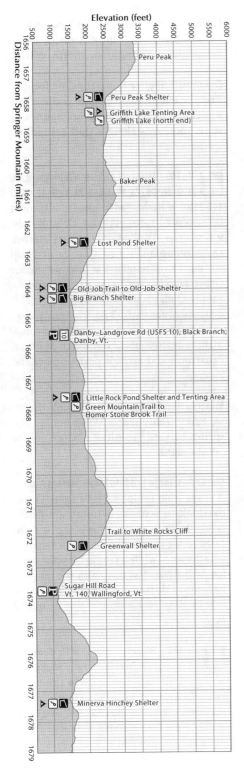

Distance from Springer Mountain (miles)

Elevation (feet)

Peru Peak

Peru Peak Shelter

Griffith Lake Tenting Area
Griffith Lake (north end)

Baker Peak

Lost Pond Shelter

Old-Job Trail to Old-Job Shelter
Big Branch Shelter

Danby–Landgrove Rd (USFS 10), Black Branch;
Danby, Vt.

Little Rock Pond Shelter and Tenting Area
Green Mountain Trail to
Homer Stone Brook Trail

Trail to White Rocks Cliff
Greenwall Shelter

Sugar Hill Road
Vt. 140, Wallingford, Vt.

Minerva Hinchey Shelter

Peru Peak Shelter/Griffith Lake Campsite
(1935/1980/2000)—Sleeps 10. Privy. Overnight
fee. Camping permitted only at designated sites
within 0.5 mile of Griffith Lake. Water source
is a brook near the shelter.

Lost Pond Shelter (2009)—Sleeps 8. Privy.
Tentsites. Water source is nearby stream.

Old Job Shelter (1935/2009)—One mile on
Old Job Trail. Sleeps 8. Privy. Water source
is in front of the shelter at Lake Brook.

Big Branch Shelter (1963)—Sleeps 8. Privy.
Close to USFS 10 and receives heavy weekend
use. Good soaking pools. Water source is Big
Branch, located in front of the shelter.

Danby–Landgrove Road—*Light traffic,
may be a difficult hitch on weekdays.*
West 3.5 miles to **Danby, Vt. [P.O. ZIP 05739: M–F
7:15–10:15 & 1–4, Sa 7:30–10:30; (802) 293-5105]**.
■ *Lodging:* Silas Griffith Inn, 178 South Main
St., (802) 293-5567, <www.SilasGriffith.com>,
1891 inn owned by hiker-friendly Brian and
Cathy Preble; check in after 2 p.m.; $99D and
up, B included; pool, spa, WiFi; laundry $15;
pet-friendly, $25 shuttle to/from Trail; mail
drops accepted only for guests. ■ *Groceries:*
Mt. Tabor Country Store, Nichols Store (both
short-term resupply). ■ *Restaurants:* Emma's
Restaurant at Silas Griffith Inn, Th–Su 9–9,
reservations required. ■ *Other services:*
MVRT, (802) 773-3244, <www.thebus.com>,
Manchester-to-Rutland commuter, M–Sa $2.
Departs for Manchester from the Mt. Tabor
Country Store; for Rutland, from Brooklyn Rd.
   West 5.5 miles *via* U.S. 7 to *Campground:*
Otter Creek Campground, 1136 U.S. 7, (802)
293-5041; George and Alice Araskiewicz,
owners. Tentsites $18, coin showers, camp
store with Coleman fuel; long-term parking;
shuttle to A.T. Trailhead (USFS 10, 1–4 hikers) $20; other shuttles possible. Will hold
UPS and USPS packages addressed to the
campground.

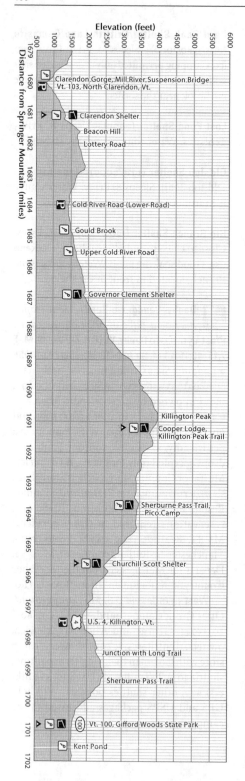

Little Rock Pond Shelter and Tenting Area (2010)—Sleeps 12. Tent platforms. Privy. Overnight fee. Spring located north on Trail.

Greenwall Shelter (1962/2009)—Sleeps 8. Privy 0.2 mile east on spur trail. Water source is a spring, prone to fail in dry seasons, 200 yards along a trail behind the shelter.

Vt. 140—West 2.8 miles to **Wallingford, Vt.** **[P.O. ZIP 05773: M–F 8–4:30, Sa 9–12; (802) 446-2140].** ■ *Restaurants:* Mom's Restaurant, B/L, open 'til 2; Sal's Pizza, L/D, Su D only. ■ *Groceries:* Wallingford Country Store & Deli, Cumberland Farms, Citgo Smart Shop (all short-term resupply). ■ *Internet access:* Gilbert Hart Library, Tu–Sa. ■ *Other services:* Family Dollar (short-term resupply); ATM; dentist; expensive B&Bs; commuter bus MVRT, (802) 773-3244, <www.thebus.com>, Manchester-to-Rutland commuter, M–Sa $2, departures and arrivals near Cumberland Farms.

Minerva Hinchey Shelter (1969/2006)—Sleeps 10. Privy. Tenting area.Water source is a spring 50 yards south of shelter; follow "Wada" signs.

Clarendon Gorge Wildlife Management Area— A suspension bridge 0.1 mile from Vt. 103 overlooks a favorite swimming hole for residents. Built in 1974, this bridge is dedicated to the memory of Robert Brugmann, who drowned while trying to cross the swollen Mill River. Swimming in the gorge is hazardous during high water. Watch for broken glass. *No camping or fires permitted in the gorge.*

Vt. 103—West 0.5 mile to ■ *Restaurant:* Qu's Whistle Stop, (802) 772-7012, Su 8–3, M–Tu 7–3, Th–Sa 7–7, closed W. ■ *Other services:* Cold River Veterinary Center, (802) 747-4076; commuter bus MVRT, (802) 773-3244, <www.thebus.com>, Bellows Falls to Rutland, $3, flag stop M–F.

West 1 mile to *Groceries:* Loretta's Good Food Deli (short term resupply), 638 Route 103, Clarendon, VT 05759; (802)772-7638, M–Sa 6–7, Su 8–4, owners Dennis and Loretta Clark; B sandwiches at 7 a.m., fresh baked goods, burgers, salads, deli, ice cream, beer, Heet, dog food, first aid, accepts mail drops (no fee), prepaid Priority Mail boxes on hand, picnic table for hikers. The Bus, with service to Rutland, stops nearby.

Clarendon Shelter (1952)—Sleeps 10. Privy. Tensites. Water source is a stream 25 yards from the shelter.

Cold River Road—East 3 miles to Pierces' Store, reopened as a community cooperative; short-term resupply, sandwiches and specials, open 10 a.m.; closed M.

Governor Clement Shelter (1929/2009)—Sleeps 12. Privy. Water source is a stream across the road and north of the shelter.

Cooper Lodge (1939)—Sleeps 16. Cooper Pooper Privy. Tent platforms. This enclosed stone cabin was built by the Vermont Forest Service. Behind the shelter is a 0.2-mile side trail to Killington Peak. Water source is a spring north of shelter on A.T.

Killington Peak—Reached by a steep 0.2-mile side trail from Cooper Lodge. At 4,241 feet, this is the highest point near the Trail in Vermont and the second-highest peak in the state. The open, rocky summit offers panoramic views, and, on a clear day, you can see the White Mountains of New Hampshire and the Adirondacks of New York. A short side trail leads from the summit to a snack bar and ski lift operated by the Killington ski resort; shops are located at the village reached by the gondola. Gondola operates Jun 27–Sep 7, 10–5, then weekends only, 10–5, until Sep 27; full operation during fall-foliage season. A GMC ridgerunner patrols the Coolidge Range (including Killington and Pico) and may be available to answer natural-history and Trail questions.

Jungle Junction–Sherburne Pass Trail—Named after a 1938 hurricane left behind a "jungle" of blowdowns (and essentially broke the A.T. as a continuous footpath a year after it opened as such). The blue-blazed Sherburne Pass Trail (former A.T.) leads 3.1 miles north to Sherburne Pass on U.S. 4, directly to the Inn at Long Trail (opened in 1938, ironically), and continues north of the inn 0.5 mile to reconnect with the A.T.

Pico Camp (1959)—Sleeps 12. Privy. An enclosed shelter located 0.5 mile east on the Sherburne Pass Trail, the former A.T. Water source is 45 yards north on the Sherburne Pass Trail.

Rutland city watershed: The western flanks of the Coolidge Range comprise a significant portion of the city of Rutland's watershed. *Fires are not permitted.* Please camp only at designated sites and use facilities provided.

Churchill Scott Shelter (2002)—Sleeps 8. Privy (composting). Tent platform. Water on spur trail downhill behind shelter.

U.S. 4—East 0.9 mile uphill along a busy thoroughfare to *Lodging:* The Inn at Long Trail, 709 Route 4, Sherburne Pass, Killington, VT 05751; (802) 775-7181; closed for innkeeper vacation mid-Apr, reopens Memorial Day weekend. The inn offers discounted rooms for hikers with full B; no dogs in the lodge. McGrath's Irish Pub serves L/D. Amenities include laundry facilities, hiker box, outside water spigot, WiFi. Only accepts UPS or Fed Ex packages. Vermont

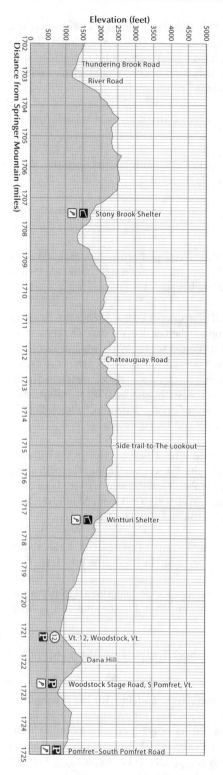

Translines, (844) 888-7267, <vttranslines.com>, runs along the U.S. 4 corridor between Rutland and White River Junction Greyhound terminal, including stops in West Lebanon and Hanover, N.H. MVRT bus service M–Sa from inn to Rutland. *A safer alternative to the roadwalk in heavy traffic is to cross Route 4 and continue on the A.T. north 1.9 miles to the northern terminus of the Sherburne Pass Trail, which will lead you 0.5 mile south directly to the inn.*

West 8.6 miles to the city of **Rutland, Vt. [P.O. 05701: M–F 8–5, Sa 8–12; (802) 773-0222]**, with all major services and chain motels; *see map.* ■ *Hostel:* Hikers Hostel at the Yellow Deli (Twelve Tribes), 23 Center St., (802) 683-9378 or (802) 773-0160, <www.hikershostel.org>, check-in at restaurant, donation accepted, includes B, common room, laundry $2, separate bunk rooms for men and women, possible shuttles, work for stay, located downtown, mail drops accepted. ■ *Groceries:* Rutland Food Coop on Wales St., Tops Market, Hannaford and Aldi on U.S. 7, Price Chopper on Merchant's Row (all long-term resupply). ■ *Restaurants:* Yellow Deli, L/D, only organic food, 15% discount to hikers, closed Sa; farmers market (Sa). ■ *Outfitters:* Mountain Travelers Outdoor Shop, U.S. 4 East, (802) 775-0814, <www.mtntravelers.com>, open M–Sa 10–6, with backpacking equipment and supplies, fuel by the ounce; Simon the Tanner, 21 Center St., (802) 282-4016, <www.simonthetanner.com>, M–Th 11–9, F 11–3, closed Sa, Su 12–7, footwear, clothing, fuel, backpacking items. Dick's Sporting Goods at Green Mountain Shopping Plaza and Eastern Mountain Sports at Diamond Run Mall both can be reached *via* local MVRT bus. ■ *Internet access:* Rutland Free Library. ■ *Bus service:* MVRT bus ($2 per ride) is available from Killington to Rutland; can be flagged anywhere along U.S. 4. The bus travels from downtown Rutland Transit Center to Killington and back approximately once every 2 hours, leaving Rutland beginning at 7:15 a.m. until 5:15 p.m. No bus service on Su. ■ *Train service:* Amtrak provides daily train service on the Ethan Allen Express, (800) USA-RAIL, from Rutland to Albany and New York City. Call for reservations and to confirm arrival and departure times. Amtrak service on the Vermonter is also available at White River

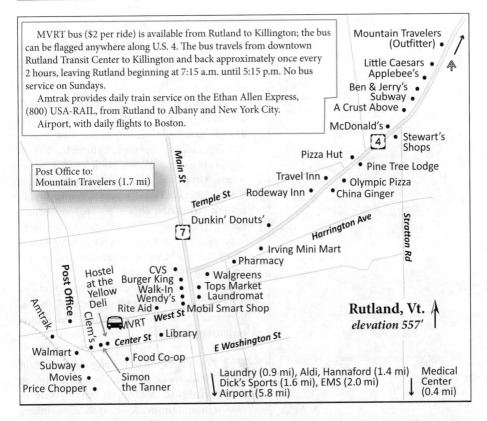

MVRT bus ($2 per ride) is available from Rutland to Killington; the bus can be flagged anywhere along U.S. 4. The bus travels from downtown Rutland Transit Center to Killington and back approximately once every 2 hours, leaving Rutland beginning at 7:15 a.m. until 5:15 p.m. No bus service on Sundays.

Amtrak provides daily train service on the Ethan Allen Express, (800) USA-RAIL, from Rutland to Albany and New York City.

Airport, with daily flights to Boston.

Mountain Travelers (Outfitter) •

Little Caesars •
Applebee's •
Ben & Jerry's •
Subway •
A Crust Above •
McDonald's •

Post Office to:
Mountain Travelers (1.7 mi)

Main St

4   • Stewart's
        Shops
Pizza Hut •
        • Pine Tree Lodge
Travel Inn •   • Olympic Pizza
Rodeway Inn • •China Ginger

Temple St
Dunkin' Donuts' •

Harrington Ave

Stratton Rd

7

• Irving Mini Mart
• Pharmacy

Post Office

Hostel   CVS •   • Walgreens
at the   Burger King • • Tops Market
Yellow   Walk-In •   • Laundromat
Deli   Wendy's •
         Rite Aid • Mobil Smart Shop
Amtrak   MVRT West St
    Clem's Center St • Library
             E Washington St

Walmart •
Subway •   Laundry (0.9 mi), Aldi, Hannaford (1.4 mi)   Medical
Movies •   Simon   Dick's Sports (1.6 mi), EMS (2.0 mi)   Center
Price Chopper • the Tanner Airport (5.8 mi)   (0.4 mi)

        • Food Co-op

Rutland, Vt.
elevation 557'

Junction, 35 miles east. ■ *Other services:* Walmart; airport with daily flights to Boston; Rutland Regional Medical Center Hospital; veterinarians; Rutland Taxi, (802) 236-3133; All Occasion Transportation, (802) 236-1966; see page 189 for public-transportation options..

Maine Junction–Willard Gap. The L.T. continues north 167.8 miles to Canada, while the A.T. diverges to the east toward New Hampshire and Maine.

Tucker-Johnson Shelter Area (1969/2009)—Located on the L.T. 0.4 mile north of Maine Junction. Shelter burned down in 2011. Tenting area. Privy. Water source is nearby Eagle Square Brook.

Kent Brook Trail Junction—This yellow-blazed 1-mile trail follows the perimeter of Gifford Woods State Park and crosses the A.T. at the halfway point. At this junction is an alternative route to the road walk along Vt. 100 to reach the Killington P.O., deli, Greenbrier Inn, and Killington Motel on U.S. 4. Directions from here are: NOBO turn right, SOBO turn left, Trail east or compass south, descend 0.2 mile south on the Kent Brook Trail to ford Kent Brook. On the south shore of the brook, immediately join and follow the Greenbrier Inn Nature Trail (black arrow in the center yellow diamond blaze). From here, it is 0.2 mile to the pool area of the Greenbrier Inn and another 500 feet to U.S. 4. (see map).

Vt. 100—The A.T. passes through Gifford Woods State Park, (802) 775-5354, with shelters, tentsites, and bathhouse visible from the Trail. *Camping:* shelters $25–$29; tentsites $18–$22 up to 4 people, cabin $48 for 4 people, two-night minimum reservation in Jul–Aug,

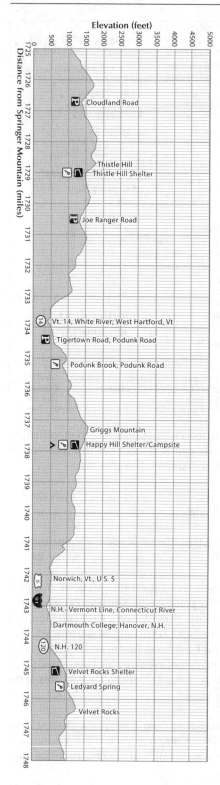

limited primitive sites $5, $1/pet/night, coin-operated showers 50¢, water spigot. Space fills up quickly during the fall "leaf season." *Shuttles:* Killington Taxi, (802) 442-9718; Gramps Shuttle, (802) 236-6600.

East 0.6 mile to U.S. 4 and **Killington, Vt. [P.O. ZIP 05751: M–F 8:30–11, 12–4:30, Sa 8:30–12; (802) 775-4247].** ■ *Lodging:* Killington Motel, (802) 773-9535, call for hiker rates, includes B, will pick up hikers as time allows, pool, WiFi, Internet access; Greenbrier Inn, (802) 775-1575, <www.greenbriervt.com>, call for rates, continental B, pool. ■ *Groceries:* Deli at Killington Corners (short-term resupply), 6:30 a.m.–7 p.m. daily, sandwiches, hot-meal specials, and ATM. ■ *Outfitter:* See below. ■ *Other services:* MVRT and VTTRANS bus stops nearby.

West 0.3 mile to *Lodging:* Grey Bonnet Inn & Resort, (802) 775-2537, (800) 342-2086, <www.greybonnetinn.com>, $89D includes full B; pub, restaurant, and pool..

Kent Pond—on A.T. *Lodging:* Mountain Meadows Lodge, 285 Thundering Brook Rd., Killington, VT 05751; (802) 775-1010, <www.mountainmeadowslodge.com>; hikers welcome, owner is a hiker; $59S $69D $20EAP includes B, tenting $10PP, if-available L/D; laundry (fee); free use of computer, dogs permitted outside; if available, hikers not staying at the lodge can have a reasonably priced B/L/D; hot tub, sauna, kayaking on Kent Pond; hiker box inside; outdoor spigot; mail drops accepted.

East 0.3 mile on side cross-country ski trail (signed marked BCO) to *Outfitter:* Base Camp Outfitters, 2363 U.S. 4, Killington, VT 05751; (802) 775-0166, <www.basecampvt.com>; on bus route to Rutland, open daily 9–6; backpacking equipment, clothing, and supplies, ice cream, freeze-dried food, fuel, disc golf, outside deck area with hiker box and recharging outlets; mail drops accepted.

East 0.6 mile to all the Killington services on U.S. 4 listed above: *A safer alternative to walking on Vt. 100.*

Thundering Falls—A 2007-8 relocation, which took 30 years from conception to completion, eliminated a road walk and added views of Thun-

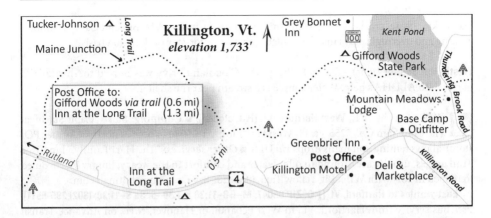

dering Falls and the Ottauquechee River. The new path descends through northern-hardwood forest to the base of high Thundering Falls and then through the open Ottauquechee River floodplain. A wheelchair-accessible bridge built by the Green Mountain Club and financed by ATC and the National Park Service crosses the river.

River Road—East 0.5 mile to Killington town offices and Johnson Recreation Center pool ($4 nonresident fee). **East** 0.7 mile to Sherburne Memorial Library, M–Sa.

Stony Brook Shelter (1997)—Sleeps 8. Privy. Water source is brook 100 yards north of shelter on A.T.

Side Trail to the Lookout—One of the few views between Killington Peak and New Hampshire. Follow side trail 0.2 mile west from A.T. to a private cabin. Use care on ladder that leads up to an observation deck. No water. The owners permit its use *as a viewpoint* by hikers; please be responsible to ensure that this privilege continues.

Wintturi Shelter (1994)—Sleeps 8. Privy. Frame shelter. Water source is a spring to the right of the shelter.

 Vt. 12—Please respect landowners at this road crossing by not camping in woods or fields near Vt. 12.

East 4.4 miles to **Woodstock, Vt. [P.O. ZIP 05091: M–F 8:30–5, Sa 9–12; (802) 457-1323]**. Services include several motels and inns, grocery (long-term resupply), restaurants, bank with ATM, doctor, dentist, pharmacy, and movie theater open F–Su. *Internet access:* library, M–Sa.

West 0.2 mile to *Groceries:* On the Edge farm stand, owners Dana and Bill, open daily in summer 10–5:30, Su 10–5; delicious home-made pies, seasonal veggies, fruit, cold drinks, ice cream, cheese, smoked meat, bread rolls, breakfast burritos, jerky, and water.

 Woodstock Stage Road (Bartlett Brook Road)—East 0.9 mile to **South Pomfret, Vt. [P.O. ZIP 05067: M–F 8–1 & 2–4:45, Sa 8:30–11:30; (802) 457-1147]**. ■ *Groceries:* Teago General Store (short-term resupply), M–Sa 7–6, Su 8–4, with deli sandwiches and P.O. inside the store. ■ *Internet access:* library, WiFi, Tu, Th, Sa.

Cloudland Road—West 0.2 mile to *Groceries:* Cloudland Farm Country Market & Restaurant, (802) 457-2599, <www.cloudlandfarm.com>; W 10–3, Th–Sa 10–5, water, cold drinks, beef jerky, cheese, crackers, ice cream. This operating farm is run by Bill and Cathy Emmons. Tenting and overnight stays may be available on a work-for-stay or donation basis.

Thistle Hill Shelter (1995)—Sleeps 8. Privy. The Cloudland privy was moved to Thistle Hill, partly with ALDHA's help. Water source is a stream near the shelter.

Vt.14—On the A.T., **West Hartford, Vt. [P.O. closed]**. ■ *Camping:* Steve "Capt. Stash" at Hartford Sign Co., 5255 Vt. 14, West Hartford, VT 05084 (4 houses north of former PO/store), allows tenting and mails drops *via* UPS. ■ *Other services:* "The Hart Family," longtime Trail angels, usually are around to offer water and comfort to the weary; library is scheduled to reopen in 2015 with WiFi; Big Yellow Taxi, (802) 281-8294, <bytaxi@hotmail.com>.

　　East 7 miles to **Hartford, Vt. [P.O. ZIP 05047: M–F 8–11:30 & 1:30–5, Sa 9–11:30; (802) 295-5511]**. Free bus service from Hartford, Vt., to West Lebanon or Hanover, N.H., on Advance Transit Green Route.

　　East 8 miles to **White River Junction**, a large town with all services. Amtrak provides daily train service on the Vermonter, (800) USA-RAIL. *Hostel:* Hotel Coolidge (Hostelling International), 39 South Main St., White River Junction, VT 05001; (802) 295-3118, (800) 622-1124, <www.hotelcoolidge.com>; $45–$65, private rooms available at higher rate; laundry, WiFi; walk to restaurants, banks, and stores.

Happy Hill Shelter (1998)—Sleeps 8. Privy. The oldest A.T. shelter (built in 1918, before the A.T.) was torn down, then burned; the debris was carried out. In 1998, a new shelter was built about 0.2 mile north of the original. ALDHA members worked on this project after the 1997 Gathering. Water source is the brook near the shelter.

U.S. 5/Norwich, Vt. [P.O. ZIP 05055: M–F 8:30–5, Sa 9–12; (802) 649-1608]—**East** 0.25 mile to *Lodging:* Norwich Inn & Brewery, (802) 649-1143, <www.norwichinn.com>; $99 hiker rate includes free pint of beer. Built in 1791 as a stagecoach inn, reportedly the inspiration for the "Newhart" TV show. ■ *Restaurants:* Norwich Inn, Tu–Su B/L/D, Su brunch. ■ *Groceries:* Dan & Whits (long-term resupply), open daily 7–9, a sprawling, eclectic general store. ■ *Internet access:* library, M–Sa. ■ *Other services:* Norwich Bookstore (on Trail); bank with ATM; free bus service to Hanover on Advance Transit Brown or Green routes.

New Hampshire

Miles from Springer	Fr Last Point	Features	Services	Miles from Katahdin	M A P	Alt. Name
1,746.5	0.4	Connecticut River (380') Vermont–New Hampshire State Line	R	442.7		
1,747.0	0.5	N.H. 10, Dartmouth College (520') **Hanover, N.H. 03755**	R, PO, C, G, L, M, O, D, V, B, sh, cl, f (E–2m L, cl; 16m H, f) (W–1.5m cl)	442.2		
1,747.7	0.7	N.H. 120 (490')	R	441.5		
1,748.5	0.8	**Velvet Rocks Shelter** (1,040') ...7.6mS; 9.7mN	W–0.2m S, nw (N–0.2m w)	440.7		
1,749.0	0.5	Ledyard Spring (1,200')...water for Velvet Rocks Shelter	W–0.4m w	440.2		
1,749.8	0.8	Velvet Rocks (1,243')		439.4		
1,751.5	1.7	Trescott Road (915')	R, P	437.7	ATC N.H.–Vt. Map 5	
1,752.9	1.4	Etna–Hanover Center Road (845')	R, P, H (E–0.9m G, f, sh)	436.3		
1,755.4	2.5	Three Mile Road (1,350')	R, P	433.8		
1,755.6	0.2	Mink Brook (1,320')	w	433.6		
1,757.2	1.6	Moose Mountain (South Peak) (2,290')		432.0		
1,758.0	0.8	**Moose Mountain Shelter** (1,850') ...9.7mS; 5.9mN	S, C, w	431.2		
1,759.2	1.2	Moose Mountain (North Peak) (2,300')		430.0		
1,759.9	0.7	South Fork, Hewes Brook (1,100')	w	429.3		
1,761.2	1.3	Goose Pond Road (952')	R, P	428.0		
1,763.2	2.0	Holts Ledge (1,930')...peregrine falcon rookery		426.0		
1,763.7	0.5	**Trapper John Shelter** (1,345') ...5.9mS; 6.9mN	W–0.2m S, C, w	425.5		
1,764.6	0.9	Dartmouth Skiway, Lyme–Dorchester Road (880') **Lyme, N.H. 03768**	R, P (W–3.2m PO, G, L, M)	424.6		
1,766.5	1.9	Grant Brook (1,090')	w	422.7		
1,766.6	0.1	Lyme–Dorchester Road (1,100')	R, P, w	422.6		
1,770.3	3.7	Smarts Mountain Tentsite (3,200')	C, w	418.9		LAMBERT RIDGE TRAIL
1,770.4	0.1	**Firewarden's Cabin** (3,230') ...6.9mS; 5.6mN Fire Tower	S, w	418.8	ATC N.H.–Vt. Map 4	
1,774.3	3.9	South Jacob's Brook (1,450')	w	414.9		J TRAIL
1,774.7	0.4	Eastman Ledges (2,010')		414.5		KODAK TRAIL
1,775.7	1.0	**Hexacuba Shelter** (1,980') ...5.6mS; 16mN North Jacobs Brook	w (E–0.3m S)	413.5		
1,777.1	1.4	Mt. Cube (south summit) (2,909') Cross Rivendell Trail Junction		412.1		MT. CUBE TRAIL
1,777.3	0.2	Mt. Cube, side trail to north summit (2,911')		411.9		
1,778.8	1.5	Brackett Brook (1,400')...ford	w	410.4		

Miles from Springer	Fr Last Point	Features	Services	Miles from Katahdin	M A P	Alt. Name
1,780.6	1.8	N.H. 25A (900') **Wentworth, N.H. 03282**	R, P (E–4.8m PO, G)	408.6		MT. CUBE TRAIL
1,782.2	1.6	Cape Moonshine Road (1,400')	R (E–1m C, sh)	407.0		ATWELL HILL TRAIL
1,782.8	0.6	Ore Hill Campsite (1,720')	E–0.1m C, w	406.4		ORE HILL TRAIL
1,785.1	2.3	Ore Hill (1,850')		404.1		
1,785.4	0.3	N.H. 25C, Ore Hill Brook (1,550') **Warren, N.H. 03279**	R, P (E–4m PO, G, M, D, cl)	403.8		
1,787.9	2.5	Mt. Mist (2,200')		401.3		WACHIPAUKA POND TRAIL
1,788.3	0.4	Hairy Root Spring, Webster Slide Trail (1,600')	w	400.9		
1,788.4	0.1	Wachipauka Pond (1,493')	w	400.8		
1,790.3	1.9	N.H. 25, Oliverian Brook (1,000')... *ford, road bypass if high water* **Glencliff, N.H. 03238**	R, P, w (E–0.4m PO, H, sh, cl, f)	398.9	ATC N.H.–Vt. Map 4	
1,791.4	1.1	**Jeffers Brook Shelter** (1,350') *...16mS; 6.9mN*	S, C, w	397.8		TOWN LINE TRAIL
1,791.8	0.4	USFS 19, Long Pond Road (1,330')	R	397.4		
1,792.1	0.3	High Street (1,480')	R, P	397.1		GLENCLIFF TRAIL
1,792.5	0.4	Hurricane Trail (1,680')		396.7		
1,795.1	2.6	Mt. Moosilauke (south peak) (4,460')		394.1		
1,796.0	0.9	Mt. Moosilauke (north peak) (4,802') Gorge Brook Trail to DOC Ravine Lodge		393.2		MOOSILAUKE CARRIAGE ROAD
1,796.4	0.4	Benton Trail (4,550')		392.8		
1,797.9	1.5	Asquam Ridge Trail (4,050')		391.3		
1,798.3	0.4	**Beaver Brook Shelter** and **Campsite** (3,750')...*6.9mS; 9mN*	S, C, w	390.9		BEAVER BROOK TRAIL
1,798.7	0.4	Beaver Brook Cascades (3,000')	w	390.5		
1,799.8	1.1	N.H. 112; Kinsman Notch (1,870') **North Woodstock, N.H. 03262** **Lincoln, N.H. P.O. 03251**	R, P (E–0.3m w; 5m PO, H, G, L, M, cl, f; 6m PO, all)	389.4		
1,800.4	0.6	Dilly Trail (2,650')		388.8		
1,803.1	2.7	Gordon Pond Trail (2,700')		386.1		
1,804.4	1.3	Mt. Wolf (East Peak) (3,478')		384.8		
1,806.3	1.9	Reel Brook Trail (2,600')		382.9		KINSMAN RIDGE TRAIL
1,806.8	0.5	Power Line (2,625')		382.4		
1,807.3	0.5	**Eliza Brook Shelter** and **Campsite** (2,400')...*9mS; 4.1mN*	S, C, w	381.9	ATC N.H.–Vt. Map 3	
1,808.7	1.4	Harrington Pond (3,400')		380.5		
1,809.8	1.1	South Kinsman Mountain (4,358')		379.4		
1,810.7	0.9	North Kinsman Mountain (4,293')		378.5		
1,811.1	0.4	Mt. Kinsman Trail (3,900')		378.1		
1,811.3	0.2	Kinsman Pond Trail (south) to +AMC **Kinsman Pond Shelter** and **Campsite** (3,750')...*4.1mS; 15.3mN*	E–0.1m S, C, w	377.9		
1,813.2	1.9	+AMC Lonesome Lake Hut (2,760')	L, M, w	376.0		FISHIN' JIMMY TRAIL
1,814.1	0.9	Kinsman Pond Trail (north) (2,294')		375.1		CASCADE BROOK TRAIL
1,814.6	0.5	Basin–Cascade Trail; Cascade Brook (2,084')...*ford*	w	374.6		

Miles from Springer	Fr Last Point	Features	Services	Miles from Katahdin	MAP	Alt. Name
1,815.7	1.1	Whitehouse Brook (1,610')	w	373.5		CASCADE BROOK TRAIL
1,815.9	0.2	Pemi Trail (1,520')		373.3		
1,816.1	0.2	I-93, U.S. 3,Franconia Notch (1,450') ...underpass Pemigawassest River **North Woodstock, N.H. 03262 Lincoln, N.H. 03251**	R (E–0.7m B; 0.8m M; 5.8m PO, H, G, L, M, cl, f; 7.3m PO, all) (W–2.1m B, C; 8m G, L, M, B)	373.1		
1,816.1	0.0	Franconia Notch paved bike path east to Liberty Springs hiker parking and shuttle;and beyond to The Flume Visitor Center; west to +Lafayette Place Campground (1,450')	(E–0.7m P, B; 0.8m M, ph) (W–2.5m C, B, w)	373.1		LIBERTY SPRING TRAIL
1,816.7	0.6	Flume Side Trail (1,800')		372.5		
1,818.7	2.0	+AMC Liberty Springs Tentsite (3,870')	C, w	370.5		
1,819.0	0.3	Franconia Ridge Trail (4,260')...0.3m to Mt. Liberty		370.2		
1,820.8	1.8	Little Haystack Mountain; Falling Waters Trail (4,800')...above treeline for next 2.5 miles north on Franconia Ridge		368.4		FRANCONIA RIDGE TRAIL
1,821.5	0.7	Mt. Lincoln (5,089')		367.7		
1,822.5	1.0	Mt. Lafayette; Greenleaf Trail to +AMC Greenleaf Hut (5,260')	(W–0.2m w; 1.1m L, M, w)	366.7		
1,823.3	0.8	Skookumchuck Trail Jct (4,680')... above treeline for the next 2.5 miles south on Franconia Ridge		365.9	ATC N.H.–Vt. Map 3	GARFIELD RIDGE TRAIL
1,825.3	2.0	Garfield Pond (3,860')	w	363.9		
1,826.0	0.7	Mt. Garfield (4,500')		363.2		
1,826.2	0.2	Garfield Trail (4,180')		363.0		
1,826.4	0.2	+AMC **Garfield Ridge Shelter** and **Campsite** (3,900')...15.3mS; 6.4mN	W–0.1m S, C, w	362.8		
1,826.9	0.5	Franconia Brook Trail (3,420')		362.3		
1,828.5	1.6	Gale River Trail (3,390')		360.7		
1,829.1	0.6	+AMC Galehead Hut, Twin Brook Trail (3,780')	L, M, w	360.1		
1,829.9	0.8	South Twin Mountain, North Twin Spur (4,902')		359.3		
1,831.9	2.0	Mt. Guyot (4,580'); +AMC **Guyot Shelter** and **Campsite** via Bondcliff Trail...6.4mS; 9.8mN	E–0.8m S, C, w	357.3		
1,833.2	1.3	Zealand Mountain (4,250')		356.0		THE TWINWAY
1,834.4	1.2	Zeacliff Pond Trail (3,800')	E–0.1m w	354.8		
1,834.8	0.4	Zeacliff Trail (south) (3,700')		354.4		
1,834.9	0.1	Zeacliff (3,700')...overlook to the east		354.3		
1,836.0	1.1	Lend-a-Hand Trail, Whitewall Brook (2,750')	w	353.2		
1,836.1	0.1	+AMC Zealand Falls Hut (2,630')	L, M, w	353.1		
1,836.3	0.2	Zealand Trail Jct. (2,460')...former railroad bed		352.9		
1,837.6	1.3	Zeacliff Trail (north) (2,448')		351.6		

Miles from Springer	Fr Last Point	Features	Services	Miles from Katahdin	M A P	Alt. Name
1,838.4	0.8	Thoreau Falls Trail (2,460')		350.8		ETHAN POND TRAIL
1,838.9	0.5	Shoal Pond Trail (2,500')	E–0.8m w	350.3	ATC N.H.–Vt. Map 3	
1,840.9	2.0	+AMC **Ethan Pond Shelter** and **Campsite** (2,860')...9.8mS; 17.4mN	S, C, w	348.3		
1,841.9	1.0	Willey Range Trail (2,680')		347.3		
1,842.2	0.3	Kedron Flume Trail (2,450')		347.0		
1,843.3	1.1	Arethusa–Ripley Falls Trail (1,600')		345.9		
1,843.5	0.2	Railroad Tracks, Willey House Station Road (1,440')	R, P	345.7		
1,843.8	0.3	U.S. 302, Crawford Notch, Presidential Range (1,275') **Bartlett, N.H. 03812**	R, B (E–1.8m C, cl, sh; 3m C, sh; 10m PO) (W–1m M; 3.7m L, M, B, sh)	345.4		WEBSTER CLIFF TRAIL
1,843.9	0.1	Saco River (1,350')...*footbridge*		345.3		
1,844.0	0.1	Saco River Trail (south) (1,350')	W–1.2m M	345.2		
1,844.1	0.1	Saco River Trail (north) (1,400')	E–2m C, cl, sh	345.1		
1,845.7	1.6	Webster Cliffs (3,025')		343.5		
1,847.1	1.4	Mt. Webster (3,910')		342.1		
1,848.5	1.4	Mt. Jackson (4,052')		340.7		
1,850.2	1.7	+AMC Mizpah Spring Hut, +AMC Nauman Tentsite (3,800')	C, L, M, w	339.0		
1,851.0	0.8	Mt. Pierce (Mt. Clinton) (4,312')... *above treeline for the next 12.7 miles north*		338.2		
1,851.9	0.9	Spring (4,350')	w	337.3		
1,852.7	0.8	Mt. Eisenhower Loop Trail (north); Edmands Path (4,475')		336.5		CRAWFORD PATH
1,853.2	0.5	Spring (4,480')	w	336.0	ATC N.H.–Vt. Map 2	
1,853.8	0.6	Mt. Franklin (5,004')		335.4		
1,854.8	1.0	Mt. Monroe Loop Trail (north) (5,075')		334.4		
1,854.9	0.1	+AMC Lakes of the Clouds Hut (5,125') ..."The Dungeon"	L, M, w	334.3		
1,855.7	0.8	Davis Path; Westside Trail (south) (5,625')		333.5		
1,856.1	0.4	Gulfside Trail (6,150')		333.1		
1,856.3	0.2	Mt. Washington (6,288'), Mt. Washington Auto Road **Mt. Washington, N.H. 03589** (not recommended)	R, P, PO, M (8m via Auto Road to N.H. 16)	332.9		
1,856.3	0.0	Tuckerman Ravine Trail (6,288') to + **AMC Hermit Lake Shelter** ...17.4S; 7.1mN to Pinkham Notch at N.H. 16	E–2m S; 4.2m R, P, B, G, L, M, sh, f	332.9		GULFSIDE TRAIL
1,856.5	0.2	Trinity Heights Connector (6,100')		332.7		
1,856.6	0.1	Cog Railroad Tracks (6,090')		332.6		
1,856.7	0.1	Great Gulf Trail (5,925')		332.5		
1,857.2	0.5	Westside Trail (5,500')		332.0		
1,857.3	0.1	Mt. Clay Loop Trail (south) (5,400')		331.9		

Miles from Springer	Fr Last Point	Features	Services	Miles from Katahdin	M A P	Alt. Name
1,857.6	0.3	Jewell Trail (5,400')		331.6		
1,858.1	0.5	Greenough Spring (5,100')	w	331.1		
1,858.2	0.1	Sphinx Col; Mt. Clay Loop Trail (north) (5,025')		331.0		
1,858.3	0.1	Sphinx Trail (4,975')		330.9		
1,858.8	0.5	Cornice Trail; Monticello Lawn (5,325')		330.4		
1,859.3	0.5	Six Husbands Trail (5,325')		329.9		GULFSIDE TRAIL
1,859.6	0.3	Mt. Jefferson Loop (north) (5,125')		329.6		
1,859.8	0.2	Edmands Col; Gulfside Spring; Spaulding Spring (4,938')	w (W–0.2m w)	329.4		
1,860.5	0.7	Israel Ridge Path (5,475') to +RMC The Perch Shelter and Campsite... 7.1mS; 2.7mN	W–0.9m S, C, w	328.7		
1,861.1	0.6	Thunderstorm Junction (5,490'); Trail to +RMC Crag Camp Cabin; Lowe's Path to Mt. Adams and +RMC Gray Knob Cabin...2.7mS; 23.2mN	W–1.1m and 1.2m S, w	328.1		
1,861.6	0.5	Air Line Trail (south) (5,125')		327.6		
1,862.0	0.4	+AMC Madison Spring Hut (4,825')	L, M, w	327.2		
1,862.0	0.0	USFS Valley Way Tentsite (3,900')	W–0.6m C, w	327.2		
1,862.5	0.5	Mt. Madison (5,366')		326.7	ATC N.H.–Vt. Map 2	
1,862.7	0.2	Howker Ridge Trail (5,100')		326.5		
1,863.0	0.3	Osgood Junction; Parapet Trail; Daniel Webster Scout Trail (4,822')		326.2		OSGOOD TRAIL
1,863.7	0.7	Osgood Ridge (4,300')...above treeline for the next 12.7 miles south		325.5		OSGOOD CUTOFF
1,865.0	1.3	USFS Osgood Campsite (2,540') Osgood Cutoff	C, w	324.2		
1,865.6	0.6	The Bluff at Parapet Brook (2,450') Great Gulf Trail	w	323.6		GREAT GULF TRAIL/ MADISON GULF TRAIL
1,865.8	0.2	Madison Gulf Trail (2,300') West Branch of the Peabody River	w	323.4		
1,865.9	0.1	Great Gulf Trail (north) (2,290')		323.3		MADISON GULF TRAIL
1,867.7	1.8	Low's Bald Spot (2,875')...rock dome		321.5		
1,867.9	0.2	Mt. Washington Auto Road (2,675')	R, P	321.3		
1,868.0	0.1	Raymond Path (2,625')		321.2		
1,868.8	0.8	George's Gorge Trail (2,525')		320.4		OLD JACKSON ROAD TRAIL
1,869.3	0.5	Crew Cutoff Trail (2,075')		319.9		
1,869.8	0.5	N.H. 16, Pinkham Notch, Pinkham Notch Visitor Center,+AMC Joe Dodge Lodge (2,050') North Conway, N.H. Gorham, N.H.	R, P, B, G, L, M, sh, f (E–16m L, O; 18m G, L, M O, D) (W–11m Gorham, N.H.)	319.4		
1,869.9	0.1	Square Ledge Trail (2,020')		319.3		LOST POND TRAIL
1,870.7	0.8	Wildcat Ridge Trail to Glen Ellis Falls (1,990')		318.5		
1,871.5	0.8	Open Ledge, Sarge's Crag (3,000')		317.7		WILD- CAT RIDGE TRAIL
1,871.8	0.3	Spring (3,250')		317.4		

Miles from Springer	Fr Last Point	Features	Services	Miles from Katahdin	M A P	Alt. Name
1,872.8	1.0	Wildcat Mountain, Peak D (4,020')... gondola		316.4		WILDCAT RIDGE TRAIL
1,873.9	1.1	Wildcat Mountain, Peak C (4,298')		315.3		
1,874.3	0.4	Wildcat Mountain, Peak B (4,330')		314.9		
1,874.8	0.5	Wildcat Mountain, Peak A (4,442')		314.4		
1,875.7	0.9	Nineteen Mile Brook Trail (3,350') Carter Notch, +AMC Carter Notch Hut	E–0.2m L, M, w	313.5		CARTER–MORIAH TRAIL
1,876.4	0.7	Spring (4,300')	w	312.8		
1,876.9	0.5	Carter Dome, Rainbow Trail (4,832')		312.3		
1,877.3	0.4	Black Angel Trail (4,600')		311.9		
1,877.7	0.4	Mt. Hight (4,675')		311.5		
1,878.3	0.6	Zeta Pass (3,890')	w	310.9		
1,879.1	0.8	South Carter Mountain (4,458')		310.1		
1,880.4	1.3	Middle Carter Mountain (4,610')		308.8	ATC N.H.–Vt. Map 2	
1,880.7	0.3	Mt. Lethe (4,584')		308.5		
1,881.0	0.3	North Carter Mountain (4,539')		308.2		
1,882.9	1.9	+AMC Imp Shelter and Campsite (3,250')...23.2mS; 6.3mN	W–0.2m S, C, w	306.3		
1,883.6	0.7	Stony Brook Trail; Moriah Brook Trail (3,127')		305.6		
1,885.0	1.4	Carter Moriah Trail to Mt. Moriah (4,000')		304.2		
1,886.2	1.2	Middle Moriah (3,640')		303.0		KEN-DUSKEAG TRAIL
1,886.4	0.2	Kenduskeag Trail (3,300')		302.8		
1,887.5	1.1	Rattle River (1,700')		301.7		RATTLE RIVER TRAIL
1,888.6	1.1	East Rattle River (1,500')...difficult in high water		300.6		
1,889.0	0.4	Rattle River Shelter and Campsite (1,260')...6.3mS; 13.9mN	S, C, w	300.2		
1,890.9	1.9	U.S. 2 (780') Gorham, N.H. 03581 Berlin, N.H.	R, P, H, w (W–1.8m H, C, G, cl, sh; 3.6m PO, H, B, G, L, M, O, cl, f; 5.6m G; 8m D)	298.3		
1,891.2	0.3	North Road, Androscoggin River (750')	R	298.0		CENTENNIAL TRAIL
1,891.4	0.2	Hogan Road (760')...unpaved	R	297.8		
1,892.4	1.0	Brook (1,350')	w	296.8		
1,894.5	2.1	Mt. Hayes, Mahoosuc Trail (2,555')		294.7		MAHOOSUC TRAIL
1,896.7	2.2	Cascade Mountain (2,631')		292.5	ATC N.H.–Vt. Map 1	
1,897.8	1.1	Trident Col Tentsite (2,020')	W–0.1m C, w	291.4		
1,898.8	1.0	Trident Pass, Page Pond (2,240')		290.4		
1,899.4	0.6	Wockett Ledge (2,780')		289.8		
1,900.5	1.1	Dream Lake inlet, Peabody Brook Trail (2,610')	w	288.7		
1,902.0	1.5	Moss Pond (2,630')	w	287.2		
1,902.7	0.7	Austin Brook Trail Jct. to Gentian Pond Shelter and Campsite (2,166')...13.9mS; 5.7mN	E–0.2m S, C, w	286.5		

Miles from Springer	Fr Last Point	Features	Services	Miles from Katahdin	M A P	Alt. Name
1,905.5	2.8	Mt. Success (3,565')		283.7	N.H.–Vt. Map 1	MAHOOSUC TRAIL
1,906.1	0.6	Success Trail (3,170')		283.1		
1,907.4	1.3	New Hampshire–Maine State Line (2,972')		281.8		

+ Fee charged   *RMC = Randolph Mountain Club*

At Hanover, southbounders will have already experienced the White Mountains. Northbounders should gear up for the conditions ahead.

Considered one of the most challenging states, it is also one of the most rewarding. As the trees get shorter and the views get longer, you've entered the krummholz zone, where trees are stunted with flag-like tops due to stress from the wind and cold. Boreal bogs are home to local carnivorous plant species, sundew and pitcher plants. Hardy, yet delicate alpine flowers—Labrador tea, bunchberry, mountain sandwort, and cloudberry—may be in bloom when you pass through. Spruce grouse, winter wren, dark-eyed junco, and the white-throated sparrow will greet you along the way.

Much of the Trail is above timberline, where the temperature may change very suddenly; snow is possible in any season. Snow falls on Mt. Washington every month of the year. High winds and dense fog are common. Most shelters and campsites charge a fee.

Tenting is prohibited within 200 feet of the A.T. from the Connecticut River (Vermont state line) to the summit of Mt. Moosilauke.

Many water sources in southern New Hampshire are not always reliable, including sources at, or adjacent to, shelters.

Dartmouth Outing Club—DOC maintains the 53.3 miles from the Connecticut River to Kinsman Notch in New Hampshire. Correspondence should be sent to DOC Box 9, Hanover, NH 03755; (603) 646-2428; <www.dartmouth.edu/~doc>. The DOC no longer uses orange-and-black paint for blazes, although many are still visible. The DOC does continue to use orange and black on trail signs.

Hanover, N.H. [P.O. ZIP 03755: M–F 8:30–5, Sa 8:30–12, lobby opens at 7 a.m.; (603) 643-5201]—Home of Dartmouth College. The A.T. passes through the center of Hanover, and most services are along the route of the Trail. At the center of town and the Dartmouth Green, a blue-blazed side trail leads (Trail-west) to Robinson Hall and the office of the Dartmouth Outing Club (DOC) in Room 113, (603) 646-2428, <www.dartmouth.edu/~doc/>. DOC has student volunteers (DOC tours), Su–Th 2–6, phone, and Internet access. This is a good place to begin in town. The college does not allow nonstudents to stay in student housing. Dartmouth College security has reported problems with improper use of college facilities and buildings by hikers; hikers must not enter dormitories, offices, laundry rooms, *etc.*, without permission or try to sleep overnight in those locations, including the DOC building. Public (on-street) consumption of alcohol is illegal downtown. ■ *Hostel:* Stray Kat's AT Hillton-Hanover, c/o Steve Lake, 365 Choate Rd., Canaan, NH 03741; (603) 252-8295, <athikershuttle@gmail.com>, $45PP (local pick-up), bunk-style lodging includes fresh linens, shower, WiFi, CATV, picnic table, BBQ grill. Hearty dinner with salad/dessert ($10) and country

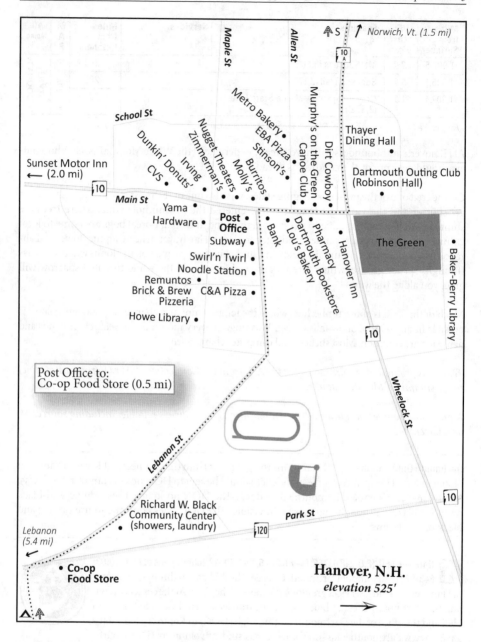

Hanover, N.H.
elevation 525'

breakfast ($7.50) by request. Laundry $4. Hostel rates for pick-up between Vt. 12 (Woodstock, Vt.) and N.H. 25A (Wentworth, N.H.) are higher. Only 6-8 hikers per night on first come/first served basis. Other shuttles available. Mail drops accepted. ■ *Camping:* Tenting is permitted in the woods, past the soccer fields, *if you are 200 feet from the Trail and on Forest Service land.* ■ *Groceries:* Hanover Food Co-op (long-term resupply), bulk and natural foods; Irving Food Stop, CVS Pharmacy, and Stinson's Village Store (all short-term resupply). ■ *Restaurants:* Ramunto's Pizza; Everything But Anchovies, L/D; Lou's Bakery & Restaurant, B/L; Thayer Hall, the Dartmouth dining hall, B/L/D; C&A Pizza; Noodle Station; Boloco Burritos; Jewel of India; Dirt Cowboy Café; The Canoe

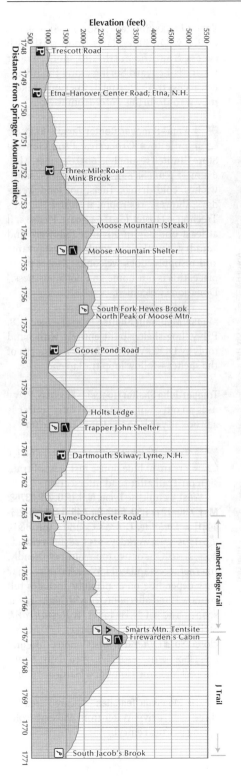

Club Restaurant; Murphy's. ■ *Internet access:* Howe Public Library and DOC. ■ *Outfitters:* Zimmermann's, sells primarily North Face clothing and packs; CamelBak. In West Lebanon: EMS, (603) 298-7716; Omer and Bob's Sport Shop; and L.L.Bean Outlet, (603) 298-6975—take "Orange" bus route, switch to "Red," and ask the driver to let you off at the Powerhouse Mall. ■ *Other services:* Laura's Place, (603) 727-8187, 1 mile out of town near bus line, call for arrangements 8–8; True Value Hardware, Coleman fuel, denatured alcohol; Richard Black Recreation Center, Lebanon and Park streets, shower and laundry for hikers M–F during summer; College Cleaners on Allen Street offers "wash, dry, and fold"; One Clean Place, 1.5 miles north on N.H. 10 on "Brown" bus route, has coin laundry; bookstores; dentist; doctor; hospital; movie theater; optician; banks with ATM; pharmacy; barber shop; Hanover Veterinary Clinic, (603) 643-3313, (603) 643-4829 after hours; Hanover Hot Tubs. ■ *Bus service:* Advance Transit is a local bus service, 6 a.m. to 6 p.m., M–F only. All routes are free; can be picked up outside the Hanover Inn (going north) or in front of Dartmouth Bookstore on Main St. (going south); offers transportation throughout Hanover and to White River Junction, Vt. (where there is an Amtrak station), Lebanon, and West Lebanon, with all major services. Bus schedules available in the bookstore. Bus service to Boston by Dartmouth Coach, (800) 637-0123, and Greyhound, (800) 231-2222. ■ *Long-term parking:* available for hikers in "A" lot, east of campus. Call parking operations, (603) 646-2204, for directions and to make arrangements. ■ *Shuttles:* Trail Head Shuttle, (802) 477-2048; Big Yellow Taxi, (603) 643-8294; "Stray Kat" (see Hostel entry above).

 East (south)—2.0 miles to *Lodging:* Sunset Motor Inn, (603) 298-8721, on N.H. 10, on the "Orange" bus route, $69–$99 through May, $74–$93 Jun–Sep, no pets, no smoking, CATV, continental B, shuttle and laundry may be available if you ask the owners; Super 8 Motel in White River Junction, Vt., (802) 295-7577, on the "Orange" bus route; Days Inn in Lebanon, N.H., (603) 448-5070, on the "Blue" bus route.

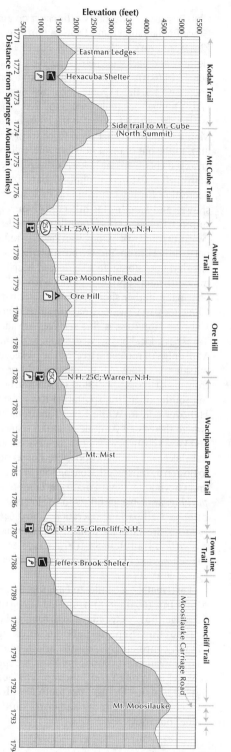

Velvet Rocks Shelter (1980s/2006)—Sleeps 6. Privy. On blue-blazed loop trail with access from the north and south. Water source is Ledyard Spring along the northern access trail. During dry periods, hikers may want to bring water from town.

Etna–Hanover Center Road—East 0.7 mile to ■ *Groceries:* Etna General Store (limited resupply), (603) 643-1655, M–F 6 a.m.–7 p.m., Sa 8–7, Su 8–6, snacks, sandwiches, cold drinks, fuels, hot food weekdays, showers, restroom. ■ *Hostel:* Tigger's Treehouse Hostel, (603) 643-9213. Please call at least one day in advance. Showers and laundry, shuttle into town for restaurants and resupply, dogs welcome. "Not a party place; this is our home and not a business." Donations welcomed.

Moose Mountain Shelter (2004)—Sleeps 8. Privy. Log shelter built entirely with hand tools by DOC. Water is on the A.T. north of the shelter—follow loop trail to end.

Trapper John Shelter (1990s)—Sleeps 6. Privy uses an old chair. Tentsites. Water source is a brook 15 yards to the left of the shelter.

Lyme–Dorchester Road—Water and ice cream at blue house just west of trail; sign on Trail after road intersection.
    West 3.2 miles to **Lyme, N.H. [P.O. ZIP 03768: M–F 7:30–12 & 1:30–5:15, Sa 7:45–12; (603) 795-4421].** ■ *Lodging:* Dowd's Country Inn B&B, (603) 795-4712; weekdays $75S, $85D; weekends $95S, $115D. One or two rooms are pet-friendly. Internet access and WiFi. Weekend prices may vary depending on availability. Includes full country B and afternoon tea with home-made scones and all N.H. taxes. ■ *Restaurant:* Stella's Italian Kitchen & Market, L/D M–Sa, closed Su. ■ *Other services:* Country store and deli (short-term resupply), open daily; banks with ATM; Lyme Home and Hardware store.

Smarts Mountain Tentsites—Cleared area for three tents. Privy. Water from Mike Murphy Spring (see next entry).

Smarts Mountain Firewarden Cabin—Sleeps 8. Privy. Panoramic views from the abandoned firetower on Smarts Mountain summit. Water source is Mike Murphy Spring 0.2 mile north of cabin on blue-blazed Daniel Doan Trail.

Hexacuba Shelter (1989)—Sleeps 8. Tentsites. Privy (penta-style). Water source is an unreliable stream at the blue-blaze junction to the shelter. Alternative source is 0.3 mile south on the A.T. at North Jacobs Brook.

N.H. 25A—**East** 0.1 mile to lake with beach for swimming; 4.8 miles to **Wentworth, N.H.** **[P.O. ZIP 03282: M–F 7–1 & 2:45–4:45, Sa 7:15–12; (603) 764-9444]**. *Groceries:* Shawnee's General Store (long-term resupply), (603) 764-5553, M–Th 5 a.m.–8 p.m., F 5–9, Sa 6–9, Su 7–8.

Cape Moonshine Road—**East** 1 mile to *Work for stay:* Dancing Bones Village, <www.dancingbones. net>, an independent community that offers hikers tentsites, showers, and sometimes meals in exchange for light work.

Ore Hill Shelter Area (2000)—Shelter burned down in late 2011; camping with privy (medieval-style). Water source is a spring on the path 100 yards in front of the former shelter foundation.

N.H. 25C—**East** 4 miles to **Warren, N.H. [P.O. ZIP 03279: M–F 7:30–9:30 & 3–5, Sa 7:30–12; (603) 764-5733]**. ■ *Groceries:* Warren Village Market (long-term resupply), open daily 6 a.m.–8 p.m. (7 on Su), ATM, restrooms. ■ *Restaurants:* Calamity Jane's, B/L/D, (603) 764-5288, open M–W 6 a.m.–2 p.m., Tu–Sa 6 a.m.–8 p.m., Su 8–3; Greenhouse Restaurant, (603) 764-5708, "hiker pizza challenge," M 3–8, Th–F 3–11, Sa 12–10, Su 12–8. ■ *Other services:* hardware store, doctor, and coin laundry. See Warren's "Mystery Missile"—according to the *Boston Globe*, it is one of New England's eight most bizarre roadside attractions.

N.H. 25—**East** 0.4 mile to **Glencliff, N.H. [P.O. ZIP 03238: M–F 12–2, Sa 7–1; (603) 989-5154]**. This is a prudent mail drop for northbounders to pick up cold-weather gear before entering the high country of the White Mountains. *Hostel:* The Hikers Welcome Hostel, 1396 N.H. 25, (603) 989-0040 or (203) 605-9430, <www.hikerswelcome.com>, located at the base of Mt. Moosilauke; $20 hostel/bunk includes shower; $15 tenting includes shower; hot outdoor shower $2.50; laundry)$2.50 wash, $2.50 dry); hiker snacks, denatured alcohol and Coleman fuel by the ounce, free phone and wireless Internet, shuttles. Mail drops *via* USPS (P.O. Box 25), UPS, and FedEx. Resupply, ATM, and restaurants in Warren (5 miles; see above).

Oliverian Brook—The brook can be a difficult ford after rain. Be careful.

Jeffers Brook Shelter (1970s)—Sleeps 10. Privy. Located on a spur trail. Water source is Jeffers Brook, located in front of the shelter.

The White Mountains—One of the most impressive sections of the A.T., the Whites offer magnificent views with miles of above-treeline travel. Extra caution should be exercised while above treeline, due to rapidly changing weather and the lack of protection from it. Carry cold-weather gear, even in the middle of summer. Winter weather, including sleet, snow, and ice, is possible on these high ridges year-round. Each year, carelessness ends in death for a few visitors to the Whites. Pay close attention at Trail intersections. The Appalachian Mountain Club (AMC) maintains many trails that cross the A.T., and the A.T. route is commonly referred to on signs and in guidebooks by the name of the local trail it follows, such as "Franconia Ridge Trail." (And, to add to the confusion, sections above treeline from Mizpah Hut to Madison Hut are often marked with yellow blazes on rock cairns, to stand out in the snow.)

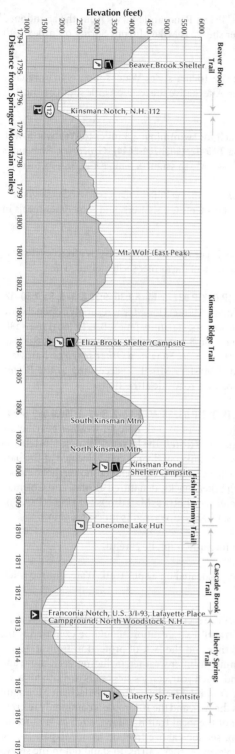

When above treeline, stay on the Trail. This alpine zone is home to very fragile plants. One misplaced bootstep can destroy them.

Backcountry regulations—Each summer, AMC serves tens of thousands of backpackers and campers at its backcountry shelters and campsites in the White Mountain National Forest. To prevent the Whites from being "loved to death," the USFS, in conjunction with AMC and the New Hampshire state parks agency, established a strict set of backcountry rules for the White Mountains. Please follow the rules. Hikers should be aware of all pertinent rules and regulations pertaining to camping in these areas and should not be surprised if they are rigorously enforced by ridgerunners and rangers. This especially applies to those who choose to camp immediately adjacent to huts, shelters, caretaker campsites, and road crossings. Hikers who ignore posted warnings may well receive hefty tickets. You will encounter forest protection areas (FPAs), where camping and fires are prohibited. The following regulations apply in those areas: no camping above treeline (where trees are less than eight feet high); no camping within 0.25 mile of huts, shelters, or tentsites except at the facility itself; no camping within 200 feet of the Trail. Groups of 6 or more should contact AMC Group Notification System, <www.outdoors. org>, (603) 466-2721 x8150, so it can effectively manage all large groups that stay at AMC sites. AMC-managed sites can accommodate groups of up to 10. USFS parking fees are established throughout the Whites; be prepared to pay if you park at Forest Service trailheads.

Mt. Moosilauke—The north side of Mt. Moosilauke is slick, particularly in rain. Be careful! Sections use rebar, rock steps, and wooden blocks for footing. For northbounders, it is the first mountain above treeline. For southbounders, the meadow at the base of the southern side is the first pastureland they encounter on the A.T. From the summit, Franconia Ridge, as well as the rest of the Whites, can be seen to the northeast; the Green Mountains are visible to the west.

Remnants of the 1860 Prospect House, a tourist spot that burned down in 1942, can still be seen at the summit.

Beaver Brook Shelter (1980s)—Sleeps 10. Privy (composting). Completed by DOC and ALDHA members, site includes 2 small tent pads and a nice view of Franconia Ridge. Water source is Beaver Brook on the spur trail to the shelter.

Appalachian Mountain Club—AMC maintains most of the A.T. and many of the surrounding trails between Kinsman Notch and Grafton Notch in Maine, a total of 120 miles; (603) 466-2721; <www.outdoors.org>.

AMC Tentsites, Shelters, and Campsites—"Tentsites" have designated tenting areas and platforms or pads. "Shelters" are three- or four-sided structures. "Campsites" have designated tenting areas *and* a shelter. See below for description of "huts," where reservations are required. Tentsites, shelters, and campsites are on a first-come, first-served basis. Caretakers are in residence at the following tentsites, shelters, and campsites, where an $8 overnight fee is charged: Kinsman Pond Campsite, Liberty Spring Tentsite, Garfield Ridge Campsite, 13 Falls Tentsite, Guyot Campsite, Ethan Pond Campsite, Nauman Tentsite, Imp Campsite, and Speck Pond Campsite (Maine). A caretaker works at those sites due to the locations' popularity and the fragility of their resources. The remaining tentsites, shelters, and campsites, except those operated by the Randolph Mountain Club (see below), are available to backcountry travelers at no charge. *All AMC campsites now have metal bear boxes available while a caretake is on site.*

A *work-for-stay option* is possible for thru-hikers at the tentsites and shelter sites that have caretakers. This is at the discretion of the caretaker and may not always be available. A maximum of two thru-hikers per night can be accommodated in that way at each site, and each will be expected to contribute an hour of work.

AMC Huts—These large, enclosed lodges sleep from 36 to 90 people and are open with full service from Jun to early Sep or early Oct, depending on the hut. Rates range from $98 to $118, depending on the day, AMC membership, and the hut. Lonesome Lake, Carter Notch, and Zealand Falls huts are self-service from fall to the following Jun; Mizpah, Galehead, and Greenleaf are self-service the last 3 weeks of May. A crew ("croo") staffs these facilities during the full-service season. An overnight stay includes bunk space, pillow, blanket, bathroom privileges (no showers), and potable water. If you plan to stay three consecutive nights, there is a discounted package rate, available all summer. Rates for self-service seasons are significantly less ($35–$39) than full-service seasons. Each hut has trained wilderness first-aid staff, and the facilities' crews give natural- and cultural-history evening programs. The huts also contain excellent libraries and displays on cultural and natural history.

If you plan to pay for a stay in one of the huts, make reservations, (603) 466-2727, especially for the weekends, when bunk spaces fill quickly. *Call AMC or check <www.outdoors. org> to verify the huts' opening and closing dates as well as rates and make reservations.* You may also be able to make a reservation by having a caretaker at one of the other huts or campsites radio ahead for you. The huts cater mainly to families and weekend hikers. AMC had wells drilled at all the huts, so you can look forward to water that meets state health standards. During the self-service season, a caretaker is at Lonesome Lake, Zealand, and Carter huts. Schedules vary from hut to hut; check individual listings for specific dates.

Work exchange at the huts—Thru-hikers can sometimes arrange with the croo to work off stays at the full- or self-service huts. Most huts can accommodate one or two working thru-hikers each night—except for Lakes of the Clouds Hut, which takes up to four thru-hikers—but availability of work is never guaranteed. Work-for-stay is at the discretion of the hut croo. When work is available, thru-hikers are asked to put in two hours either at night or in the morning; when work is not available, the full fee may be charged. Please give other thru-hikers a chance to work off their stay, and limit your use of the work-for-stay option to no more than three huts.

The AMC *Thru-Hiker's Guide to AMC-Maintained Trails & Facilities in the White Mountains & Mahoosucs* is a resource written for those who plan to stay at the fee sites (both backcountry and hospitality). It is not a tool for thru-hikers who correctly follow backcountry regulations and camp through this area; see <www.outdoors.org/thru-hikers>.

AMC Shuttle—603-466-2727, <www.outdoors.org/lodging/lodging-shuttle>, daily Jun 1–Sep 15, weekends only Sep 21–Oct 13; $18 AMC members ($22 nonmembers), reservations strongly recommended; walk-ons accepted on a space-available basis, see driver; drop-offs on route between scheduled stops may be arranged with driver. Stops include trailheads at Liberty Spring/A.T. on I-93, Lafayette Place Campground, Old Bridle Path, Gale River, Zealand Falls, Ammonoosuc Ravine, Highland Center at Crawford Notch, Webster Cliff/A.T. at U.S. 302, Pinkham Notch Visitors Center, 19-Mile Brook Trail, Gorham information booth, Valley Way/Appalachia. Check Web site for further details.

N.H. 112/Kinsman Notch—**East** 0.3 mile to Lost River Gorge and Boulder Caves, a series of streams, caves, and waterfalls owned by the Society for the Protection of New Hampshire Forests. Self-guided tour of gorge, ecology trail, and nature garden, $16, daily 9–5, from mid-May to mid-Oct, last ticket sold at 4 p.m. Snack bar. Phone available during business hours, with permission and a phone card.

  East 5 miles to **North Woodstock, N.H. [P.O. ZIP 03262: M–F 9:30–12:30 & 1:30–4:30, Sa 9–12; (603) 745-8134]**, which also is accessible from Franconia Notch (below). ■ *Hostel:* The Notch Hostel, 324 Lost River Rd., North Woodstock, NH 03262 ; (978) 602-7218, <www.notchhostel.com>, new farmhouse hostel opens Aug. 1, 2015; $30PP includes bunk, fresh linens, towel, shower, laundry, denatured alcohol, coffee/tea; overflow tenting $20PP; pick-up from Kinsman Notch and Franconia Notch; call ahead for shuttle details; basic B $5, pizza, ice cream, and some supplies sold on site; Internet/WiFi, sauna, kitchen, large yard; mail drops accepted. ■ *Lodging:* Woodstock Inn, (603) 745-3951 or (800) 321-3985, shared bath $94PP, private bath $112S/D, $25EAP, rates vary on weekends and holidays, no pets, includes B, nonsmoking rooms, pool at Alpine Village, brew pub, restaurant L/D; Autumn Breeze, (603) 745-8549, $72–$90, nonsmoking rooms, no dogs, rooms have kitchenettes; Carriage Motel, (603) 745-2416, $68–$82, game room, gas grills, picnic tables, pool, hiker box, deli, ATM, laundry, and P.O. across street. ■ *Groceries:* Wayne's Market (long-term resupply), deli and grinders. ■ *Restaurants:* See map. ■ *Shuttles:* The Hiker Shuttle Connection, (508) 889-8515, 6 a.m.–2 a.m. year-round; from A.T. in Franconia Notch, follow Rt. 3 south to Exit 34A for shuttle pick-up on Rt. 3.
  East—6 miles to **Lincoln, N.H.** (see below).

Eliza Brook Shelter/Campsite (2010)—Shelter sleeps 8. Privy (composting). Four hardened tent pads. Water source is Eliza Brook.

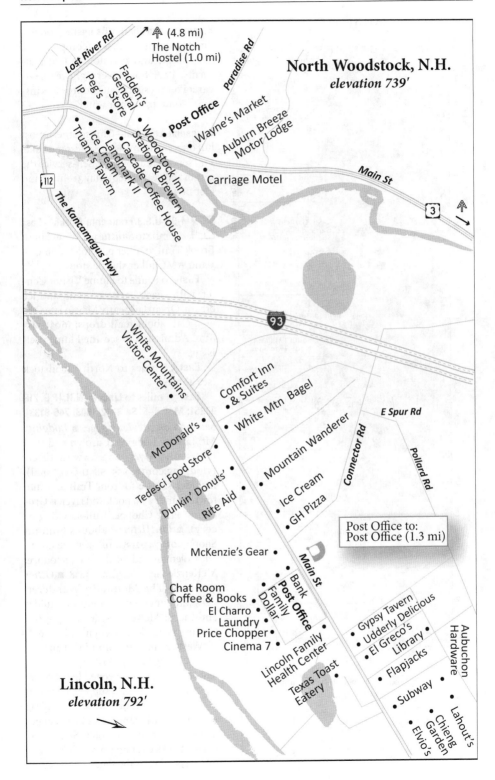

North Woodstock, N.H.
elevation 739'

↑ (4.8 mi)
The Notch
Hostel (1.0 mi)

Lost River Rd
Paradise Rd
Peg's
IP
Fadden's General Store
Post Office
Wayne's Market
Woodstock Inn Station & Brewery
Auburn Breeze Motor Lodge
Ice Cream
Landmark II
Cascade Coffee House
Truant's Tavern
Carriage Motel
Main St
112
The Kancamagus Hwy
3
↑

93

White Mountains Visitor Center
Comfort Inn & Suites
White Mtn Bagel
E Spur Rd
McDonald's
Mountain Wanderer
Connector Rd
Pollard Rd
Tedesci Food Store
Ice Cream
Dunkin' Donuts'
GH Pizza
Rite Aid

Post Office to:
Post Office (1.3 mi)

McKenzie's Gear
Main St
Bank
Post Office
Chat Room Coffee & Books
Family Dollar
El Charro
Laundry
Price Chopper
Cinema 7
Lincoln Family Health Center
Gypsy Tavern
Udderly Delicious
El Greco's
Library
Aubuchon Hardware
Flapjacks
Texas Toast Eatery
Subway
Lahout's
Chieng Garden
Elvio's

Lincoln, N.H.
elevation 792'

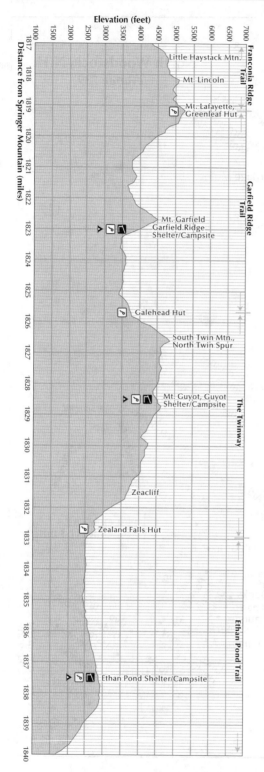

Kinsman Pond Shelter/Campsite (2007)—Shelter sleeps 15. Privy (composting). Two single and two double tent platforms. Bear box. Overnight fee $8PP, caretaker on site. Water source is Kinsman Pond; treat your water.

Lonesome Lake Hut—This southernmost hut offers swimming in Lonesome Lake. Full service Jun 3–Oct 17. Self-service the rest of the year except May 31–Jun 2 and Oct 18–19.

I-93/U.S.3/Franconia Notch—East 0.7 mile to *Shuttle via* Whitehouse Brook Trail to hiker parking lot on U.S. 3 and AMC hiker shuttle stop.

East—0.8 mile to Flume Visitor Center, with snack bar/restaurant, and ice cream. Open daily early May to late Oct, 9–5. Call about mail drops; (603) 745-8391. Admission to see The Flume itself is $15.

East 5.8 miles to North Woodstock (see above).

East 7.3 miles to **Lincoln, N.H. [P.O. ZIP 03251: M–F 8–5, Sa 8–12; (603) 745-8133].** *See map on previous page.* ■ *Lodging:* Mt. Liberty Lodging, Carolyn and Paul Peterson, (603) 745-3600, <www.mtlibertylodging.com>, $55–$85D (seasonal), includes shuttle to/from Trail and into town, laundry $5, pool, and river. ■ *Groceries:* Price Chopper (full-service grocery). ■ *Outfitter:* Lahout's Summit Shop, (603) 745-2882, full-service outfitter, Coleman and alcohol by the ounce; McKenzie Gear, (603) 745-3438. ■ *Other services:* The Mountain Wanderer, <www.mountainwanderer.com>, guides and maps; McKenzies, (603) 745-3438, Coleman and alcohol, open daily 9–6.

West 2.1 miles to *Camping:* Lafayette Place Campground, (603) 823-9513, with tentsites $25D, coin-operated hot showers $1, store (short-term resupply), Coleman fuel by the quart, outside soda vending machine. Park rangers hold packages mailed to Franconia Notch State Park, Lafayette Place Campground, Franconia, NH 03580. Write the date you expect to arrive on the package. Open mid-May to Columbus Day. Campground is usually filled by noon on weekends. AMC shuttle stop.

West 8 miles to Franconia; I-93 North at N.H. 18. ■ *Lodging:* Gale River Motel, 1 Main St., Franconia, N.H. 03580, (603) 823-5655 or (800) 255-7989, <www.galerivermotel.com>, <info@galerivermotel.com>, $90–$125 Jun–Sep, $95–$220 foliage season, $45–$95 in between and ski season, shuttle to and from Trail when available, seasonal pool, hot tub, Internet access, laundry, call ahead for mail drops; White Mountain Best Western, $90–$110, indoor pool, hot tub, Internet access. ■ *Groceries:* Mac's Market (long-term supply). ■ *Internet access:* library. ■ *Other services:* pizza, restaurant, bank, ATM, Concord Coach bus service.

Liberty Springs Tentsite—Privy (composting). Seven single and three double tent platforms. Overnight fee $8PP, caretaker on site. Water source is the spring on the A.T.

Franconia Ridge—In any kind of weather, this ridge walk will leave you awestruck. Beautiful views from the summit of Mt. Liberty can be reached from the A.T. *via* a side trail.

Greenleaf Hut—Visible from the summit of Mt. Lafayette, it is 1.1 miles on the Greenleaf Trail to the hut. Self-service May 1–May 30. Full service Jun 3–Oct 17.

Garfield Ridge Shelter/Campsite (2011)—Shelter sleeps 12. Privy (composting). Two single and five double tent platforms. Bear box. Overnight fee $8PP, caretaker on site. Water source is a spring at the junction to the campsite.

Galehead Hut—Rebuilt 1999–2000, with wheelchair-accessible design. Self-service May 1–May 30. Full service Jun 3–Oct 17.

Guyot Shelter/Campsite (1977)—Shelter sleeps 12. Privy (composting). Four single and two double tent platforms. Bear box. Located 0.7 mile east on Bondcliff Trail. Overnight fee $8PP, caretaker on site. Water source is a spring at the campsite.

Zealand Falls Hut—Next to beautiful falls. Full service Jun 3–Oct 17. Self-service the rest of the year except May 31–Jun 2 and Oct 18–19.

Ethan Pond Shelter/Campsite (1957)—Shelter sleeps 10. Privy (composting). Three single and two double tent platforms. Bear box. Overnight fee $8PP, caretaker on site. Water source is the inlet brook to the pond.

U.S. 302/Crawford Notch—East 1.8 miles to ■ *Camping:* Dry River Campground, (603) 374-2272, $25D, dogs welcome, coin laundry, and showers 25¢. Trail access to A.T. Mail drops accepted at P.O. Box 177, Twin Mountain, NH 03595 (Crawford Notch State Park). ■ *Shuttle*: AMC shuttle stop at Webster Cliff/A.T. Trailhead.

East 3 miles to *Camping:* Crawford Notch Campground, <www.crawfordnotch.com>, (603) 374-2779; coin-operated shower; dogs; campsites $30D, additional fee for up to 4 people; laundry for overnight guests only.

East 10 miles to the small town of **Bartlett, N.H. [P.O. ZIP 03812: M–F 8:30–1 & 1:30–4:45, Sa 8:30–12; (603) 374-2351].**

West 1 mile to the Willey House, with snack bar (ice cream, cold drinks, fudge, sandwiches) and hiker message board, tent repair and seam sealer, open daily mid-May to mid-Oct, 9–5. Mail drops accepted at P.O. Box 177, Twin Mountain, NH 03595 (Crawford Notch State Park).

West 3.7 miles to ■ *Lodging:* AMC's Highland Center, Route 302, Bretton Woods, NH 03575; (603) 278-4453, <www.outdoors.org>, limited hiker supplies, AYCE B $14, 6:30–10; *a la carte* L

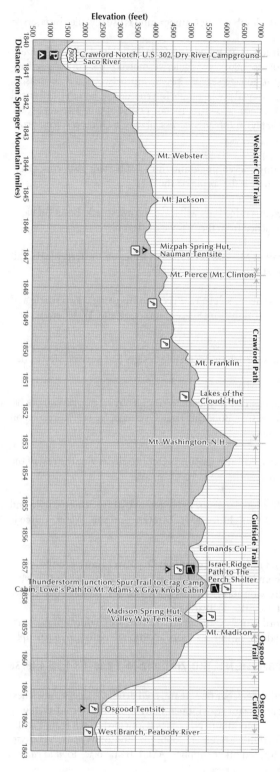

$8–$15, 10–4; 4-course D $28, reserve seat by 6; bunk room in lodge $77–$99PP, includes B/D; private room in lodge $91–$144PP, includes B/D; Shapleigh Bunkhouse, $39PP AMC member, $47PP nonmember, includes bunk, shower, towel, and B. Facilities generally are for overnight guests only. Mail drops accepted. ■ *Shuttle:* AMC shuttle stop. ■ *Other services:* Showers at the visitors center, 9–5 Memorial Day–Columbus Day, coin-operated, towel rental $2.

Presidential Range—The highest part of the Trail in New Hampshire, with 25 miles of ridge-walking between Crawford Notch and Pinkham Notch, most of which is above treeline (about 4,400 feet). The A.T. skirts many peaks, which can be reached by short side trails leading to, and often over, the summits.

Mizpah Spring Hut & Nauman Tentsite—Self-service May 1–26 and May 29–30; full-service Jun 3–Oct 17. Tentsite, five single and three double tent platforms. Composting privy. Bear box. Overnight fee $8PP. Water source for tentsite is a stream or potable water from hut (if open).

Lakes of the Clouds Hut—Constructed in 1915 at an elevation of 5,050 feet, the highest, largest, and most popular hut. Full-service Jun 3–Sep 19, with no self-service operation. "The Dungeon," a small basement shelter, is available to thru-hikers for $10, with access to hut restroom and the common area; it sleeps only 6, first-come/first-served, no reservations. "The Dungeon" is an emergency-only shelter when the hut is closed; must not be used as a destination.

Mt. Washington Auto Road/Mt. Washington—The highest peak in the Northeast (6,288 feet). Since it is also accessible by the Auto Road and a cog railroad, more touristy services are here than one might expect. *Note: In 2007, 8 hikers were arrested for mooning said cog railroad; take heed.* The summit building is operated by the New Hampshire Division of Parks and Recreation and houses Mt. Washington Observatory, <www.mountwashington.org>; Mt. Washington Museum ($2 admission); a snack bar; a post office. The state park is open daily 8–8 early May–early Oct, weather permitting. A hiker room is downstairs, with a table, restroom, and a space to rest. (Absolutely no overnight stays are allowed.) Over the years, many buildings have come and gone on the summit, including a 94-bedroom hotel completed in 1873 and destroyed by fire in 1908. The summit is under cloud cover about 55 percent of the time. Average summertime high is 52 degrees, and the average wintertime high is 15 degrees. On April 12, 1934, an on-land wind speed of 231 mph was recorded, which still stands as the world's record. If you see a staff meteorologist, ask about the "Century Club." The upper plateau is home to large grassy areas, strewn with rocks but known as "lawns." These lawns hold many species of plants and animals otherwise found only on high mountain peaks and in tundra areas hundreds of miles to the north.

Mt. Washington, N.H. [P.O. ZIP 03589: (603) 846-5570]—The post office in the summit building is *not* recommended as a mail drop. Its hours are limited, and it caters to those who visit the summit and desire to have the distinguished Mt. Washington postmark; since there is little space for storing mail drops, they may be redirected to other New Hampshire post offices, well off the Trail.

East 8 miles *via* Auto Road to N.H. 16.

Tuckerman Ravine Trail—A steep, 4.2-mile route from Mt. Washington to Pinkham Notch. In bad weather, you may wish to use this trail to get below treeline and bypass the exposed northern loop of the Presidential Range, but this precarious route is no picnic in icy conditions.

Hermit Lake Shelters—At the base of the Tuckerman Ravine bowl, 2 miles downhill, with some steep rock- and boulder-scrambling from the summit; 8 lean-tos, 3 tent platforms, $15PP; pets are not permitted overnight in the shelters; caretaker year-round.

Edmands Col—Just down to the east in the col is a reliable spring and the site of the former Edmands Col emergency shelter. Also, look for a bronze tablet in memory of J. Rayner Edmands, who was instrumental in the construction of most of the graded paths through the northern Presidentials.

Randolph Mountain Club—RMC maintains the 2.2 miles from Edmands Col north of Mt. Washington to Madison Spring Hut; <www.randolphmountainclub.org>.

Crag Camp/Randolph Mountain Club (RMC) Cabins and Shelters—Randolph Mountain Club was named an A.T. maintaining club by ATC in Oct 2010. In addition to the 2.2 miles of the A.T. north of Edmands Col, RMC maintains a network of 100 miles of hiking trails, principally on the northern slopes of Mounts Madison, Adams, and Jefferson in the Presidential Range of the White Mountain National Forest and on the Crescent Range in the town of Randolph. The RMC maintains several cabins and shelters below treeline in the Presidential Range that are often used by A.T. hikers seeking shelter from the exposed ridgeline. Crag Camp and Gray Knob are cabins. The Perch and the Log Cabin are lean-tos. All camps are available to the public on a first-come, first-served basis. If a site is full, the caretaker may ask visitors to move to another RMC facility, if space is available. Groups are limited to 10. To maintain serenity, cellular phones may not be used at any of the camps. Gas stoves at both cabins are available to the public; at all other times, users must bring their own stoves. Year-round, the weather is far harsher and colder here than "below the notches." RMC

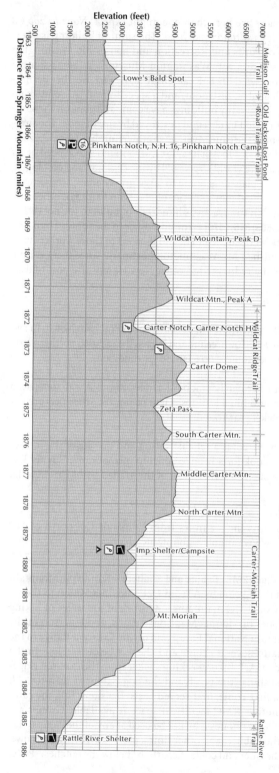

relies on visitors to carry out their trash and help keep the cabin and woods clean. To support the caretakers' wages and maintain the camps, fees are charged on a per-night basis. If the caretaker is absent, please mail fees to: Treasurer, RMC, Randolph, NH 03570.

The Perch (1948)—Shelter sleeps 8. Privy. Four tent platforms, $7PP fee. Water source is crossed *en route* to the shelter.

RMC The Perch (1948)—Shelter sleeps 8. Privy. Four tent platforms, $10PP fee. Water source is crossed *en route* to the shelter.

RMC Crag Camp Cabin (1909/1993)— Sleeps 20. Water is available from a spring, approximately 0.25 mile west on the Gray Knob Trail. Caretaker in Jul–Aug; $20PP.

RMC Gray Knob Cabin (1905/1989)— Sleeps 15. Water is available from a spring, approximately 0.25 east on the Gray Knob Trail. Resident caretaker year-round; $20PP.

RMC Log Cabin (1985)— Sleeps 10. Privy. Water near shelter. Located 1 mile below Gray Knob Cabin. This is a shelter, not a cabin as the name may suggest. No fires permitted; $10PP.

Madison Spring Hut—Located in a col 0.5 mile south of the summit of Mt. Madison. Full service Jun 3–Sep 26, with no self-service operation.

Valley Way and Osgood Tentsites— These two no-fee U.S. Forest Service tentsites, below treeline on Mt. Madison, are often used by hikers starting or finishing the traverse of the Presidential Range. Valley Way Tentsite is off the A.T., 0.6 mile west of Madison Springs Hut, with two large tent platforms and a privy. Osgood Tentsite is 3 miles north of the hut, along the A.T., and has three tentsites, privy, and spring.

N.H. 16/Pinkham Notch—Pinkham Notch Visitors Center; front desk, (603) 466-2721. AMC's New Hampshire headquarters, located on the A.T., offers a store with limited hiker supplies, restroom, coin-operated showers (open 24 hours), AMC shuttle stop, and Concord Coach bus service (see below). The center holds packages sent to AMC Visitors Center, c/o Front Desk, N.H. 16, Gorham, NH 03581. ■ *Restaurant:* Cafeteria with AYCE $12 B, deli L (not AYCE) 9:30–4, trail L $13, $23 D (thru-hikers get member rates). ■ *Lodging:* Joe Dodge Lodge, (603) 466-2727, $62 includes B/D. Prices can change; contact AMC for the most current rates.

East 13–16 miles to Intervale, N.H. ■ *Outfitter:* Ragged Mountain Equipment, (603) 356-3042, open daily, backpacking gear and repair service. ■ *Lodging:* Cranmore Mountain Lodge, 859 Kearsage Rd., Kearsarge, NH 03847; (603) 356-2044, $79D includes B, seasonal heated pool, spa, mail drops accepted. ■ *Other services:* Peter Limmer & Sons Shop, (603) 356-5378, located on N.H. 16A, home of legendary hand-made hiking boots, will repair many brands of boots and hiking gear with priority to thru-hikers; closed Su.

East 18 miles to North Conway, N.H., a tourist town with most major services, including several outfitters, a supermarket, cobbler, coin laundry, bank, ATM, hospital, veterinarian, pharmacy, one-hour photo, movie theater, hotels, and restaurants.

West 2 miles to the Wildcat Mountain Gondola, daily mid-Jun to mid-Oct, 10–4:45, and offers rides to and from the A.T. on the top of Wildcat Mountain; $15 round-trip, $7.50 one way; special round-trip with lunch (deli) available for $22.

West 11 miles to Gorham, N.H. (see below).

Concord Coach Bus Service—Service between Boston and Pinkham Notch, as well as Gorham, Berlin, and Conway, (800) 639-3317, <www.concordcoachlines.com>. Departs Pinkham Notch daily at 8:07 a.m. and arrives at Boston South Station at 12:20 p.m. The bus to Pinkham Notch departs Boston at 4:15 p.m. and arrives at Pinkham Notch at 8:15 p.m. One-way, $33; round-trip, $62.

Carter Notch Hut—The northernmost hut, located on the banks of two small lakes in Carter Notch. It is the original hut, built in 1914. Full service Jun 3–Sep 19; self-service rest of year except May 31–Jun 2 and Sep 20–21.

Imp Shelter/Campsite (1981)—Shelter sleeps 16. Privy (composting). Four single, one double tent platform. Bear box. Overnight fee $8PP, caretaker on site. Water is stream near shelter.

Rattle River Shelter (1980s)—Sleeps 8. Privy. Shelter built by USFS. Water source is Rattle River.

U.S. 2—*Hostel:* Adjacent to Rattle River Trailhead, White Mountains Lodge & Hostel, 592 State Route 2, Shelburne, NH 03581; (603) 466-5049, <www.whitemountainslodge-andhostel.com>, $33PP with B, fresh linens, laundry, Internet, microwave, refrigerator, fuel, shuttles to town, slackpacking from Pinkham with shuttle, smoking outdoors, credit cards accepted, no pets, rates and services may vary; all mail drops accepted.

West 1.8 miles to *Hostel:* The Birches Loft at White Birches Camping Park, owners Bob/Janet Langlands, 218 State Rt. 2, Shelburne, NH 03581; (603) 466-2022, <www.whitebirches-campingpark.com>, <whbirch@ncia.net>; May 1–end of Oct, tentsites $14s, hostel $15s per night, private cabins. Hot showers and laundry for guests only, limited resupply, microwave, refrigerator, dogs welcome, local restaurants deliver, swimming pool, mail drops accepted for guests, limited shuttle to town/trailhead for guests only, slackpacking, Visa/MasterCard/Discover.

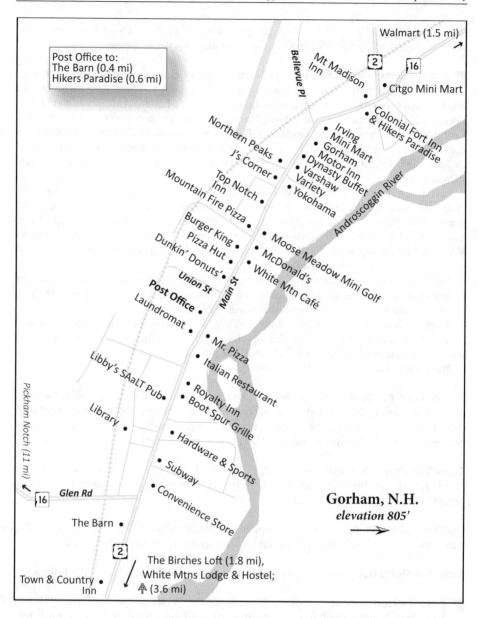

Post Office to:
The Barn (0.4 mi)
Hikers Paradise (0.6 mi)

Walmart (1.5 mi)

Bellevue Pl

Mt Madison
Inn

Citgo Mini Mart

Colonial Fort Inn
& Hikers Paradise

Northern Peaks

Irving
Mini Mart

Gorham
Motor Inn

Dynasty Buffet

Varshaw
Variety

J's Corner

Top Notch
Inn

Mountain Fire Pizza

Yokohama

Moose Meadow Mini Golf

Androscoggin River

Burger King

Pizza Hut

McDonald's

Dunkin' Donuts

White Mtn Café

Union St

Post Office

Main St

Laundromat

Mr. Pizza

Italian Restaurant

Libby's SAaLT Pub

Royalty Inn

Boot Spur Grille

Library

Pickham Notch (11 mi)

Hardware & Sports

Subway

Glen Rd

Convenience Store

Gorham, N.H.
elevation 805'

The Barn

Town & Country
Inn

The Birches Loft (1.8 mi),
White Mtns Lodge & Hostel;
(3.6 mi)

West 3.6 miles to **Gorham, N.H. [P.O. ZIP 03581: M–F 8:30–5, Sa 8:30–12; (603) 466-2182].** The postmaster requests that all packages include your legal name and ETA; use bold letters/colors and have ID; can knock on door inside lobby to pick up mail drops after hours. ■ *Hostels:* Hikers Paradise Hostel at Colonial Fort Inn, 370 Main St., (603) 466-2732, <www.hikersparadise.com>, <paradise@hikersparadise.com>; owners Mary Ann and Bruno Janicki, 3 hostel units, $23PP, each with bath, kitchen, phone, linen, and heat; motel rooms available; no pets, no mail drops; limited shuttle service to Trailhead, laundry, Coleman fuel and denatured alcohol; B at motel restaurant. The Barn Hostel, 55 Main St., (603) 466-2271, <theskilift@aol.com>, at Libby House B&B offers room in the hostel, $20PP; WiFi,microwave, TV, shower, shuttles, no pets, $5 laundry; free mail drops for guests ($15 nonguests). ■ *Lodging:* Libby

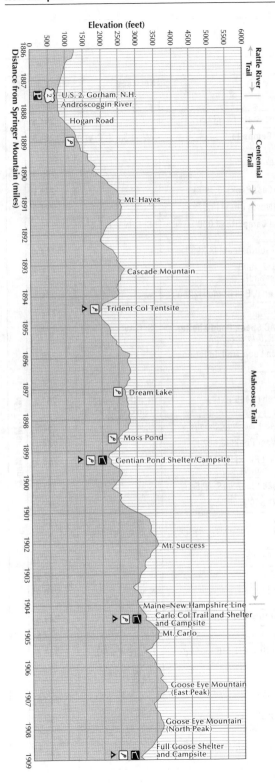

House B&B, (603) 466-2271 or (603) 723-6129, beginning at $70S, $85D, includes continental B; Royalty Inn, (603) 466-3312, <www.royaltyinn.com>, $83S, $89D; Northern Peaks, (603) 466-3374, $46 per room, dogs welcome, a/c, pool; Town & Country Inn, U.S. 2, (603) 466-3315, $50–60S, $74–84D, $6EAP, pets welcome, mail drops accepted. ■ *Groceries:* Super Walmart (long-term resupply) located 1.5 miles north of town on N.H. 16. ■ *Restaurants:* Mr. Pizza, J's Corner, and various fast-food options. ■ *Outfitter:* Gorham Hardware/Sports Center, (603) 466-2312, boots and hiker gear, Coleman fuel and alcohol by the ounce. ■ *Internet access:* public library, M, W, F, 10–7, Tu, Th 10–8, closed weekends, located near railroad, nominal fee. ■ *Other services:* Trail Angels Hiker Services, (978) 855-9227, <www.trailangelshikerservices.com>, shuttles, mail drops, guide service, *etc.*; coin laundry; bank with ATM; dentist; free concerts on the common Tu evenings; TriCounty CAP Transit, local Berlin–Gorham shuttle bus, (888) 997-20920, <www.tccap.org>, no Su service, stops at Walmart.

West 8 miles to small city of Berlin, N.H., and the Androscoggin Valley Hospital.

Trident Col Tentsite—Four tent pads. Privy (composting). Water source is an intermittent spring on a side trail.

Gentian Pond Shelter/Campsite (1974)—Shelter sleeps 14. Privy (composting). Three single and one double tent platform. Water source is the inlet brook of Gentian Pond.

Maine

Miles from Springer	Fr Last Point	Features	Services	Miles from Katahdin	M A P
1,907.4	1.3	New Hampshire–Maine State Line (2,972')		281.8	
1,907.9	0.5	**Carlo Col Shelter** and **Campsite** (2,945')...5.7mS; 4.7mN Carlo Col Trail	W–0.3m S, C, w	281.3	
1,908.3	0.4	Mt. Carlo (3,565')		280.9	
1,910.1	1.8	Goose Eye Mountain (East Peak) (3,790')		279.1	
1,911.3	1.2	Goose Eye Mountain (North Peak) (3,675')		277.9	
1,912.3	1.0	**Full Goose Shelter** and **Campsite** (3,030') ...4.7mS; 5.1mN	S, C, w	276.9	
1,912.8	0.5	Fulling Mill Mountain (South Peak) (3,395')		276.4	
1,913.8	1.0	Mahoosuc Notch Trail (2,400') Mahoosuc Notch (west end)	w	275.4	
1,914.9	1.1	Mahoosuc Notch (east end), Bull Branch (2,150')	w	274.3	
1,916.5	1.6	Mahoosuc Arm (3,770')		272.7	
1,917.4	0.9	Speck Pond Trail, +AMC **Speck Pond Shelter** and **Campsite** (3,500')...5.1mS; 6.9mN	S, C, w	271.8	
1,918.5	1.1	Old Speck Trail, Grafton Loop Trail Junction (3,985')		270.7	
1,920.9	2.4	Brook (2,500')	w	268.3	
1,922.0	1.1	Maine 26, Grafton Notch (1,495')	R, P (E–5.5m C; 13m C, g, M, sh, f)	267.2	
1,924.3	2.3	**Baldpate Lean-to** (2,645')...6.9mS; 3.5mN	S, w	264.9	
1,925.1	0.8	Baldpate Mountain (West Peak) (3,662')		264.1	
1,926.0	0.9	Baldpate Mountain (East Peak) (3,810') Grafton Loop Trail Junction		263.2	
1,927.8	1.8	**Frye Notch Lean-to** (2,280')...3.5mS; 10.5mN	S, w	261.4	
1,931.5	3.7	Dunn Notch and Falls (1,350')	w	257.7	
1,932.3	0.8	East B Hill Road (1,485') **Andover, Maine 04216**	R, P, C (E–8m PO, H, G, L, M, f; 11m H)	256.9	
1,934.1	1.8	Surplus Pond (2,050')...outlet	w	255.1	
1,937.0	2.9	Wyman Mountain (2,920')		252.2	
1,938.3	1.3	**Hall Mountain Lean-to** (2,635') ...10.5mS; 12.8mN	S, w	250.9	
1,939.7	1.4	Sawyer Notch, Sawyer Brook (1,095')...ford	w	249.5	
1,940.6	0.9	Moody Mountain (2,440')		248.6	
1,942.4	1.8	South Arm Road, Black Brook (1,410')...ford **Andover, Maine 04216**	R, w (E–9m PO, H, G, L, M, f; 12m H) (W–3.5m C, G, cl, sh)	246.8	
1,945.2	2.8	Old Blue Mountain (3,600')		244.0	
1,948.4	3.2	Bemis Stream Trail (3,350')		240.8	
1,949.4	1.0	Bemis Range (West Peak) (3,580')		239.8	
1,951.1	1.7	**Bemis Mountain Lean-to** (2,790') ...12.8mS; 8.3mN	S, w	238.1	

MATC Maine Map 7

Miles from Springer	Fr Last Point	Features	Services	Miles from Katahdin	M A P
1,954.9	3.8	Bemis Stream (1,495')...*ford*	w	234.3	
1,955.7	0.8	Maine 17 (2,200') **Oquossoc, Maine 04964**	R (W–11m PO, G, M, f)	233.5	
1,957.3	1.6	Moxie Pond (2,400')	w	231.9	
1,959.1	1.8	Long Pond (2,330')...*sandy beach*	w	230.1	
1,959.4	0.3	**Sabbath Day Pond Lean-to** (2,390') *...8.3mS; 11.2mN*	S, w	229.8	
1,964.0	4.6	Little Swift River Pond Campsite (2,460')	C, w	225.2	
1,966.7	2.7	South Pond (2,174')	w	222.5	
1,968.8	2.1	Maine 4 (1,700') **Rangeley, Maine 04970**	R, P (W–0.3m L; 9m PO, H, G, L, M, O, D, cl, f; 15m Oquossoc)	220.4	
1,968.9	0.1	Sandy River (1,595')	w	220.3	
1,970.6	1.7	**Piazza Rock Lean-to** (2,080')...*11.2mS; 8.9mN*	S, C, w	218.6	
1,972.5	1.9	Eddy Pond (2,616')	w	216.7	
1,974.5	2.0	Saddleback Mountain (4,120')		214.7	
1,976.1	1.6	The Horn (4,020')		213.1	MATC Maine Map 6
1,976.8	0.7	Reddington Stream Campsite (3,170')	C, w	212.4	
1,978.1	1.3	Saddleback Junior (3,655')		211.1	
1,978.5	0.4	Stream (3,200')	w	210.7	
1,979.5	1.0	**Poplar Ridge Lean-to** (2,920')...*8.9mS; 8mN*	S, w	209.7	
1,982.2	2.7	Orbeton Stream (1,550')...*ford*	w	207.0	
1,985.3	3.1	Lone Mountain (3,260')		203.9	
1,986.4	1.1	Mt. Abraham Trail (3,184')		202.8	
1,987.5	1.1	**Spaulding Mountain Lean-to** (3,140') *...8mS; 18.6mN*	S, w	201.7	
1,988.3	0.8	Spaulding Mountain (4,000')		200.9	
1,989.0	0.7	Bronze Plaque (3,500')...*1937 completion of the final two miles of the A.T.*		200.2	
1,990.4	1.4	Sugarloaf Mountain Trail (3,540')	E–0.3m w; 0.6m to summit	198.8	
1,992.6	2.2	South Branch Carrabassett River (2,100')...*ford*	w	196.6	
1,992.7	0.1	Caribou Valley Road (2,220')	R, P	196.5	
1,993.7	1.0	Crocker Cirque (2,710')	w (E–0.2m C)	195.5	
1,994.8	1.1	South Crocker Mountain (4,040')		194.4	
1,995.8	1.0	North Crocker Mountain (4,228')		193.4	
2,001.0	5.2	Maine 27 (1,450') **Stratton, Maine 04982**	R, P (E–2m G) (W–5m PO, H, G, L, M, cl, f)	188.2	
2,001.8	0.8	Stratton Brook Pond Road (1,250')	R, P	187.4	MATC Maine Map 5
2,002.0	0.2	Stratton Brook (1,230')	w	187.2	
2,002.9	0.9	Cranberry Stream Campsite (1,350')	C, w	186.3	
2,004.2	1.3	Bigelow Range Trail, Cranberry Pond (2,400')	W–0.2m w	185.0	
2,005.9	1.7	Horns Pond Trail (3,200')		183.3	
2,006.1	0.2	**Horns Pond Lean-tos** (3,160')...*18.6mS; 10.2mN*	S, C, w	183.1	

Miles from Springer	Fr Last Point	Features	Services	Miles from Katahdin	M A P
2,006.6	0.5	South Horn (3,831')		182.6	
2,008.7	2.1	Bigelow Mountain (West Peak) (4,145')		180.5	
2,009.0	0.3	Bigelow Col, Fire Warden's Trail (3,850') Avery Memorial Campsite	C, w	180.2	
2,009.2	0.2	Spring (3,900')	w	180.0	
2,009.4	0.2	Bigelow Mountain; Avery Peak (4,090')		179.8	
2,011.3	1.9	Safford Brook Trail (2,260')		177.9	
2,011.4	0.1	Safford Notch (2,230')	E–0.3m C, w	177.8	
2,014.6	3.2	Little Bigelow Mountain (east end) (3,010')		174.6	
2,016.3	1.7	**Little Bigelow Lean-to** (1,760') ...*10.2mS; 7.7mN*	S, C, w	172.9	MATC Maine Map 5
2,017.7	1.4	East Flagstaff Road (1,200')	R	171.5	
2,017.8	0.1	Bog Brook Road, Flagstaff Lake (1,150')...*inlet*	R, P, w	171.4	
2,018.8	1.0	Campsite (1,210')	C, w, privy	170.4	
2,020.5	1.7	Long Falls Dam Road (1,225')	R	168.7	
2,022.2	1.7	Roundtop Mountain (1,760')		167.0	
2,023.3	1.1	West Carry Pond (west side) (1,320')	w	165.9	
2,024.0	0.7	**West Carry Pond Lean-to** (1,340') ...*7.7mS; 10mN*	S, w	165.2	
2,024.7	0.7	West Carry Pond (east side) (1,320')	w	164.5	
2,026.6	1.9	Sandy Stream, Middle Carry Pond (1,229')... *inlet*	w	162.6	
2,028.1	1.5	East Carry Pond (north end) (1,237')	w	161.1	
2,029.8	1.7	Logging Road (1,300')	R	159.4	
2,030.5	0.7	North Branch of Carrying Place Stream (1,200')	w	158.7	
2,034.0	3.5	**Pierce Pond Lean-to** (1,150')...*10mS: 9.7mN*	S, w	155.2	
2,034.4	0.4	Trail to Harrison's Pierce Pond Camps (1,100')	R (E–0.3m L, M, w)	154.8	
2,037.7	3.3	Kennebec River (490')...*ferry*	w	151.5	
2,038.0	0.3	U.S. 201 (520') **Caratunk, Maine 04925**	R, P (E–0.3m PO; 1m H, G, L, sh, cl; 16.5m G, L, M, cl) (W–2m C, L, M, sh, cl; 7m G, f)	151.2	
2,040.7	2.7	Holly Brook (900')	w	148.5	MATC Maine Map 4
2,043.3	2.6	Boise-Cascade Logging Road (1,400')	R, P	145.9	
2,043.7	0.4	**Pleasant Pond Lean-to** (1,320')...*9.7mS; 9mN*	S, w	145.5	
2,045.0	1.3	Pleasant Pond Mountain (2,470')		144.2	
2,049.9	4.9	Moxie Pond (south end) (970')		139.3	
2,052.7	2.8	**Bald Mountain Brook Lean-to** (1,280') ...*9mS; 4.1mN*	S, w	136.5	
2,054.7	2.0	Moxie Bald Mountain (2,629')		134.5	
2,056.8	2.1	**Moxie Bald Lean-to** (1,220')...*4.1mS; 8.9mN*	S, w	132.4	
2,058.9	2.1	Bald Mountain Pond (1,213')...*outlet*	w	130.3	
2,062.6	3.7	West Branch Piscataquis River (900')...*ford*	w	126.6	

Miles from Springer	Fr Last Point	Features	Services	Miles from Katahdin	MAP
2,065.7	3.1	**Horseshoe Canyon Lean-to** (880')...*8.9mS; 12mN*	S, w	123.5	
2,068.0	2.3	East Branch Piscataquis River (650')...*ford*	w	121.2	
2,068.4	0.4	Shirley–Blanchard Road (850')	R, P	120.8	MATC Maine Map 4
2,071.4	3.0	Blue–blaze to Pleasant St., Monson (900')	C (E–0.3m R, P; 2m Monson)	117.8	
2,074.7	3.3	Maine 15 (1,215') **Monson, Maine 04464**	R, P (E–4m PO, H, G, L, M, cl, sh, f) (W–10m G, L, M, O, D, V, f)	114.5	
2,074.8	0.1	Spectacle Pond (1,163')...*outlet*	w	114.4	
2,075.9	1.1	Bell Pond (1,278')	w	113.3	
2,076.6	0.7	Lily Pond (1,130')	w	112.6	
2,077.7	1.1	**Leeman Brook Lean-to** (1,060')...*12mS; 7.4mN*	S, w	111.5	
2,078.5	0.8	North Pond (1,000')...*outlet*		110.7	
2,081.3	2.8	Little Wilson Falls (850')		107.9	
2,081.5	0.2	Little Wilson Stream (750')...*ford*	w	107.7	
2,084.4	2.9	Big Wilson Stream (600')...*ford*	w	104.8	
2,084.7	0.3	Montreal, Maine & Atlantic RR Tracks (850')		104.5	
2,085.1	0.4	**Wilson Valley Lean-to** (1,000')...*7.4mS; 4.7mN*	S, w	104.1	
2,089.0	3.9	Long Pond Stream (620')...*ford*	w	100.2	MATC Maine Map 3
2,089.8	0.8	**Long Pond Lean-to** (930')...*4.7mS; 4.4mN*	S, w	99.4	
2,092.9	3.1	Barren Mountain (2,660')		96.3	
2,093.8	0.9	**Cloud Pond Lean-to** (2,420')...*4.4mS; 7.3mN*	E–0.4m S, w	95.4	
2,095.9	2.1	Fourth Mountain (2,380')		93.3	
2,098.4	2.5	Third Mountain, Monument Cliff (1,920')		90.8	
2,099.0	0.6	West Chairback Pond Side Trail (1,770')	w	90.2	
2,100.3	1.3	Columbus Mountain (2,325')		88.9	
2,100.7	0.4	**Chairback Gap Lean-to** (2,000') ...*7.3mS; 9.9mN*	S, w	88.5	
2,101.2	0.5	Chairback Mountain (2,180')		88.0	
2,103.4	2.2	East Chairback Pond Side Trail (1,630')	W–0.2m w	85.8	
2,104.6	1.2	Katahdin Iron Works Road (750')	R (E–20m C, G) (W–1.5m L; 6.1m L)	84.6	
2,105.1	0.5	West Branch Pleasant River (680')...*ford*	w	84.1	
2,105.4	0.3	The Hermitage (695')	(E–0.7m C, w)	83.8	
2,106.4	1.0	Gulf Hagas Trail (950')	w	82.8	
2,107.1	0.7	Gulf Hagas Cut-off Trail (1,050')	w	82.1	MATC Maine Map 2
2,110.6	3.5	**Carl A. Newhall Lean-to** (1,860') ...*9.9mS; 7.2mN*	S, w	78.6	
2,111.5	0.9	Gulf Hagas Mountain (2,683')		77.7	
2,112.4	0.9	Sidney Tappan Campsite (2,425')	C (E–0.2m w)	76.8	
2,113.1	0.7	West Peak (3,178')		76.1	
2,114.7	1.6	Hay Mountain (3,244')		74.5	
2,115.3	0.6	White Brook Trail (3,125')		73.9	

Miles from Springer	Fr Last Point	Features	Services	Miles from Katahdin	M A P
2,116.4	1.1	White Cap Mountain (3,650')		72.8	
2,117.8	1.4	**Logan Brook Lean-to** (2,480')...*7.2mS; 3.6mN*	S, w	71.4	
2,119.4	1.6	West Branch Ponds Road (1,650')	R	69.8	
2,121.4	2.0	**East Branch Lean-to** (1,225')...*3.6mS; 8.1mN*	S, w	67.8	
2,121.7	0.3	East Branch Pleasant River (1,200')...*ford*	w	67.5	
2,123.3	1.6	Mountain View Pond (1,597')...*outlet*	w	65.9	
2,123.6	0.3	Spring (1,580')	w	65.6	
2,124.9	1.3	Little Boardman Mountain (1,980')		64.3	
2,126.3	1.4	Kokadjo-B Pond Road (1,380')	R, P	62.9	
2,127.2	0.9	Crawford Pond (1,240')...*outlet*	w	62.0	MATC Maine Map 2
2,129.5	2.3	**Cooper Brook Falls Lean-to** (880') ...*8.1mS; 11.4mN*	S, C, w	59.7	
2,133.2	3.7	Jo-Mary Road (625')	R, P, C, w (E–6m C, G, cl, sh; 17m Maine 11)	56.0	
2,136.1	2.9	Mud Pond (508')..*outlet*	w	53.1	
2,137.4	1.3	Antlers Campsite (500')	C, w	51.8	
2,139.1	1.7	Sand Beach, Lower Jo-Mary Lake (580')	w	50.1	
2,140.9	1.8	**Potaywadjo Spring Lean-to** (710') ...*11.4mS; 10.1mN*	S, w	48.3	
2,141.5	0.6	Pemadumcook Lake (580')...*southwest shore*	w	47.7	
2,143.2	1.7	Mahar Tote Logging Road (580')		46.0	
2,145.2	2.0	Nahmakanta Stream Campsite (600')	C, w	44.0	
2,146.7	1.5	Tumbledown Dick Trail (625')		42.5	
2,148.4	1.7	Nahmakanta Lake (south end) (650')	R, w	40.8	
2,151.0	2.6	**Wadleigh Stream Lean-to** (685") ...*10.1mS; 8.1mN*	S, w	38.2	
2,152.9	1.9	Nesuntabunt Mountain (1,520')		36.3	
2,155.3	2.4	Crescent Pond (west end) (980')	w	33.9	
2,156.7	1.4	Pollywog Stream (682')...*logging road, bridge*	R, P, w	32.5	
2,159.1	2.4	**Rainbow Stream Lean-to** (1,020') ...*8.1mS; 11.5mN*	S, C, w	30.1	
2,161.1	2.0	Rainbow Lake (west end) (1,080')...*sidetrail*	w	28.1	
2,162.9	1.8	Rainbow Spring Campsite (1,100')	C, w	26.3	MATC Maine Map 1
2,166.3	3.4	Rainbow Lake (east end) (980')	w	22.9	
2,168.1	1.8	Rainbow Ledges (1,517')		21.1	
2,170.6	2.5	**Hurd Brook Lean-to** (710')...*11.5mS; 13.7mN*	S, w	18.6	
2,174.0	3.4	Golden Road (Greenville–Millinocket Road) (600')	R	15.2	
2,174.1	0.1	Abol Bridge over West Branch of Penobscot River, junction with International A.T., Abol Bridge Campground and Store (588') **Millinocket, Maine 04462**	R, P, C, G, sh (E–20m PO, H, G, L, M, D, O, cl)	15.1	
2,174.8	0.7	Abol Stream, Baxter Park Boundary (620')		14.4	
2,174.9	0.1	Hiker Kiosk, registration for "The Birches Campsite"; Blueberry Ledges Trail junction (620')		14.3	
2,175.2	0.3	Katahdin Stream (620')	w	14.0	

Miles from Springer	Fr Last Point	Features	Services	Miles from Katahdin	M A P
2,178.2	3.0	Pine Point (640')	w	11.0	
2,178.7	0.5	Lower Fork Nesowadnehunk Stream (630')...*ford*	w	10.5	
2,179.6	0.9	Upper Fork Nesowadnehunk Stream (800')...*ford*	w	9.6	
2,180.4	0.8	Big Niagra Falls (900')	w	8.8	
2,181.7	1.3	+Daicey Pond Campground Road; Ranger Station (1,100')	R, P (E–0.1m L, w)	7.5	
2,183.9	2.2	Cross Perimeter Road (Tote Road) (1,070')	R	5.3	
2,184.0	0.1	+Katahdin Stream Campground, Ranger Station; (1,070')+**The Birches Campsite**... *13.7mS*	R, P, S, C, w (E–0.25m S, C)	5.2	MATC Maine Map 1
2,185.0	1.0	The Owl Trail (1,570')		4.2	
2,185.2	0.2	Katahdin Stream Falls (1,550')	w	4.0	
2,186.8	1.6	Hunt Spur, Treeline at Base of "The Boulders" (3,400')		2.4	
2,187.6	0.8	Gateway to Tablelands (4,600')		1.6	
2,188.2	0.6	Thoreau Spring (4,627')	w	1.0	
2,189.2	1.0	Katahdin, Baxter Peak (5,268')...*sign, plaque, cairn*		0.0	

+ Fee charged, ~ Northbound long-distance hikers only at The Birches

Hikers in Maine encounter approximately 282 miles of lakes, bogs, moose, loons, hand-over-hand climbs, and a 100-mile wilderness that is neither 100 miles nor truly a wilderness. It is a mystical, magical place to begin or end your A.T. journey.

No camping is allowed above treeline on the A.T. in Maine.

Carlo Col Shelter and Campsite (1976)—Shelter sleeps 8. Off trail 0.3 mile west. Privy (composting). Two single and one double tent platforms. Bear box. Water source is a spring left of the lean-to.

Full Goose Shelter and Campsite (1978)—Shelter sleeps 8. Privy (composting). Many hikers choose to stay here before or after Mahoosuc Notch. Three single and one double tent platforms. Bear box. Water source is stream behind shelter.

Mahoosuc Notch—Famous for ice in deep crevices throughout the year. Many call this scramble under, around, over, and between boulders the most difficult mile on the Trail.

Speck Pond Shelter and Campsite (1968)—Shelter sleeps 8. Privy (composting). Three single and three double tent platforms. Cookstoves only. Bear box. Overnight fee $8PP. Speck Pond is the highest body of water in Maine. Water source is a spring on the blue-blazed trail behind the caretaker's yurt.

Maine 26/Grafton Notch—Difficult hitch, very light traffic. **East** 5 miles to *Camping:* Grafton Notch Camp Ground, 1471 Bear River Rd., Newry, ME 04261, (207) 824-2292, <www.campgrafton.com>, wooded sites with fire pit and picnic table, hot showers and flush toilets, $25 per site (up to 2, $5EAP), shower only $5, leashed dogs, open mid-May through Columbus Day.

East 13 miles to Stony Brook Recreation, 3036 Main St., Hanover, ME 04237, (207) 824-2836, convenience store & restaurant; tentsites, lean-tos, showers, laundry, mini-golf, shuffleboard, zip line, pool (in season), canoe & kayak rentals, shuttles with reservation. Open year round.

Maine Appalachian Trail Club—MATC maintains the 267.2 miles from Grafton Notch to Katahdin. Correspondence should be sent to MATC Box 283, Augusta, ME 04332-0283; <www.matc.org>.

Baldpate Lean-to (1995)—Sleeps 8. Privy. Water source is a spring behind the lean-to.

Frye Notch Lean-to (1983)—Sleeps 6. Privy. Water from Frye Brook in front of the lean-to.

East B Hill Road/Andover—**East** 8 miles to **Andover, Maine [P.O. ZIP 04216: M–F 8:30–1:30 & 2–4:30, Sa 8:30–12:15; (207) 392-4571]**. Andover also can be reached *via* South Arm Road, 9.5 miles north on the A.T. Neither road has much traffic. ■ *Hostel:* Pine Ellis Hiking Lodge, 20 Pine St. (P.O. Box 12), (207) 392-4161, <www.pineellislodging.com>; hiker-friendly hosts Ilene Trainor and David Rousselin; located near P.O. and stores; large shared room in house or bunk-house in backyard $25PP, private rooms $45S, $65D, $75T, all stays include shower, laundry (loaner clothes), morning coffee, house privileges, Internet/WiFi, CATV, and use of kitchen. For a fee: shuttle to/from Trailhead ($6), slackpacking from Grafton Notch to Rangeley, denatured alcohol, and Coleman. Credit cards accepted; mail drops accepted. Also, camping cabin 3 miles from lodge, Paul's A.T. Camp, accommodates up to 4 for $60, EAP extra, includes shower and round-trip shuttles from lodge ■ *Groceries:* Andover General Store & Diner, 5 a.m.–9 p.m., B/L/D, ATM, Heet; Mills Market, 7 days, 5 a.m.–9 p.m. (10 p.m. Sa–Su), resupply, deli, pizza. ■ *Internet access:* Andover Public Library, Tu–Th, Sa 1–4:30. ■ *Other services:* Little Red Hen Diner & Bakery, Tu–Th 6:30–2, F–Sa 6 a.m.–8 p.m. (Sa AYCE pizza), Su 7–2, WiFi; massage therapist Donna Gifford, (207) 357-5686.

   East 11 miles to East Andover and *Lodging:* The Cabin, (207) 392-1333, owned by Margie and Earle Towne (Honey and Bear); log cabin with bunkroom and private room. Reservations only; alumni always welcome.

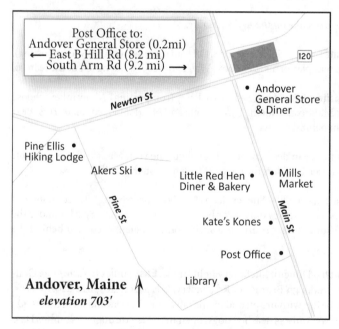

Post Office to:
Andover General Store (0.2mi)
← East B Hill Rd (8.2 mi)
    South Arm Rd (9.2 mi) →

120

Newton St

• Andover
  General Store
  & Diner

Pine Ellis •
Hiking Lodge

Akers Ski •

Little Red Hen •
Diner & Bakery

• Mills
  Market

Pine St

Kate's Kones •

Main St

Post Office •

Andover, Maine   Library •
elevation 703'

Hall Mountain Lean-to (1978)—Sleeps 6. Privy. Water source is a spring south of the lean-to on the A.T.; might have to walk downstream.

South Arm Road— **East** 9 miles to Andover, Maine (see above).
   West 3.5 miles to *Camping:* South Arm Campground, (207) 364-5155, open mid-May to mid-Sep; $15 per site, up to 4. Campstore (short-term resupply); showers 25¢; coin laundry; canoe, kay-ak, and boat rentals. No credit cards. Packages accepted at P.O. Box 310, Andover, ME 04216.

Bemis Mountain Lean-to (1988)—Sleeps 8. Privy. Water source is a small spring to the left of the lean-to.

Maine 17—West 11 miles to **Oquossoc, Maine [P.O. ZIP 04964: M–F 8–10 & 2:15–4:15, Sa 9–12; (207) 864-3685].** ■ *Groceries:* Carry Road Country Store (short-term resupply), with deli and bakery. ■ *Restaurants:* Gingerbread House, B/L/D with vegetarian specials; Four Seasons Café, daily 11–11, serves Mexican and vegetarian specialties, L/D.

Sabbath Day Pond Lean-to (1993)—Sleeps 8. Privy. A sandy beach, 0.3 mile south on the A.T., provides an excellent swimming opportunity. Water source is Sabbath Day Pond in front of the lean-to.

Little Swift River Pond Campsite (1975)—Privy. Water from piped spring near pond. Sometimes a canoe is available; be sure to leave it upside-down after use.

Maine 4—West 0.3 mile to the Hiker Hut, 2 Pine Road, (207) 897-8984, <hikerhut@gmail. com>, a rustic shelter for A.T. hikers beside the Sandy River, $25PP includes meal, bunk with linens, shower, shuttle into Rangeley (other shuttles available); mail drops ($5 nonguests) to: c/o Stevwe Lynch, 2 Pine Rd., Sandy River Plantation, ME 04970.

West 9 miles to **Rangeley, Maine [P.O. ZIP 04970: M–F 9:30–12:30 & 1:30–4:15, Sa 9:30–12; (207) 864-2233]**, where services are spread along Maine 4. ■ *Hostel:* Farmhouse Inn, (207) 864-3113, mail drops accepted at 2057 Main Street, Rangeley, ME 04970; bunks start at $30, (2) queen $50, studio $80, laundry $5 load, use of kitchen and dining room, fire pit, nonguest showers $5; complimentary shuttles, trailhead pick-up, debit/credit cards accepted. ■ *Lodging:* Rangeley Inn, (800) MOMENTS or (207) 864-3341, $84–$99; Saddleback Motor Inn, (207) 864-3434, $90D, WiFi; Town and Lake Motel, (207) 864-3755, $85S, $99D; North Country Inn B&B, (207) 864-2440, <www.northcountrybb.com>, $99–$149, full B. ■ *Groceries:* IGA Supermarket

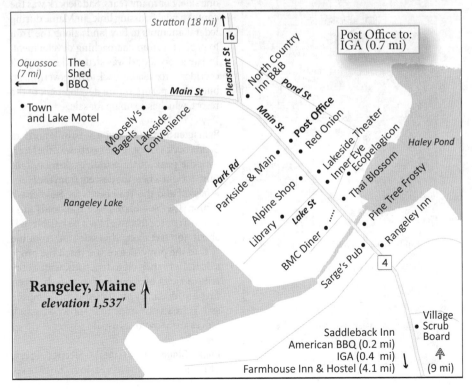

Stratton (18 mi)

16

Post Office to:
IGA (0.7 mi)

Oquossoc
(7 mi)
←

The
Shed
● BBQ

Pleasant St

North Country
Inn B&B

Pond St

Main St

● Town
and Lake Motel

Mooseley's
Bagels

Lakeside
Convenience

Main St

Post Office

Red Onion

Lakeside Theater

Inner Eye

Ecopelagicon

Haley Pond

Park Rd

Parkside & Main ●

Rangeley Lake

Alpine Shop ●

Lake St

Thai Blossom

Pine Tree Frosty

Rangeley Inn

Library ●

BMC Diner ●

Sarge's Pub ●

4

Rangeley, Maine
elevation 1,537'

Village
● Scrub
Board

Saddleback Inn
American BBQ (0.2 mi)
IGA (0.4 mi)
Farmhouse Inn & Hostel (4.1 mi)

(9 mi)

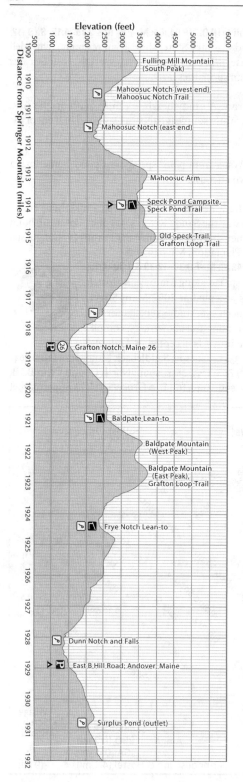

Elevation (feet)

Distance from Springer Mountain (miles)

Fulling Mill Mountain
(South Peak)

Mahoosuc Notch (west end),
Mahoosuc Notch Trail

Mahoosuc Notch (east end)

Mahoosuc Arm

Speck Pond Campsite,
Speck Pond Trail

Old-Speck-Trail,
Grafton Loop Trail

Grafton Notch, Maine 26

Baldpate Lean-to

Baldpate Mountain
(West Peak)

Baldpate Mountain
(East Peak),
Grafton Loop Trail

Frye Notch Lean-to

Dunn Notch and Falls

East B Hill Road; Andover; Maine

Surplus Pond (outlet)

(long-term resupply). ■ *Restaurants:* Parkside Main Café, L/D; Sarge's Pub & Grub, L/D; Red Onion, L/D; BMC Diner, B/L; The Shed BBQ, L/D. ■ *Outfitters:* Alpine Shop, (207) 864-3741, Coleman fuel and alcohol by the ounce; Ecopelagicon, 7 Pond St., (207) 864-2771, freeze-dried meals, backpacker supplies, fuel, ATC publications, slackpacking/shuttles. ■ *Internet access:* Rangeley Public Library. ■ *Other services:* banks with ATM; Village Scrub Board coin laundry; doctor; Rangeley Region Health Center, (207) 864-4397; dentist; bookstore.

West 15 miles to Oquossoc (see entry above).

Piazza Rock Lean-to (1993)—Sleeps 8. Privy; two-seater with cribbage board. Tent platforms. Water source is the stream that passes through the campsite. MATC caretaker in residence.

Saddleback Mountain—One of the most spectacular above-treeline stretches of the Trail in Maine; you may not notice the ski resort on one side. For many years, Saddleback was the controversial "missing link" in Maine during federal attempts to buy lands along the Trail to protect it from encroaching development. In late 2000, a deal was struck to sell a Trail corridor across Saddleback to the government, but it does permit future development of the resort, which is again up for sale.

Redington Stream Campsite—0.9 mile north of Saddleback's Horn, at the east base of the Horn (middle peak of the Saddleback mountain range), right where the descent from the Horn levels off and the Trail heads for Saddleback Junior. The blue-blazed side trail leads 1,100 feet to a source that might not be reliable. It is about 400 feet along this side trail from the A.T. to the privy. Before you reach the privy, side trails branch off to tent pads, with a current capacity of about two tents each. Open fires are *absolutely prohibited* at this campsite as it is in a very vulnerable softwood stand. Stoves are allowed, as usual.

Poplar Ridge Lean-to (1961)—Sleeps 6. Privy. This shelter uses the increasingly rare "base-

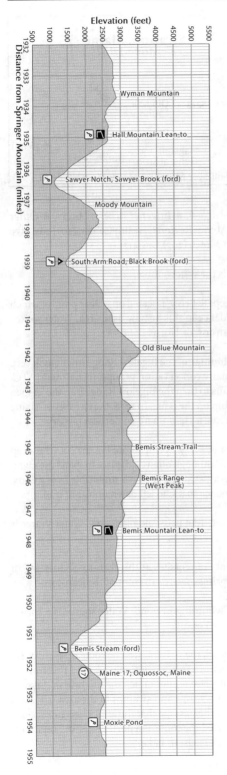

Elevation (feet)

Distance from Springer Mountain (miles)

Wyman Mountain

Hall Mountain Lean-to

Sawyer Notch, Sawyer Brook (ford)

Moody Mountain

South Arm Road, Black Brook (ford)

Old Blue Mountain

Bemis Stream Trail

Bemis Range
(West Peak)

Bemis Mountain Lean-to

Bemis Stream (ford)

Maine 17; Oquossoc, Maine

Moxie Pond

ball bat" design for its sleeping platform. Water source is the brook in front of lean-to.

Spaulding Mountain Lean-to (1989)—Sleeps 8. Privy. Water source is a small spring to right of lean-to.

Sugarloaf Mountain—A 0.6-mile side trail to the east leads to the summit of Sugarloaf, where, on clear days, panoramic views include glimpses of Katahdin and Mt. Washington. Cool spring water can be found at 0.3 mile. This side trail was the last section of the original A.T. to open, in August 1937.

Crocker Cirque Campsite (1975)—Privy. Numerous campsites; east on a 0.2-mile side trail, one large group platform, 2 small platforms. Water source is the spring.

Maine 27—East 2 miles to *Groceries:* Mountainside Grocers (long-term resupply), (207) 237-2248, at the base of Sugarloaf access road; open 7:30–6.

West 5 miles to **Stratton, Maine [P.O. ZIP 04982: M–F 8:30–1 & 1:30–4, Sa 9–11:30; (207) 246-6461].** *See map on next page.* ■ *Hostel:* Stratton Motel & Hostel Box 284, (207) 246-4171, <www.thestrattonmotel.com>, owned by Susan Smith; hostel $25PP includes hiker kitchen, free Internet/WiFi and long-distance phone; motel rooms $60s, $70D, $10EAP; $5 shuttle to Trail at Maine 27, local shuttles and slackpacking available; $5 laundry for nonguests; accepts mail drops. ■ *Lodging:* Spillover Motel, (207) 246-6571, $69S, $89D, pets okay with a $20 deposit and $5 charge, continental B, located south of town; White Wolf Inn, Main St. (P.O. Box 590), (207) 246-2922, closed Tu (call for room), weekdays $60S/D, weekends $70S/D, dogs $10, accepts packages; Diamond Corner B&B, 8 Rangeley Road (P.O. Box 176), (207) 246-2082, rooms $70–$100, includes B, shuttle to Trail, home-made pie, accepts mail drops. ■ *Groceries:* Fotter's Market (long-term resupply), with deli, Coleman fuel and denatured alcohol by the ounce, M–Sa 8–8 Su 9–5; Northland Cash Supply (short-term resupply), 152 Main St., pizza, daily 5–9, hiker box, accepts packages; Copeland Co-op, organic groceries. ■ *Restaurants:* White Wolf Café, L/D (closed Tu, D-only W, B F–Su); Stratton Plaza, Tu–Sa 11–9, Su 12–5,

pizza, L/D; The Looney Moose Café, B/L/D, W–Su 7–8. ■ *Internet access:* library. ■ *Other services:* Old Mill Coin laundry; bank; ATM; Mt. Abram Regional Health Center, (207) 265-4555, located in Kingfield. ■ *Shuttles:* Susan at Stratton Motel, (207) 246-4171.

Cranberry Stream Campsite (1995)—Privy. Stream is the water source.

Horns Pond Lean-tos (1997)—Two lean-tos; each sleeps 8. Privy. Located on a clear pond at which fishing is permitted. A MATC caretaker is in residence in this heavily used area. Water source is an often-dry spring on the A.T., north of the lean-tos, or Horns Pond.

Bigelow Mountain—Known as Maine's "Second Mountain," the Bigelow Range might look very different today had it not been for the efforts of many conservation groups, including MATC. During the 1960s and '70s, land developers had plans to turn the Bigelow Range into the "Aspen of the East," but opponents forced a state referendum on the issue. In 1976, the citizens of Maine decided to have the state purchase the land and create a 33,000-acre wilderness preserve.

Bigelow Col/Avery Memorial Campsite—Tent platforms. Privy. Spring located in the col. This deep cleft between West Peak and Avery Peak is a beautiful (although often cold) place to spend the night. You can catch the sunset or sunrise views from either peak. The spring is unreliable in dry years; one maintained water site is behind the red maintenance shack, to left down unblazed trail.

Safford Notch Campsite—Privy. Located 0.3 mile east. Tent pads and platforms. Water source is Safford Brook, downhill from the campsite.

Little Bigelow Lean-to (1986)—Sleeps 8. Privy. Plenty of tentsites at this lean-to. Swimming in "the Tubs" along the side trail. Water source is a spring 50 yards in front of the lean-to.

West Carry Pond Lean-to (1989)—Sleeps 8. Privy. Swimming in pond. Water source is a spring house located to the left of the lean-to or West Carry Pond.

Arnold Trail—From West Carry to Middle Carry Pond, the A.T. follows the route of the historic Arnold Trail. In 1775, Benedict Arnold and an army of 1,150 Revolutionaries used this trail *en route* to Quebec, where they hoped to mount a surprise winter attack on the British. Like so many hikers, the army literally bogged down in the streams and swamps of the area, and, as a result, the remaining 650 men were so weakened by the passage that the attack was unsuccessful. Prior to Arnold's transit, the Abenaki Indians used the route as a portage around rapids on the Dead River, the waters of which now fill artificial Flagstaff Lake.

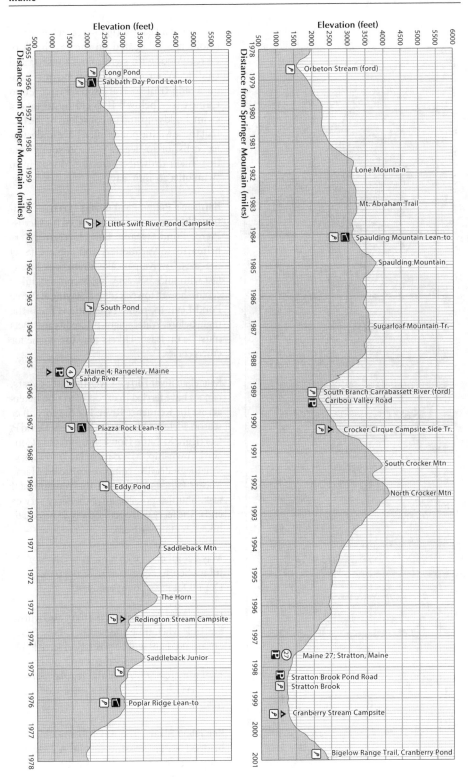

Elevation (feet)

Distance from Springer Mountain (miles)

Long Pond
Sabbath Day Pond Lean-to

Little Swift River Pond Campsite

South Pond

Maine 4; Rangeley, Maine
Sandy River

Piazza Rock Lean-to

Eddy Pond

Saddleback Mtn

The Horn

Redington Stream Campsite

Saddleback Junior

Poplar Ridge Lean-to

Elevation (feet)

Distance from Springer Mountain (miles)

Orbeton Stream (ford)

Lone Mountain

Mt. Abraham Trail

Spaulding Mountain Lean-to

Spaulding Mountain

Sugarloaf Mountain Tr.

South Branch Carrabassett River (ford)
Caribou Valley Road

Crocker Cirque Campsite Side Tr.

South Crocker Mtn

North Crocker Mtn

Maine 27; Stratton, Maine

Stratton Brook Pond Road
Stratton Brook

Cranberry Stream Campsite

Bigelow Range Trail, Cranberry Pond

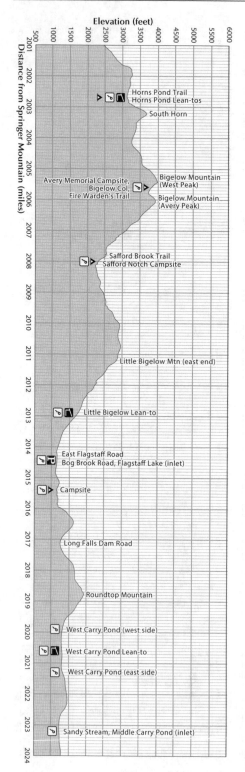

Elevation (feet)

Distance from Springer Mountain (miles)

Horns Pond Trail
Horns Pond Lean-tos
South Horn

Avery Memorial Campsite,
Bigelow Col,
Fire Warden's Trail

Bigelow Mountain
(West Peak)

Bigelow Mountain
(Avery Peak)

Safford Brook Trail
Safford Notch Campsite

Little Bigelow Mtn (east end)

Little Bigelow Lean-to

East Flagstaff Road
Bog Brook Road, Flagstaff Lake (inlet)

Campsite

Long Falls Dam Road

Roundtop Mountain

West Carry Pond (west side)

West Carry Pond Lean-to

West Carry Pond (east side)

Sandy Stream, Middle Carry Pond (inlet)

Pierce Pond Lean-to (1970)—Sleeps 6. Privy (moldering). Located on the east bank of Pierce Pond, with swimming, sunsets, and wildlife. Water source is the pond or stream on a side trail to Harrison's Pierce Pond Camps (see below). If deciding to take a swim, buddy-up and be conscious of the fact that these Maine ponds often have underwater "cells" of 40-degree water. A young 2012 thru-hiker drowned here after diving in to swim off a 20-mile day.

Harrison's Pierce Pond Camps (1934)—Traditional Maine camp on blue-blazed trail across Pierce Pond Stream. Tim Harrison caters primarily to vacationers and anglers; (207) 672-3625. Twelve-pancake lumberjack breakfast with juice, $8; eggs, $9; bacon, $10; hiker cabin, shower, towel, $30PP. If staying at Pierce Pond Lean-to, make reservations for B the night before. Water spigot; no credit cards; pets must be on leash. Hikers may use phone for emergencies.

Kennebec River Ferry—Over the last 25 years, canoes have ferried in excess of 22,000 hikers across the Kennebec River. For the 2015 hiker season, Fletcher Mountain Outfitters, David P. Corrigan, 82 Little Houston Brook Rd., Concord Township, ME 04920, (207) 672-4879, <maineguide@live.com>, a registered Maine Master Guide, will handle this monumental task. Shuttles possible after the ferry service ends. The ferry will operate daily, at no cost to hikers, tentatively from:

May 22–Jul 9	9–11 a.m.
Jul 10–Sep 30	9–11 a.m. & 2–4 p.m.
Oct 1–Oct 12	9 –11 a.m.

In early May and late Oct, the ferry also will be available when time and weather allow. Exact hours and dates will be posted at Pierce Pond and Pleasant Pond lean-tos and on line at <www.matc.org>. After the regular season, ferry service is available for a fee of $50 for 1–2 hikers.

Kennebec River—The most formidable unbridged water-crossing on the A.T. Ironically, the Indian word "Kennebec" means

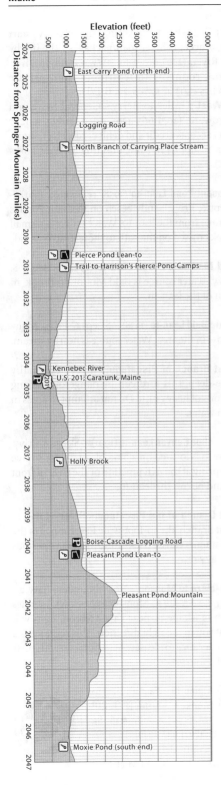

Elevation (feet)

Distance from Springer Mountain (miles)

East Carry Pond (north end)

Logging Road

North Branch of Carrying Place Stream

Pierce Pond Lean-to
Trail to Harrison's Pierce Pond Camps

Kennebec River
U.S. 201; Caratunk, Maine

Holly Brook

Boise-Cascade Logging Road
Pleasant Pond Lean-to

Pleasant Pond Mountain

Moxie Pond (south end)

"long, quiet water." A thru-hiker drowned in 1985 trying to ford the river, and many other hikers have had close calls. Dangers include rocks, strong currents, and unpredictable water levels due to releases from the dams upstream. ATC and MATC strenuously urge hikers not to attempt to ford the river. *Purists also should note that a ferry is the official "white-blaze" route,* as well as the original, historical route of the A.T. across the Kennebec. This is a free service funded by ATC and MATC. Hikers need to arrive a half-hour before the ferry ceases operation. If late, be prepared to wait, and note that camping and fires are prohibited on both banks of the river. You will be required to sign a release form before crossing, wear a life jacket during the crossing, and follow the instructions of the ferry operator; please cooperate in these matters. If river conditions or weather make the crossing dangerous, the service will be discontinued until conditions improve. The ferry is for hiker and pack—the operator will not carry your pack so you can attempt to ford.

U.S. 201—East 0.3 mile on Main Street to **Caratunk, Maine [P.O. ZIP 04925: M–F 7:30–11:30 & 12–3:45, Sa 7:30–11:15; (207) 672-3416].**

East 1 mile on U.S. 201 to *Lodging and resupply:* The Sterling Inn, 1041 U.S. 201 (P.O. Box 129), (207) 672-3333, <www.maine-sterlinginn.com>. Bunk room $25; private rooms $40–$70, includes B and free shuttle to/from Trailhead, post office, or brew pub. Free WiFi, computer, and LD calling. Call from free phone near PO for pick-up. Debit/credit cards accepted, multinight discounts, well-behaved pets okay. Long-term resupply, showers, laundry, mail drops, and shuttle service available for guests and nonguests.

East 16.5 miles to the small town of Bingham, with restaurants, coin laundry, pharmacy, and grocery stores (all long-term resupply). *Lodging:* Bingham Motor Inn, (866) 806-6120, <www.binghammotorinn.com>, $61S, $81D, $91T.

West 2 miles to *Lodging:* Northern Outdoors Resort, 1771 U.S. 201, The Forks, ME 04985, (800) 765-7238; rates begin at $57.25/room for lodge rooms (max 4 persons, subject to availability), cabin tents at $10.70PP; tent sites at $6.42PP; include all taxes; B/L/D, Kennebec River Pub & Brewery, shuttle to the A.T. (ask ahead), coin laundry, free showers, free Internet access, hot

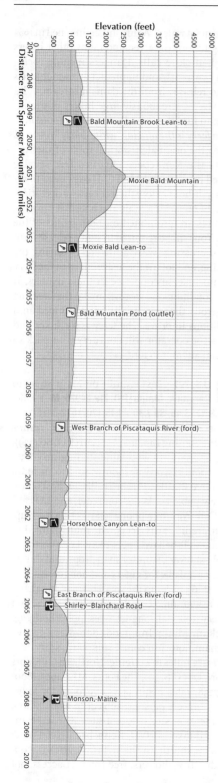

Elevation (feet)

Distance from Springer Mountain (miles)

Bald Mountain Brook Lean-to

Moxie Bald Mountain

Moxie Bald Lean-to

Bald Mountain Pond (outlet)

West Branch of Piscataquis River (ford)

Horseshoe Canyon Lean-to

East Branch of Piscataquis River (ford)
Shirley–Blanchard Road

Monson, Maine

tubs, Kennebec River rafting trips (class IV) start at $79, accepts hiker mail/packages . The Inn by the River, (207) 663-2181, <www.innbytheriver. com>, rooms with whirlpools and private porches start at $79–$129, B/L/D.

West 7 miles to Berry's General Store and Hardware, (207) 663-4461, open daily 5 a.m.–7 p.m., accepts credit and debit cards; Heet, short-term resupply; in same building as West Forks P.O.

Pleasant Pond Lean-to (1958, renovated 1991)— Sleeps 6. Privy. Sandy beach on Pleasant Pond is 0.2 mile from the lean-to. Water source is a small brook crossed on the path to the lean-to or pond.

Bald Mountain Brook Lean-to (1994)—Sleeps 8. Privy. Water source is Bald Mountain Brook, in front of the lean-to.

Moxie Bald Lean-to (1958)—Sleeps 6. Privy. Many moose in the area. Water source is nearby stream.

West Branch of Piscataquis River—Normally knee-deep, this ford can be dangerous during periods of heavy rain. Do not attempt to cross in high water.

Horseshoe Canyon Lean-to (1991)—Sleeps 8. Privy. Lean-to is located on a blue-blaze. Water source is a spring at the A.T. junction or the river in front of, and below, the lean-to.

East Branch of the Piscataquis River—Like its West Branch, the 50-foot-wide East Branch of the Piscataquis can be tricky fording during periods of heavy rain.

Blue-blaze to Monson—Northbounders have an alternative route to Monson (see below), 3.3 miles south of Maine 15, near Lake Hebron; signs will point you in the right direction. This route leads a short distance to Pleasant St., where you will go left 2 miles into town.

Maine 15—East 4 miles to **Monson, Maine [P.O. ZIP 04464: M–F 8–1 & 2:15–4:15, Sa 7:30–11; (207) 997-3975].** Post office accepts debit cards with *limited* cash back. ATM at Mo-

bile Mart. ■ *Lodging:* Shaws' Lodging, 37 years serving hikers, 17 Pleasant St. (P.O. Box 72), (207) 997-3597, <www.shawslodging.com>; owners Dawn MacPherson-Allen and Sue Stevens; open May 15–Oct 15, no credit cards; tenting $12PP, bunkhouse and bunkroom $25PP, guest rooms $35S $56D, semiprivate $28PP; advance reservations accepted; B $9 (outside guests welcome); dogs welcome in bunkhouse; campstore, WiFi and Internet; nonguest showers, laundry, and mail drops $5 each. Shuttles, slackpacking, and food drops available. Mail drops free for guests. Lakeshore House Lodging & Pub Box 215, (207) 997-7069, (207) 343-5033, <www.thelakeshorehouse.com>, open year-round, credit cards accepted; owner Rebekah Anderson. Bunks $25, private rooms $40S $50D; coin-oper-

ated shower for nonguests; dogs OK; work for stay (3 hours work); WiFi and loaner laptop for guests; pub hours Tu–Sa 12–9, Su 12–8, bar open later; AYCE specials on W and F; live music Su 2–5; free Trailhead pick-up and drop-off; no charge for parking; hiker store (long-term resupply); mail drops accepted. 100 Mile Wilderness Adventures and Outfitters; Phil Pepin, regis-

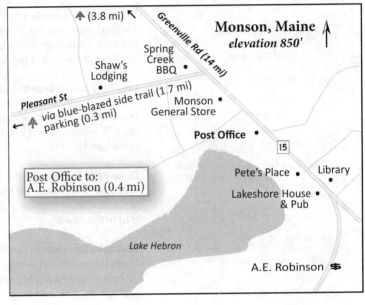

tered Maine guide; 349 Pleasant St. (P.O. Box 47), (207) 991-7030, <www.100milewilderness.info>; bunkhouse $25PP, private cabins $50, private tentsites $15. Stays include full use of facilities including free WiFi/Internet, laundry $5, campstore, free long-term parking for section-hikers, midwilderness resupply options, shuttle services from Rangeley to Baxter Park and Bangor; open May 15–Oct 15. ■ *Groceries:* A.E. Robinson Mobil Mart (short-term resupply), M–Su 5 a.m.–10 p.m., pizzas, hiker-sized calzones, hot sandwiches, ATM. ■ *Restaurants:* Spring Creek BBQ, Th–F 10–8, Su 8–6; Pete's Place, open daily. ■ *Internet access:* Monson Public Library, M–W–F 1–4. ■ *Shuttles:* Buddy Ward, cell (207) 343-2564, home (207) 997-3792; Phil Pepin, (207) 991-7030; Shaw's; and Lakeshore House.

West 10.3 miles to Greenville, Moosehead Lake's main tourist town and gateway to Maine's North Woods. ■ *Lodging:* Indian Hill Motel, (207) 695-2623, <indianhillmotel@gmail.com>, $69S/D, $12EAP. ■ *Groceries:* Indian Hill Trading Post (long-term resupply). ■ *Restaurants:* Kelly's Landing, AYCE B on Su; Auntie Em's Family Restaurant; The Stress-Free Moose Pub; The Blue Loon Café; The Black Frog Pub; Flatlanders Rod and Reel. ■ *Outfitter:* Northwoods Outfitters, (207) 695-3288, <www.maineoutfitter.com>, daily 7–7, Internet (fee), and coffee at the Hard Drive Café inside store. ■ *Other services:* Indian Hill Trading Post, <www.indianhill.com>, (800) 675-4487; banks with ATM; Harris Drug Store, (207) 695-2921; Charles A. Dean Memorial Hospital, 24-hour ER, (207) 695-5200; Greenville Veterinary Clinic, (207) 695-4408.

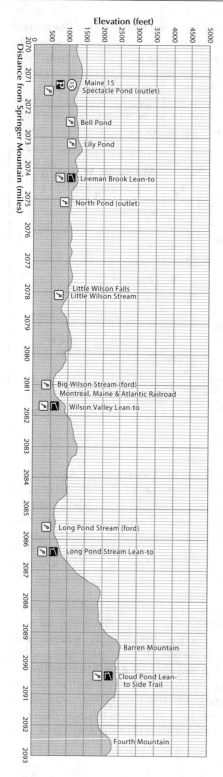

"100-Mile Wilderness"—Signs at each end of this section proclaim this area's remoteness and warn the unprepared hiker to stay away, but don't be intimidated. Hikers should remember to bring cash for Baxter State Park.

Leeman Brook Lean-to (1987)—Sleeps 6. Privy. Water source is the stream in front of the lean-to.

Wilson Valley Lean-to (1993)—Sleeps 6. Privy. Located north of Big Wilson Stream. Water source is a small spring in front of the lean-to, on the opposite side of the A.T.

Long Pond Stream Lean-to (1991)—Sleeps 8. Privy. Swimming in the scenic Slugundy Gorge and falls located 0.1 mile south, on a side trail 150 yards off the A.T. Water source is a small stream to the left of the lean-to.

Cloud Pond Lean-to (1992)—Sleeps 6. Privy 0.4 mile east. Water source is Cloud Pond, in front of the lean-to, or a spring to the north of the side trail to the lean-to.

Chairback Gap Lean-to (1954)—Sleeps 6. Privy. Water source, a small spring downhill and north of the lean-to 25 yards, is prone to go dry in drier years.

Katahdin Iron Works (KIW) Road/West Branch of Pleasant River—Just east of the A.T., on the KIW logging road, is a parking lot for Gulf Hagas.

West on KIW Road to *Lodging:* AMC Gorman Chairback Lodge (0.3 mile to left on Gorman Chairback Camp Rd., 1.2 mile to lodge) and Little Lyford Pond Cabins (4.9 mile to left on Frenchtown Rd., 1.2 mile to lodge), (603) 466-2727; <www.outdoors.org>; $96 for bunkroom space, *possible* two-night minimum, B/L/D included; accepts mail drops at P.O. Box 310, Greenville, ME 04441.

East 20 miles to Maine 11 and Brownville Junction. ■ *Groceries:* The General Store and More (short-term resupply), (207) 965-8100, <www.thegeneralstoreandmore.com>, deli, live outdoor music on summer weekends, primitive camping available. ■ *Shuttle:* Kathy Preble, contact well in advance, (207) 965-8464, <svivor@midmaine.com>.

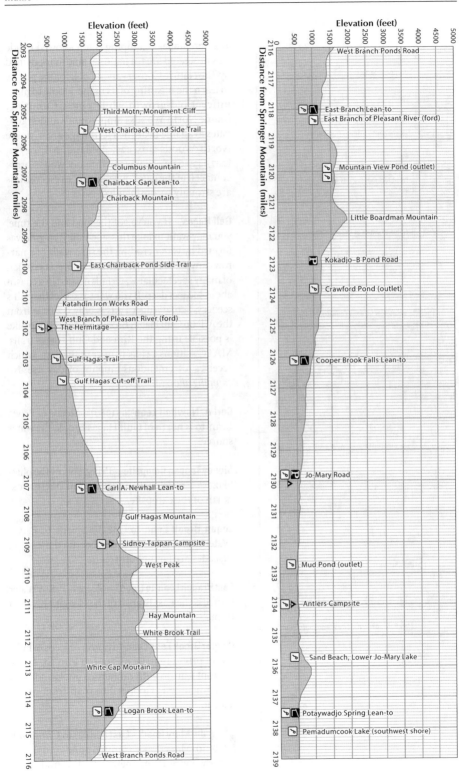

Elevation (feet)

Distance from Springer Mountain (miles)

Third Motn, Monument Cliff
West Chairback Pond Side Trail
Columbus Mountain
Chairback Gap Lean-to
Chairback Mountain
East Chairback Pond Side Trail
Katahdin Iron Works Road
West Branch of Pleasant River (ford)
The Hermitage
Gulf Hagas Trail
Gulf Hagas Cut-off Trail
Carl A. Newhall Lean-to
Gulf Hagas Mountain
Sidney-Tappan Campsite
West Peak
Hay Mountain
White Brook Trail
White Cap Moutain
Logan Brook Lean-to
West Branch Ponds Road

Elevation (feet)

Distance from Springer Mountain (miles)

West Branch Ponds Road
East Branch Lean-to
East Branch of Pleasant River (ford)
Mountain View Pond (outlet)
Little Boardman Mountain
Kokadjo–B Pond Road
Crawford Pond (outlet)
Cooper Brook Falls Lean-to
Jo-Mary Road
Mud Pond (outlet)
Antlers Campsite
Sand Beach, Lower Jo-Mary Lake
Potaywadjo Spring Lean-to
Pemadumcook Lake (southwest shore)

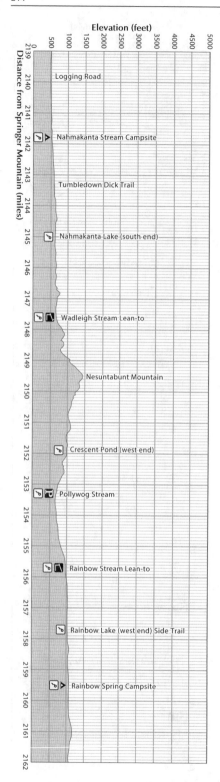

The Hermitage—Camping is not allowed inside this protected area, a national landmark owned by The Nature Conservancy. Look for the plaque to learn the meaning of its name. Home to magnificent old-growth white pines. *Camping:* Maine North Woods campgrounds and $7 tentsites available near the Hermitage area. Maine North Woods Box 425, Ashland, ME 04732, (207) 435-6213, <www.northmainewoods.org>; contact it at the gatehouse; advance reservations are strongly recommended.

Gulf Hagas—If you've got the food and the time, you may want to take this side trail. The gulf was formed by water eroding the slate walls of a narrow canyon. The result of this sculpting is a stretch of many spectacular waterfalls nestled in a chasm about 500 feet deep. If you want a taste of the gulf's scenery, Screw Auger Falls is only 0.2 mile from the A.T. on Gulf Hagas Brook. A 5.2-mile loop hike is possible using the Rim and Gulf Hagas trails. MATC stations a ridgerunner in the area, which receives a tremendous amount of day use. *No camping allowed.*

Carl A. Newhall Lean-to (1986)—Sleeps 6. Privy. Lean-to is north of Gulf Hagas Brook, the water source.

Sidney Tappan Campsite—Privy. Follow the blue-blaze 0.2 mile east to water; trail begins just north of the campsite.

Logan Brook Lean-to (1983)—Sleeps 6. Privy. Water source is Logan Brook behind the lean-to; cascades are farther upstream.

East Branch Lean-to (1996)—Sleeps 8. Privy. Water source is the East Branch of the Pleasant River, in front.

Cooper Brook Falls Lean-to (1956)—Sleeps 6. Full-moon privy. Tentsite on trail to lean-to. A waterfront lean-to with numerous pools and falls. Water source is Cooper Brook in front of the lean-to.

Jo-Mary Road—**East** 6 miles to *Camping:* Jo-Mary Lake Campground, (207) 723-8117, <www.northmainewoods.org>, mid-May–

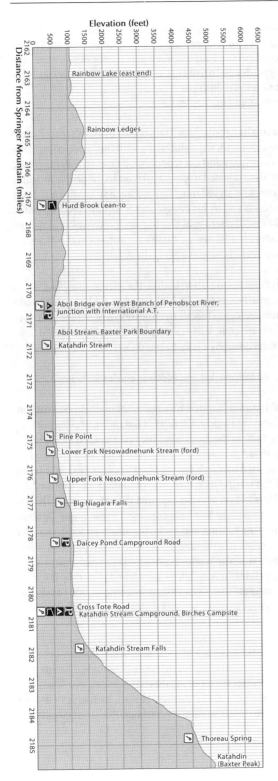

Oct 1, campsites $20, campstore B/L, showers, laundry, shuttle, dogs welcome. The A.T. crossing of Jo-Mary Road is 17 miles from Maine 11 and Brownville Junction.

Antlers Campsite—Campsites are on the edge of Lower Jo-Mary. Fort Relief privy to the west of the Trail. Water source is Jo-Mary Lake.

Potaywadjo Spring Lean-to (1995)—Sleeps 8. Privy. Water source is the 15-foot-wide Potaywadjo Spring, to the right of the lean-to.

Nahmakanta Stream Campsite—Privy. Water is a stream in front of the campsite.

Wadleigh Stream Lean-to (1981)—Sleeps 6. Privy. Located 0.5 mile north of Nahmakanta Lake, which has a sandy beach. Water source is a spring on the beach.

Rainbow Stream Lean-to (1971)—Sleeps 6. Privy. Home of the A.T.'s best totem pole; often crowded with hiker groups. Good tenting and hammocking above and behind the lean-to. Water source is Rainbow Stream, in front.

Rainbow Spring Campsite—Privy. Water source is a flowing spring at the shore of Rainbow Lake.

Hurd Brook Lean-to (1959)—Sleeps 6. Privy. During high water, Hurd Brook, 50 feet south of the lean-to, can be deep and swift, and the ford dangerous. Area is frequented by hunters. Water source is Hurd Brook. Southbounders might want to tank up at the spring 0.7 mile north of the lean-to.

"Golden Road"/Abol Bridge. ■ *Camping:* Abol Bridge Campground, open May 15–Oct 1, privately run and located along the road on the West Branch of the Penobscot River, campsites $12PP ($24 minimum) or single-hiker special of $17, coin-op showers for guests ($5 for nonguests), all visitors must register; Department of Conservation's Abol Pines, seasonal, tentsite or space in one of two six-person lean-tos, $9PP plus tax for out-of-state residents, reached by following a dirt road 75 yards east in front of the camp store. ■ *Groceries:* Abol Bridge Store (short-term resupply), restaurant, credit cards accepted.

East 20 miles to Millinocket, Maine, near end of chapter.

Baxter State Park—The northern terminus of the Appalachian Trail, hosted by Baxter State Park, is Baxter Peak on Katahdin, Maine's highest mountain. Katahdin, along with the surrounding landscape, is part of a 209,644-acre wilderness sanctuary and forest preserve, Baxter State Park; <www.baxterstateparkauthority.com>. The lands were donated in perpetual trust to the people of Maine by former Governor Percival Proctor Baxter, who served from 1921 to 1924. BSP is self-supporting, in large part due to Baxter's endowment funds and by his design, and is administered separately from any other agency or state park in Maine. Baxter's goal was to place preservation of natural resources as a priority over their recreational use, so some of BSP's regulations and policies are markedly different from what may be encountered elsewhere along the A.T.

Most of Baxter's A.T.-related rules stem from the weather. Unlike the surrounding landscape south, Katahdin is exposed to extreme weather, including high winds, and has gotten snow during every month of the year. No shelters are located above treeline (north of Katahdin Stream Campground), and all trails to the summit are completely exposed. On humid, unsettled, late-summer days, for example, it is wise to start down by 1 p.m. to avoid electrical storms.

Dogs—Dogs are **not** allowed in the park. See Millinocket and Medway entries for kennels.

Katahdin—The translation of the Abenaki word is "greatest mountain." Maine's Penobscots considered the mountain a holy place and believed in Pamola, the deity of Katahdin, who purportedly would destroy any man who ventured too close to the mountain. The first recorded ascent of Katahdin by Euroamericans came on Aug 13, 1804, when a party led by Charles Turner, Jr., reached the summit by the same rocks-and-roots route used by the A.T.—the Hunt Trail (named after Irving Hunt, a sporting-camp owner who cut the trail). Since then, the mountain has captured the imagination of many, including Henry David Thoreau, who explored the area in 1846. Thoreau Spring on the Tableland bears his name, although he likely never made it there. From Katahdin Stream Campground, it is a 10.4-mile trip to the summit and back. The ascent packs an elevation gain of 4,000 feet into 5 miles. Backpacks may be left at the ranger station at the campground, where you can borrow a daypack and obtain information on weather conditions. The park posts recommended "cut-off" times for beginning your climb: In Aug, hikers are advised to start by 11 a.m.; in Sep, by 10 a.m.; in Oct, by 9 a.m. Park rules require that you sign in at the campground before your climb and sign out on your return. Don't forget to make your final, or first, register entry on the ranger station's front porch.

Weather—Baxter State Park posts daily weather reports and trail-status alerts during the hiking season at 7 a.m. Before Memorial Day and anytime after late Sep, it is not uncommon for some trails to be closed for public-safety reasons or to protect the alpine-plant communities. The "class day" system has been discarded. Going forward, the mountain either will be open for hiking or it won't. Hikers who choose to hike on closed trails are subject to a court summons, fine, and revocation of park-visitation privileges.

Register—Every hiker must register with a ranger upon entering BSP. An information kiosk is located on the A.T. 1 mile north of Abol Bridge. The 12 hikers using The Birches (see below) must sign up at the Abol Stream kiosk and also with the ranger at Katahdin Stream Campground. A Baxter Park "A.T. Steward" patrols the area to help hikers with information on the A.T. and the park.

Reservations—A "rolling reservations" policy is available four months in advance of the day you wish to stay within the park. If you want Jun 3, you need to know your reservation will not be processed before Feb 3. The traditional opening day to make walk-in reservations is the closest business day to Jan 15. Please call the park at (207) 723-5140, or check the Web site for updates. More information, and a chart outlining when reservations can be made, is at <www.baxterstateparkauthority.com>. The site provides the many different ways reservations may be secured; you are strongly advised to review those options.

The overnight camping season is May 15–Oct 15 each year. After Oct 15, overnight camping is prohibited anywhere within the park. You may camp at the private Abol Bridge campground or the Maine DOC Abol Pines Campground downriver and across the road from Abol Bridge. Both charge fees. Your hike to the summit is then 15 miles one way from this area outside the park. Another option when BSP is closed for camping is to stay in Millinocket and hire one of the local shuttle services to transport you in and out of Baxter on the day of your hike. Southbounders should note that the A.T. from Katahdin Stream Campground to Baxter Peak might not be open until Jun 1. Northbounders should note that they can check reservation availability by either going on-line or calling, and then sending in their request. With other mail requests coming in daily, that may not guarantee a spot. Between Jun 16 and Oct 15, campsite reservations may be made with a credit card *via* phone or Internet for any unreserved site in the park for any date. If you can't get camping space at one of the reservation-only campgrounds or the 12-slot Birches (see below), a very fit and fast thru-hiker, with 2,000 miles under her (or his) belt, might try leaving from and returning to Abol Bridge *via* the Blueberry Ledges Trail, a 19.2-mile round-trip to Katahdin's summit that includes the most challenging ascent and descent on the entire A.T. It wouldn't be a very leisurely way to end your thru-hike.

Pamphlet—*Long-Distance Hiking in Baxter State Park*, a pamphlet, is available on request from BSP. It has a map of the A.T. and the Blueberry Ledges Trail, a wealth of information about the park, and a message from park management.

Mail and Messages—BSP does not accept mail or packages. Mail drops should be arranged through the Millinocket post office.

Trail closings on Katahdin—It is advised to plan to reach BSP by Oct 1 or arrange to climb Katahdin before Oct 15; park officials emphasize that, in this northerly climate, chances are significantly high that you will be unable to successfully finish your hike at Katahdin's summit after this date. Winter hiking season is Dec 1–Mar 31; during that period, you must obtain a permit from the park to climb Katahdin.

In some years, access to the park road and trails up Katahdin can be closed by snowstorms for up to two weeks *before* Oct 15. On those days, the A.T. up to Baxter Peak is open only when conditions permit (see above). Each day at 7 a.m., park rangers post the weather forecast and trail alerts. Trail closures are not uncommon in late Sep–Oct. When the trails are closed, anyone hiking beyond the designated Trailhead is subject to a court summons and fine, and revocation of park privileges. If you must be rescued, assistance will be delayed until the rescuers can proceed safely; you could be found negligent and liable for all costs of search and rescue.

After Oct 15, Baxter State Park is open for day use only (sunrise to sunset), conditions permitting. Vehicular access to the park after Oct 15 is at the discretion of the park director and should not be planned on after Nov 1. Call park headquarters if you have questions about road access before May 15 or after Oct 15.

Beginning at Katahdin—Southbound thru-hikers beginning their trek at Katahdin should make reservations for campsites well in advance of their starting dates. During July and Aug, campsites normally are booked to maximum levels.

Ending at Katahdin—Northbounders who plan to have family and friends meet them at the park should reserve campsites in advance. Labor Day weekend is especially busy, with a traditional native-American event reserving the entire Katahdin Stream Campground. If driving into the park, there is a $14 fee at the gate for out-of-state residents. Advise those who are meeting you that a new day-use parking reservation system is in effect at Katahdin Trailheads. You can compete to make a reserva-tion on-line (<www.baxterstateparkauthority.com>) for a $5 fee for the Trailhead of your choice. Out-of-state residents can reserve a spot no earlier than two weeks before arrival; Maine residents can reserve anytime after Apr 1. When parking lots fill, visitors will be directed to open lots and alternate trailheads by the rangers at the gatehouse. **Park regulations limit hiking groups to no more than 12 individuals; larger groups will be required to separate themselves into separate groups of 12 with at least a mile of trail between them. This regulation is designed to prevent large groups from dominating the experience at Baxter Peak.** The park asks, "Please assist us in respect-ing the spectacular natural setting Percival Baxter generously preserved by complying with this new regulation." Plan ahead!

Southbounders, it is suggested you reserve a site for the nights before and after climbing Katahdin. For reservations and information, contact BSP, 64 Balsam Dr., Millinocket, ME 04462, (207) 723-5140.

Camping in Baxter State Park—Two 4-person lean-tos and tenting space for 4 additional people are available at a site called **The Birches**, not far from Katahdin Stream Campground. Advance reservations are not required; the fee to stay there is $10PP. At reservation campgrounds, the fee is $30 for either lean-to or tentsite (4- to 6-person capacity). *Cash only inside park.*

The Birches is 9.9 miles from Abol Bridge *via* the A.T. or 4.4 miles from Abol Bridge *via* the Blue-berry Ledges Trail. Use of The Birches is limited strictly to 12 long-distance or thru-hikers who have hiked at least 100 contiguous miles up to and including entering the BSP. Stays at The Birches are limited to one night. Park authorities have posted a sign-up sheet for long-distance hikers at the information kiosk just north of Abol Bridge. If all 12 spaces are claimed for the night that you planned to stay at The Birches, you need to stay elsewhere. Your choices include the Abol Bridge private campground; the nearby Maine Department of Conservation Abol Pines site on the West Branch of the Penobscot (both are fee sites); standard-reservation campsites in the park at Katahdin Stream Campground, Foster Field Group Campsite, or any other available site of your choice in the park, if they are not already full; or staying in a campground or motel near Millinocket, if available. In Jul and Aug, and on fall weekends, it is difficult to get a site at Katahdin Stream or anywhere in the park, because sites are often reserved months in advance. However, Labor Day–Oct 15, it is possible (although not certain) that you will find vacant sites at Katahdin Stream during the week. *Beware:* In 2012, the park implemented a new policy of opening up all unreserved sites after Jun 16 for online reservations for the remainder of the camping season. That means that many sites previously ob-tained with ease at the last minute may become more difficult to reserve if you wait too long.

2,000-Miler Certificate Applications—ATC has asked Katahdin Stream Campground rangers to hand out forms to all northbounders who are about to finish the Trail, in an effort to expedite the processing of 2,000-miler certificates. See requirements on page xii.

Reaching Baxter State Park—No public transportation is available to and from BSP. Unless you have someone meeting you at the park, you'll need to hitch 24 miles from the Trail to Millinocket. Rides are usually easy to find, since almost everyone headed out of the park must go through Millinocket.

Baxter State Park Road—BSP Togue Pond Visitors Center, M–Th 7–3, F–Su 7–6; maps, guidebooks, additional information; beach, and picnic area (no camping).

East 2 miles from the park's south gate to *Lodging:* Maine Timberland Company's Katahdin Forest Cabins, (877) 622-2467, log cabin on Sunday Pond, spectacular view of Katahdin, $87 per night, sleeps 6, with gas heat, stove, and privy; advance reservations necessary.

East 2.6 miles to *Camping:* Penobscot Outdoor Center on Pockwockamus Pond, (207) 723-3580, tentsites, showers, sauna, hot tub, restaurant, and lounge; call for rates.

East 7 miles to Golden Road junction (8 miles from here to Abol Bridge).

East 8.3 miles to ■ *Groceries:* Northwoods Trading Post (short-term resupply), (207) 723-4326, open 7–9, last gas station and ATM before entering BSP. A.T. maps, books, trail guides, patches, and souvenirs. ■ *Lodging:* Big Moose Inn, (207) 723-8391, <www.bigmoosecabins.com>, inn room with shared bath weekday $53, weekend $56; camping $10PP; lean-to $13PP; cabins, call for rates; restaurant and bar open W–Su, B available Sa–Su, no pets.

East 15.6 miles to *Camping:* Hidden Springs Campground, (888) 685-4488 or (207) 723-6337, <www.hiddenspring.com>, tentsites $10PP/night, shower without stay $3.

East 17 miles from the park's south gate to **Millinocket, Maine [P.O. 04462: M–F 9–4, Sa 9–11:30; (207) 723-5921]**. *See map on next page.* The Trail's End Festival will be Sep 18–20, with a Hard Core project on Sep 18. BSP Headquarters, (207) 723-5140, 64 Balsam Dr., park reservations, publications, maps, and general information. ■ *Lodging:* Appalachian Trail Lodge, 33 Penobscot Ave., (207) 723-4321, <www.appalachiantraillodge.com>, owners Paul (OleMan) & Jaime (NaviGator) Renaud, $25 bunkroom, $35S, $55D, family suite (private bath) $95 (sleeps 4; $10EAP); showers for nonguests $5; WiFi; insured shuttle service to and from bus in Medway, into 100-mile wilderness or Monson, free daily shuttle from Baxter Sep 18–Oct 15 for guests (others $10PP); no pets; accepts credit cards and mail drops for guests; closes Oct 15. Katahdin Inn & Suites, (207) 723-4555, $69S, $79D, $89 king & sofa pull-out, dogs $10/night, continental B, indoor pool and hot tub, WiFi, computer access, fitness center, laundry. Baxter Park Inn, (207) 723-9777, $79S, $89D, $10EAP, dogs welcome $10, continental B. Pamola Motor Lodge, (800) 575-9746, (207) 723-9746, <www.pamolamotorlodge.com>, $59S, $69D, dogs okay 410, continental B, Internet access, hot tub, lounge, laundry service. Hotel Terrace, (207) 723-4525, $47S, $56D, $5EAP. The Young House B&B, 193 Central Ave., (207) 723-5452, <www.theyounghousebandb.com>, $95, credit cards accepted, WiFi, mail drops accepted. Joe Fish Inn, (207) 723-9999, <www.icefishinn.com>, $120–$135, pet-friendly, WiFi, hot tub, multiple B options. ■ *Restaurants:* Appalachian Trail Café, owned by Paul and Jaime Renaud, B/L/D, home of the Sundae Summit Challenge, gift shop, free Internet access, showers $5; Hotel Terrace, L/D, AYCE only on weekends; Hang Wong at Pamola Inn, M–Sa AYCE L; Angelo's Pizza Grille, B/L/D; BBQ House; others shown on map. ■ *Outfitter:* Ole Man's Gear Shop, open 10–4, gear, fuel, *etc.* ■ *Other services:* Most major services are available in town, including supermarkets, coin laundrys, and banks with ATM; LanMan's Lounge, 28 Hill St., pack lockers $5/day, TV, snacks, soda, ice cream, restrooms, across from library; Town Taxi, (207) 723-2000, provides service to the bus station ($15) in Medway and ($55) to Baxter State Park; Millinocket Regional Hospital, (207) 723-5161. Millinocket has no bus service, but Cyr Bus Lines of Old Town, Maine, serves nearby Medway (see below).

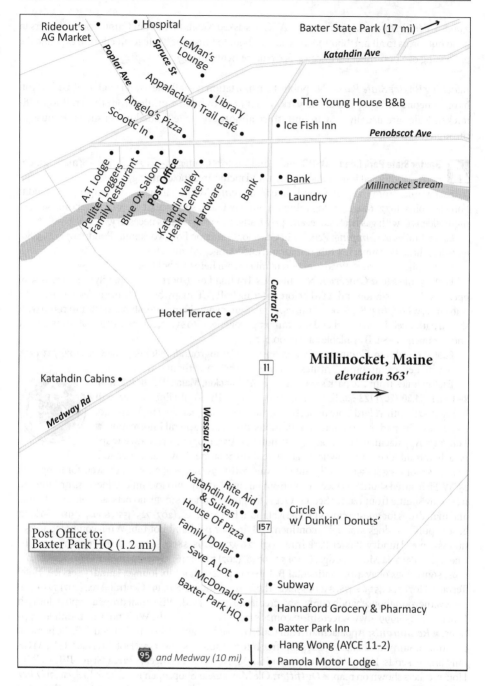

Rideout's AG Market

Hospital

LeMan's Lounge

Spruce St

Poplar Ave

Appalachian Trail Café

Angelo's Pizza

Scootic In

Library

The Young House B&B

Ice Fish Inn

Katahdin Ave

Baxter State Park (17 mi)

Penobscot Ave

A.T. Lodge

Pelliter Loggers Family Restaurant

Blue Ox Saloon

Post Office

Katahdin Valley Health Center

Hardware

Bank

Bank

Laundry

Millinocket Stream

Hotel Terrace

Katahdin Cabins

Medway Rd

Central St

Wassau St

11

Millinocket, Maine
elevation 363'

Post Office to:
Baxter Park HQ (1.2 mi)

Katahdin Inn & Suites

House Of Pizza

Family Dollar

Save A Lot

McDonald's

Baxter Park HQ

Rite Aid

157

Circle K
w/ Dunkin' Donuts'

Subway

Hannaford Grocery & Pharmacy

Baxter Park Inn

Hang Wong (AYCE 11-2)

Pamola Motor Lodge

95 *and Medway (10 mi)*

■ *Kennel services:* Connie McManus, (207) 723-6795, will pick up at Abol Bridge and house dogs for thru-hikers.

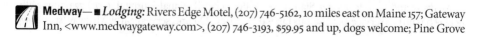

Medway— ■ *Lodging:* Rivers Edge Motel, (207) 746-5162, 10 miles east on Maine 157; Gateway Inn, <www.medwaygateway.com>, (207) 746-3193, $59.95 and up, dogs welcome; Pine Grove

Campground and Cottages, (207) 746-5172, <www.pinegrovecamping.com>, tentsites, fully equipped cottages, dogs welcome, free use of canoe and kayak for guests, will pick up at bus station. ■ *Outfitter:* Nicatau Outfitter, <www.mainecampingtrips.com>, (207) 746-3253 or (207) 746-3251, call ahead for shuttles or boarding pet. ■ *Bus service:* Cyr Bus Lines of Old Town, Maine, serves northern Maine; 10 miles east on Maine 757, (207) 927-2335, (207) 827-2010, or (800) 244-2335, <www.cyrbustours.com>. A bus departs Bangor at 6:00 p.m. and arrives at Medway at 7:40 p.m.; departs Medway at 9:30 a.m. and arrives at Bangor at 10:50 a.m.; fee $11.50 one way. ■ *Shuttle:* Maine Quest Adventures, (207) 746-9615, <www.mainequestadventures.com>; from Medway bus stop to Baxter SP or Abol Bridge, $55 (2 persons), $5EAP; will shuttle to all points in 100-mile Wilderness and to/from all Maine airports.

Bangor—A city with all major services, <www.bangorinfo.com>. For those traveling to or returning from BSP, Bangor has a bus station and airport. The Chamber of Commerce, (207) 947-0307, can provide information as you prepare for your hike or return. For information on local transportation in the Bangor area: BAT Commuter Connection, (207) 992-4670, <www.bangor-maine.gov>. ■ *Lodging:* Many motels and a mall are near the airport, including Days Inn, (207) 942-8272; Econo Lodge, (207) 945-0111; Fairfield Inn, (207) 990-0001; Howard Johnson's, (207) 947-3464; Holiday Inn, (207) 947-0101. ■ *Outfitters:* Epic Sports, 6 Central St., (207) 941-5670, <www.epicsportsgear.com>, M–Sa 9–8, Su 9–5; Dick's Sporting Goods, (207) 990-5932, located in the Bangor Mall. ■ *Bus service:* Concord Coach, (800) 639-3317; Cyr Bus Lines with daily transportation to Medway, (800) 244-2335 (see above).

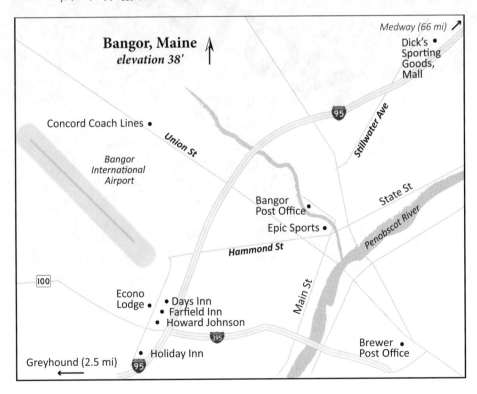

NOTES

Post Offices along the A.T.

Post offices are listed here in south-to-north order. *Note: Many post offices (perhaps all) have been shaving one hour or more off their daily hours, typically some in the morning, some in the afternoon, and some at lunch time.* Changes we have verified are reflected here, but please take this development into account in your planning for picking up packages—call ahead! **Also, at the time of publication, the fates of a couple post offices for 2015 were undecided; check before you mail (or walk)!**

Local post office telephone numbers can be verified by calling (800) 275-8777 (ASK USPS) or consulting <www.usps.com>.

Post offices printed in **bold** are located on, or within one mile of, the Trail.

Town	ZIP Code	Hours Phone
Suches, GA	30572	M–F 12:15–4:15 p.m. (706) 747-2611
Helen, GA	30545	M–F 9–12:30, 1:30–4, Sa 9–12 (706) 878-2422
Hiawassee, GA	30546	M–F 8:30–5, Sa 8:30–12 (706) 896-3632
Franklin, NC	28734	M–F 8:30–5, Sa 9–12 (828) 524-3219
Bryson City, NC	28713	M–F 9–5, Sa 10–12 (828) 488-3481
Fontana Dam, NC	28733	M–Th 11:45–3:45, closed F–Su (828) 498-2315
Gatlinburg, TN	37738	M–F 9–5, Sa 9–11 (865) 436-5464
Cherokee, NC	28719	M–F 9–4:30 (828) 497-3891
Hot Springs, NC	**28743**	M–F 9–11:30 & 1–4, Sa 9–10:30 (828) 622-3242
Erwin, TN	37650	M–F 8:30–4:45, Sa 10–12 (423) 743-9422
Unicoi, TN	37692	M–F 8:45–12 & 1–3:45, Sa 8:30–10:30 (423) 743-4945
Elk Park, NC	28622	M–F 7:30–12 & 1:30–4:15, Sa 7:30–11 (828) 733-5711
Roan Mountain, TN	37687	M–F 8–12 & 1–4, Sa 7:30–9:30 (423) 772-3014
Hampton, TN	37658	M–F 7:30–11:30 & 12:30–4, Sa 8–10 (423) 725-2177
Shady Valley, TN	37688	M–F 8–12–3:30, Sa 8–10 (423) 739-2073
Damascus, VA	**24236**	M–F 8:30–1 & 2–4:30, Sa 9–11 (276) 475-3411
Troutdale, VA	24378	M–F 9–1, Sa 8:15–11:30 (276) 677-3221

Sugar Grove, VA	24375	M–F 8:30–12 & 2–4, Sa 8:15–10:30 (276) 677-3200
Marion, VA	24354	M–F 9–5, Sa 9:30–12 (276) 783-5051
Atkins, VA	24311	M–F 8:30–12:30 & 1:45–3:45:, Sa 9–10:45 (276) 783-5551
Bland, VA	24315	M–F 8:30–11:30 & 12–4, Sa 9–11 (276) 688-3751
Bastian, VA	24314	M–F 8–12, Sa 8:15–11 (276) 688-4631
Pearisburg, VA	**24134**	M–9–4:30, Sa 10–12 (540) 921-1100
Catawba, VA	**24070**	M–F 9–12:30 & 2:30–5, Sa 8:30–11 (540) 384-6011
Daleville, VA	**24083**	M–F 8–5, Sa 8–12 (540) 992-4422
Troutville, VA	24175	M–F 9–12 & 1–5, Sa 9–11 (540) 992-1472
Buchanan, VA	24066	M–F 9–1 & 2–4, Sa 10–12 (540) 254-2178
Big Island, VA	24526	M–F 8–12 & 2–4, Sa 8–10 (434) 299-5072
Glasgow, VA	24555	M–F 8–11:30 & 12:30–4:30, Sa 8:30–10:30 (540) 258-2852
Buena Vista, VA	24416	M–F 8:30–4:30, closed Sa (540) 261-8959
Lexington, VA	24450	M–F 9–5, Sa 10–12 (540) 463-6449
Montebello, VA	24464	M–F 10–2, Sa 10–12 (540) 377-9218
Waynesboro, VA	22980	M–F 9–5, closed Sa (540) 942-7320
Elkton, VA	22827	M–F 8:30–4:30, Sa 9–11 (540) 298-7772
Luray, VA	22835	M–F 8:30–4:30, closed Sa (540) 743-2100
Front Royal, VA	22630	M–F 8:30–5, Sa 8:30–1 (540) 635-7983
Linden, VA	22642	M–F 8–12 & 1–5, Sa 8–12 (540) 636-9936
Bluemont, VA	20135	M–F 10–1 & 2–5, Sa 8:30–12 (540) 554-4537
Harpers Ferry, WV	**25425**	M–F 8–4, Sa 9–12 (304) 535-2479
Boonsboro, MD	21713	M–F 9–1 & 2–5, Sa 9–12 (301) 432-6861
Smithsburg, MD	21783	M–F 8:30–1 & 2–4:30, Sa 8:30–12 (301) 824-2828
Cascade, MD	21719	M–F 10–1 & 2–5, Sa 8–12 (301) 241-3403
Blue Ridge Summit, PA	17214	M–F 8–4, Sa 9–11:30 (717) 794-2335
Rouzerville, PA	17250	M–F 8:30–1 & 2–4:30, Sa 8:30–11:30 (717) 762-7050

Waynesboro, PA	17268	M–F 8:30–5, Sa 9–12 (717) 762-1513
South Mountain, PA	17261	M–F 12–4, Sa 8:30–11:30 (717) 749-5833
Fayetteville, PA	17222	M–F 8–4:30, Sa 8:30–12 (717) 352-2022
Mt. Holly Springs, PA	17065	M–F 8–1 & 2–4:30, Sa 9–12 (717) 486-3468
Boiling Springs, PA	**17007**	M–F 8–12 & 1–4:30, Sa 8–12 (717) 258-6668
Duncannon, PA	**17020**	M–F 8–11, 12–4:30, Sa 8:30–12:30 (717) 834-3332
Bethel, PA	19507	M–F 8–12, 1:15–4:30, Sa 8:30–10:30 (717) 933-8305
Pine Grove, PA	17963	M–F 8:30–4:30, Sa 9–12 (570) 345-4955
Port Clinton, PA	**19549**	M–F 7:30–12:30 & 2–5, Sa 8–11 (610) 562-3787
Hamburg, PA	19526	M–F 9–5, Sa 9–12 (610) 562-7812
Slatington, PA	18080	M–F 8:30–5, Sa 8:30–12 (610) 767-2182
Walnutport, PA	18088	M–F 8:30–5, Sa 8:30–12 (610) 767-5191
Palmerton, PA	18071	M–F 8:30–5, Sa 8:30–12 (610) 826-2286
Danielsville, PA	18038	M–F 8:30–12 & 2–4:30, Sa 8–12 (610) 767-6882
Wind Gap, PA	**18091**	M–F 8:30–5, Sa 8:30–12 (610) 863-6206
Delaware Water Gap, PA	**18327**	M–F 8:30–12 & 1–4:45, Sa 8:30–11:30 (570) 476-0304
Branchville, NJ	07826	M–F 8:30–5, Sa 8:30–1 (973) 948-3580
Unionville, NY	10988	M–F 8–11:30 & 1–5, Sa 9–12 (845) 726-3535
Glenwood, NJ	07418	M–F 7:30–5, Sa 10–2 (973) 764-2616
Vernon, NJ	07462	M–F 8:30–5, Sa 9:30–12:30 (973) 764-9056
Greenwood Lake, NY	10925	M–F 8–5, Sa 9–12 (845) 477-7328
Warwick, NY	10990	M–F 8:30–5, Sa 9–4 (845) 986-0271
Southfields, NY	10975	M–F 8:30–12, 1–5, Sa 8:30–11:30 (845) 351-2628
Bear Mountain, NY	**10911**	M–F 8–10, closed Sa (845) 786-3747
Ft. Montgomery, NY	**10922**	M–F 8–1 & 2:30–5, Sa 9–12 (845) 446-8459
Peekskill, NY	10566	M–F 9–5, Sa 9–4 (914) 737-6437
Stormville, NY	12582	M–F 8:30–5, Sa 9–12 (845) 226-2627

Poughquag, NY	12570	M–F 8:30–5, Sa 8:30–12:30 (845) 724-4763
Pawling, NY	12564	M–F 8:30–5, Sa 9–12 (845) 855-2669
Wingdale, NY	12594	M–F 8–5, Sa 8–12:30 (845) 832-6147
Gaylordsville, CT	06755	M–F 8–1 & 2–5, Sa 8–12 (860) 354-9727
Kent, CT	**06757**	M–F 8–1 & 2–5, Sa 8:30–12:30 (860) 927-3435
Cornwall Bridge, CT	**06754**	M–F 8:30–1 & 2–5, Sa 9–12 (860) 672-6710
West Cornwall, CT	06796	M–F 8:30–12 & 2–4:30, Sa 9–12 (860) 672-6791
Sharon, CT	06069	M–F 9:30–4:30, Sa 9:30–12:30 (860) 364-5306
Falls Village, CT	**06031**	M–F 8:30–1 & 2–5, Sa 8:30–12 (860) 824-7781
Salisbury, CT	**06068**	M–F 8:30–1 & 2–5, Sa 9–12 (860) 435-5072
South Egremont, MA	01258	M–F 8:15–12 & 12:30–4, Sa 9–11:30 (413) 528-1571
Sheffield, MA	01257	M–F 9–4:30, Sa 9–12 (413) 229-8772
Great Barrington, MA	01230	M–F 8:30–4:30, Sa 8:30–12:30 (413) 528-3670
Monterey, MA	01245	M–F 8:30–1 & 2–4:30, Sa 9–11:30 (413) 528–4670
Tyringham, MA	**01264**	M–F 9–12:30 & 4–5:30, Sa 8:30–12:30 (413) 243-1225
Lee, MA	01238	M–F 8:30–4:30, Sa 9–12 (413) 243-1392
Becket, MA	01223	M–F 8–4, Sa 9–11:30 (413) 623-8845
Dalton, MA	**01226**	M–F 8:30–4:30, Sa 9–12 (413) 684-0364
Cheshire, MA	**01225**	M–F 7:30–1 & 2–4:30, Sa 8:30–11:30 (413) 743-3184
Adams, MA	01220	M–F 8:30–4:30, Sa 10–12 (413) 743-5177
North Adams, MA	01247	M–F 8:30–4:30, Sa 10–12 (413) 664-4554
Williamstown, MA	01267	M–F 8:30–4:30, Sa 9–12 (413) 458-3707
Bennington, VT	05201	M–F 8–5, Sa 9–2 (802) 442-2421
Manchester Center, VT	05255	M–F 8:30–4:30, Sa 9–12 (802) 362-3070
Danby, VT	05739	M–F 7:15–10:15 & 1–4, Sa 7:30–10:30 (802) 293-5105
Wallingford, VT	05773	M–F 8–4:30, Sa 9–12 (802) 446-2140
Rutland, VT	05701	M–F 8–5, Sa 8–12 (802) 773-0301

Killington, VT	05751	M–F 8:30–11, 12–4:30, Sa 8:30–12 (802) 775-4247
Pittsfield, VT	05762	M–F 8–12 & 2–4:30, Sa 8:30–11:30 (802) 746-8953
Woodstock, VT	05091	M–F 8:30–5, Sa 9–12 (802) 457-1323
South Pomfret, VT	**05067**	M–F 8–1 & 2–4:45, Sa 8:30–11:30 (802) 457-1147
Hartford, VT	05047	M–F 7:45–10:45 & 2:15–5:15, Sa 7:30–10:15 (802) 295-5511
Norwich, VT	**05055**	M–F 8:30–5, Sa 9–12 (802) 649-1608
Hanover, NH	**03755**	M–F 8:30–5, Sa 8:30–12 (603) 643-5201
Lyme, NH	03768	M–F 7:45–12 & 1:30–5:15, Sa 7:45–12 (603) 795-4421
Wentworth, NH	03282	M–F 7–11 & 2:45–4:45, Sa 7:15–12 (603) 764-9444
Warren, NH	03279	M–F 7:30–9:30 & 3–5, Sa 7:30–12 (603) 764-5733
Glencliff, NH	**03238**	M–F 12–2, Sa 7–1 (603) 989-5154
North Woodstock, NH	03262	M–F 9:30–12:30 & 1:30–4:30, Sa 9–12 (603) 745-8134
Lincoln, NH	03251	M–F 8–5, Sa 8–12 (603) 745-8133
Bartlett, NH	03812	M–F 8:30–1 & 1:30–4:45, Sa 8:30–12 (603) 374-2351
Mt. Washington, NH	**03589**	M–Sa 10–4, not recommended for mail drop (603) 846-5570
Gorham, NH	03581	M–F 8:30–5, Sa 8:30–12 (603) 466-2182
Andover, ME	04216	M–F 8:30–1:30 & 2–4:30, Sa 8:30–11:30 (207) 392-4571
Oquossoc, ME	04964	M–F 8–10 & 2:15–4:15, Sa 9–12 (207) 864-3685
Rangeley, ME	04970	M–F 9:30–12:30 & 1:30–4, Sa 9:30–12 (207) 864-2233
Stratton, ME	04982	M–F 8:30–1 & 1:30–4, Sa 8:30–11 (207) 246-6461
Caratunk, ME	**04925**	M–F 7:30–11:30 & 12–3:45, Sa 7:30–11:15 (207) 672-3416
Monson, ME	04464	M–F 8–12 & 2:15–4:15, Sa 7:30–11 (207) 997-3975
Millinocket, ME	04462	M–F 9–4, Sa 9–11:30 (207) 723-5921

Mail Drops

Many thru-hikers use "mail drops" to send themselves supplies. The *Companion* lists U.S. Postal Service (USPS) offices and also establishments that accept packages from shippers such as UPS and FedEx. Mail drops can be sent to both types of locations, but it is important to address them differently. Post offices accept only mail; a post office will not accept a

FedEx or UPS package, generally speaking (the carriers have arrangements in some areas for this). Only post offices will accept packages addressed to a "General Delivery" address. USPS will forward unopened first-class and "priority" items at no additional fee. **UPS and FedEx packages cannot be sent to "General Delivery"**—you must provide a physical address other than a post office, such as a street number, and (for FedEx) a telephone number for those shipments. Please assist the businesses and post offices by printing legibly and practicing the following labeling instructions:

> Your Full Name (no nicknames or Trail names)
> c/o the business (*General Delivery* if a post office)
> City/State/ZIP Code
> *Please Hold for Thru-hiker or Section-Hiker*
> (and estimated date of arrival)

To obtain prefilled/printed labels for the most frequently used locations, try AT Mailing Labels, <www.soruck.net/at>.

At the post office, be prepared to show a photo ID when you pick up your package. Postmasters are one of a thru-hiker's best friends on the Trail. Help them help you and other hikers by following the labeling instructions above for all your mail. Send a postcard if you leave the Trail for any reason, to let the post office know what to do with your package.

To ensure that your food parcels don't pick up any "unwanted visitors" before you arrive, we suggest that hikers double-bag and securely seal all parcels.

Hostels, Camping & Showers

The first thing that comes to a hiker's one–track mind when she/he hits town is FOOD and lots of it, followed by a good hot shower and affordable accommodations. In the pursuit of just food, shower, and laundry, some hikers want to minimize the town experience and return to the Trail as soon as possible, usually the same day. This list provides low–cost options and will help you to keep the grunge at bay. Campgrounds were chosen for their proximity to the Trail, and consideration was given if they allowed nonguest showers, while keeping in mind travel by foot. There are many other campgrounds listed in the *Companion* that are best reached by car or require a longer walk.

The A.T. Passport program was developed by hostel owner Jeff Taussig as a way for hikers to document their journeys with "stamps" from participating establishments, with any proceeds going to the ATC. The passport can be bought at <www.atctrailstore.org>. More information can be found at <www.atpassport.com>.

Establishments printed in **bold** are located on or within one mile of the Trail.

NA=not available

n/c= no charge

S = shelter; H = hostel; C = camping; L = lodging; B = bunk

State	Location; Establishment	Guest Fee	Nonguest Shower–only fee	A.T. Passport
Ga.	**Amicalola Falls State Park**	C $75–$175, L $60+		P
Ga.	Suches; A.T. Hiker Hostel Wolfpen Gap Country Store Hostel	H $18 H $15	$5	P
Ga.	**Neel Gap**; Walasi–Yi Center	H $15	$3.50	P
Ga.	Dicks Creek Gap; Top of Georgia	H $20		P
N.C.	Rock Gap; Standing Indian Campground	C $16	$2	
N.C.	Burningtown Gap; Aquone Hostel	H $20		P
N.C.	**Wesser; Nantahala Outdoor Center**	H $20		P
N.C.	**Fontana Dam Visitors Center**		n/c	
Tenn.	**Green Corner Rd**; Standing Bear Farm	H $20/$15		P
N.C.	**Hot Springs**; The Sunnybank Inn The Hostel at Laughing Heart Lodge	L $20 H $17 L $28		P P
Tenn.	**Greeneville**; Hemlock Hollow	L $25–$60 B $20 C $12	$3	
Tenn.	Erwin; **Nolichucky Hostel and Outfitters**	H $20 C $10	$4	P
Tenn.	**Greasy Creek Gap**; Greasy Creek Friendly	H $10/$15 C $7.50	$3	P
Tenn.	**U.S. 19E**; Mountain Harbour B&B/ Hostel	C $10 B $22	$4	P
Tenn.	**Roan Mtn; Vango Memorial Hostel**	H $5–$10 L $20s–$30D		

Tenn.	**Dennis Cove**; Kincora Hostel Black Bear Resort	H $5 C $10 H $15 L $40		P P
Va.	**Damascus**; The Place Dave's Place, MRO Hiker's Inn Crazy Larry's Woodchuck	H $7 H $21 (2) H $25 H $25 H $25	$3	P P P P P
Va.	**USFS Hurricane Campground**	C $16	$2	
Va.	Va. 16; Troutdale Baptist Church	H donation	n/c	
Va.	**Va. 606**; Trent's Grocery Store	C $6	$3	
Va.	**Sugar Run Rd**; Woodshole Hostel	H $15 C $10		P
Va.	**Pearisburg**; Holy Family Church Hostel	H $5		
Va.	**U.S. 11**; Day Stop Inn (Travel Centers of America)		$10	
Va.	Va. 624; Four Pines Hostel	H donation		P
Va.	Va. 614; Middle Creek Campground	C $26/4 L $65/4	$5	
Va.	Buena Vista; Glen Maury Campground Three Springs Hostel	C $5	n/c	P
Va.	Montebello; Montebello Camping and Fishing	C $10s/ $5EAP		
Va.	Tye River; Crabtree Falls Campground	C $23D	n/c	
Va.	**Waynesboro**; Grace Evangelical Lutheran Church YMCA/ALDHA Hiker Pavilion	H donation C donation	n/c n/c	P
Va.	**SNP**; Loft Mountain Campground Lewis Mountain Campground Big Meadows Campground	C $16 C $16 C $16	$1 $1 $1	
Va.	**Compton Gap Trail/ Front Royal Terrapin Hostel**	H $19		P
Va.	U.S. 522; Mountain Home Cabin	H $20		P
Va.	**Bears Den Hostel**	H $30/$17 C $10	$3	P
Va.	**Blackburn Trail Center**	H, C donations		P
W.Va.	**Harpers Ferry**; Teahorse Hostel	H $33		P
Md.	Keep Tryst Road; **Harpers Ferry Hostel**	H $18/$21 C $6	$5	P
Md.	**Gapland Rd. West; Maple Tree Campground**	C (ask for rate)		
Md.	**Dahlgren Backpack Campground**	C	n/c	
Pa.	**Caledonia State Park**	C $21 weekday; $25 weekend	$3	
Pa.	**Pa. 233; Pine Grove Furnace State Park, Ironmasters Mansion**	H $25		P
Pa.	**Boiling Springs**; Boiling Springs Pool		$1	
Pa.	**U.S. 11, Carlisle**; Flyin' J Travel Plaza		$11.50	
Pa.	**Duncannon**; Doyle Hotel	L $25s/ $7.50EAP	$7.50	P
Pa.	**Duncannon**; All–American Truck Stop		$8	
Pa.	**Port Clinton pavilion**	C n/c		

Pa.	**Hawk Mountain Road**; Eckville Hikers Center; solar shower	B, C n/c	n/c	
Pa.	Palmerton; Borough Hall	H n/c	n/c	P
Pa.	**DWG; Presbyterian Church of the Mountain Hostel**	H donation		P
N.J.	**Mohican Outdoor Center**	L $35–$40 C $12	$5	
N.J.	**High Point State Park** day–use area		n/c	
N.J.	**Sawmill Lake Campground**	C $25 + $5		
N.J.	Vernon; St. Thomas Episcopal Church	H $10		P
N.Y.	**Arden Valley Rd**; Tiorati Circle		n/c	
N.Y.	**Graymoor Spiritual Life Center**	C	n/c	
N.Y.	N.Y. 301; Clarence Fahnestock State Park	C $17.75–$21.75	n/c	
Conn.	**Cornwall Bridge**; Housatonic Meadows State Park	C $36	n/c	
Conn.	**Falls Village; Hydroelectric Plant**; Bearded Woods Hike & Dine	H $50 (w/ meals)	n/c	P
Mass.	**U.S. 7**; Dolls & Dwellings	C	n/c	
Mass.	East Mountain Retreat	H $10		
Mass.	**Dalton**; Tom Levardi's 83 Depot St.	C n/c		P
Mass.	**Cheshire**; St. Mary's Church	H donation		P
Mass.	Mass. 2; North Adams YMCA		n/c	
Mass.	Williamstown; Williams Inn		$7	
Vt.	Manchester Center; Green Mountain House	H donation		P
Vt.	Rutland; Hostel at the Yellow Deli	H $20		P
Vt.	**Vt. 100**; Gifford Woods State Park	S $25–$29 C $18–$22/4	50¢	
N.H.	**Etna–Hanover Ctr. Rd East**; Tigger's Treehouse	H donation		P
N.H.	**Cape Moonshine Rd**; Dancing Dunes Village	C work for stay		
N.H.	**Glencliff**; Hikers Welcome Hostel	H $20 C $15	$2.50	P
N.H.	I–93, U.S. 3, Franconia Notch; Lafayette Place Campground	C $25ᴅ	$1	
N.H.	U.S. 302, Crawford Notch; Dry River Campground Crawford Notch Campground AMC Highland Center	C $25ᴅ C $30ᴅ B $47	25¢	
N.H.	**N.H. 16**; Pinkham Notch Visitors Center		coin–operated	
N.H.	**U.S. 2, Shelburne**; White Mtns Lodge & Hostel The Birches Loft at White Birches Camping Park	H $33 H $15 C $14	·	P P
N.H.	Gorham; The Barn at Libby House Hikers Paradise Hostel at Colonial Fort Inn	H $20 H $23		P P
Maine	Andover; Pine Ellis Hiking Lodge South Arm Campground	B $25 C $15/4	25¢	P
Maine	East Andover; The Cabin	donation		P
Maine	Rangeley; Farmhouse Inn Hostel	H $30		
Maine	Stratton; Stratton Motel & Hostel	H $25		P

Maine	U.S. 201; Sterling Inn Northern Outdoors Resort	B $25 C $10.70/ $6.42 L $57.25/4	n/c	P
Maine	Monson; Lakeshore House Shaw's Lodging	B $25 B $25 C $12PP	coin–operated $5	P P
Maine	**Golden Road**; Abol Bridge Campground Abol Pines	C $15S C $8PP	coin–operated	
Maine	Millinocket; A.T. Lodge	B $25 $35S, $55D	$3	P

Among the additional lodging and service providers included in the A.T. Passport program are:

Survivor Dave's Trail Shuttles, Atlanta to Fontana
A.T. Kick-Off, Amicalola Falls State Park, Ga.
Budget Inn, Hiawassee, Ga.
Ron's Appalachian Trail Shuttle, Hiawassee, Ga.
Buckhead House Outfitter, Hiawassee, Ga.
Haven's Budget Inn, Franklin, N.C.
Three Eagles Outfitter, Franklin, N.C.
Outdoor 76 Outfitter, Franklin, N.C.
Bluff Mountain Outfitter, Hots Springs, N.C.
Montgomery Homestead Inn, Damascus, Va.
Mt. Rogers Outfitters, Damascus, Va.
Mt. Rogers Visitors Center, Marion, Va.
Holiday Lodge, Pearisburg, Va.
Outdoor Trails Outfitter, Daleville, Va.
Appalachian Trail Conservancy Headquarters, Harpers Ferry, W.Va.
Appalachian Trail Conservancy, Boiling Springs, Pa.
Allenberry Inn, Boiling Springs, Pa.
Appalachian Trail Museum, Gardners, Pa.
Native Landscapes, Pawling, N.Y.
The Inn at Long Trail, Killington, Vt.
Mountain Meadows Lodge, Killington, Vt.
The Hart Family, West Hartford, Vt.
Chet's One Step at a Time, Lincoln, N.H.

ALDHA Gathering

Equipment Manufacturers & Distributors

Most manufacturers and distributors stand behind their products. Companies will often replace or repair equipment while you are on the Trail. Usually, it is best to deal directly with the manufacturer rather than going through an outfitter along the Trail (except where noted below). A few telephone calls can save lost time and prevent a lot of headaches.

AntiGravity Gear	(910) 794-3308 www.antigravitygear.com
Arc 'Teryx	(866) 458-BIRD www.arcteryx.com
Asolo	(603) 448-8827, ext. 105 www.asolo.com
Backcountry Gear	(800) 953-5499 www.backcountrygear.com
Campmor	(800) 226-7667 www.campmor.com
Camelbak	(877) 404-7673 www.camelbak.com
Cascade Designs/MSR	(800) 531-9531 www.cascadedesigns.com
Cedar Tree Industry	(276) 780-2354 www.thepacka.com
Columbia	(800) 622-6953 www.columbia.com
Eastern Mountain Sports	(888) 463-6367 www.ems.com
Eureka	(888) 6EUREKA www.eurekacampingctr.com
Ex Officio	(800) 644-7303 www.exofficio.com
Feathered Friends	(206) 292-2210 www.featheredfriends.com
Frogg Toggs	(800) 349-1835 www.froggtoggs.com
Gossamer Gear	(512) 374-0133 www.gossamergear.com
Granite Gear	(218) 834-6157 www.granitegear.com
Gregory Mountain Products	(877) 477-4292 www.gregorypacks.com
Hi-Tec Sports, USA	(800) 521-1698 www.us.hi-tec.com
Jacks 'R' Better Quilts	(757) 643-8908 www.jacksrbetter.com
Katadyn	(800) 755-6701 www.katadyn.com
Kelty Pack, Inc.	(866) 349-7225, (800) 535-3589 www.kelty.com
Leki	(800) 255-9982, ext 150 www.leki.com
L.L.Bean	(800) 441-5713 www.llbean.com
Lowe Alpine Systems	(303) 926-7228 www.lowealpine.com

Marmot	(888) 357-3262 www.marmot.com
Merrell	(800) 288-3124 www.merrell.com
Mont-bell	(303) 449-5331 www.montbell.com
Montrail	(855) 698-7245 www.montrail.com
Moonbow Gear	(603) 744-2264 www.moonbowgear.com
Mountain Hardwear	(877) 927-5649 www.mountainhardwear.com
Mountainsmith	(800) 426-4075, ext. 2 www.mountainsmith.com
The North Face	(855) 500-8639 www.thenorthface.com
Osprey	(866) 284-7830 cs@ospreypacks.com
Outdoor Research	(888) 467-4327 www.outdoorresearch.com
Patagonia	(800) 638-6464 www.patagonia.com
Primus	(888) 546-2267 www.primusstoves.com
Princeton Tec	(609) 298-9331 www.princetontec.com
REI	(800) 426-4840 www.rei.com
Royal Robbins	(800) 587-9044 www.royalrobbins.com
Salomon	(800) 654-2668 www.salomonsports.com
Sierra Designs	(800) 736-8592 www.sierradesigns.com
Six Moon Designs	(503) 430-2303 www.sixmoondesigns.com
Speer Hammocks	(252) 619-8292 www.tttrailgear.com
Suunto	(855) 258-0900 www.suunto.com
Tarptent by Henry Shires	(650) 587-1548 www.tarptent.com
Teva/Deckers Corporation	(800) 367-8382 www.teva.com
The Underwear Guys/Warm Stuff	(570) 573-0209 www.theunderwearguys.com/www.warmstuff.com
ULA-Equipment	(435) 753-5191 www.ula-equipment.com
Vasque	(800) 224-4453 www.vasque.com
Western Mountaineering	(408) 287-8944 www.westernmountaineering.com
ZZManufacturing (Zipztove)	(800) 594-9046 www.zzstove.com
Complete list of major and cottage gear manufacturers	**www.soruck.net/at/gear.html**

ALDHA 2015 Membership/Registration Form

Membership open to all ◆ No prerequisites or requirements ◆ No need to be a hiker to join

Name(s)

Current ALDHA member? ☐ Yes ☐ No

Address

City, State, ZIP Code

Telephone *(with area code)*

E-mail

Trail name(s)

Trails completed and years they were hiked

Membership (choose one)
(includes four newsletters & the membership directory):

☐ Enclosed is $10 for my renewal or 2015 annual membership in ALDHA. *(It's $10 per family. Memberships run Jan. 1–Dec. 31.)*

☐ Enclosed is $20 for my 2015 and 2016 annual memberships in ALDHA.

☐ Enclosed is $200 for a lifetime membership in ALDHA. *(Membership is for life but **does not include** the Gathering fee each year.)*

☐ **2015 Gathering registration fee**

(It's $20 per person) _____ registrants X $20 = _____

☐ $_____ tax-deductible donation to ALDHA, a 501(c)(3) nonprofit organization

How would you like to receive your newsletters and directory? ☐ e-mail (color; default) ☐ paper (black & white)

Send completed form with payment (payable to ALDHA) to:

ALDHA, 10 Benning St., PMB 224, West Lebanon, NH 03784

or join on-line with debit or credit card at <www.aldha.org>.

NOTES

Message to the Class of 2015

2015 THRU-HIKER & 2,000-MILER AWARD CEREMONY

ALDHA and ATC will be working together at the 2015 Gathering to recognize both thru-hikers and section-hikers who finish their journeys this year.

You will be called up to the stage at the Friday-night meeting during the Class Years Event to receive an end-to-end certificate and a "I Hiked ALDHA Way" patch from ALDHA.

The application for the official Appalachian Trail Conservancy certificate is on line at <http://www.appalachiantrail.org/about-the-trail/2000-milers/2000-miler-application>.

Special notice to 2015 thru-hikers and 2000-Milers: Bring your Trail-worn *A.T. Thru-Hikers' Companion* (or the Maine section in its entirety) and a completed-trail form to the registration desk, and your gathering fee is on ALDHA!

NOTES

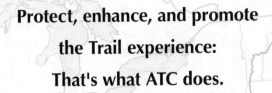

**Protect, enhance, and promote
the Trail experience:
That's what ATC does.**

You can help
by joining the
Appalachian Trail Conservancy today!

You can become a member
by going to
www.appalachiantrail.org/join
or calling
(304) 535-6331

NOTES